KU-255-635

Education, Training and Employment

Volume 2: The Educational Response

This reader is one part of an Open University integrated teaching system and the selection is therefore related to other material available to students. It is designed to evoke the critical understanding of students. Opinions expressed in it are not necessarily those of the course team or of the University

Education, Training and Employment

Volume 2: The Educational Response

A Reader edited by Geoff Esland
at the Open University

Addison-Wesley Publishing Company

Wokingham, England • Reading, Massachusetts • Menlo Park, California
New York • Don Mills, Ontario • Amsterdam • Bonn • Sydney
Singapore • Tokyo • Madrid • San Juan

in association with

The Open
University

Selection and editorial material copyright © The Open University 1991

All rights reserved. No part of this publication may be reproduced, stored in a
retrieval system, or transmitted in any form or by any means, electronic, mechanical,
photocopying, recording or otherwise, without prior written permission of the
publisher.

Many of the designations used by manufacturers and sellers to distinguish their
products are claimed as trademarks. Addison-Wesley has made every attempt to
supply trademark information about manufacturers and their products mentioned in
this book.

Cover designed by Chris Eley
and printed by The Riverside Printing Co. (Reading) Ltd.
Typeset by Columns Design and Production Services Limited, Reading.
Printed in Great Britain by Mackays of Chatham PLC, Kent.

First printed 1990.

British Library Cataloguing in Publication Data
Education, training and employment.
    Vol. 2, The educational response : a reader
    1. Great Britain.   Vocational education
    I. Esland, Geoff   II. Open University
    370.1130941

    ISBN 0–201–54430–X

Preface

This is the second of two volumes of readings entitled *Education, Training and Employment*. Volume 1 is organized around the theme *educated labour – the changing basis of industrial demand*, and Volume 2 focuses upon *the educational response*.

Both volumes – which are designed to be complementary – form part of the Open University MA Module *Education, Training and Employment* (E817), but they are also intended to appeal to a wider audience with an interest in policy development in employment-related education and training.

For much of the past two decades vocational education and training (VET) have remained high on the political agenda as the economic crises of the 1970s led to rising inflation, and the recession, industrial collapse and high levels of unemployment of the early 1980s. Crisis management characterized much of the state's response to these events giving rise to schemes and initiatives designed to limit the social damage which followed widespread de-industrialization. A major consequence of this policy has been the piecemeal and often partisan nature of public debate about the causes and effects of industrial decline and a tendency to lose sight of the wider picture. From the mid-to-late 1970s, the institutions responsible for education and training were particularly singled out for criticism as employers and government attacked what they saw as the source of an anti-industrial (and anti-capitalist) culture. Arnold Weinstock's 1976 *Times Educational Supplement* article 'I blame the teachers' (23–1–76) epitomized the antipathy of employers to education at the time.

The displacement of responsibility for economic failure and decline from the political and economic arenas to the educational and training institutions (and the individuals within them) has had the effect of distorting public policy debate about the relationship between economic change, education and employment. The concentration on changing the content of education and the attitudes of teachers and learners has led to the neglect of the part played by political and economic factors (such as the nature of Britain's industrial policy) in determining the shape and quality of the national workforce. It has also provided legitimation for the imposition of a market forces model on the education provided by schools and colleges.

One of the main objectives in compiling these readings has been to bring together analysis and research which consider employment-related education and training in a broader political–economic context than has been customary in much of the official discourse on the subject, and which provide a critical examination of the VET policies of the 1980s. The aims of these readers, as of the course itself, can be summarized as setting out:

1. to introduce a number of approaches to the analysis and understanding of education and training policies, with particular reference to their political and economic implications;
2. to consider the changes taking place in the UK economy and their implications for the nature of education, training and employment;
3. to examine recent developments in vocational education and training in schools and the further education sector.

For students on the Open University course the two Readers are accompanied by a study guide, a number of set books, and an audio cassette.

■ Outline of contents

☐ **Volume 1: *Education, Training and Employment: educated labour – the changing basis of industrial demand***

Much is heard of the British economy's need for a more highly educated and trained workforce. Higher level skills are believed to be necessary in order for Britain to compete with the knowledge-based, high-technology, high quality service economies of the advanced industrial world. The reality, however, is somewhat different, as the UK has the lowest post-16 participation rate in education and training of any of the major industrial economies.

The collection begins with an analysis of the reasons for Britain's manufacturing decline and de-industrialization and moves to a consideration of the changes in work organization required by the introduction of the methods of 'flexible specialization'. Although there is support for the view that flexible specialization leads to job enhancement for certain groups of workers, there is also evidence that other workers face increasing marginalization and de-skilling.

Discussion of these issues is followed by a group of studies which examine the importance of labour markets in the determination of employment opportunities for young people, and the factors which lead to inequalities of access. As a number of commentators have pointed out, a central feature of the political analysis of youth unemployment has been its emphasis on the so-called lack of employment skills among school leavers. In rejecting explanations which 'blame the victim', these readings underline the importance of social and geographical factors in the distribution of unemployment – particularly those pertaining to gender and ethnicity.

These are followed by two chapters which explore the history of training policy in the UK and particularly its failure to promote a shift from the 'low skill–low quality equilibrium' characteristic of British industry. Finally, we include three chapters – two of them from employers – which focus on the criteria used by companies in job recruitment. Concluding the collection is a comparative study of training in the retail industries of Britain and France.

☐   **Volume 2: *Education, Training and Employment: the educational response***

A major feature of industrial demand for reform has been the call for supply-side changes in the preparation of the workforce. The readings in Volume 2 look at a range of policy initiatives designed to make schools and colleges more aware of the 'needs of business and industry'. As a number of them make clear, this policy has met with a good deal of scepticism and criticism from educationalists.

Volume 2 begins with two chapters which discuss the relevance of economic goals to education, and the influence of 'human capital' theories on educational investment. These are followed by two studies – one of which draws comparisons between France, Britain and Germany – which examine the rise of employer demands for greater emphasis in schools on the preparation for work.

These are followed by two chapters which offer a critical examination of attempts to impose the principles of economic utility on education. The first puts forward a philosophical analysis of the differences between education and training, and the second argues that the priority given by some state education systems to the demands of their industrial lobbies raises serious questions about the nature of power and democracy in those societies.

Each of the following seven chapters focuses on a different element of the 'new vocationalism', including TVEI, the education–industry movement, enterprise, and the role of the Training and Enterprise Councils. In considering the dominant ideology underlying the vocational curriculum many of them reflect on the growing gulf between the political vision it is promoting and the principles of general education.

The following three chapters consider the operation of youth training in the UK, raising the issue as to the degree to which YTS has been an unemployment scheme rather than a source of training. The final chapter consists of a review of recent developments in EC vocational training policy.

In addition to the Open University audience for which they are intended, it is hoped that these two volumes will be of interest to many students and professionals with an interest in education and training and more general concerns of social, industrial and economic policy.

Acknowledgements

I would particularly like to thank the members of the E817 Module Team on whose behalf this Reader has been compiled and who participated in the selection of readings: Heather Cathcart, Roger Dale, Peter Raggatt and Lorna Unwin. I am also grateful for the assistance of Frank Coffield and Marten Shipman who advised the Module Team on several aspects of the development of the teaching materials. The contributions of Alison Robinson, Megan Ball and John Taylor to the preparation of this Reader have also been much appreciated.

Geoff Esland
September 1990

Introduction

In Volume 1 we were concerned to portray the pressures for change in Britain's education and training provision within a broad political and economic perspective. Too often, it was argued, public debate has tended to focus narrowly on alleged failures within education and training and to ignore the ways in which the state and industry interact with these systems and create limits on what they can achieve.

The readings in this volume focus on the nature of the *response* which the institutions for education and training have been required to make to the policy changes of the 1980s. They consider whether the objectives which have been set for vocational education and training (VET) are necessarily the appropriate ones and whether, in some cases, they are capable of being realized.

The starting point for a number of the chapters in this collection is the change which the British education system underwent after James Callaghan's Ruskin College speech of 1976. If anything, the passage of time has strengthened the perception of this speech as a major turning point in post-war education. Considered superficially, it can be read as an expression of mild prime ministerial censure of the professional priorities and methods of schools and teachers: the country was in economic crisis, youth unemployment was rising rapidly and the education system needed to be reminded of its responsibilities towards young people in preparing them for work in a rapidly changing economy.

However, what distinguishes this speech from many similar addresses of politicians on the state of the body politic is that it was intended as the opening shot of a protracted political struggle for control over an education service perceived as being too autonomous from the requirements of 'the national interest' (Callaghan, 1987; Donoughue, 1987; Ranson, 1984). In effect it was putting down a marker for the establishment of a new agenda entailing the transfer of authority and influence over educational decision-making from the 'producers' of education – among whom the teacher unions were seen as a primary target – to employers and parents.

The process inaugurated by these events has continued in a variety of guises through the education policy changes that have followed, and the location and exercise of political control in education are still major issues. In the last years of the 1974–79 Labour government, the changes heralded by the Great Debate amounted to little more than some loosely coordinated pressures for a greater emphasis on economic awareness and education for employment within the curriculum; but with the change of government in 1979, it was a relatively easy task for the tentative steps already established by Labour to be taken further by a Conservative government intent on diminishing the influence not just of educational professionals but increasingly of the LEAs as well.

During the early eighties, the main instrument for advancing the establishment of greater centralized control was the Manpower Services Commission. With the announcement of the TVEI scheme by David (now Lord) Young in November 1982, the relationship between the state and the education service entered a new phase in which the MSC took a more directive role in the determination and management of VET policy. Unconstrained by the constitutional limitations which fettered the activities of the DES, the MSC assumed the role of licensing authority for LEAs and schools wishing to avail themselves of the largesse which it was able to distribute for TVEI. The centralized control obtainable through targeted funding and the contractual requirement on schools and LEAs to account for their use of TVEI resources according to agreed objectives represented a significant step towards reducing the autonomy of LEAs in their control over educational budgets.

The culmination of the process begun in 1976 was the passage of the Education Reform Act (ERA) in 1988. Imposed on the educational service with a minimum of consultation (Simon, 1988; Haviland, 1988), the ERA established the requirement on schools to compete in the market for pupil and parental support. At the same time, schools were obliged to take on the responsibility for their own financial management under the regulations for the Local Management of Schools (LMS) and encouraged ultimately to opt out of LEA control altogether.

One of the major consequences of these political changes has been a marked breakdown of consensus over educational values. As the Conservative governments of the eighties have sought to construct an education service consistent with their political commitment to a free market economy and individual enterprise, major differences of educational ideology now divide the political parties. This process has been reinforced by the abandonment of close consultation between government and educational professional bodies and a lack of concern for formulating policy on the basis of consensus. Instead, the government has preferred to impose its policies on teachers and educationalists who have been obliged to implement them. Inevitably this means that some of the educational reforms of the past decade have been strongly contested. It also means that difficulties of implementation have arisen as teachers have tried to incorporate the prescribed changes into their professional practice.

The issue of the economic relevance of education has therefore, perhaps more than any other, constituted the main driving force and source of legitimation for the movement towards centralized political control in the determination and management of educational policy. At the same time, it has been responsible for the prominence given to employers in the governance of education and the development of those parts of the curriculum for which economic applications are considered relevant. For both school and college management purposes as well as the professional development of teachers, increasing emphasis is placed on the importance of forming links between the business community and education. The introduction of industrial governors, business placements for teachers, industrial ambassadors, partnerships between schools and companies, and joint participation between business and education in the Training and Enterprise Councils (Local Enterprise Companies in Scotland) are just some of the current examples of employer participation in the educational process.

A number of the readings collected in this volume reflect upon and assess the VET initiatives introduced during the past decade, among them YTS, TVEI, the education–industry movement, enterprise and partnerships. Inevitably, the contested nature of the 'new vocationalism' – both in its educational and political forms – features prominently in some of the analysis, where there is a fundamental concern as to the appropriateness of using the educational process for the promotion of national economic goals, particularly when the gap between political rhetoric and reality is perceived to be large. A good deal of this concern centres on the low levels of skill development which have been built into some of the training programmes – YTS particularly – and there are underlying doubts as to the validity of the widely-expressed belief that the British economy of the future will require a much larger proportion of the population to have higher level, knowledge-based skills. The pressures on employers to drive down labour costs in the pursuit of greater efficiency may well lead to job enhancement for a few, but for the majority the pattern of casualization, de-skilling and redundancy is all too familiar. It is in recognition of this, and the fact that in some labour markets youth unemployment will remain high, that a number of commentators are concerned that much of the new vocationalism amounts to little more than a programme for teaching people 'to know their place'.

To some degree or other, most industrialized nation states make use of 'human capital' assumptions in their decisions about educational planning and the allocation of resources. Some of the readings in this volume might wish to draw the lines differently as between equity and efficiency or between what are sometimes called the intrinsic and extrinsic goals of education, but that a line of some kind has to be drawn is politically inescapable.

We therefore begin with a consideration of human capital approaches to educational planning. In the first chapter, 'Educational Policy and Economic Goals', White takes as his starting point the assumption 'that educational policy should be developed, in part, in order to achieve goals of an economic character', and goes on to assess the British economy's longer-term requirements for higher level skills in the labour force. White takes the view that the expanding sectors of manufacturing industry as well as many of the service industries are likely to require greater numbers of more highly educated personnel, claiming that 'it is hard to visualize any reversal or even slackening in the demands for high-quality services and products'. Acknowledging that there is controversy as to the skill implications of particular cases, he suggests that 'at the aggregate level the trends are clearly to higher rather than lower levels of skill. . . . We appear to be in a period in which demand for higher occupations will continue to expand.'

This assessment leads White to support a policy strategy which tries to develop the capacities of individuals through a programme of general education at least to the age of 18. Such is the gap between the UK and its industrial competitors in the numbers of 18-year-olds attaining a general education qualification, that in the next two decades Britain will need to more than double the proportion of people reaching such a level of achievement just to reach the position which France held at the end of the 1980s. As to whether current education and training policies are commensurate with this strategy, White is doubtful, arguing that reliance on the market as prescribed by the ERA will do nothing to check its biases (particularly those of class, race and gender), nor is any attention paid to the importance of increasing the motivation of young people to stay on in education. He is also critical of pursuing work-based training as an alternative to general education because it is likely to bolster and recycle the lower level skills that are in need of transformation.

Human capital approaches to educational expenditure have played a significant part in educational planning since the concept was first given prominence by Theodore Schultz in his 1960 Presidential Address to the American Economics Association. Although it has been widely used – particularly by supra-national organizations such as the World Bank – it continues to be controversial, and there is still an issue as to whether there might be a greater social return from investment in physical capital.

In Chapter 2, Woodhall summarizes some of the arguments surrounding human capital theory, drawing attention to the considerable difficulties of finding an effective measure for social rates of return on investment in education. The problem has been compounded by the fact that, in its early years of development, the cost–benefits of human capital investment were calculated on the basis of the *private* rates of return in the form of individual levels of income – a measure which is now largely discredited. Woodhall also refers to the belief of some economists of education that because these are often used by employers as a screening device for occupational recruitment, higher educational qualifications cannot necessarily be assumed to lead to higher productivity.

The issue as to whether the changes taking place in the UK economy will in fact require higher level skills is touched on by Finn in Chapter 3, in which he reviews the background political events associated with the Ruskin

College speech and the Great Debate. Finn's assessment of the future requirement for higher level skills is generally pessimistic. For Finn, the problem is more often one in which school leavers are *over-educated* for the low-level skills needed by many employers, and he suggests that a part of the hidden agenda of the Great Debate was a concern to lower the employment expectations of school leavers. Citing a number of reports published during the mid-70s, Finn argues that the real problem facing the government at the time was not the declining quality of young workers but the collapse of the job market. In the growing surplus of labour over jobs, caused partly by industrial decline and partly by the substitution of technology for labour, young people were particularly vulnerable to long-term unemployment.

According to Finn, 'the political crisis of youth unemployment was transformed into an *educational* crisis'. Education was made to take the responsibility for economic forces beyond its control. In addition, the Youth Opportunities Programme– like the Youth Training Scheme which succeeded it – was essentially an unemployment scheme designed to limit the potential damage to society that could be inflicted by a large number of unemployed young people. Finn goes on to argue that the blaming of school leavers for their own unemployment has had the effect of diverting attention from the low quality as well as the declining number of jobs available.

The tendency to hold education responsible for economic failure was not restricted to the UK. In Chapter 4, Noah and Eckstein compare industrial involvement in education in Britain, France and Germany, and find a high degree of consensus in the views of their respective business communities. Employers in France and Germany, as well as the UK, have been critical of the emphasis placed by schools on academic education, while simultaneously complaining of inadequate attention paid to basic skills. There have also been requests by the business communities of the three countries for greater employer involvement in curriculum development and educational governance. However, the forms which this involvement have taken vary considerably, the most extensive arrangements being found in the German system.

The pressure exerted by politicians and employers on schools to supply a more vocationally relevant curriculum has led some educationalists to fear that what is really intended is the substitution of the principles of training for those of education. In Chapter 5, 'Education and Training', Dearden sets out to explore what he sees as the conflation of the concepts of education and training in the various vocational initiatives of the 1980s, and argues for maintaining a clear conceptual distinction between them. In restating the principles of liberal education, Dearden underlines the importance of 'the free development of understanding' and 'critical reflectiveness', arguing that these learning goals should be applied to vocational training itself: 'In that way, vocational training might be safeguarded not only from being uneducational but even from being anti-educational.'

The degree of influence exerted on public debates on education by industrialists is the theme of Chapter 6, 'The Present Economic Sea Changes and the Corresponding Consequences for Education'. Referring principally to the United States, Brosio reviews the crises which dominated the capitalist economies of the 70s, and questions the tendency of industrial lobbies to attribute the fundamental causes of economic crisis to malfunctioning education systems. For Brosio, the denigration of liberal education and the concern to instil values more supportive of capitalist wealth creation can be seen as part of an attempt by the economically powerful to reestablish legitimacy and ideological control. For him, this practice raises questions as to the democratic accountability of industrial and military corporations which seek to exert greater control over educational culture and processes.

In advancing this argument, Brosio suggests that the 'correspondence principle' put forward by Bowles and Gintis (1976) has to some extent been misunderstood. While acknowledging that there is no place for an interpretation based on a mechanistic determinism between capitalist and educational institutions, Brosio contends that, nevertheless, schools continue to be subjected to substantial political pressure to meet specific economic demands. Moreover, the fact that education can sometimes 'fall out' of correspondence with economic interests and structures does not invalidate the correspondence principle. It merely indicates that these phases are likely to be associated with explicit pressure from governments and industrial lobbies to bring about greater congruence between education and economic needs.

The commitment of governments and employer groups to the inculcation of attitudes more favourably disposed towards industry and wealth creation is discussed by Cathcart and Esland in Chapter 7. In 'The Compliant–Creative Worker: The Ideological Reconstruction of the School Leaver', they argue that the impetus for the new vocationalism is sustained by an intention to establish greater political control over curriculum content, and suggest that 'the new educational principles being called for to support the new vocationalism are epitomized in the concept of the compliant–creative worker'. The ideal workers of the future are those who can be flexible and multi-skilled, able to work in teams, and who are at the same time enterprising; but these same ideal workers are not expected to direct this desired creativity towards challenging the policies of the companies which employ them – even where these are in conflict with their interests.

Focusing on curriculum initiatives in the areas of industrial awareness and preparation for work in the education of 14–16 year olds, Cathcart and Esland argue that the concept of 'industry' which often forms the basis of this element of the curriculum is one which fails to place it in a broader, critical perspective. The authors argue that this is consistent with the tendency for vocational education to depoliticize the economic context in which wealth creation takes place.

The argument that vocational education – at least in its inception – is often founded on the desire to inculcate an uncritical acceptance of business culture and industrial work relations is the theme of Chapter 8, 'Satisfying the Needs of Industry'. Here Watkins, citing a number of studies of workplace culture and organization, suggests that the popular assumption that the advanced economies of the future will require larger numbers of highly skilled employees is based on a mis-perception of employment practice. The pressures on employers are such that senior managers are constantly looking for ways of reducing labour costs and are prepared to tolerate their dependency on skilled workers only under conditions favourable to the company. Watkins goes on to argue that an increasingly important aspect of the new styles of management consists of strategies designed to foster the acceptance by employees of company culture and identity. According to Watkins, programmes of vocational education are likewise often expected to confirm rather than to examine existing conditions of business practice.

In similar critical vein, Stronach, in Chapter 9, 'Education, Vocationalism and Economic Recovery: The Case against Witchcraft' undertakes a detailed examination of the discourses of vocationalism which have featured in the policy developments of the UK. He begins by reminding us that the official reason for the priority attached to vocational education is Britain's failing economic performance, and goes on to argue that this belief is often translated into public messages which are intellectually untenable. Citing as an example the 1986 White Paper *Working Together – Education and Training*, Stronach argues that economic decline is often attributed to the motivational failings of individuals – a view which totally ignores structural and political factors. The author suggests that the creation of public myths of this kind serves as a social ritual which dramatizes and reinforces the notion of the individual as 'standing for' economic prosperity.

In Chapter 10, we return to the theme of the place of industrialists in education. Here Jamieson reviews the schools–industry movement as it developed after the Great Debate, and considers whether in practice the greater involvement of employers in the school curriculum is leading to domination by business interests. His verdict, although made before the passing of the Education Reform Act, is that there is little evidence for such an interpretation. He suggests that, in the first place, teachers usually regard industry as an *educational* resource and not as a vehicle for promoting the interests of industry. Secondly, through their participation in school activity, employers themselves often 'become incorporated into the educational world'.

In Chapter 11, 'The Curriculum and the New Vocationalism', Pring offers a critical overview of the vocational education programmes of the 1980s, and examines the sometimes confused rationales on which they were based. His underlying concern is that certain elements of the vocational curriculum are tending to diminish opportunities for young people to deepen their understanding and critical awareness. In drawing out the often contradictory demands which vocational schemes place on teachers and pupils he expresses concern at the dissolution of the boundaries between education and training and at the tendency for an emphasis on skills to take the place of education-based approaches to learning. Furthermore, in Pring's view, some of the assumptions about appropriate skills which underlie YTS, CPVE and TVEI, for example, reflect both an impoverished view of working life and an inadequate conception of future economic requirements. For Pring there is a danger that vocational education will degenerate into vocational *training* – an outcome which will serve neither the cause of economic progress nor the personal development of young people.

The most significant vocational education initiative of the past two decades has undoubtedly been TVEI, announced in November 1982. In the manner of its launch, in its administrative structure and its educational methodology, TVEI represents a quite unique venture in post-war education. In Chapter 12, Dale reviews the political context of the establishment of TVEI and assesses its educational significance. He argues that TVEI does not conform to any of the established models of educational innovation, but suggests that 'it follows a business or commercial model, moving resources into a new "line" when the existing one is proving ineffective'. TVEI was also imposed on the education service without prior consultation and it changed dramatically the relationship between schools/colleges, LEAs and government. In spite of its centralized and regulated structure, TVEI in practice has led to considerable diversity of outcome. A much-debated issue concerns the degree to which schools and LEAs simply used the resources on offer to further the policies to which they were already committed. In the final part of the chapter, Dale considers the nature of the 'TVEI effect'. Although in origin TVEI was presented as a necessary instrument for changing attitudes towards 'preparation for work', it has in practice become a catalyst for significant change in school organization and development as well as in the teacher–learner relationship.

One of the ideological mainsprings of the VET policies of the 80s has been the notion of 'enterprise'. In Chapter 13, 'From the Decade of the Enterprise Culture to the Decade of the TECs', Coffield traces the institutional growth of the 'enterprise movement' in vocational education and training initiatives and critically assesses its ideological import. Describing the concept of 'enterprise' in practice as 'a farrago of "hurrah" words', Coffield argues that 'it is best understood . . . as a short-hand way of referring to a clutch of values such as individualism, self-reliance, competition, self-employment, profitability, minimal government and capitalism unfettered by rules and regulations on the US model'.

The most significant of the Conservative government's enterprise initiatives has undoubtedly been the setting up of a network of Training and Enterprise Councils (TECs) in England and Wales. In the second part of his chapter, Coffield assesses various aspects of their constitution and remit. Describing them as 'a national network of independent companies, led by chief executives from private industry in order to deliver training and enterprise locally', Coffield expresses serious doubts as to their capacity to meet national (as distinct from local) training requirements, and argues that present arrangements permit the large numbers of employers who will not be participating in the TEC structure to ignore their training obligations with impunity.

Chapters 14–16 focus on the Youth Training Scheme in the UK. The first by Chandler and Wallace, 'Some Alternatives in Youth Training: Franchise and Corporatist Models', compares the training philosophies and approaches of Britain and West Germany. The authors describe the West German system of training as following a 'corporatist' model 'involving a high degree of collaboration between industry and the state'. The British approach, on the other hand, is described as a 'franchise' model 'whereby youth training has been subcontracted to small and mostly private agencies but at public expense'. Chandler and Wallace argue that although the original intention was that YTS should train young people in transferable skills for occupational labour markets, in practice, employer control has led to a system of training for the internal labour markets of companies. Although critical of some of the rigidities of the West German system, Chandler and Wallace do not support the decision to devolve responsibility for training to local TECs. They argue that such a policy will mean that training in Britain will be 'tied to short-term economic goals rather than long-term national interests'. They maintain that Britain requires a nationally coordinated system of education and training – a need that will become more apparent as Britain becomes part of the European labour market in 1992, and British workers have to compete with those from Germany.

The quality of training provided under the auspices of YTS is one of the main concerns of Chapter 15, 'The Youth Training Scheme and Core Skills: an Educational Analysis', by Jonathan. Focusing on the transferable core skills element of the YTS programme, she argues that it is consistent with the claims made for YTS that it be evaluated both as an educational and as a training programme. Through a close analysis of the prescribed core skills, Jonathan concludes that many of them are rudimentary to the point of vacuity, and suggests that her brief examination 'should demonstrate that not only is there nothing here for trainers to teach . . . there is nothing for trainees to learn, at least in the cognitive sense'. The core skills element of YTS is indicted by Jonathan as anti-educational: 'what is offered to these young people is indeed mere information rather than knowledge and understanding, and information selected in such a way that possibilities for the development of understanding are foreclosed'.

The view of YTS as a scheme for unemployment tends to be confirmed by Raffe and Courtenay in Chapter 16, '16–18 on Both Sides of the Border'. In their analysis of the Scottish experience of YTS, the authors consider the effects of the institutional differences in school to work transition which operate north of the border. Although the transition process in Scotland is more flexible and staggered than it is in England and Wales, Raffe and

Courtenay argue that this has only a marginal effect on the respective destinations of school leavers. They claim that one of the key factors influencing the take-up of YTS in Scotland has been the nature of the Scottish labour market where levels of unemployment were (and continue to be) higher than those south of the border. The experience of YTS in Scotland tends to confirm the widespread perception in England and Wales that it was an unemployment rather than a training scheme.

In the final chapter, 'Policy and Response: Changing Perceptions and Priorities in the Vocational Training Policy of the EEC Commission', Neave outlines the evolution of vocational education policies within the EC. At first perceived as a temporary feature of the economic recession of the 70s, youth unemployment within the European Community was increasingly seen as a structural problem requiring a wider range of social and economic measures. The broadening of the intellectual and bureaucratic base of vocational education and training in the EC brings into focus the relative responsibilities of member states in relation to the Community. As the political and cultural distance between member states progressively diminishes during the 1990s, the issues of responsibility and power-sharing will assume much greater importance. The impact on the British systems of education and training is likely to be substantial.

References

Bowles, S. and Gintis, H. (1976) *Schooling in Capitalist America*. London: Routledge.

Callaghan, J. (1987) *Time and Chance*. Glasgow: Collins.

Donoughue, B. (1987) *Prime Minister: the conduct of policy under Harold Wilson and James Callaghan*. London: Cape.

Haviland, J. (ed.) (1988) *Take Care, Mr Baker! A selection from the advice on the Government's Education Reform Bill which the Secretary of State for Education invited but decided not to publish*. London: Fourth Estate.

Ranson, S. (1984) 'Towards a tertiary tripartism: new codes of social control and the 17+' in Broadfoot, P. (ed.) *Selection, Certification and Control: social issues in educational assessment*. Lewes: Falmer.

Simon, B. (1988) *Bending the Rules: the Baker 'reform' of education*. London: Lawrence & Wishart.

Contents

xx **Contents**

Chapter 1

Educational Policy and Economic Goals

M. White

This mid-1980s have witnessed developments in educational policy in England and Wales[1] more extensive than any since the 1940s. The purpose of this paper is to assess whether these developments are likely to help achieve long-term goals of economic adaptation.

At the time of writing, the centre of the stage is held by the Education Reform Bill (ERB) (HMSO, 1987b). The avowed aim of this legislation is to increase the strength of market forces within education, or to reduce the insulation of the education system from market forces. Such an aim reflects the central thrust of Thatcherist policy. At the same time, important curricular developments are taking place, the original inspiration for which was from within the education profession. The Technical and Vocational Education Iniative (TVEI), although sponsored by the present Government, was the creation of educationists. Moreover, 1988 is the first year in which sixteen year olds throughout England and Wales will be taking the General Certificate of School Education (GCSE). The GCSE has had a gestation period of at least fifteen years, and its conceptualization owes more to liberal values among educationists than to any desire to create a homogeneous market in qualifications. The GCSE in its turn propels further changes in education between sixteen and eighteen.

The main focus of the paper is upon education for the fourteen–eighteen age group, where the provisions of the ERB intersect with major developments in the curriculum. Earlier stages of education, though important in providing foundations to build upon, are excluded from consideration because to discuss them would require a different approach to that adopted here. Higher education policy is not considered in its own right, but only in terms of its influence in motivating educational

Source: © Oxford University Press and OREP 1988. Reprinted from the *Oxford Review of Economic Policy* vol. 4 no. 3 (1988) by permission of Oxford University Press.

development for the fourteen–eighteen year olds. However, the focus upon education in the fourteen–eighteen age range is not arbitrary. It is here that crucial results, on which both higher education and the economy depend, are achieved or not achieved.

The paper assumes that educational policy should be developed, in part, in order to achieve goals of an economic character. It proceeds by sketching those aspects of the long-term economic context which seem to have the most important implications for educational policy. In the light of this context, and of some international comparisons, it then proposes broad, long-term quantitative targets towards which policy should be steering the educational system. The quantification of the targets is not essential to the argument, but has the advantage of creating a sharper perspective within which current educational policy (and other related policy) can be appraised. In essence, we consider whether current policy is likely to facilitate or obstruct achievement of the targets which link education to economic adaptation.

In order to carry out the appraisal in a systematic manner, it is helpful to have some general model or framework of how policy could affect educational outcomes. A simple conceptual framework of this kind is described and applied. This framework uses notions drawn from educational production functions and from rational choice theory. Evidence from research on educational effectiveness is also used to help the appraisal. In conclusion, suggestions are put forward to remedy apparent shortcomings in current policy.

■   Economic goals

It does not seem necessary to justify the assumption that education should serve economic goals, among others. But we cannot begin without some brief explanation of the kinds of goals of which we are speaking.

Economic thought revolves around the twin poles of 'efficiency' and 'equity'. Education can be regarded as important, from an economic viewpoint, to the extent that it contributes to these. Of course, it is not easy to obtain general agreement on what constitutes either of the concepts. It has been suggested, however, that education, regarded as an investment, meets the criterion of efficiency if it yields as good a long-term return to individuals and to society as other investments. Similarly, one might suggest that the criterion of equity is met if individuals have equal opportunities to invest in education, after making allowance for innate capacities. (Exactly what allowance one should make for innate capacities, however, is a difficult problem.)

Over the past three decades, the notion of education as an investment has been particularly developed in human capital theory

(Becker, 1964, 1975): but almost wholly on the side of efficiency. An assumption of this approach has been that education is economically important because it increases productivity. Since productivity is reflected in earnings, people choose to undergo additional education in order to increase future streams of income. More education will be worthwhile when these future additional payoffs, suitably discounted, outweigh the costs incurred and current income foregone during education. According to human capital theory these individual choice processes are inherently rational, so that an efficient educational policy will be one which permits them to take place unobstructed.

This view is over-simple. Some kinds of education directly increase productivity (one cannot be a doctor without learning medicine), but the economic value of much, perhaps most, education is less direct. For education, however immediately irrelevant to particular occupations, increases the capacity to learn and thereby increases the cost-effectiveness of later training, a point now being made with increasing clarity by industrialists and employers. In addition, education sorts and labels people with certificates, which help employers and individuals to find one another in the job market. So far as individuals' educational choices are concerned, they are usually formed under more complex influences than human capital theory contemplates (Gambetta, 1987). For example, the objectively measured costs and returns are not subjectively equal to members of different social classes. Most important, perhaps, the impression of precision given by rate of return analyses based on historical or cross-sectional data is largely misleading if applied to individual (or public) decisions which have to assess future prospects. This task can only be carried out in broad and far from precise terms because of the inevitable uncertainties both about the changing context and about the choices to be made by other individuals.

Despite these reservations, human capital theory and rate of return analysis provides notions which are worth keeping in an economic assessment of educational policy. These include the contribution of education to productivity growth; the influence of individuals' expectations of future returns to education; the importance of the earnings foregone in order to continue education; and the possible role of distortions of individual choices resulting from the policies of educational institutions, employers, or governments.

On this last point, the distinction drawn within rate of return analysis between the 'private' and 'social' returns to education remains important. The social differ from the private returns in taking account of the full costs of educational provision and of grants or other subsidies. In Britain, for example, individuals' education at universities or polytechnics receives far more favourable support than that of most other groups, making higher education a relatively attractive option. At the same time, this is countered by a complex institutional system of rationing of places, so that a substantial proportion of initial choices is frustrated (Redpath and Harvey, 1987).

It is partly because government, and other institutions, are so heavily implicated in the structuring and financing of education that, in the end, efficient and equitable outcomes cannot be expected from the autonomous workings of individual choice. With long time-lags involved, government must choose structures and allocate finances on the basis of its own judgement of the future requirement for education. Its choices for education (and indeed its broader economic policies) then provide signals which affect individuals' educational choices. Moreover, the shape of government subsidies can have a great influence upon the equity of the education system, either in correcting the unequal costs of education which fall upon different groups, or in accentuating these differences.

■   The economic context

Educational policy has to address long-term considerations if it is to engage with economic goals. Economic opportunities and hazards to be expected over (say) the next few decades constitute the economic context for educational policy. Naturally, this economic context is itself continuously changing and evolving. Because of inevitable uncertainties, policy can only consider the long-term in a broad, strategic way.

Government has, over recent years, emphasized the importance for educational policy of the context of growing international competition and of technological change. Educational policy has been advanced as, to some extent, a response to this context. However, the link between context and policy has remained vague. We propose to focus upon two aspects of the economic context, themselves shaped by competition and technology, which may provide this missing link. The first, representing economic opportunity, is the expansion of the higher occupations. The second, reflecting economic hazard, is the high level of unemployment, and especially of youth unemployment.

Since 1950, employment in manual occupations has steadily contracted as a proportion of total employment; and employment in higher occupations (professional, scientific, technical, managerial and administrative) has increased rapidly (Goldthorpe, 1980; Whitley et al., 1980; Goldthorpe and Payne, 1986). Underlying this upward shift in the occupational structure, two influences can be postulated: an income and wealth effect and an effect of technology.

The growth of real income and the spread of the ownership of wealth leads both to a demand for more sophisticated products and for an increased range of services. The growth of health, welfare and education services has constituted one of the main elements in occupational change, creating a substantial class of professional public servants. Equally, the widening ownership of private wealth has led to a burgeoning of financial services. And the demand for novel and superior products leads to the increased relative employment, not only of industrial scientists and design engineers, but of many specialists in production, marketing and distribution. Higher occupations minister to raised expectations.

It is more difficult to characterize the influence of technology, of which many aspects remain puzzling (for a review of evidence, see Freeman and Soete, 1987). But at the risk of some over-simplification, it seems possible to discern two post-war phases. In the first, which lasted until the middle or late 1960s, technology played an expansionary role. The industries with high expenditures on R&D and on capital plant were those that provided a large part of economic growth (see, for example, Terlecky, 1974), and both R&D and capital expansion required more industrial scientists, engineers and technicians, together with more sophisticated management and administration.

Since the late 1960s, on the other hand, markets for important products such as vehicles have become mature, or constrained by a less favourable climate for world trade, and have offered slow growth at best. Yet even in these cases techniques of production have continued to improve. Investment for expansion has taken a smaller share of total investment, but investment for labour-saving or for quality enhancement has grown: it has been a period of 'capital deepening'. In mature industries, total employment has fallen very substantially, but often the absolute numbers of higher-level posts have increased. At the same time, those manufacturing industries which remain expansionary, such as electronics, instrumentation and office equipment and computers, have exceptionally high proportions of higher-level and white-collar workers.

So far as the income and wealth effect is concerned, it is hard to visualize any reversal or even slackening in the demands for high-quality services and products. As for the technology effect, the central question for the future concerns the resolution of changes induced by communications, computers and microelectronics ('information technology'). There has been much controversy over the skill implications in particular cases, but at the aggregate level the trends are clearly to higher rather than lower levels of skill (see, for example, Daniel, 1987). We appear to be in a period in which demand for higher occupations will continue to expand.

Long-term or chronic unemployment is the reverse side of the same developments, in that it too is occupational in character. Long-term unemployment is almost wholly concentrated in manual occupations (including those which are regarded as skilled), and (to a lesser extent) in the under-qualified margins of lower non-manual occupations (White, 1983; White and McRae, 1988). It is closely associated, then, with occupational strata characterized by below-average educational attainments. Since the mid-1960s in Britain, each economic downswing has propelled larger numbers into unemployment, and each upswing has failed to redress the balance. The consensus of economic forecasters is that unemployment in the late 1980s will stabilize at about 2.5 million, which will be 1 million above the level existing before the preceding recession. A crucial question is whether future recessions will continue the established pattern and leave still larger residues in unemployment.

In principle, it should be possible to adapt displaced workers to the opportunities in the recovery following recession, through additional training or retraining. But this redistribution is obstructed because the low educational attainments of those in the lower strata (not just the unemployed) make it expensive to train or retrain them to the standards required for jobs in, say, financial services, computing or servicing of electronic equipment. Moreover, the lower-level jobs which the unemployed formerly occupied may either have permanently disappeared or have been pre-empted by new entrants with better qualifications. In a job market increasingly controlled by the signals provided by educational qualifications, the unqualified or less qualified may be screened out so as not to receive serious consideration from prospective employers, even if they have worthwhile skills and experience to offer.

Whether one considers the opportunities for higher occupations provided by rising incomes and changing technologies, or the dangers to employment posed by competition and structural change, the fundamental, adaptive response appears to require capable and flexible people. The creation of personal capacity and flexibility is the broad task of education.

■ Specific targets for education

The review of the economic context leads us to propose two specific targets relevant to educational policy over, say, the next two decades.

□ Education for the higher occupations

There is likely to be continuing scope for growth in the higher occupations. The opportunities for economic development embodied in this growth may be taken to a lesser or greater extent. There will be corresponding repercussions upon national productivity and upon individual incomes. Moreover, the distribution of access to higher occupations will have a large influence upon the degree of social equity achieved. What, in these respects, would be the nature of an appropriate educational target?

In the first place, one should put aside any temptation to formulate educational provision in terms of specific occupations. The fallacies of this form of manpower planning have been criticized in classic papers by

Table 1.1 Average years of education for population aged 15–64 in 1950, 1973 and 1984 for six advanced nations. (*Source*: Maddison (*Journal of Economic Literature*, 1987, p. 688), q.v. for definitions and original sources.)

| | Secondary | | | Higher | | |
	1950	1973	1984	1950	1973	1984
France	3.04	4.11	4.89	0.18	0.47	0.90
FGR	4.37	5.11	5.17	0.14	0.20	0.31
Japan	2.08	3.79	4.56	0.16	0.39	0.59
Netherlands	1.17	2.49	3.34	0.24	0.39	0.58
UK	3.27	3.99	4.50	0.13	0.25	0.42
USA	3.40	4.62	5.10	0.45	0.89	1.62

Boulding (1970) and by Blaug (1967). A review by Psacharopoulos (1986) documents the failures of manpower planning in education to achieve its hopes of preparing supply to match forthcoming demand. In an era of much structural change, there is little reason to expect that past performance in this respect can be improved upon.

A more sensible strategy is to develop the capacities of young people through general education, to an extent which permits them to move quite flexibly into opportunities which later arise. Methods of supporting individual flexibility include post-graduate conversion courses, professional post-graduate training (as in accountancy), continuing education and professional updating, and training provided internally by employers. Moreover, many highly qualified young people already move away from their original occupation of choice, and this can either be stimulated or reduced by salary and career incentives. In short, no policy is likely to be superior to one of providing high levels of general education, and allowing supply and demand supported by flexible institutions to work things out thereafter.

The crucial practical question, however, concerns how much growth of general education is necessary over the next decade or two to provide the foundation for this kind of flexible higher-level work-force. Nearly all higher occupations now recruit either after tertiary education, or into their own vocational courses at age eighteen. In short, widespread general education to age eighteen appears essential as a foundation for a long-term productive expansion of the higher occupations.

Historically, Britain has been slow to expand education relative to other advanced industrial nations. Direct evidence of this is provided in Table 1.1, which is adapted from a recent review of economic growth accounting by Maddison (1987).

The analysis shows comparisons for the post-war period covering six advanced industrial nations, including the United Kingdom. In 1984 the UK came fifth out of six in terms of average years of secondary education, exceeding only the Netherlands. It also came fifth out of six on average years spent in higher education, exceeding only West Germany. On change measures (1950–84) it came fifth on increase in secondary education, and fourth on increase in higher education.

Of course, comparisons based on such global measures can be misleading, without appreciation of the structural and qualitative differences between education systems in different countries. For example, the low level of tertiary education in West Germany has to be placed alongside an extremely strong system of vocational and professional training which provides a genuine alternative route to higher occupations (an approach also well developed in Switzerland and Sweden).

The most useful comparisons may, perhaps, be made with France, a nation of closely similar population, and with a similar economic structure, to Britain. Like Britain, also, France has compulsory education to age sixteen, and a system largely reliant on state funding to the age of eighteen. How do the two countries compare in providing general education to age eighteen? For Britain, this includes those studying A-levels in Colleges of Further Education, after transferring from school at sixteen or seventeen, as well as those taking A-levels at school. In France, this means those studying for the *Baccalaureat*, including its more recently developed technological versions.

The annual flow into the '*Bac*' is about 375,000–400,000 (*Ministère de l'Education Nationale*, 1984). The annual flow at age sixteen–seventeen into A-level courses in Britain is not available, but a sensible estimate, based on both attainment and failure rates published in Department of Education and Science statistics for school leavers and for further education, might be 250,000. Hence France, with a marginally larger population, sends about one-and-a-half times as many through general education to eighteen plus. Moreover, two-thirds of the French pupils are awarded the *Baccalaureat*, based on achievement across a range of six or seven subjects. In Britain, only one half of those taking A-levels within schools passes three or more subjects, while in Colleges of Further Education, the average number of A-level passes per student is just over one.

It is possible to argue that A-levels represent a higher standard than the *Baccalaureat*, and on a subject-for-subject basis, that is almost certainly true. But that gain has to be offset against the losses resulting from excluding many who could have benefited from general education to the age of eighteen. These losses may have adverse implications both for efficiency and for equity. Moreover, nobody would suggest that the *Baccalaureat* represents a dysfunctionally low standard: on the contrary, it enjoys international repute for its excellence within the category of broad-based educational qualifications.

The first target for British educational policy, therefore, might reasonably be specified as to increase the proportion achieving a general educational qualification at age eighteen by about one-half over its present level. This target would only bring British education to where France now stands. By the time this could be achieved, France may well have moved on. Indeed, there is a lively debate in France concerning schemes to broaden general education by the early years of the 21st century, so as to permit up to 80 per cent to remain in general education until eighteen (a shift towards the US or Japanese model of universal general education). We would therefore suggest a doubling of present British levels of education to age eighteen as a more desirable target.

A target increase of 50–100 per cent over two decades represents an annual increase of around 2.0–3.5 per cent. Some data from recent history are summarized in Figure 1.1, and suggest that the target rate proposed need not be considered wildly unrealistic. In the twelve years from 1966 to 1977, the proportion of the relevant age group obtaining A-levels in England and Wales rose by about 55 per cent. After 1977, statistics were prepared separately for England, and the basis for the calculation was changed. The trough-to-peak growth in the proportion, on the new basis and for England only, in the eight years 1978–1985, was 12 per cent, much more modest than in the earlier period. However, an important part of this growth was contributed by Colleges of Further Education, where the rate of increase was about three times the overall rate (see Figure 1.2).

Moreover, there is evidence that many young people who could take good advantage of general education from sixteen to eighteen are not doing so. In the early 1980s, about 80,000 children *per annum* were leaving school at sixteen or seventeen with five O-levels of grades A–C. Although exact figures are lacking, it seems likely that only about one-half of these took A-levels at Colleges of Further Education, with perhaps a further one-third following vocational courses and the remainder entering the job market. If all these young people followed a general education to eighteen, this would increase the present inflow by about 15 per cent.

More generally, of all those who finished school with one or more O-levels (grades A–C) in 1985, about one-half had five or more subjects, and one-half from one to four. Exact figures of destinations by examination results are not available, but some reasonable inferences and estimates can be made. While the great majority of those with five or more passes stayed in full-time education, it is doubtful if as many as one in four of those with one to four O-levels continued their education beyond sixteen. Yet, this very large group has already demonstrated a potential capacity for further education, by success at an 'academic' standard in one or more subjects.

There is little reason to believe, therefore, that the potential for young people to remain in general education beyond sixteen has been exhausted, even if we did not have the example of other countries to

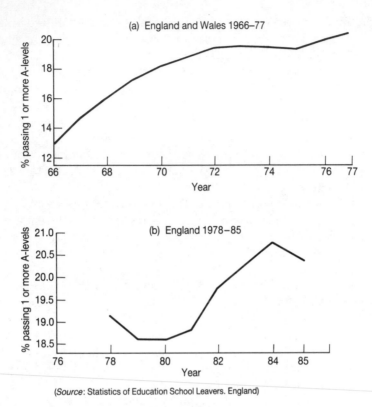

(*Source*: Statistics of Education School Leavers. England)

Figure 1.1   A-levels in the 18 year old age group 1966–85: schools and Colleges of Further Education.

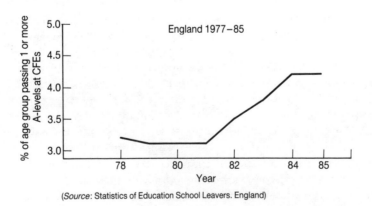

(*Source*: Statistics of Education School Leavers. England)

Figure 1.2   A-levels among 18 year olds: Colleges of Further Education.

suggest what might be possible. Even within the educational structure existing before 1988, expansion was possible.

□   **Alternatives for fourteens to eighteens**

At present, a little more than one-half leave school for the labour market at age sixteen. Many of these, we have just suggested, could be and should be drawn into general education to age eighteen. But the majority of the group only has lower qualifications (grade 2 or below on the old Certificate of Secondary Education (CSE)), or no qualifications at all. On entering the labour market, a little more than one-half again (about 30 per cent of the total age-group) are initially drawn into the Youth Training Scheme (YTS), with the remainder split between jobs and unemployment. For this group, the goal of a general education to age eighteen (which most could expect to obtain if they lived in Japan or Taiwan) seems unrealistic, without fundamental structural change unlikely to be achieved in the next two decades. However, to leave their education in its present condition seems a wholly inadequate response to the economic changes which we have sketched.

Against this judgement, it has customarily been argued in the past that less academically inclined young people will be gaining more by entering the labour market and acquiring practical training and experience, than they would by remaining in education. Or, to update the argument, it could be said that the YTS is the appropriate response to the needs of this group, and that the emphasis should be placed upon getting more young people into that scheme. This counter-argument has two flaws. The first is that, whatever the merits of purely practical and vocational training, it does not equip people either for the opportunities provided by occupational change nor for the hazards posed by unemployment and by a labour market based on credentials. The flexibility required by this occupational context can only be supplied and accredited by *educational* means.

Secondly, the YTS itself is *not* a scheme of education. Significantly, it was included in the 1987 Conservative Manifesto only under the heading of 'helping unemployed people into jobs'. Early planning for the YTS did, commendably, place considerable stress upon the quasi-educational aim of 'training in generic skills', but available evidence suggests that this aspect could not be widely implemented (see, for example, Roberts *et al.*, 1986). In practice, the low level of funding for training within YTS, and the reliance on employers to deliver most of the training, have confined the scheme to narrow vocational objectives. Only one in four of the young people passing through YTS obtains recognized qualifications, the better of which represent stages towards apprenticeships (Grey and King, 1986). There is also a low level of continuity from YTS to employment, a circumstance which militates against continuing development. Entry to sub-schemes of the YTS leading to qualifications, or to permanent employment with the chance of continued development, is itself governed by selection based largely on educational criteria (Roberts *et al.*, 1986). While YTS can be acknowledged as a worthwhile initiative to redevelop occupational training after its collapse in the late 1970s, it is unfair to expect it to make good the deficiencies of general education as well.

In France, levels of educational participation and qualification have been greatly increased by the introduction of an extreme form of vocationalism. Nearly one-half of young people there are currently completing vocational courses, the majority of which continue to age eighteen. However, this gain is purchased at the cost of streaming at the age of thirteen and of quite severely narrowing the education of those in the vocational streams. Such characteristics do not seem ideal for an age of substantial economic and technical change. What the French experience does provide, however, is a demonstration of the power of vocational education to provide *an alternative in which most pupils can participate*.

What is required, perhaps, is an injection of vocational content which does not lead to an undue narrowing of general education. Education then becomes partly vocationalized, but not wholly vocational. The vocational element is not only valuable in its own right but helps to sustain the general element of education which is so important for long-term flexibility and for upward mobility. In fact, a development with such characteristics already exists in Britain, in the form of the TVEI, a scheme explicitly intended to provide a mixed general and vocational education from fourteen to eighteen. TVEI itself offers no new qualification, but is flexible enough to take advantage of the whole range of qualifications available to the age group. These include both the main academic courses, and the Certificate of Pre-Vocational Education (CPVE), a sixth-form course with a strong vocational orientation. Although still operating on a modest scale, it has been shown that TVEI can and does encompass a wide range of abilities. And it is popular with its participants, a vital consideration if more young people are to be induced to invest in education. Slim though the evidence is at this stage, it seems a sufficient encouragement for the goal of a more comprehensive development along these lines, especially if the changes in curricula initiated by the GCSE succeed in the aim of making education more interesting to fourteen–sixteen year olds.

Within twenty years, the target should be to develop schemes of this kind to provide for as many as possible of those now not following the path of general education to eighteen. Such schemes would need to cater for at least 40 per cent of young people, and perhaps as many as 50 per cent, to draw them both towards improved standards of general education and towards pursuit of vocational qualifications.

The idea of developments along these lines has been criticized by educationists as diluting educational content and diverting educational resources into vocational subjects which could be learned better elsewhere (at work, for example). These criticisms are probably valid so long as vocationalized education is merely an alternative path for those already committed to remaining in education. The broader the application of the scheme, however, the less valid this criticism becomes. The aim should be to enlarge education, especially post-sixteen, for the many who would otherwise receive only the narrowest vocational preparation.

Taken together, the two targets for educational policy which we have proposed would constitute a balanced response to economic opportunity and hazard, and would seek to encompass the great majority of young people. Although derived from economic considerations, the targets are little different from those which might be proposed on general cultural or social grounds: to raise educational participation and attainment, by offering worthwhile opportunities to all young people. What an economic perspective adds, perhaps, is a sense of scale and of urgency to that task.

■ Methods of raising educational attainment

Current educational debates often suffer from lack of clarity about means of change and their efficacy. Even a rather simple model of educational attainment may prove helpful in analysing the available means of change. Educational attainment can be thought of as the output or measurable result of a process of learning. Apart from innate capabilities or qualities of the individual, there are three chief influences upon this process:

(1) *teaching* (coming from other individuals, notably teachers, and from the environment in as much as that provides information and stimulation);

(2) *motivation* of the individual (to learn, or to use learning as a means to other ends); and

(3) *time* (the period for which the process of learning continues).

The effect of *teaching* on educational attainment has probably been the main centre of research with an economic or cost–benefit orientation (for a recent review, see Hanushek, 1986). But it has proved much more difficult to demonstrate that teaching affects educational attainment than might have been expected. Common sense would suggest, for example, that educational budgets, class size, and the qualifications and experience of teachers, would be important, but extensive research (Hanushek collated 147 studies) shows that within the ranges of these variables which are met in practice, that is not the case.

The best that research has been able to do is to demonstrate that, after controlling for other inputs including family background, class or school composition, and prior attainment, there are differences between the *outputs* achieved by different teachers (Hanushek, 1971) and by different schools (Smith and Tomlinson, 1988). Indeed, these studies show that the differences in outputs are large. So we know that teaching matters, both at the level of individual teachers and of the educational establishment, but we know little about how or why this is so. This lack of knowledge is an important consideration from the viewpoint of policy.

The importance of *motivation* for attainment is not in doubt. Of the many formulations of motivation across the social sciences, one of the most useful is that of subjectively rational choice, which extends the more customary notion of private returns to education. Using this formulation leads one to consider both the payoffs and opportunity costs of staying in education, and the *probabilities* (as subjectively perceived) of obtaining the payoffs in question.

For example, rational choice theory would suggest that increased proportions of sixteen year olds would remain in education to take A-levels in response to such developments as (a) employers offering more jobs, or better pay and prospects to those with A-levels, (b) less employment, or lower pay, being available to those without A-levels, (c) easier availability of financial support during the period of studying for A-levels, (d) better chances of succeeding in A-level examinations, because of (say) changes in curriculum or teaching.

Considerations such as these have been rather successfully used to explain long-term changes in educational participation at an aggregate level (Halsey *et al.*, 1980). At a more descriptive level, commentators have frequently remarked that strong motivation for university education is achieved in Japan by making entry to most higher occupations (and to favourable employment conditions) open only to graduates. Or again, the strength of the West German apprenticeship system may depend in part upon (a) the virtual certainty of obtaining a place once necessary preliminary qualifications have been obtained, and (b) the high probability of being retained in employment after completion of the apprenticeship.

Time spent in education is so obviously important to educational attainment that one of the measures most commonly used by social scientists is number of years in education. There are two main ways in which increases in time devoted to education may come about: either from individual choice, or from institutional changes which improve access to education. Since individual choice has already been considered under the heading of motivation, it is on access that we focus here. Increases of educational provision under statutory enforcement (the growth of public sector education, raising of the minimum school-leaving age, or the Robbins principle in higher education) constitute expansions of access. Changes in selection criteria or in the curriculum may also represent important increases (or decreases) in access. Hence the main growth in numbers of students in higher education in Britain over the past decade has taken place in polytechnics through CNAA degrees, and through the Open University (HMSO, 1987a). Flexibility over the timing of examinations represents another practical addition to access. In France in 1983, no less than 56 per cent of pupils taking the *Baccalaureat* had repeated a year on the way, a degree of flexibility which goes far to explain both the high proportions taking the academic path and the small loss through drop-outs there (*Ministère de l'Education Nationale*, 1984).

■ Assessing educational policy

By what means does current British educational policy seek to change educational attainments? Are the policies of sufficient force to achieve increases in attainments of the order which we have earlier argued is desirable? We are at least in a position to sketch answers to these questions.

The Government's strategy, as noted at the beginning of this paper, can be characterized as one of opening education to market forces. Market forces are particularly represented, here, by parents of school-age children, and in a subsidiary but significant role, by employers. The implicit model of the educational system is one of a protected enclave unresponsive to the influences of change and to the demands of those whom it should serve. Among the most important indications of this unresponsiveness, it is argued, has been the continuance of schools which are unpopular with parents or have educational attainments considerably lower than could reasonably be expected.

This protected position of schools is to be removed through the Education Reform Bill (ERB), especially by means of the following provisions:

(1) encouragement for schools to leave local education authority control;

(2) financial responsibility for each school, and funding in proportion to size;

(3) greatly increased influence and power for parents and governing bodies of schools;

(4) exposure of unpopular schools by freeing enrolments of artificial constraints;

(5) exposure of ineffective schools by introduction of a compulsory system of testing of pupil attainments;

(6) creation of a less regulated job market for teachers;

(7) development of the City Technology Colleges, which will provide a competing model to established forms of education.

Rather different in concept, but still compatible with a strategy of opening education to market forces, is the National Curriculum for five–sixteen year olds. Statutory control or standardization of a service, it can be argued, helps the functioning of certain types of markets by reducing information costs to the users of the service. It also makes it more difficult for local education authorities or schools to reduce expenditure by providing a low service level.

It is claimed by government that this opening of the school system to various forms of competition will increase levels of educational attainment. According to our analysis, *it could only do so through changes to teaching, motivation, or access,* and we will consider each of these in turn.

☐   Teaching

Competition will place increased pressures on schools and upon individual teachers to improve teaching. If schools have low attainment levels and fail to improve them, they will run a higher risk of closure than at present. If teachers perform badly, they will face greater risks of dismissal and reduced chances of re-employment. Conversely, schools with high levels of performance will on average attract more pupils, obtain corresponding resources, and offer better prospects to their staff. In short, the ERB offers fairly clear incentives for improved teaching.

The main question is whether currently less effective head teachers and teachers will know how to respond to these incentives. Effectiveness in teaching, as noted earlier, appears hard to define or to communicate. If improved effectiveness is veiled from the perception of these head teachers and teachers, then average effectiveness can only be raised by forced closures or dismissals.

Here one encounters one of the difficulties of reconstituting the school system as a market. One of the most important forms of market competition is through flexibility of capital investment and divestment. This is much less available in a system supported from public funds. If less effective schools close, then the capacity of schools in an area may become exhausted, and in that case both the reality of choice for parents and the reality of incentives for schools and for teachers will disappear. Spare capacity is essential both for choice and for incentives. It could only be restored, after a period of forcing-out of ineffective schools, either by permitting successful schools to increase their capacity through capital investment, or by opening new schools. The former would lead to an increase in average size of school, the educational effect of which cannot readily be gauged. The latter would involve a capital cost likely to be unacceptable in terms of public budgeting, if on a scale sufficient to make a substantial impact on aggregate educational attainment. Yet another possibility which one might envisage is of schools being in some sense 'privatized' when facing closure, so that they could be continued 'under new management' with grant-aided status.

Similar problems exist concerning the removal of ineffective teachers from the profession. At present the supply of teachers is limited by central provision of training places, coupled with strict constraints on teacher qualification. If many teachers are removed from the profession, the cost to the public budget of teacher training will increase significantly. Alternatively, constraints on teacher recruitment and training could be relaxed. For example, one might envisage schools providing their own 'in-house' training, rather than relying upon a national system. Such a move, however, would meet with strenuous professional opposition.

In short, the path of incentive-based improvements in 'teaching' is a dubious one, because of the fundamental uncertainty about what is involved in effective teaching. The alternative path to improvements through *structural* change would be beset by institutional, budgetary and capacity constraints: these might be overcome, but only by permitting a high degree of flexibility in capital budgets, school sizes, recruitment and training, or ownership arrangements. The degree of instability and experimentation which would be needed to raise teaching standards through restructuring could well be opposed by parents, who tend to seek secure and stable environments for their children's education.

☐ **Motivation**

It is difficult to find any aspect of the ERB which affects returns to educational investment or otherwise bears upon the rational choices made by pupils or their parents concerning continuation of education. Some aspects of 'access' within the Bill, which are discussed below, may however feed back positively upon motivation.

This neglect of economic motivation appears to be a major limitation in a strategy based upon the development of a stronger market. As has been pointed out in a recent report to the (then) Manpower Services Commission (Deloitte Haskins & Sells, 1987), the structure of financial subsidies to young people in the sixteen to twenty-one age group is a mass of inconsistencies and anomalies. To note only the largest: (1) sixteen–eighteen year olds at school or college attract only Child Benefit payments; (2) sixteen–eighteen year olds on the Youth Training Scheme receive an allowance, not means-tested, which is similar in value to the highest level of mandatory grants received by first degree students under means-testing; (3) those studying advanced vocational and professional courses receive either nothing, or discretionary grants usually of less than half the value of mandatory grants, or mandatory grants, dependent upon the course and their area of residence.

If educational provision beyond sixteen were to become more responsive to market forces, then an important step would be to ensure that relative subsidies (including the absence of subsidies for those families most affected by earnings foregone for education) did not distort the choices made by individuals. While the strategy of the ERB does not appear to address issues of educational motivation, it may be that other aspects of government policy, or other aspects of the economic context, are relevant, and this we will consider later.

☐   **Time: access to education**

The ERB seeks directly to increase access to education, and in other respects may indirectly have the same effect.

The introduction of a statutory National Curriculum will increase access to certain kinds of education up to age sixteen. Many pupils until now have been excluded, or permitted to withdraw, from some subjects which are to become mandatory: notably science and foreign languages. Previous experience has shown that, where children are required to participate in a subject up to a certain age, the probability of choosing to continue with that subject thereafter increases.

City Technology Colleges are evidently intended to increase access, both in providing a longer school week, and in actively fostering commitment to education until the age of eighteen (Taylor, 1988). Whether the latter will change actual access in the aggregate, however, will depend largely on selection procedures. Although City Technology Colleges are required to provide for 'pupils of different abilities' (ERB, clause 80) they could meet this modest requirement with an ability mix which was highly skewed towards those who would, in any case, remain in education. If, however, these Colleges recruit *proportionately* across the ability range, and offer a mix of post-sixteen educational courses to meet the needs of all groups, then access will have been increased compared with current average practice. The success of such educational practices could then diffuse to other schools.

Still more important, the Bill would provide substantial incentives to schools to persuade more children to remain after sixteen, and to offer courses accordingly. The incentives arise because local authority funding of each school (or the equivalent central funding for the new grant-maintained status) is to be in general proportionate to numbers and ages of pupils; and because schools will have direct management of these funds. Presumably, the funding formulae will have to take account of the higher average cost of pupils in the sixth form. In many cases, moreover, the marginal cost of additional sixth-form pupils will be considerably below the average cost, since there will be relatively small subject classes with spare teaching capacity. Under these circumstances schools will tend to become more willing to facilitate inward transfer of new pupils at the sixth-form stage; and conversely, they will have more incentive to be responsive to the needs of existing pupils in order to reduce movement out.

Although we have pointed out some of the limits on the notion of an educational market-place, the Government's overall strategy of opening schools to market forces does contain possibilities for increasing educational attainment. Removing inefficient schools or teachers is one possibility, but it will soon encounter practical constraints and could be destabilizing in its effects. The surer influence is likely to be through increased access to education, stimulated through the National Curriculum, the City Technology Colleges, and inter-school competition to maintain rolls and finances. This competition will provide the real increases of power and choice for parents. But will the potential of competition driven by power be sufficient to achieve the specific goals we have proposed?

A weakness in the Government's competition strategy for schools is that effective market power may be taken by the section of parents interested only in the academic route for children. Because educational attainment and occupational aspiration is so strongly influenced by parents' education and occupation (Gambetta, 1987; Rudd, 1987), parents of children with lower academic aspirations and attainments may themselves have low levels of interest in education, and accordingly will be less likely to make demands on schools. The effective pressures upon schools will in that case reflect only part of the market, and those pressures may well tend to reinforce the entrenched traditions of the British educational system, rather than stimulating change. The market will thus support development only in that segment of education where growth is already well established. It will not provide the impetus for the more difficult changes needed to develop improved provision within education for those now likely to leave with low qualifications; for there will be less parent pressure to achieve this. Indeed, if one section of parents is more active in the educational market than others, then educational development could be systematically distorted to serve one-sided interests.

Such an outcome would fail to provide one half of young people with the capacity to adapt to economic change and to survive economic hazards. It would be economically wasteful, reducing the potential productive contribution which these young people could make in the kind of future which we have sketched. It would also constitute an aggravation of the existing inequitable structure of educational opportunity. If, on the other hand, the ERB succeeded, against these expectations, in drawing a broad cross-section of all parents into the educational market-place, so that new voices with new demands were heard, that would be a great achievement.

■ Other educational policy

As was stressed at the beginning of this paper, the Government's market-making strategy for education constitutes only part of educational policy. We now turn to other developments to see what prospects they offer. The main policies of relevance are those concerned with the curriculum and those relating to higher education.

A significant possibility, in terms of access to sixteen–eighteen general education, will be the progressive adoption of the AS syllabus. This offers young people the alternative of less specialized and less intensive courses than those provided under the A-level system, and should help to retain more in general education beyond sixteen. The Government has expressed hopes that the acceptance of AS qualifications by higher education will in turn broaden access to degree courses (HMSO, 1987a). However, the recommendations of the Higginson Committee (HMSO, 1988) that A-levels themselves should be broadened to a five-subject standard, with more emphasis upon 'flexibility' and 'accessibility', have met with immediate rejection from the Secretary of State for Education and Science. With government policy in this area lacking coherence, the impact of AS levels will depend largely upon the responses of educators.

The *utility* of sixteen–eighteen education depends, in part, upon consequent access to higher education. The Government's urging of HE institutions to be more open in their admission policy, together with its adherence to the 'modified Robbins principle' of providing places for all who can benefit from higher education and wish to do so, suggest that it is prepared to be expansionist. But conservative forecasts of growth in demand for higher education have been emanating from the DES (Department of Education and Science, 1986), and funding remains tight. The signals remain obscure, as do the workings of the rationing system for places, so there is little fresh impetus for young people from this quarter.

For those young people unlikely to pursue general education to eighteen or beyond, both the GCSE and the TVEI may prove to be important developments. Both appear to offer some progress through both increased *motivation* and enlarged *access*, to young people who would otherwise have had few educational aspirations not only at sixteen–eighteen, but even at fourteen–sixteen.

The GCSE in principle increases the average value of a qualification at sixteen by removing the sharp distinction which existed between O-levels and CSEs. There has been real injustice, and consequent disincentive, through labelling under the O-level and CSE regime: CSE grades 1, 2 and 3 were intended to equate with grades C, D and E at O-level, but never acquired the same public status. Moreover, the *probability* of obtaining a GCSE qualification is, in principle, increased by the introduction of continuous assessment alongside assessment by examination, and by assessment of a wider range of attainments (for example, attainment in oral as well as written modes of presentation). These potentially important features of GCSE would be given much greater reality by the replacement of norm-referenced grading by criterion-referenced grading (that is, of relative standards by absolute standards). At present the progress towards that aim is painfully slow.

Access may be affected by more specific curriculum developments under GCSE. For example, there is some reason to expect that the Broad Science syllabus already introduced in some areas will increase access to scientific education; and may be more likely to be widely adopted under the pressure of the National Curriculum.

The potential impact of the TVEI also seems to be chiefly through enlargement of *access*. It offers no new or different qualification, but encourages the formation of new educational routes from fourteen to eighteen. Although each local implementation has different particulars, the common feature of schemes is a blending of general with vocational education, and freedom to mix both kinds of qualification. Its flexibility of form appears suited to encouraging a wide range of young people to enlarge their investments in both educational and vocational qualifications.

■ The impact of non-educational policies

Non-educational policies affect educational attainment through their effects on *motivation*, a link which is made particularly apparent when motivation is presented in terms of rational choice. Individuals, according to this formulation, will be more likely to pursue a continuation of education when the expected long-term rewards offered by such a path are sufficiently greater than alternative paths (after taking account of the costs as well).

Government affects the real returns to education by its economic and industrial policies. It also affects the opportunity costs of education through the relative rates of subsidization which it offers for education compared with alternative paths.

Since 1979, gross earnings differentials in Britain have widened while taxation differentials have narrowed. It is possible that as a result *motivation* has been increased for education to eighteen and beyond, which gives access to the occupations offering high earnings. But large proportions of those in higher education enter teaching, medicine, nursing and other public services, the pay and prospects of which may have been adversely affected by the Government's policy in the public sector. More generally, Government's desire to foster a culture of incentives and enterprise may create tensions with securing a continuing supply to the public service professions, which take a large part of the higher-qualified output of the education system.

Government sponsorship of various business groups may well increase educational flows into certain élite occupations (for Department of Trade and Industry sponsorship of the accountancy profession, see Cooper *et al.*, 1988). Similarly, the Government's policies in regard to defence, to aerospace, and more broadly to public sector R&D, affect career opportunities for many higher occupations, especially those of a scientific or technological type. Here there may again be a tension between the policy of stimulating scientific and technological education on the side of access,[2] while reducing motivation by restricting the scientific expenditure of the state (the largest employer of scientists). This tension can only be resolved if private sector employers sufficiently expand their demand.

Relative subsidization of educational and other paths is particularly crucial for an objective of raising the attainments of those who now leave education for the labour market at the age of sixteen. An important influence in this case is the Youth Training Scheme, which offers its participants a level of financial support which even first degree students are unlikely to exceed unless they have industrial sponsorship. Participation in full-time education after the age of sixteen has declined following the introduction of the two-year YTS (Department of Education and Science, 1987). This is an example of the divergence between the social and private returns to education which can result from state subsidy. The YTS in its turn may soon face severe difficulties because, with a sharp fall in the numbers of school leavers in the 1990s, it will become easier for them to obtain jobs. There may be a temptation to raise the allowance to YTS participants, in order to save the scheme, but this will lead to further distortions of educational choice.

Another source of distortion is the high rate of subsidization for first degree students, which ensures that the private returns to such education are considerably higher than the social returns. It could be argued that a switch of subsidization from degree students to pupils aged sixteen–eighteen would result in a better matching of private and social returns. However, the reduced attractiveness of tertiary education might in turn reduce the motivation to continue education beyond sixteen. This is a complex field which we cannot explore further, but its importance, and the need for further review, are evident.

■ Conclusions

For the foreseeable future, both skilled and less-skilled manual jobs which were the mainstay of employment for so long are likely to decline. The economy, a generation on, will require much greater numbers of knowledge, versatile and adaptable people capable of continuing to learn, as changing technology and rising consumer demands will require of them. The most important economic goal for educational policy is simply the education of more young people to high standards so that they will be sufficiently flexible to respond to the opportuities, and cope with the hazards, of this future.

Comparison with competitor nations shows how much further we have to go; and consideration of the existing shape of educational pathways suggests that two specific goals should be pursued. The first is to increase the proportion of those continuing general education to eighteen, or beyond. The second, and more difficult, is to provide a broad vocationalized (as opposed to narrow vocational) education for as many of the remainder as possible.

Educational policies intended to raise attainments can be assessed in terms of three possible influences on the learning process: *teaching*, *motivation* and *time* (access to education). The Government's market-making Reform Bill, when examined in this way, appears at first sight to offer some powerful influences upon the quality and organization of *teaching* resources (teachers and schools). But, because it is difficult to improve teaching directly, reliance may have to be placed upon structural change such as the closure of unpopular schools. This could develop in unpredictable ways (ranging from slow constrained change to explosive change), and the effects on educational attainment are impossible to assess. Both government policy and public opinion may have over-estimated the scope for improving teaching through incentives and sanctions applied to teachers and head teachers.

Increased access to educational opportunities, especially at sixteen–eighteen, does seem likely to be provided by the government strategy. The National Curriculum, City Technology Colleges, and the financial arrangements for schools, will all encourage pressures for enlargement of access to education. The new arrangements will offer an increase in market power for parents. However, this power is more likely to be used effectively by parents seeking access to general education for their children beyond the age of sixteen, than by parents with lower educational aspirations for their children. Market pressures are in themselves relatively unlikely to lead to expansion of provision for those now poorly catered for through education beyond the age of sixteen.

Curriculum reforms (notably the GCSE, the TVEI and the AS examination) will also contribute to the goals of increased attainment. Again, this will largely be through enlarged access. The TVEI offers a hopeful model for education for a large section of fourteen–eighteen year olds, but its success depends upon that of the courses from which it is blended, especially the GCSE, which will occupy the central place in education for at least the next decade.

Of the three main influences upon educational attainment, it is motivation (to continue in education) which current changes neglect. 'In a society where there is no automatic right to State support for students who stay at school beyond the minimum leaving age, there will always be young people who ... feel that they have to leave as soon as they can because they and their families would otherwise have to make unacceptable financial sacrifices' (HMSO, 1988). The pessimism of this remark reflects the persistent failure of policy to deal with the financial distortions of educational choice.

Nevertheless, the combination of existing trends, curriculum reform, and the Government's market-making strategy, appear sufficient to support quite ambitious goals of expansion of general education to the age of eighteen. Of course, it is still possible that the 'market' for education will fail: parents, children, employers may all fail to see the opportunities. But it will be difficult for them to say that the opportunities were not there.

The position is different for the development of an alternative path from fourteen to eighteen to encompass most of those now leaving at sixteen. Parent power is less likely to be an effective stimulus here: indeed, it may in practice be concentrated in such a way as to obstruct the development of this alternative path. The TVEI is still a modest scheme, operating for minorities in selected schools. The City Technology Colleges have everything to prove. Progress is complicated by the existence of the YTS, with its low-level and narrow vocationalism and its high subsidization. It is difficult to see the present plans for the expansion of TVEI being sufficient. It should be driven forward and made into an integrated large-scale scheme. Financial arrangements between school-based and work-based vocational education need to be harmonized to remove disincentive effects for the former. Then a genuine dual system incorporating both school and work-place, the best of TVEI and YTS, might be developed.

The distinction between the two main goals which we have discussed here is between one which is achievable through stimulation of existing processes, and one which requires a more radical transformation of education. In examining these two goals, one sees both the potential for market-like stimulation of education, and the need for a more systematic and sustained expansion of access.

Notes

1.   Scotland, with no less extensive developments, but a substantially different education system, is excluded from the scope of the paper. Nevertheless, for convenience's sake, we often speak of 'Britain'.

2.   The most notable example of such direct intervention is the Engineering and Technology Programme. It is notable that, despite this intervention, the number of engineering students has declined.

References

Becker, G. S. (1964, 1975) *Human Capital* (1st edn, 1964; 2nd edn, 1975) (New York: Columbia University Press).

Blaug, M. (1967) 'Approaches to educational planning', *The Economic Journal* (June), reprinted in *The Economics of Education and the Education of an Economist* (Aldershot: Edward Elgar, 1987).

Boulding, K. E. (1970) 'An economist's view of the manpower concept', *Beyond Economics* (Ann Arbor: University of Michigan).

Cooper, D., Lowe, T., Puxty, T., Robson, K. and Willmott, H. (1988) 'Regulating the UK accounting profession', paper presented at the *ESRC Workshop on The State and the Professions in British Industry and Commerce: A Changing Relationship, London*.

Daniel, W. W. (1987) *Workplace Industrial Relations and Technical Change* (London: Frances Pinter/PSI).

Deloitte Haskins & Sells Management Consultancy Division (1987) 'The funding of vocational education and training: a consultation document' (London: Manpower Services Commission).

Department of Education and Science (1986) 'Projections of demand for higher education in Great Britain 1986–2000' (London: DES).

Department of Education and Science (1987) *Statistical Bulletin, 6/87* (London: DES).

Freeman, C. and Soete, L. (eds) (1987) *Technical Change and Full Employment* (Oxford: Basil Blackwell).

Gambetta, D. (1987) *Were They Pushed or Did They Jump? Individual Decision Mechanisms in Education* (Cambridge: Cambridge University Press).

Goldthorpe, J. H. (1980) *Social Mobility and Class Structure* (Oxford: Clarendon Press).

Goldthorpe, J. H. and Payne, C. W. (1986) 'Intergenerational social mobility in England and Wales 1972–83'. *Sociology*, 20.

Grey, D. and King, S. (1986) 'The Youth Training Scheme: the first three years', *Manpower Services Commission Research and Development No. 35* (London: Manpower Services Commission).

Halsey, A. H., Heath, A. F. and Ridge, J. M. (1980) *Origins and Destinations: Family, Class and Education in Modern Britain* (Oxford: Clarendon Press).

Hanushek, E. A. (1971) 'Teacher characteristics and gains in student achievement: estimation using micro data'. *American Economic Review*, 61.

Hanushek, E. A. (1986) 'The economics of schooling: production and efficiency in public schools'. *Journal of Economic Literature*, 24.

HMSO (1987a) 'Higher education: meeting the challenge', *Cm. 114* (London: HMSO).

HMSO (1987b) 'Education reform. A bill to amend the law relating to education' (London: HMSO).

HMSO (1988) 'Advancing A levels' (Report of the Higginson Committee) (London: HMSO).

Maddison, A. (1987) 'Growth and slowdown in advanced capitalist economies'. *Journal of Economic Literature*, 25.

Manpower Services Commission (1985) *Technical and Vocational Education Initiative Review* (London: Manpower Services Commission).

Ministère de l'Education Nationale (1984) *Repères et Références Statistiques sur les Enseignements et la Formation* (Paris: SIGES).

Psacharopoulos, G. (1986) 'Links between education and the labour market: a broader perspective'. *European Journal of Education*, 21.

Redpath, B. and Harvey, B. (1987) *Young People's Intentions to Enter Higher Education* (London: HMSO).

Roberts, K., Dench, S. and Richardson, D. (1986) 'The changing structure of youth labour markets', *Research Paper No. 59* (London: Department of Employment).

Rudd, E. (1987) 'The educational qualifications and social class of the parents of undergraduates entering British universities in 1984'. *Journal of the Royal Statistical Society, Series A*, 150.

Smith, D. and Tomlinson, S. (1988) *Success and Failure in Secondary Schools* (London: PSI).

Taylor, C. (1988) 'Climbing towards a skilful revolution'. *Times Educational Supplement*, January 22.

Terlecky, N. (1974) *The Effect of R&D on Productivity Growth in Industries* (Washington, D.C.: National Planning Association).

White, M. (1983) *Long-term Unemployment and Labour Markets* (London: PSI).

White, M. and McRae, S. (1988) *Long-term Unemployment among 18–24 Year Olds* (London: PSI).

Whitley, J. D., Wilson, R. A. and Smith, D. J. E. (1980) 'Industrial and occupational change', in Lindley, R. M. (ed.), *Economic Change and Employment Policy* (London: Macmillan).

Chapter 2

Human Capital Concepts

M. Woodhall

The concept of human capital refers to the fact that human beings invest in themselves, by means of education, training, or other activities, which raises their future income by increasing their lifetime earnings. Economists use the term 'investment' to refer to expenditure on assets which will produce income in the future, and contrast investment expenditure with consumption, which produces immediate satisfaction or benefits, but does not create future income. Assets which will generate income in the future are called capital. Traditionally, economic analysis of investment and capital tended to concentrate on physical capital, namely machinery, equipment, or buildings, which would generate income in the future by creating productive capacity. However, a number of classical economists, notably Adam Smith, pointed out that education helped to increase the productive capacity of workers, in the same way as the purchase of new machinery, or other forms of physical capital, increased the productive capacity of a factory or other enterprise. Thus, an analogy was drawn between investment in physical capital and investment in human capital.

The concept was not fully developed, however, until the early 1960s when the US economist Theodore Schultz analysed educational expenditure as a form of investment (Schultz, 1961), the *Journal of Political Economy* in the US published a supplement on 'Investment in human beings' in 1962, and Gary Becker published a book with the title *Human Capital* (Becker, 1964, 1975) which developed a theory of human capital formation and analysed the rate of return to investment in education and training.

Since that time the concept of human capital has dominated the

Source: Woodhall, M. (1987) 'Human capital concepts', in Psacharopoulos, G. (ed.), *Economics of Education: Research and Studies*, Pergamon, Oxford, pp. 21–24.

economics of education and has had a powerful influence on the analysis of labour markets, wage determination, and other branches of economics, such as the analysis of economic growth, as well as expenditure on health care and the study of migration. For it is recognized that these also represent investment in human capital, since they can help to determine the earning capacity of individuals, and therefore increase their lifetime incomes.

However, investment in human capital remains a controversial issue. Attempts to measure the rate of return to investment in education have been attacked by critics who argue that education does not increase the productive capacity of workers but simply acts as a 'screening device' which enables employers to identify individuals with higher innate ability or personal characteristics which make them more productive. A summary of this controversy is given below, together with a brief review of research on investment in education and some other applications of the concept of human capital.

■ Measuring the rate of return to investment in human capital

When economists refer to expenditure on education and training as investment in human capital, they are doing more than pointing to analogies between education and investment in physical capital. They are asserting that it is possible to measure the profitability of investment in human capital using the same techniques of cost–benefit analysis and investment appraisal that have been traditionally applied to physical capital.

The profitability, or rate of return on investment, is a measure of the expected yield of the investment, in terms of the future benefits, or income stream generated by the capital, compared with the cost of acquiring the capital asset. Cost–benefit analysis is designed to express all the costs and benefits associated with an investment project in terms of a single figure, the rate of return, which shows the rate of interest at which the present discounted value of future income is exactly equal to the present discounted value of costs. This enables different projects to be compared and an optimum investment strategy consists of identifying and investing in projects offering the highest rate of return, or profitability.

If money devoted to education, training, or health care is regarded as investment in human capital, since it raises the lifetime earnings of workers who are better educated and trained or more healthy than other workers, then techniques of cost–benefit analysis can be used to compare the economic profitability of different types or levels of education, of on-the-job compared with off-the-job training, or of different types of medical treatment. It should also be possible to compare rates of return to investment in human capital and physical capital, in order to discover whether it is more profitable to invest in men and women or machines.

Investment in human capital produces benefits both to the individual and to society as a whole. The individual who takes part in education or vocational training benefits by increasing his or her chances of employment and by increased lifetime earnings. These additional earnings, after allowance for payment of taxes, can be compared with the direct and indirect costs of education that must be borne by the individual, including fees, expenditure on books or equipment, and earnings forgone while in school, college, or university. This provides a measure of the private rate of return to investment in education or other form of human capital.

Both the costs and benefits of education also affect society as a whole, since society benefits from the increased productivity of educated workers. Throughout the world this is recognized by governments who pay some or all of the costs of education, and provide free or subsidized tuition in schools or higher education institutions. The costs and benefits to society can be compared by means of the social rate of return.

The question of the profitability of different types and levels of education and training, and the question of the relative yield of investment in human capital and physical capital, have attracted a considerable amount of research activity since the 1960s, as well as provoking fierce disagreements among economists and educational planners. Psacharopoulos has reviewed attempts to measure the social and private rate of return to investment in education in 32 countries (Psacharopoulos, 1973) and more recently has updated this survey of research on the returns to education by analysing the results of cost–benefit analysis of education in 44 countries (Psacharopoulos, 1981). Estimates of social and private rates of return to educational investment, based on surveys of the earnings of workers of different educational levels in 44 countries in the period from 1958 to 1978 reveal, according to Psacharopoulos (1981, p. 326), four underlying patterns:

(1) the returns to primary education (whether social or private) are the highest among all educational levels;

(2) private returns are in excess of social returns, especially at the university level;

(3) all rates of return to investment in education are well above the 10 per cent common yardstick of the opportunity cost of capital;

(4) the returns to education in less developed countries are higher relative to the corresponding returns in more advanced countries.

■ The profitability of human capital *versus* physical capital

The rates of return that are reviewed by Psacharopoulos are summarized in Table 2.1, which shows the average private and social rate of return for primary, secondary, and higher education in less developed, intermediate, and economically advanced countries. These rate of return estimates refer to single years, and therefore do not show how rates of return change over time, although the average rate of return is calculated from estimates for years which range over a 20-year period. However, there are very few countries for which it is possible to calculate rates of return on an historical time-series basis. Data exist on earnings of workers in the USA classified by educational level since 1939. Estimates of rates of return to secondary and higher education between 1939 and 1976 suggest that the returns to education are falling, although not by a large amount. Data from Colombia also suggest that between 1963 and 1974 the returns to education declined, but still remained profitable.

The results of all these studies confirm that expenditure on education does represent investment in human capital, and that it is a profitable investment, both for the individual and for society, although some critics deny that the earnings of educated workers provide an adequate measure of the economic benefits of education. It is difficult, however, to answer the question of whether human or physical capital represents the more profitable form of investment.

An early attempt to answer this question was called 'Investment in men *versus* investment in machines' (Harberger, 1965), and this is still a question that is of vital concern to economists and planners. Psacharopoulos examined estimates of the returns to physical capital in both developed and developing countries and concluded: (a) the returns to both forms of capital are higher in developing countries, which reflects the differences in relative scarcities of capital in either form in developed and developing countries; and (b) human capital is a superior investment in developing countries but not in developed countries, as indicated by the reversal of the inequality signs in Table 2.2 (Psacharopoulos, 1973, p. 86).

■ How does human capital increase workers' productivity?

The earliest explanations of the concept of human capital suggested that education or training raised the productivity of workers, and hence increased their lifetime earnings, by imparting useful knowledge and skills.

Table 2.1 The returns to education by region and country type (per cent).

Region or country type	N^a	Private			Social		
		Prim.[b]	Sec.[c]	High.[d]	Prim.	Sec.	High.
Africa	9	29	22	32	29	17	12
Asia	8	32	17	19	16	12	11
Latin America	5	24	20	23	44	17	18
LDC average	22	29	19	24	27	16	13
Intermediate	8	20	17	17	16	14	10
Advanced	14	e	14	12	f	10	9

[a] N = Number of countries in each group. [b] Prim. = primary educational level. [c] Sec. = secondary educational level. [d] High. = higher educational level. [e] Not computable because of lack of a control group of illiterates. [f] *Source*: Psacharopoulos (1973, p. 86).

However, this assumption was soon attacked by critics who argued that the higher earnings of educated workers simply reflected their superior ability, rather than the specific knowledge and skills acquired during the educational process. In addition, it was argued that highly educated workers are more likely to come from higher social class groups in society, and to work in urban rather than rural areas. Many estimates of rates of return to education therefore adjust the observed earnings differentials of educated people to allow for the influence of other factors on earnings.

Since ability is one of the main factors that may determine earnings, this is often called the 'ability adjustment' or alternatively the 'alpha coefficient', where 'alpha' (α) represents the proportion of the extra earnings of the educated, which is assumed to be due to education.

Table 2.2 The returns to alternative forms of capital by level of economic development. (*Source*: Psacharopoulos, 1981, p. 329.)

Level of development	Physical capital		Human capital
Per capita income under $1,000 (7 countries)	15.1	<	19.9
Per capita income over $1,000 (6 countries)	10.5	>	8.3

Regression analysis and earnings functions suggest that an appropriate value for the α coefficient is between 0.66 and 0.8 (Psacharopoulos, 1975).

More recently, however, critics have gone further, and have argued that education does not improve productivity by imparting necessary knowledge and skills, but simply acts as a screening device, which enables employers to identify individuals who possess either superior innate ability or certain personal characteristics, such as attitudes towards authority, punctuality, or motivation, which employers value and which are therefore rewarded by means of higher earnings.

This argument is called by various names in the literature, including the 'screening' or 'filtering' hypothesis, or alternatively the 'certification' or 'sheepskin' argument, since it is suggested that education simply confers a certificate, diploma, or 'sheepskin', which enables the holder to obtain a well-paid job without directly affecting his or her productivity. This argument has attracted considerable controversy, but has been refuted by a number of economists who argue that while a 'weak' version of the screening hypothesis is undoubtedly true, since employers do use educational qualifications in selecting employees, as a proxy for other characteristics, there is no evidence to support the 'strong' versions of the hypothesis, that education has no direct effect on productivity. The fact that employers continue to pay educated workers more than uneducated throughout their working lives refutes this (Psacharopoulos, 1979).

Even if the 'strong' version of the screening hypothesis is rejected, and it is difficult to see why no cheaper means of identifying workers with desired characteristics has not been developed if education really had no effect on productivity, it is nevertheless true that the idea of education as a screen or filter has been important in influencing recent directions in research in the economics of education. Blaug (1976) in a review of research on investment in human capital, which he describes as a 'slightly jaundiced survey' of the empirical status of human capital theory, predicts that

> in time, the screening hypothesis will be seen to have marked a turning point in the 'human investment revolution in economic thought', a turning point to a richer, still more comprehensive view of the sequential life cycle choices of individuals. (Blaug, 1976, p. 850)

The reason why the screening hypothesis is important is that it has focused attention on the precise way in which education or other forms of investment in human capital influence productivity, and has served as a reminder that education does far more than impart knowledge and skills. The reason why employers continue to prefer educated workers is that not only does the possession of an educational qualification indicate that an individual has certain abilities, aptitudes, and attitudes, but the educational process helps to shape and develop those attributes. In other words, it is now increasingly recognized that education affects attitudes, motivation, and other personal characteristics, as well as providing knowledge and skills.

This means that the concept of investment in human capital is still valid, but it must be extended to include activities which affect personal attributes as well as skills, and it must recognize that such activities increase workers' productivity in complex ways.

■ Other forms of investment in human capital

Other forms of investment in human capital also develop the personal attributes that help to determine a worker's productivity. On-the-job training and work experience and the process of job search, including migration, as well as health care, can all increase earning capacity, and can therefore be regarded as investment in human capital. Blaug's survey of research on human capital links all these activities together.

> The concept of human capital, or 'hard core' of the human-capital research program is the idea that people spend on themselves in diverse ways, not for the sake of present enjoyments, but for the sake of future pecuniary and non pecuniary returns .... All these phenomena – health, education, job search, information retrieval, migration and in-service training – may be viewed as investment rather than consumption, whether undertaken by individuals on their own behalf or undertaken by society on behalf of its members. What knits these phenomena together is not the question of who undertakes what, but rather the fact that the decision-maker, whoever he is, looks forward to the future for the justification of his present actions .... The human-capital research program has moved steadily away from some of its early naive formulations ... [but] it has never entirely lost sight of its original goal of demonstrating that a whole range of apparently disconnected phenomena in the world are the outcome of a definite pattern of individual decisions having in common the features of forgoing present gains for the prospect of future ones. (Blaug, 1976, pp. 829, 850)

Not only does research in human capital now link those apparently disparate activities together, but many programmes that have been developed in recent years in response to high levels of unemployment among young people are increasingly concerned to forge closer links between education, training, and work experience. Programmes such as the Youth Opportunities Programme and Youth Training Scheme in the United Kingdom and a number of programmes for young people in Europe are designed to provide alternating periods of vocational education, training, and work experience, recognizing that all these activities represent investment in human capital (CEDEFOP, 1982).

References

Becker, G. S. (1964, 1975) *Human Capital: A Theoretical and Empirical Analysis, with Special Reference to Education* (1st edn, 1964; 2nd edn, 1975) (Princeton, New Jersey: Princeton University Press).

Blaug, M. (1976) The empirical status of human capital theory: a slightly jaundiced survey. *J. Econ. Lit.*, 14, pp. 827–55.

CEDEFOP (European Centre for the Development of Vocational Training) (1982) *Alternance Training for Young People: Guidelines for Action* (Berlin: CEDEFOP).

Harberger, A. C. (1965) 'Investment in men *versus* investment in machines: The case of India', in Anderson, C. A. and Bowman, M. J. (eds), *Education and Economic Development* (Chicago: Aldine).

Psacharopoulos, G. (1973) *Returns to Education: An International Comparison* (Amsterdam: Elsevier).

Psacharopoulos, G. (1975) *Earnings and Education in OECD Countries* (Paris: Organization for Economic Cooperation and Development).

Psacharopoulos, G. (1979) 'On the weak *versus* the strong version of the screening hypothesis'. *Econ. Letters*, 4, pp. 181–185.

Psacharopoulos, G. (1981) 'Returns to education: an updated international comparison'. *Comp. Educ.*, 17, pp. 321–341.

Schultz, T. W. (ed.) (1961) *Investment in Human Beings* (Chicago: University of Chicago Press).

Chapter 3

The Great Debate on Education, Youth Employment and the MSC

D. Finn

As a new generation of working class youth became acclimatized to an extended period of compulsory schooling, the educational consensus out of which RSLA had been created was disintegrating. Rather than opportunities for social mobility, an increasing number of minimum age school leavers were confronted with more or less extended periods of unemployment. It seemed that young people had become less acceptable to employers and their exclusion from the labour market was to generate problems of social control and political legitimacy.

The 1970–4 Conservative government had implemented RSLA, presided over large schemes of comprehensive reorganisation and in its first White Paper in 1972 declared its commitment to 'a framework for expansion'. The Conservatives accepted many of the terms of the social democratic consensus. However, the assumptions of that period were now under attack from a wide variety of groups from across the political spectrum (Education Group, 1981, chapter 9).

Crucially, economic decline undermined the claim that an expanding education system contributed to economic growth and efficiency. An aggressive new school of economics began to assert that educational expenditure, as part of an ever growing public sector, was actually precipitating the decline of British capitalism. The New Right in and around the Conservative Party identified school reform and progressive teaching methods as important causes of the moral and political malaise of the period.

Source: Finn, D. (1987) *Training without Jobs*, Macmillan, London and Basingstoke, chapter 5, pp. 103–129.

The most important pressure group in this new politics was the alliance created through the pages of the Black Papers on Education, whose first report in 1969 had been laughingly dismissed by the educational establishment. By 1975, it had helped to discredit the achievements, purposes and resource arguments of the educational world as they had been expressed in the 1960s. It was campaigning for new controls to be imposed on schools and in the process was changing the terms of reference of the debate about educational means and ends.

In the 1975 edition, which was marked by the emergence of Dr Rhodes Boyson as co-editor, the analysis of schooling's failure was given a political dimension. A more populist argument emerged; parental involvement in the work of the schools became a basic element of the programme. This contrasted the concerns and anxieties of parents with the anonymity of the state and insularity of the professionals who worked for it. It exploited the fears of parents who were apprehensive about their children's futures and harnessed the dissatisfaction that was felt by many who saw that schools were unable to develop the abilities and talents their children possessed.

Populist definitions of the purposes of education, and of the most appropriate teaching methods, were invoked against the alleged orthodoxy of progressivism as practised by 'trendy' teachers owing responsibility to no-one outside the school. The demand was for higher standards, to be secured by making teachers more accountable. The central challenge to the legitimacy of schooling – for both school leavers and their parents – was the changing relationship between qualifications and jobs. With rising unemployment it became more difficult to sustain the argument that if they attended, behaved well and worked hard in school, then young people would get access to better job opportunities. This not only affected those incarcerated by the extra year but increasingly blighted the prospects of the achievers, whose qualifications seemed to have less and less value on the labour market.

Under the 1974–79 Labour government this crisis of education resulted in a major attempt to redefine the nature and purposes of schooling. In attempting to explain this transformation, I want to concentrate on the way in which schools were held responsible for the growth of youth unemployment and how this argument created the political space which allowed for a rapid expansion of special unemployment measures organized by the Manpower Services Commission (MSC). These were to be rationalized in 1978, to produce the Youth Opportunities Programme (YOP), which was intended to remedy the faults of the young working class and provide them with a route into jobs.

New definitions of the relationship between education and work-based training were to be explored through the concept of *vocational preparation*. In place of day release for purposes of general education, the objective of reform became preoccupied with making young workers more acceptable to employers. Early in 1979, proposals were put forward (DES/DE, 1979) for creating a national system of traineeships which would be extended to all those young workers who received no further education or training at work.

■ The Great Debate: education and working life

The Great Debate on education, initiated by James Callaghan at Ruskin College in October 1976, marked at the highest political level the end of the phase of educational expansion which had been largely promoted by his own party, and signalled a public redefinition of educational objectives. As the Tories took up the arguments popularized by the Black Paper writers, Callaghan was to 'steal their clothes' and undermine the polemical force of their critique of Labour's educational past. The debate was also a response to more immediate events – the acute economic crisis, escalating unemployment, cuts in public expenditure, and the anticipated fall in pupils as the number of infants started to decline.

This intervention by the Prime Minister represented an attempt to win political support and secure a new educational consensus. It marked a clear shift on the part of the Labour leadership towards policies which would facilitate greater government control of the education system. This was required because it was now assumed that the quality of the labour force was a major problem encountered by industry in the economic crisis. The new educational consensus was to be constructed around a more direct subordination of education to what were perceived to be the needs of the economy. As the subsequent Green Paper made the point:

> It is vital to Britain's economic recovery and standard of living that the performance of manufacturing industry is improved and that the whole range of government policies, including education, contribute as much as possible to improving industrial performance and thereby increasing the national wealth. (DES, 1977, para. 1.16)

The core theme of education's relationship to economic performance did not attain its prominent position on the agenda of the Great Debate as the result of some natural process. It was defined as a central issue within a wider debate about Britain's economic and social problems. Constructed over a number of years, and articulated in various reports and media, consistent complaints about falling standards, progressive teachers and education's lack of relevance to working life were transformed into a wide-ranging critique of the 1960s developments.

The relationship between reforms in secondary schooling, the characteristics of young workers, and the nature of work discipline were highlighted by the growth in youth unemployment and by the complaints of employers. It was argued that because of developments within schooling, the pattern of educational control and the habits and characteristics it created were actually developing in opposition to the patterns of behaviour required at work. In an early paper, which first outlined the objectives of vocational preparation, the MSC underlined the extent of these changes:

> In recent years the social environment in a number of schools, with more emphasis on personal development and less on formal instruction, has been diverging from that still encountered in most work situations, where the need to achieve results in conformity with defined standards and to do so within fixed time limits call for different patterns of behaviour. The contrast is more marked where changes in industrial processes have reduced the scope for individual action and initiative. (MSC/TSA, 1975, p. 15)

Accumulating evidence suggested that this contradiction between the demands of employers and the characteristics of young workers was getting worse.

A major survey of employers' reactions to young workers was carried out by the National Youth Employment Council (NYEC) in 1974. Drawing on evidence from a wide variety of bodies, including the CBI and the Institute of Careers Officers, the report concluded that employers were placing increasing emphasis on 'motivation': 'coupled with the fact that a large minority of unemployed young people seem to have attitudes which, whatever their cause or justification, are not acceptable to employers and act as a hindrance to young people in securing jobs' (NYEC, 1974, p. 29). Most employers complained of a change of attitude in young people who were now 'more questioning', 'less likely to respect authority', and 'tend to resent guidance about their appearance' (p. 74).

These perceived changes in the characteristics of young workers, and the implicit criticisms of the education system, were dramatically expressed in the period immediately preceding the Great Debate. In a marked break from post-war tradition, some of the major contributions to this critique of the schools came from representatives of industrial capital. Given prominence in the media, the criticisms of Sir Arnold Weinstock (Managing Director, GEC), Sir John Methven (Director General of the CBI), Sir Arthur Bryant (Head of Wedgwood Pottery), and others, portrayed unaccountable teachers, teaching an irrelevant curriculum to young workers who were poorly motivated, illiterate and innumerate.

By the time of Callaghan's speech, rather than there being an assumed loose fit between school and work, it had become commonly asserted that there was a mismatch. The Prime Minister was concerned that some schools 'may have over-emphasized the importance of preparing boys and girls for their roles in society compared with the need to prepare them for their economic roles.' Teachers were ignorant about the world of work; they were directing their pupils into the wrong subject areas (too much arts and humanities) and prejudicing them against industrial employment. More fundamentally, he echoed complaints from indus- trialists that young people left school without 'the basic tools to do the job'. He concluded that there was 'no virtue in producing socially well adjusted members of society who are unemployed because they do not have the skills' (quoted in *Times Educational Supplement*, 22 October 1976).

The Great Debate had a dual purpose. Not only were the aims and objects of education redefined but, at the same time, the *actual processes* of the education system were being restructured both to achieve those new goals and to fit the new patterns of reduced state expenditure. However, this restructuring of the social relations of schooling was necessarily a long- term process – with contradictions and potential resistances. In the meantime, increasing youth unemployment meant that the need to ensure a disciplined, productive and malleable labour force, or as the MSC's Holland Report (1977) put it, 'building a workforce better adapted to the needs of the 1980s,' was too important to be left to the vagaries of the labour market and the streets, or in the hands of an unreformed and now suspect educational apparatus.

■ There's work to be done? The rise of the MSC and special measures for the unemployed

The MSC was created by the Employment and Training Act 1973, which gave it power to make arrangementes for 'assisting people to select, train for, obtain and retain employment, and for assisting employers to obtain suitable employees' (HMSO, 1973, p. 2). It was given two executive arms, the Employment Services Agency (ESA) and the Training Services Agency (TSA), through which it would modernize and rationalize existing provision.

The Commission was given control over its own budget, con- siderable administrative powers and a broad remit. It became responsible for a wide range of services and institutions ranging from the ITBs and Skill Centres, through to the Job Centres. It was required to organize any training activities of 'key importance to industries or the national economy'. The actual Commission was made up of an equal number of TUC and employer representatives. These were not delegates, and the individuals involved were expected 'to take decisions without continual reference back' (HMSO, 1973, p. 1).

The apparent powers of the MSC were subordinate to those of the

Secretary of State for Employment who set the Commission its targets but was under no obligation to accept any recommendations it might come back with. The Secretary of State was given power to 'direct' the Commission and even 'modify' its functions: the possible duties that the Commission could be asked to perform were open-ended and allowed space to take up any new 'directions' that the Secretary of State thought suitable. Through the Commission, the government could not effectively – if indirectly – control training and any unemployment measures it chose to introduce.

At the same time that the 1973 Act created greater centralized control, it also weakened the previously autonomous, more directly interventionist, industry-based training agencies. In responding to the pressure of the small firms lobby, the Conservative government replaced the levy grant system by which ITBs raised their funds with a levy–grant exemption system which had the effect of making the Boards far more dependent on direct exchequer support, and less able to intervene in individual employers' training practices.[1]

As unemployment began to creep upwards the MSC (which was formally launched on 1 January 1974) commissioned, as one of its first acts, a study from the Cambridge economist Santosh Mukherjee in order 'to prepare contingency plans against the possibility of unemployment rising to a higher level and for a longer period than we have had since the war' (MSC, 1974, p. 3). The report's ironic title, 'There's work to be done', suggested that even in a context of escalating unemployment there were plenty of tasks waiting to be done.

As Britain's industrial decline accelerated in the mid-1970s, the Conservative, then Labour, governments had attempted to alleviate its effects on employment by introducing a series of direct financial subsidies and inducements to employers to salvage and preserve existing jobs. Mukherjee and the MSC now proposed a new kind of programme where the waste of resources represented by the unemployed could be transformed into 'an opportunity' to fulfil otherwise unmet social needs. The ensuing Job Creation Programme (JCP) was introduced in October 1975, with an initial budget of £30 million to create some 15,000 temporary jobs. Special emphasis was given to recruiting the two age groups hardest hit by unemployment – those under twenty and those over fifty.

At the same time, the Department of Employment introduced a Recruitment Subsidy for School Leavers (RSSL), which offered employers £5 a week for six months for recruiting an unemployed school leaver. It was to have mixed effects. It displaced unemployment on to other groups, it failed to benefit those school leavers most affected by unemployment, and it created very few extra jobs (Casson, 1979, p. 111). As a resut, it was replaced in October 1976 by a Youth Employment Subsidy (YES), paying £10 a week for *any* young person under twenty who had been unemployed for more than six months. This also encountered problems and the evidence 'suggests that it was no more successful than the RSSL in increasing net employment' (Casson, 1979, p. 111).

There was considerable criticism of the JCP for not reaching the groups most at risk from prolonged unemployment. Contrary to expectations, for example, it ended up employing a high number of unemployed graduates, and not enough of the young long-term unemployed. In September 1976, JCP was supplemented by the creation of a Work Experience Programme (WEP). This scheme provided work experience places for six months for unemployed young people under the age of nineteen, who received an allowance of £16 a week. It was envisaged that the programme would cost £19 million and provides places for 30,000 young people. Early evidence indicated that few WEP schemes had been fully subscribed and, as with JCP, about half the participants left during the course of the programme.

As unemployment stubbornly refused to fall in line with government policy it became evident that these *ad hoc* responses would need to be rationalized. It also seemed that employers were ignoring the exhortations of government to recruit more of the young unemployed. An MSC survey of 13,000 employers found that most of them 'were not prepared to support' government-aided schemes for reducing youth unemployment. Seventy-eight per cent of the employers interviewed said they would not increase their recruitment of young workers. Even if their businesses expanded by 10 per cent they would rely on getting more out of their existing workforce. If they had to increase recruitment, most put youth at the bottom of their list of potential recruits (*Observer*, 12 June 1977).

At the same time that Mr Callaghan launched the Great Debate, the MSC published 'Towards a comprehensive manpower policy', its first major policy statement. This spelled out what the Commission understood as its primary objectives. It described what already existed, set out future projections, and made many administrative and programmatic recommendations. It also emphasized that there was an ideological dimension to its activities:

> It is the Commission's task to define and articulate ... a comprehensive manpower policy .... It would however be wrong to suppose that there is some magic list of extra manpower measures .... *The task is rather to create a new attitude to manpower* (MSC, 1976, p. 6, my emphasis).

Within its proposals for the future, the MSC identified the vocational preparation of young workers as an issue of particular concern, which had been accentuated by youth unemployment. The policy statement outlined the various youth initiatives it was involved in, including those which it now ran directly for the Department of

Employment. The JCP and WEP would come to an end in 1977, and would need to be replaced. It proposed 'ambitiously', that it should have the objective of ensuring: 'that all young people of 16 to 18 years of age who have no job or who are not engaged in further or higher full time education should have the opportunity of training, of participation in a job creation programme or of work experience' (MSC, 1976, p. 22). A working party was set up in October 1976, chaired by Geoffrey Holland, which reported in May 1977. The proposals were accepted by the Secretary of State for Employment in June, who wanted them to come into effect by April 1978.

The Youth Opportunities Programme (YOP) replaced the older schemes with courses designed to: 'prepare young people for work and different kinds of work experience.' It aimed to provide 130,000 places, to accommodate 234,000 youngsters a year by 1978. The adult unemployed were given their own Special Temporary Employment Programme (STEP),[2] and YOP was restricted to sixteen–eighteen year olds who were to receive an allowance of £18 a week. The programme consisted of Work Preparation courses – from employment induction (two weeks) to Short Training courses (three months); and Work Experience – from six months on employers' premises, to one year in training workshops or community service. It was intended, given the emphasis on placing youngsters in conventional jobs, that work experience with employers would constitute the dominant element of the programme.

What started out as contingency plans were assuming increasing importance in the MSC and transforming its objectives and structure. A further 'Special Programmes' division was added to the already existing Employment Services and Training Divisions. New mechanisms for local delivery were to be created, and the scheme had to be marketed to an ever-growing number of sponsors and potential trainees.

■ The DES and the MSC

This rapid expansion of MSC programmes soon had a direct impact on the most work-related element of the education sector, the Colleges of Further Education. As apprentices disappeared, they were gradually replaced by a new client group. In evidence to a House of Commons Select Committee in 1976, the Commission emphasized that its leading role in responding to youth unemployment was inevitably changing the nature of what took place in colleges: 'it is a fact that we have been expanding our training activities … much more rapidly than education activity has been expanding', and 'much of the initiative in terms of new plans and progress has come from our side of the fence rather than theirs' (HMSO, 1976, p. 400). NATFHE, the college lecturers' union, argued in their evidence that the MSC was now posing 'fundamental issues of educational principle'

(p. 238). The Commission was both offering its own solution to the problem of young people and work, and it was bypassing the political relationship between central government and local authorities through which educational change had previously been negotiated.

During the proceedings of the Select Committee it became clear that far from dictating educational policy, central government was significantly hamstrung in its activities. Policies had to be translated into practice via the financial and political autonomy of Local Education Authorities (LEAs). This barrier posed acute problems for any national policies. This was especially the case in trying to evolve a coherent and unified response to the education, training and employment provision of the sixteen–eighteen year age group. There was also intense competition between government departments.

The Select Committee concluded that the 'DES and the Department of Employment are in a sense competing for resources and liable to be judged one against the other by result.' The DES was thought to be 'less nimble in a situation where objectives themselves are changing' than in more routine matters, and that the MSC 'has moved at a tempo which DES could not (and indeed should not try to) emulate.' The Committee welcomed the 'enthusiasm displayed by the MSC' (p. xxviii).

It is in this context that we have to see the rise to power of what was called 'manpower-servicedom'. Unfettered by the political and financial constraints on the education sector, and more ideologically in tune with the then government's industrial strategy, the MSC was able to win control over this whole area of institutional expansion.

Despite this success, there was a central ambiguity in the MSC's approach to young people. On the one hand, it was attempting to reform work-based training and extend it to all minimum age school leavers. On the other hand, it was expanding provision for the young unemployed. This distinction made sense only if the assumption that youth unemployment was a cyclical phenomenon could be sustained, and YOP was originally designed as a temporary programme with a five-year life span. However, as youth unemployment continued to grow, it became apparent that it was not merely caused by the recession or poor quality of school leavers, but was part of a more fundamental shift in employment patterns. The conclusion increasingly drawn was that the nature of the relationship between minimum age school leavers and the labour market required a permanent change.

■ Cyclical and structural youth unemployment

During the 1950s and 1960s the average rate of recorded unemployment was 1.5 per cent; between 1971 and 1975 this rose to 3.5 per cent, and this continued to increase under the Labour government until 1977 when unemployment exceeded 1.3 million. There was a slow decline thereafter, but at its lowest point in September 1979 it still exceeded 1.2 million, or 5.1 per cent of the labour force. Job prospects for young people changed dramatically. In the early 1960s the youth unemployment rate was not dissimilar to that of adults, but afterwards the relative position of young workers grew steadily worse (MSC, 1974, p. 28). Between January 1972 and January 1977, for example, overall unemployment increased by 45 per cent, but for those under twenty it had risen by 120 per cent.

Evidence showed that young people were being disproportionately affected by *cyclical* unemployment – due to the recession and other short-term factors, such as young people's propensity to change jobs rapidly; trade union insistence on 'last in first out' and no recruitment policies; and employers' reluctance to take on marginal workers in response to demand because they would be covered by employment protection. Research carried out for the Department of Employment, which reviewed the evidence up to 1976, concluded that 'changes in youth unemployment are closely associated with changes in overall unemployment, but move with a greater amplitude' (Makeham, 1980, p. 235). There were other factors, but it was overall levels of unemployment and the general condition of the local economy which provided 'the major explanation of variations in youth unemployment' (p. 236). The policy implication was that if significant changes in youth unemployment were to be effected, then there needed to be an improvement in the economy as a whole.

However, there were aspects to youth unemployment which could not be explained by cyclical factors (Casson, 1979). There were significant structural causes of youth unemployment. The most obvious was the growth in the number of young people coming on to the labour market; this was expected to increase every year until 1981, when it would total 50,000 more than in 1976. With an anticipated increase in the number of women looking for work, the total labour supply was expected to increase from 25.75 million in 1976 to 26.5 million in 1981. Even if unemployment stabilized, 150,000 *extra* jobs per year would have been required merely to stop it getting worse.

The general decline in the manufacturing sector and the reduction in jobs for unskilled manual workers also undermined the demand for young people, especially those without qualifications. In evidence submitted to the National Youth Employment Council, attention was drawn to the closure of large establishments, especially in the traditional industries of coalmining, shipbuilding, steel and railways. The apprenticeship system was collapsing. In engineering and shipbuilding, the number of apprentices almost halved ebtween 1964 and 1974, falling from 140,000 to less than 80,000. In construction, apprenticeships fell from over 129,000 to just over 93,000 (NYEC, 1974, p. 20).

The point was made that the newer industries established were often capital-intensive, or preferred employing older women as part-timers. Revealing their preoccupation with the threat posed by male unemployment, this report concluded that 'all over the country firms were improving productivity, and the tea boy, van boy, the messenger boy and the office boy had been weeded out in the process' (NYEC, 1974, pp. 56–57).

A 1976 Department of Employment study, a 'View of occupational employment in 1981', showed that whereas up to that point changes in the relative sizes of different industries were the key to changing occupational patterns, it was now technical changes *within* industries which were of increasing significance. Manual workers were subject to two important economic changes. They suffered from *displacement*, where jobs were lost without any prospect of new investment or job creation; but they also lost out from the *creation* of new plants, processes and jobs, which tended to be more capital-intensive and used less manual labour (examples quoted were the docks, railways, gas and telecommunications). For the British Youth Council, 'all of these factors ... make the plight of the young worker ... even more severe' (BYC, 1977).

Beyond this absolute decline in the number of jobs available for young people, the 1970s were to witness a change in employers' perceptions of the kind of young workers they were interested in. Traditionally, many young workers had been typified as irresponsible, poorly motivated and quick to change jobs. They found work in casual, blind alley trades, where they were controlled by direct discipline and supervision; they learnt their skills on the job, 'sitting by Nellie'. However, as unemployment increased, and more steady adult workers became available, the balance of costs tilted towards them. The return of married women to the labour market, which had been increased by the recession and by other changes in women's roles, also gave employers access to a supply of stable workers, many of whom were willing to accept part-time work. It seemed that young people and older female workers were competing for similar types of jobs: unskilled light manual or clerical work, predominantly in service industries (Casson, 1980).

Reviewing evidence on employers' recruitment practices in Coventry, Simon Frith concluded in 1977 that:

> Young workers today enter a labour market in which there are fewer and fewer openings for either skilled craftsmen or for unskilled casual labourers. The dominant demand is for generalised, semi skilled labour power. The shifting employment opportunities resulting from the rise of service occupations, technological changes in production, the decline of small firms means, too, shifting modes of labour control. It is in this context that the young compete unequally with experienced adults. They lack commitment and discipline and 'realism'. These are the qualities which schools have 'failed' to instil.These are the qualities which have to be instilled by the

State, as it takes on responsibilities for the now lengthy period of transition from school to work (Frith, 1977, p. 4).

■ The political crisis of youth unemployment

The government's response to youth unemployment reflected more than a concern with their numbers. The extent and speed of state intervention was a product of the fears then expressed about the social and political unrest which might follow prolonged unemployment. At a Summit meeting held in London in 1977 the Heads of Western Governments declared their concern about the consequences and promised action. In Britain this apprehension was increased following the Carnival Riots in Notting Hill which in August 1976 were to open up a decade of riot and urban revolt by black British youth.

Attention was drawn to the emergence of black and white youth subcultures which were making sense of life without work, and to the alienation and despair of other young people excluded from the labour market. Youth unemployment itself reflected and recreated broader social inequalities. If you were black, a minimum age unqualified school leaver, or if you lived in certain towns or regions, your chances of obtaining work were more severely curtailed. The British Youth Council reported that between February 1975 and 1976, youth unemployment among ethnic minority groups increased by 110 per cent for males and 275 per cent for females: unemployment among West Indian youth was twice the national average (BYC, 1977, p. ix).

The MSC 'declared its fear' that the failure of young people to get a job could 'permanently alienate them from the world of work and from society'. Not only did this 'bode ill for the future productivity of the country's potential labour force, but it is also likely to cause high levels of crime and social unrest' (BYC, 1977).

The special employment measures introduced in the mid-1970s depended on more than administrative, financial or logistical considerations. They required a political and ideological realignment of the purposes and defined function of education and training; an amplification of causes and promotion of explanations of the crisis rather than a simple accommodation of its effects. If there was work to be done, that work lay as firmly in the political and ideological terrain as it did in the application of technocratic procedures to the operations of the labour market.

In this sense, a key feature of unemployment among the young was that theirs was not politically or ideologically equivalent to unemployment as it affected older groups in the labour market. Their predicament was not susceptible to the same explanations nor vulnerable to the same political critique. Novel explanations of their situation were required. The pursuit of such an explanation saw attention move away from employment towards the changing nature of young people as they emerged on to the labour market. The political crisis of youth unemployment was transformed into an *educational* crisis.

■ The crisis in education

In the crisis of education of the late 1970s I have emphasized the significance of two key policy developments – the growing involvement of the state in training, epitomized by the creation of the MSC, and the increasing pressure on schools to be responsive to the needs of industry. Both these policies were attempts to grapple with the effects of recession and the collapse of youth employment.

For the government, the most dramatic problem posed by the young workless was that of social and political unrest. The educational problem, however, was employability. The state had to ensure that the young unemployed would be good workers when they did eventually get jobs.

The immediate consequence of youth unemployment was that the transition from school to work now lasted a long time. School leavers no longer got immediate work experience and so schools and training programmes had to become the source of something like the work ethic; the state was to be held responsible for the processes of work socialization that used to be a normal part of leaving school and getting a job. Some of this new responsibility was to be taken up by the MSC, but schools were also expected to put a new emphasis on vocational preparation.

Substantial changes were to be promoted in schools, designed to create a new relationship between education and work. Two national curriculum projects were set up, one by the Confederation of British Industry (CBI), the other by the Schools Council. A host of local developments were initiated including opportunities for teacher secondment to industry and school–industry twinning schemes, where teachers and employers discussed the curriculum and the expansion of work experience. Unconnected with any established academic discipline, and given official blessing by the Great Debate, this growing curricular input was able to bypass the traditional gatekeepers of school knowledge, especially the examination boards (Bates, 1984). The central preoccupation was with inculcating positive social attitudes to industry and the 'wealth-making' process. Indeed, the Schools Council Careers Education and Guidance Project was directly censored; they were told that industry should be presented in a more 'positive' light and that their materials placed too much emphasis on the 'exploitation of young people': the materials were subsequently modified (Bates, 1984, p. 202).

At issue in all these developments was not the schools' usual role in the classification and qualifying of young workers, but a concept of education as a direct preparation for work. Schooling for unemployment was to involve, paradoxically, more efficient education for employment; teachers were expected to instil the work ethic deeply enough for it to survive lengthy periods of non-work. The stress was on a particular kind of realism. Work experience schemes became as important as lessons in Maths and English. All teachers were expected to become employment-conscious, assessing their subjects and their pupils with reference to local job opportunities.

The impact this new orientation had on actual classroom practice is hard to assess. However, the analysis itself had considerable potency, not only in explaining youth unemployment but also in explaining the disaffection of a large number of school leavers. It suggested that the reluctant stayers should be given a more work-related curriculum in a new exchange, which would both meet their expressed interests and make them more acceptable to employers. For the achievers it suggested that they should be taking courses which were more directly relevant to their future employment rather than dominated by the academic preoccupations of the examination boards. Schools were to become more directly involved in preparing young people for work. The conventional distinction between education and training had been blurred, and was in the process of being redefined.

Before evaluating that process of redefinition, which was to be expressed in the concept of vocational preparation, it is worth exploring in some detail why employers were dissatisfied with young people. What were these needs and requirements they had which schools and young people were failing to meet?

■ Employers' needs and young workers' attitudes

On examination, it turned out that employers' educational needs were extremely ambiguous. They could in fact be contradictory, confused or simply unknown. Even though it carried out its review of education, training and industrial performance from a single point of view – from 'the "needs" of the world of work' – a 1980 Think Tank report had to conclude that:

> There are quite serious difficulties about interpreting what the needs of industry are .... These [needs] are far from uniform; there are inconsistencies between what employers say they want and the values implicit in their selection process; their conception of their needs, present and future, is frequently not explicit and clearly formulated (CPRS, 1980, p. 7).

There are also significant differences between industrial interests and the interests of other employment sectors. The issue is not so much a question of the needs of employers as the logics of capitals. A very different educational logic will attach to businesses with a high ratio of technically or commercially skilled labour – say the banking or telecommunications industries – to businesses which have found a way of exploiting casual labour by, for example, a reversion to domestic outwork. The former represents educational requirements at their most advanced, the second an extension of nineteenth-century modes of exploitation which were crudely anti-educational in their effects. Yet both forms co-exist in one society and under the same state.

Employers may require certain technical and scientific skills in their labour force at any given time, but the range and pace of innovation in modern industrial processes soon makes specific skills redundant. Employers have an interest in minimizing training costs and gearing it to their immediate requirements. For them, training needs to be as brief as possible for jobs which are likely to change or disappear in a short space of time. Yet time-serving methods of apprenticeship training preserved trade union organization and recreated a now unwanted division of labour. As they adapted to international competition and new technologies, manufacturing companies were abandoning their traditional ways of recruiting young workers.

Employers now required skilled workers with the flexibility, adaptability and disciplines which would enable them to be quickly trained (and retrained) for specific jobs over relatively short periods of time. There is a real sense in which employers cannot know what *particular* skills they require from their workers' general education and training. Moreover, the actual evidence on the skill requirements of many working class jobs shows that their educational demands are very limited. Blackburn and Mann (1979) in their study of the working class labour market in Peterborough, estimated that 85 per cent of the workers could do 95 per cent of the jobs surveyed. They pointed out that most workers exercised more skill in driving or getting to work than they actually used while there. The experience of women during the world wars, where they were involved in taking over areas of production from men, also demonstrated the ease with which apparently untrained, unprepared or 'weaker' groups can function in the production process without great problems. In reality, the skills required across a very wide sector of the labour market are relatively easy to acquire, and are well within the grasp of most workers.

What are articulated as the needs of employers are never a straightforward or unproblematic expression of the needs of the labour process. Individual employers have specific requirements of their workforce, but the translation of these needs into a coherent set of demands on the state, and their resolution in certain policies, is a political process and involves far wider issues than the simple representation of objective problems encountered in workplaces.

■   Ignorance or knowledge?

On closer examination it turned out that the comments on falling educational standards were inextricably entwined with an argument about attitudes. Not only were school leavers barely literate or numerate, but they also 'don't know what working life is about.' The Holland Report linked employers' complaints about literacy and numeracy with simultaneous comments about poor motivation (MSC, 1977, p. 17). Most employers, it seemed, were looking 'for a greater willingness and a better attitude to work from young people' (MSC, 1977, p. 17). The criticism of schools for producing ignorant workers was simultaneously a criticism of school for producing unwilling workers.

What was at issue here, as Simon Frith (Frith, 1977) pointed out at the time, was not ignorance but knowledge: what was worrying employers was that their young recruits knew all too well what work was about. Theresa Keil, for example, in her 1976 study of the transition from school to work in Leicestershire, found that 'young people have a wide range of knowledge about their work situations' (Keil, 1976, p. 49), acquired before starting their jobs from friends, relatives and neighbours. Their biggest area of ignorance was actually about the role of trade unions.

A study of 200 young workers at GEC in Rugby in 1977 found that 'the expectations of many young people that industrial work is boring and repetitive are broadly realistic' (Simon, 1977, p. 64). The research exposed a key contradiction faced in the management of young workers in that if young people had high expectations of their jobs they tended to become disillusioned and dissatisfied with the reality they went on to experience, whereas if they had lower, more realistic expectations they showed little interest in the job at all (Simon, 1977, p. 5).

A comprehensive review of evidence about 'Young people and their working environment' was published by the International Labour Organization (ILO, 1977). It provided evidence about the conditions which confronted many young people in industry. It drew attention to the lack of congruence between education and work, but emphasized that 'many of the jobs now available in industry are unsuited to most workers' standard of education' (p. 2). The report pointed out that despite their education or training, many school leavers found themselves in semi-skilled jobs, usually in a secondary labour market. Their jobs had a catalogue of disadvantages going with them, ranging from low wages and poor career prospects through to their greater exposure to accidents and experience of monotonous or menial jobs. Wage discrimination against young people was common to all countries, especially in industry. Young people were often required to accept the same working conditions and obligations as adults, but were frequently lower paid. As a result 'young people's lives are fraught with insecurity', especially in the case of those who had left home.

Young workers had a catalogue of complaints. What they most disliked about their working environments were 'cold, heat, noise, dirt, incorrect posture, carrying heavy loads, the loneliness and monotony which came from job fragmentation and repetitive tasks, and the lack of independence and responsibility' (p. 9). Poignantly, they found the wish for freedom, interesting work and comfort, was commonest in the youngest workers of all, who had not had time to realize what working life actually involved: 'older workers expect no more than they know they are likely to get' (p. 20).

Not surprisingly, they found the swift emergence of an instrumental orientation to the working situation, 'young people are first and foremost realists' and 'model their ambitions . . . on the opportunities given them' (p. 19). In response to work, which was devoid of interest, and where their future was uncertain, they tended to concentrate their interests on life outside the workplace. They were interested in work only insofar as it gave them the wage which they valued because it was 'the only means of getting the things that seem to them essential in a consumer society' (p. 19). Although their attitudes to industrial work varied greatly, 'it can safely be said that in almost every country they are predominantly negative' (p. 18).

At the heart of the problem was young people's attitudes to work. In the UK, however, these characteristics were not viewed as a realistic assessment by the young of the possibilities which awaited them, instead they were now defined as a pathology. The young employed were ignorant, their attitudes were wrong, they lacked even basic skills, and these characteristics explained why they were unemployed. By 1976, it was to be axiomatic for Sir Richard O'Brien, then chairman of the MSC, to announce that 'the expectations, aptitudes and attitudes of young people are often out of balance with those of employers and the world of work.' This was by now an established fact which all should deplore. Reforming the priorities and practices of schooling was only part of the solution. There was also the problem of what happened to school leavers when they started work.

■ Day release education and vocational preparation

The absence of systematic training for most young workers had been criticized by the OECD, and had been commented upon unfavourably in many other international comparisons. The National Training Survey in 1975 showed that 30 per cent of those under twenty-five had never received any work-based training. Part-time courses, usually on day release from work, were the most common form of contact with the formal education system, but in 1975–76 only one in five boys in work and one in eighteen girls under nineteen years of age were attending such courses (*Department of Employment Gazette*, November 1980).

The younger the school leaver, the more likely he or she was to enter employment which did not provide significant training. Although vocational training was concentrated on young people, about a third of all training received by those questioned by the National Training Survey had lasted less than one month, and a further quarter for one month to a year. Young people with no educational qualifications were more likely to receive basic or initial training than further training, to be trained on the job rather than off the job, and to have a shorter duration of training.

Following the achievements of RSLA, many educational groups and the broader labour movement were to renew their demands for better provision for young unskilled workers, but they still stressed educational rather than training provision. In the 1960s it had been anticipated that the Industrial Training Boards (ITBs) would have been able to extend day release provision to all young workers, but such illusions were shortlived.

The basic problem concerned employers' reluctance to make any provision for the young unskilled. At the same time that the apprenticeship system was contracting, it was hardly surprising that employers were less than convinced of the benefits of giving day release to all their young workers. In 1972, the Engineering ITB commented on the naive optimism of the education service in assuming that the Industrial Training Act would result in an expansion of day release. It argued that although day release education may have been a desirable objective, the costs of what was essentially a social programme should be met by government, not by employers (FECDRU, 1980, p. 24). In 1972 the Director of Education and Training at the CBI specifically rejected the accusation that they were failing to create universal day release education:

> it seems fair to ask whether this situation is directed to the right Act. There is no doubt that the resentment caused in industry by a tendency to seek the achievement of purely educational objectives through the Industrial Training Act and also to use it to seek to shift costs from the educational system to industry, has done a great deal of damage (FECDRU, 1980, p. 24).

It was to transform those educational objectives into terms acceptable to employers that the MSC began to construct the concept of vocational preparation. In its original 1975 discussion document it sketched out the elements of a new relationship between education and training. In deference to employers' priorities it replaced the historical emphasis on general education with a concern about how to make young people more effective and productive workers:

> it seems certain that properly conceived vocational preparation would raise substantially the ability of many of these young workers. More important still, the experience of 'learning to learn' things relevant to work would help them to adapt to change more readily and therefore work more effectively throughout their lives. Proper training for young people would in fact raise the whole potential of the workforce (MSC/TSA, 1975, p. 19).

Proposals were made to modernize apprenticeship training in ways which would prevent skill shortages occurring in the future. The report called for the introduction of development projects aimed at creating new forms of vocational preparation for the unskilled and semi-skilled; and short industrial courses to be provided by ITBs for the young unemployed.

The report echoed many of the themes feeding into the Great Debate. It suggested that those aspects of general school education which had vocational relevance should be extended and, without suggesting actual job training in schools, asked whether 'a directly vocational element should be included in the curriculum' (p. 21). The authors called for an extension of work experience and observation at school, and for a careful examination of 'where the balance should be struck between the responsibilities of secondary education and the role of industrial training' (p. 21).

These arguments provoked a sharp response from the TUC, which was unhappy about the dominance of the employers' perspective which pervaded the discussion document. The General Council rejected the assertion that schools should prepare for work. Young people should be encouraged to have a critical awareness of life at work, but schools must 'give overriding consideration to the personal development of their pupils and must create learning situations that reflect *the varied needs of their pupils not those of industry*' (TUC, 1975c, p. 2, my emphasis).

At a delegate conference, held in November 1975, the TUC agreed that 'the introduction of day release education for all young workers was perhaps the single greatest priority for the trade union movement in this area' (TUC, 1975a, p. 2). They argued that a single Department of Education *and* Training was necessary to coordinate this policy. In their own discussion document on day release, the TUC argued that the voluntary route of persuading employers had 'manifestly failed' and it would be 'futile' to pursue it further. They called for legislation to place a statutory requirement on employers to release all their young employees so that they could 'attend courses of their choice according to their individual needs' (1975b, p. 5). They consistently rejected 'vocationalism' in favour of a broad education related to the individual young person's needs:

> General education at this stage will necessarily have to have some reference to the occupations and employments in which young workers find themselves, but will be concerned with the personal rather than the vocational development of individual young people. Young workers requiring specifically vocational education to complement sustained occupational training should receive additional release for that purpose (TUC, 1975b, p. 1).

The DES, which could have resisted the pervasive vocationalism of the MSC, was by this time trying to outdo it. Having lost the ideological initiative in the Great Debate and the practical initiative when the Commission had been given the resources to develop programmes for the unemployed, the DES was by now advertising its support for the government's industrial strategy. In its 1978 Annual Report, for example, the DES stressed how in 'its efforts to expand educational opportunity and participation the Department concentrated on the 16 to 18 year old age group, with the aim of producing a much more coherent approach to the central question of giving young people a better start in working life' – a set of objectives directly rivalling the broader objectives of the MSC (quoted by Tapper and Salter, 1981, p. 218).

The pilot programme of unified vocational preparation (UVP) which was introduced in 1976–77 represented a compromise. The programme was jointly administered by the DES and MSC. A constant theme in the government's initial statement on UVP was on the necessity to achieve a 'careful blend', a 'real synthesis of education and training.' By 1979, when the Labour government was proposing a national system of traineeships, the concept of vocational preparation replaced older definitions of education and training:

> The terms 'training' and 'education' have been commonly used as a rough and ready means of distinguishing between learning to perform specific vocational tasks (training) and the general development of knowledge, moral values and understanding required in all walks of life (education). But such definitions have obvious shortcomings .... The concept of vocational preparation treats the entire process of learning, on and off the job, as a single entity, combining elements of training and education to be conceived and planned as a whole (DES/DE, 1979, p. 10).

While it was possible to create a new perspective which ideologically resolved the tension between education and training, translating that perspective into an employment reality was a different proposition. Employers had already demonstrated their reluctance to take on what they considered to be the social objectives of day release education and the government's original statement on UVP acknowledged that the case was 'still not recognized.' The government conceded that 'the economic gain from improved vocational preparation is not precisely quantifiable', but they appealed to employers' enlightened self-interest and assured them that there was 'no doubt' that vocational preparation would improve young people's attitudes and productivity (DES, 1976, p. 5). The government hoped that a series of pilot programmes would convince employers.

Few employers, however, made efforts to increase provision for their young workers. The MSC's 1978–79 *Annual Report* records just over 100 schemes with about 3,000 trainees; a year later it records some 250 schemes involving 3,500 trainees. Most of these experiments were sponsored by employers involved with the Distributive and Rubber and Plastics ITBs.

■ A national system of traineeships

1978 witnessed the emergence of YOP, of pilot UVP schemes, of reforms to the apprenticeship system, and experiments with grants for young people staying on at school. This chaotic pattern of provision was criticized by many organizations because it was leading 'to a plethora of dead-ends' and was characterized by a complete absence of 'common objectives' (RPPITB, 1978, p. 5).

The TUC put considerable pressure on the government. In February 1978, it called for a commission of enquiry to examine provision for the age group and to come back, as a matter of urgency, with comprehensive proposals. It demanded a mandatory system of educational maintenance allowances for all those staying on at schools or colleges, and for the government to commit itself to introducing vocational preparation for all young workers. As an indication of the developing consensus, the contrast between vocational preparation and general education disappeared from the TUC's concerns, and it even considered that YOP 'might well provide the foundations of a permanent scheme of work preparation for young people' (*Guardian*, 2 February 1978).

The pressure for some kind of overall policy statement resulted in the publication of a consultative paper just before the 1979 General Election. This outlined proposals for a comprehensive system of trainee-ships for all sixteen–eighteen year olds starting work. These traineeships would be aimed at the 250,000 or so young people who were entering jobs with no further education or training.

Like apprenticeships, the traineeships would be work-based, but would be shorter, lasting from three to twelve months. They would offer 'an integrated programme of education and training both on and off the job.' Trainees would be given an induction to the job and to industry and working life generally, and taught both job skills and social skills. A certificate recording the content and coverage of the programme would be issued at the completion of the traineeship (DES/DE, 1979).

The scheme was to start on a voluntary basis, with employers being encouraged to participate with training grants. By the time the scheme was in full operation – covering about a third of the target group – the cost would be between £35 and £50 million a year, though this would be 'pump-priming' finance. It was anticipated that eventually the programme would become self-financing with employers meeting the costs themselves.

The period which had been initiated by the Great Debate and which ended with the fall of the Labour government was marked by a transformation of the debate about educational mans and ends. As youth unemployment multiplied, and employers complained about the quality of young people, schools were blamed for not preparing their pupils adequately for the world of work. The MSC was able to colonize this area of institutional expansion because of its sensitivity to employers' needs and because it was directly controlled by central government. It evolved a special programme for the young unemployed which was described (by Albert Booth, Labour's Employment Secretary) as a new deal, and was intended to act as a testbed for new forms of work preparation.

By 1979, the Labour government was proposing to introduce a new comprehensive form of provision, its new synthesis of vocational preparation. This would realize the Labour movement's historical demand for day release provision for all young workers and meet employers' complaints about the attitude and willingness of their young recruits. Before these proposals were put into practice, however, they were to be swept aside in the public expenditure cuts initiated by the Conservative Party after their victory in 1979. It seemed that the monetarists in the new government were hostile to the MSC and were against this experiment in social engineering and the expansion in the role of the state it involved.

Notes

1.   The government had wanted to eliminate the levy–grant system entirely, but met resistance from the TUC and CBI who feared a total loss of control over training to a centralized state agency. The compromise was the levy–grant exemption system which formalized small company eligibility for grants and state provision without a levy obligation. In addition, companies could win levy exemption by internal evaluation of their training activity compared with company requirements. That is, company-specific criteria for training quality replaced industry-imposed standards. The 1973 Act marked a retreat from the position of 1964, and undermined the ability of ITBs to provide counter-cyclical training when individual employers were experiencing financial constraints (Goldstein, 1984, p. 97).

2.   The Job Creation Programme came to an end in December 1978, and was replaced by YOP for sixteen–eighteen year olds, and the Special Temporary Employment Programme for unemployed adults. STEP was to

provide 25,000 places and was open to people aged nineteen–twenty-four who had been unemployed for more than six months or those aged over twenty-five who had been continuously unemployed for more than a year. Participants were to be employed by sponsors, normally for a maximum of 52 weeks, on projects of benefit to the community, which would not otherwise be carried out.

References

Bates, I. (1984) 'From vocational guidance to life skills: historical perspectives on careers education', in Bates, I. *et al.*, *Schooling for the Dole? The New Vocationalism* (Basingstoke: Macmillan).

Blackburn, R. M. and Mann, M. (1979) *The Working Class in the Labour Market* (Basingstoke: Macmillan).

BYC (British Youth Council) (1977) *Youth Unemployment: Causes and Cures* (London: BYC).

Casson, M. (1979) *Youth Unemployment* (Basingstoke: Macmillan).

CPRS (Central Policy Review Staff (Think Tank)) (1980) *Education, Training and Industrial Performance* (London: HMSO).

DES (1976) *Unified Vocational Preparation: a Pilot Approach, a Government Statement* (London: DES).

DES (1977) 'Education in schools: a consultative document', *Cmnd 6869* (London: HMSO).

DES/DE (1979) *16–18: Education and Training for 16–18 Year Olds*. A Consultative Paper presented by the Secretaries of State for Education and Science, for Employment and for Wales (London: DES).

Education Group (1981) *Unpopular Education: Schooling and Social Democracy in England since 1944* (London: Hutchinson).

FECDRU (Further Education Curriculum Development and Review Unit) (1980) *Day Release – a Desk Study* (London: FECDRU).

Frith, S. (1977) *Education, Training and the Labour Process*. Unpublished paper given to the CSE Education Group, Birmingham.

Goldstein, N. (1984) 'The new training initiative: a great leap backward'. *Capital and Class*, 23, Summer.

HMSO (1973) 'Employment and training: government proposals', *Cmnd 5250* (London: HMSO).

HMSO (1976) *Policy Making in the Department of Education and Science: Tenth Report from the Expenditure Committee*. House of Commons, Session 1975–76 (London: HMSO).

ILO (1977) *Young People in their Working Environment* (Geneva: ILO).

Keil, E. T. (1976) *Becoming a Worker* (Leicester: Leicestershire Committee of Education).

Makeham, P. (1980) 'The anatomy of youth unemployment'. *Employment Gazette*, March.

MSC (1974) *There's Work to be Done* (Santosh Mukherjee) (London: MSC).

MSC (1976) *Towards a Comprehensive Manpower Policy* (London: MSC).

MSC (1977) *Young People and Work: Report on the Feasibility of a New Programme of Opportunities for Unemployed Young People* (Holland Report) (London: MSC).

MSC/TSA (1975) *Vocational Preparation for Young People* (London: MSC).

NYEC (National Youth Employment Council) (1974) *Unqualified, Untrained and Unemployed: Report of a Working Party set up by the National Youth Employment Council* (London: HMSO).

RPPITB (1978) *Work and Learning: Proposals for a National Scheme for 16–18 Year Olds at Work.* Third Report of the Study Group on the Education/ Training of Young People, Rubber and Plastics Processing (London: Industrial Training Board).

Simon, M. (1977) *Youth into Industry: a Study of Young People's Attitudes to Work in a Large Midlands Factory* (London: NYB).

Tapper, T. and Salter, B. (1981) *Education, Politics and the State: the Theory and Practice of Educational Change* (Grant McIntyre).

TUC (1975a) *Training and Education of Young Workers: Report of TUC Consultative Conference held on 4 November 1975* (London: TUC).

TUC (1975b) *Day Release for Further Education: a Discussion Paper Prepared by the TUC* (London: TUC).

TUC (1975c) *Note of Comment on Training Services Agency Paper 'Vocational Preparation for Young People'* (London: TUC).

Chapter 4

Business and Industry Involvement with Education in Britain, France and Germany

H. J. Noah and M. A. Eckstein

This chapter examines the involvement of business and industry with the education and training of young people aged 14–18 (middle and upper secondary level) in three industrialized countries: Britain, France and the Federal Republic of Germany. It is concerned with the two broad categories of this involvement: what employers and their associations say about the schools, and how they actually participate in education and training.

■ Business/industry criticisms

Employers have been complaining about deficiencies of formal schooling ever since the establishment of national systems of education. Their criticisms of the schools continue unabated, and are directed at both the schools' curricula and at their organization and management practices.

With respect to the curriculum, in Britain, France and Germany, as in the USA, the most frequent criticism voiced is that schools provide an inadequate and inappropriate preparation for entry into work. Thus, a

Source: Noah, H. J. and Eckstein, M. A. (1987) 'Business and industry involvement with Education in Britain, France and Germany', in Langlo, J. and Lillis, K. (eds), *Vocationalizing Education*, Pergamon, Oxford.

memorandum submitted by the British Manpower Services Commission to a House of Commons committee observed:

> There are a number of common specific points raised by employers in criticism of school curricula. A frequently heard concern is that the standard of school leavers' literacy and numeracy is well below what it should be. When pressed to be more specific about standards of literacy, employers point to illegible writing, limitations of vocabulary, weakness of grammar and syntax and poor presentation. Lack of facility in mathematical skills means that many school leavers are unable to cope with craft training without remedial education and this gives widespread cause for concern. (Great Britain, House of Commons, 1983, p. 361, para. 3.9)

The Association of British Chambers of Commerce has also complained that employers remain unconvinced that the schools are equipping their leavers with the sort of numeracy needed in the workplace. They fault the schools for giving too little attention to equipping students for group work and deplore 'the stranglehold which academic selection for universities has on the schools' ability to provide either a broadly-based, relevant or practical education for high attainers' (Association of British Chambers of Commerce, 1984, paras 15, 16).

Similarly, in France:

> Employers do not mince their words when criticizing the training of young workers and employees, especially those graduating from the *Lycées d'Enseignement Professionel* (LEPs): absence of necessary workskills; lack of practical training; ignorance of working conditions, limits and norms characteristic of the enterprise. (Cans and Coutty, 1982, p. 10)

German employers offer parallel criticisms of their educational system. It is alleged that the recent reforms intended to improve access to middle and upper secondary education have increased the emphasis on general academic schooling to the neglect of preparation for work; and that the needs of employers and the demands of the work-place are ignored and vocational schooling is disparaged (Goebel, 1984, p. 71).

Citing the results of a survey of British employers, Jamieson and Lightfoot report:

> the vast majority [of local industrialists] had particular grievances about the [educational] system which they felt should be redressed. Three of the most common criticisms of the school system were, in rough order of importance, pupil attitudes towards work (including attitudes towards the disciplines of work of any kind as well as specific attitudes towards industry); the maths problem; the literacy and communications problems. (Jamieson and Lightfoot, 1982, p. 105)

It is argued that attempts to improve the school system may have made important things worse. Business interests in Germany claim that reforms in both the organization and content of secondary schooling have led to a deterioration in general education (Goebel, 1984, p. 34).

The British Chamber of Commerce and Industry makes the following summary criticisms:

> the education system has not hitherto proved flexible enough in adapting to the changing needs of the community which it serves .... There is too much choice in the curriculum of most secondary schools. (Association of British Chambers of Commerce, 1984)

In apparent paradox, employers fault the schools for being too academic while at the same time failing to equip young people with adequate basic educational skills. In addition, it is alleged, students lack the skills of cooperation and communication needed for successful work in a business environment. Making a more ideological point, British employers especially have complained that schools do not inculcate in school-leavers positive attitudes toward business/industry, but instead even promote negative attitudes to authority, entrepreneurial activity and the fundamental concept of a market-driven, profit-oriented economic system (Confederation of British Industry, 1984).

In a memorandum submitted by the Confederation of British Industry to a House of Commons Education, Science and Arts Subcommittee in 1981, similar views were expressed:

> Employers therefore strongly support the case for vocational elements within the school curriculum particularly in the later years of compulsory education. By this we do not mean specific vocational courses as an entry into particular trades or occupations, but a general vocational approach leading to an orientation across the whole of school life which encourages the development of attitudes, skills and knowledge of relevance to adult society ....
>
> We believe that young people should leave school with an adequate understanding of how wealth is created in our society and an appropriate evaluation of the essential role of industry and commerce. (Confederation of British Industry, 1981, p. 117)

In similar vein, a French employers' group (the *Chambres de Commerce et d'Industrie*) complains of the 'excessive segregation between the world of the schools and the outside world' (*Mission Education-Entreprises*, 1985, p. 2).

Part of the problem, observes Otto Esser, President of the Confederation of German Employers, has to do with the way school textbooks portray the economic aspects of society:

It would not be right to present an idealized version lest cynicism immediately overtake the new entrant into the workforce. But it is equally untrue and irresponsible to show it only as negative and marked by conflict. (Cited in Goebel *et al.*, 1980, p. 332)

A second set of criticisms refers to employers' concerns about the operation and governance of the educational system. They allege persistent wasteful practices that lead to high costs per unit of 'output', for example, the proliferation of elective subjects and courses. As far as the external efficiency of the school system is concerned, employers everywhere complain about a lack of response to the changing needs of the work-place. Plans for school reforms completely omit consideration of market mechanisms (Goebel *et al.*, 1984, p. 71). Where the schools provide skill-specific training, waste is said to occur because the training tends to be extremely expensive and the skills provided too often do not conform well to those needed in the work-place. French employers' criticisms are particularly pointed (Cans and Coutty, 1982, p. 14).

Moreover, and notably in Britain, employers state that the credentials gained through schooling are poor predictors of an employee's eventual performance, and that where new credentials have been introduced during recent years they are difficult to understand.

In England, France, and Germany, employers point to what they consider to be excessive red tape and government interference in both school-based and out-of-school vocational training. Efforts to improve education by more planning have resulted in inefficiency and bureaucratization. At the same time, they view the schools as insular, dominated by educational professionals who pay too little regard to the realities of economic life and business people's advice. According to one German industrialist, this is a result of the poor education of teachers who are all too often unable to relate their teaching to practical experience and reality (Goebel *et al.*, 1984, pp. 31–32).

■ Business/industry recommendations

Business/industry involvement with education goes far beyond voicing complaints, and extends to making both general and specific recommendations for change. In spite of significant differences among the three countries in educational goals, structures and processes, there is remarkable similarity of view expressed by employers and their organizations in Britain, France and Germany, regarding what needs to be done in the realm of secondary education.

Business people wish to see the distance between the world of work and the world of the schools sharply diminished, and to that end they propose changes in school curriculum, in teacher training and in-service education, and in the management and structure of the school system.

As noted in many citations above, a major charge made against the secondary school curriculum is that it has been too academic, and is biased against the child with practical talents. British, French and German employers are united in their specification of the qualities they desire to see in the young people they hire:

> The qualities which employers want in school leavers are qualities which are equally valuable to those looking for work, the self employed or those training or re-training. They are: the ability to learn; the ability to get on well with other people; the ability to communicate; reliability; basic literacy and numeracy; and an understanding of how the community's wealth is created. (Association of British Chambers of Commerce, 1984, Recommendation 16)

In the hope of promoting the acquisition of such skills, business/industry recommends that it be afforded a much greater opportunity than at present to influence the content, pacing and balance of the curriculum. It argues that its influence should be used to ensure that preparation for work be made an organic element of the secondary school curriculum, and not just a mere 'add-on' subject (Association of British Chambers of Commerce, 1984, Recommendation 8). German industry in particular recommends that the upper grades of the secondary schools move away from their single-minded concentration on preparing young people for university entrance and that throughout the school system the emphasis on academic material be tempered by giving more attention to music, art and sport. French employers make explicit recommendations for a more desirable pedagogy in French schools: young people should have the experience of carrying out their own research projects and of working together in small groups. (*Charte des Apprentissages Professionels*, 1984, pp. 6, 23).

In England and Germany especially, business/industry wants a curriculum that adapts much more readily than at present to the changing needs of the economy. The key to greater flexibility, they suggest, is to adopt in education the market principles guiding the business world:

> Curriculum policy should be customer oriented instead of producer oriented. It should begin with an audit of the skill requirements which people need in their normal daily life, including their working life, followed by the matching of these requirements against what the schools are providing. (Association of British Chambers of Commerce, 1984, Recommendation 5)

Business/industry wants a good deal more knowledge of economic and business affairs incorporated in the general education curriculum, and it recommends that school subject-matter be conveyed using less abstraction and more practical applications of language, mathematics, the natural sciences and the arts. The curriculum should provide for visits to enterprises on a regular basis in the early years of schooling, and for opportunities for older children to spend periods engaged in practical work in enterprises (Letter of response, Conseil National du Patronat Français, in *Mission Education-Entreprises*, 1985, p. 152; Goebel *et al.*, 1984, p. 46). By the same token:

> Teachers with no experience of business should be encouraged to seek it. The value of such experience should be reflected in salary and career progress. (Association of British Chambers of Commerce, 1984)

The counterpart French organization recommends, specifically, that regional inspectors and teachers of geography and history should be taught the real facts about the economy, that teachers should have the opportunity to acquire continuing education through meeting business people and through visiting firms in, for example, summer courses (Assemblée Permanente des Chambres de Commerce et d'Industrie, n.d. 2).

In like manner, the *Institut der Deutschen Wirtschaft* (the Institute of the German Economy) wishes to encourage business to provide teachers with economic education and experience in the business/industry world, in both their initial and in-service training (Goebel, 1980, pp. 333–335). In the view of Paul Schnittker, President of German Handicrafts, *Arbeitslehre* (familiarization with the working world) should be a compulsory subject for all teachers undergoing their training ('Technical change triggers new discussion on education content', 1984, p. 90).

Business/industry organizations urge their members to sponsor partnerships with individual schools and groups of schools, to make available to the teachers more printed information about themselves and about the world of work, and to be as explicit as possible about the specific educational characteristics they would like to see in the young people they hire. All of this should be aimed at helping teachers overcome ignorance about and prejudice against the business world, to reduce the chance that they will impart to their students negative attitudes toward business, either consciously or unconsciously.

Business/industry recommends a sharp improvement in the management of schools, to help them become more effective users of society's resources. School administration should learn from business practice. The Institute of Directors in Britain wants at least one member of each maintained school's governing board to be appointed specifically as a representative of employers (*Times Educational Supplement*, 12 October, 1984). As in the commercial world, so in the world of education, argues the

Institute of the German Economy, competition will tie education more closely to the changing demands of the market-place, thus improving quality (Goebel *et al.*, 1980, pp. 32–33). As in the commercial world, too, teachers (as producers) should have clear, agreed, and regularly monitored objectives in mind, and should be held accountable for their performance (Association of British Chambers of Commerce, 1984). The strong State monopoly of educational provision should be tempered by strengthening non-State (private, foundation, business/industry) institutions and arrangements in education. Personnel coming from business and industry should be permitted to serve in the schools (*Assemblée Permanente des Chambres de Commerce et d'Industrie*, n.d. 2, Propositions 8–9). Wherever possible, business initiatives should be supported by tax relief, or subsidies.

Business/industry makes specific recommendations for changing the structure of the school system and rationalizing the articulation of its several levels and institutions. The recommendations differ in detail among the three countries, as each has its own established pattern of institutions. But across the three countries the general tenor of the recommendations is the same: the position and prestige of those parts of the system providing vocational training and direct preparation for work need to be enhanced *vis-à-vis* the more purely academic parts; the prestige of vocational credentials should be raised; and opportunities for students to move from one part of the system to another should be improved. British employers would like to see a reformed system of credentials, that would go far beyond a simple recitation of academic achievements, to include a student profile. They ask also for greater uniformity and systematization of what appears to them as a 'bewildering array of courses, course providers, and methods of assessment' (Association of British Chambers of Commerce, 1984).

There is widespread agreement that partnerships between enterprises and the schools should be formed, and where they exist, they should be strengthened, so that the abyss separating the world of the school from the world of work is closed. Too much preparation for work continues to be located in schools, and more should be done within enterprises.

The German dual system of vocational education, in particular the reliance on apprenticeships, finds strong support among employers, although it receives criticism from school people. Approving the example of their German counterparts, French and British employers generally recommend moving vocational education closer to the German system, but, as in Germany, they too face opposition from many spokespersons of school-based interests.

In making recommendations for desirable changes in the schools, business/industry spokespersons are wary of the schools taking over training functions that they believe are best left to business initiative. They also warn against government control of training given within firms, and (in

France, at least) they do not view government subsidies to training as justification for detailed governmental regulation of their apprenticeship programmes.

The general stance taken by business/industry toward the conditions for partnership with government and the schools is that they should be given a freer hand, with less red tape associated with getting involved with education, and with less concentration upon detailed accountability. This attitude is taken in the name of facilitating pragmatic experimentation, quick response to perceived needs, and the capacity to change direction quickly as some things are seen to work and others not (Confederation of British Industry, 1981, p. 117; Jamieson and Lightfoot, 1982, p. 106).

Although the recommendations made in the three countries are remarkably similar, both in premises and in specifics, the posture taken by business/industry toward its 'educational responsibilities' varies. In France, business organizations tend to defer more to the education authorities and the teaching profession than in the other two countries, although their claims to a voice in educational policy are growing. In Germany, where business/industry involvement in training policies is long-standing, there is no hesitation on the part of business organizations in making recommendations for far-reaching change. In Britain, business organizations, taking a relatively new stand, assert the necessity for business to get involved in setting policies for education, and even business/industry's positive right to do so. They point out that not only does the world of work have a *special* claim to be heard, but that education and business are mutually dependent, have common interests and many common purposes, and must therefore cooperate as partners (Association of British Chambers of Commerce, 1984).

■   Business/industry participation

Business/industry has become involved with the education of young people beyond simply offering criticisms and making recommendations for change. Since roughly 1975 their active participation has been stimulated by a number of increasingly important factors. The downturn in economic growth and a sharpening of economic competition among nations, combined with increasing numbers of young people in the age-groups leaving school, resulted in rapidly rising youth unemployment rates. These reached quite unprecedented levels in France, for example, where the percentage of unemployed males aged 15–19 increased from about 5 to over 20 per cent in the period from 1974 to 1982, and in the UK, from a similar level to nearly 30 per cent (OECD, 1984, p. 26). In Germany, however, the rise was much smaller, from close to 2.5 per cent to about 7 per cent. These figures were interpreted as demonstrating the extent to which the existing structures and content of secondary schooling had become outdated, despite the prolongation of schooling for many. Moreover, technical progress had apparently eliminated many low-skilled entry level jobs formerly available to school-leavers, creating a problem which had every prospect of worsening in the future. Thus there was a widespread feeling that even when economic growth rates improved, and the size of the entry level age groups fell, a severe problem of adequate education and training of the young labour force would remain.

The result has been a new focus in all three countries on the requirements of so-called 'transition education', in which business/industry would play a larger role than ever before, not only in its more usual training function but especially in an increasing contribution to general education. This has called for changes in the legislative and regulatory frameworks for education and training, for changes in financial arrangements, for novel institutional functions and provisions, and for greater acceptance of business/industry as a full partner in a total national education and training enterprise.

The following three sections are devoted to the context and the experience of each of the three countries, as business/industry participates in activities aimed at a more directly work-relevant education. These endeavours take a variety of forms, among which are: providing an increasing number of teachers and students with opportunities to observe life in the work-place and gain practical experience; twinning and partnership arrangements to improve communication and cooperative work ties between the world of learning and the world of earning; providing schools with material and human resources, and opportunities to collaborate directly with business/industry; and sponsoring many kinds of activities, local and national, designed to encourage the development of work-related skills, an appreciation of the importance of efficiency in production, and a more positive attitude toward business/industry.

☐   Britain

The distinction between educational and vocational training has been quite sharp in Britain, where vocational training has been regarded as a substantially inferior preparation to academic education. Until the passage of the Industrial Training Act of 1964 the principle of non-intervention by the State in job-training had for the most part prevailed, and business/industry was considered to have sole responsibility for preparing its own workforce. The State had assumed responsibility for providing general education, and there was little expectation that commerce and industry had any part to play, except with respect to particular craft and technical qualifications. General education remained predominantly within the jurisdiction of the local education authorities (LEAs), who guarded their prerogatives quite jealously, and who were unaccustomed to accept advice from non-professionals concerning the educational system they provided.

The 1964 legislation marked a new view of the role of employers in the education and training of young people. Since that date, legislation (for the most part permissive, and intended to encourage activities at regional and local levels) has increasingly drawn the State into the training field, while growing business concern about the quality and structure of schooling has led to greater involvement of employers and unions with schooling.

The contemporary role of British employers has been summed up in the following terms:

> Business and industry take an active part in secondary education by supporting such initiatives as the Technical Education Initiative of the Manpower Services Commission, the School Curriculum Industry Project, Understanding British Industry and in a number of school company links. (Confederation of British Industry, private communication, 2 Feb. 1985)

Employers may also exercise advisory powers, both regionally and nationally, with respect to the general education provided in LEA schools.

Apprenticeships and other types of in-company training continue to be entirely in the hands of employers' associations and trade unions, though the State, through regional Industrial Training Boards (ITBs), has played a growing part in expanding provisions for apprenticeships.

Employers (and trade unions) are represented on the numerous examination boards that award credentials in craft and technical areas. These boards are important in Britain, because their examinations serve a coordinating role in the extremely diverse system of further education and training. The examination boards in the vocational training areas have a decisive influence over the curricula of the colleges and schools preparing students for business/industry, which in turn gives ready recognition to the credentials awarded by the examining authorities. The most notable of these are: the Royal Society for the Encouragement of Arts, Manufactures and Commerce (RSA), an independent body founded in 1774, now primarily concerned with secretarial, commercial, and public administration occupations: the City and Guilds of London Institute (CGLI), the largest such examining body, with between 400,000 and 500,000 candidates a year in the manual trades and other basic skill areas; the Technician Education Council, which since 1973 has progressively assumed responsibility for the establishment of curricula and examinations for middle-level qualifications from CGLI; and the Business Education Council, established in 1974, to develop curricula and qualifications below the university level for clerical, commercial, and administrative occupations (CEDEFOP, 1984, p. 453).

Beginning in 1964, the introduction of a levy–grant system placed pressure on employers to increase the quantity of vocational training they provided. A tax of up to 1 per cent of the payroll was imposed on (larger) companies that did not have their own training schemes, and the proceeds were used to compensate companies offering training. New bodies, called Industrial Training Boards (ITBs), were established to administer the levy–grant programme. Companies thus paid the costs of on-the-job training, while the LEAs continued to cover the costs of general education.

> Anecdotal evidence indicates that company expenditure on ET [education and training] in the UK declined considerably in 1981 and 1982 and began to recover somewhat in mid-1983 . . . a first British priority is to get better value for money . . . . Without the wealth, size and 'frontier' tradition of the US, Britain may not be able to afford a process in which each company decides not only what ET it wants internally but also what it wants the public education service to supply and in which each company also has the capacity to negotiate for what it wants with the appropriate public authorities. (National Economic Development Council, 1984, p. 90)

In 1973, the Employment and Training Act established an independent Manpower Services Commission (MSC), charged with responsibility for developing a national training effort. The Act was partly a response to complaints from smaller employers that they derived little or no benefit from the levy–grant system. Since 1973, the Manpower Services Commission has increased so rapidly that it has been termed 'Britain's fastest growing quango'. ITB activities have been increasingly taken over by the MSC, and it is expected that training through ITBs will cover no more than about 25 per cent of the youth labour force, predominantly in construction and engineering. For the rest, MSC has administered a changing menu of work-subsidy and youth training programmes involving employers. The most important date from September 1983, with the establishment of the Youth Training Scheme (YTS) and the Technical and Vocational Education Initiative (TVEI).

YTS is directed at the post-16 age group, to guarantee a 12-month training period for unemployed school-leavers. MSC is currently proposing extension to two-year programmes. Training takes place either in firms (who receive public funds amounting to about $3000 per training place), or in a variety of off-the-job training establishments run by local authorities. The YTS has incorporated three or four prior government initiatives that encouraged employers to give school-leavers work experience or training, or both, although YTS' target of providing 400,000 training places has not yet been completely met.

The Technical and Vocational Education Initiative (TVEI) promotes technically-oriented and vocationally-relevant courses for the 14–18 age group in schools and colleges. Pilot courses were instituted in 14 LEAs in 1983, and the activity was extended to a further 45 LEAs the following year. By September 1984 the programme enrolled 16,000 students. Courses are intended to provide general as well as technical education, vocational preparation and work experience for young persons of all levels of ability, including senior grade students in academic secondary education (sixth-formers). The courses are intended to be attractive to those students in the post-compulsory grades who do not intend to proceed to higher education, and thus to help widen curriculum and career choices. In this connection, the new Certificate of Pre-Vocational Education (CPVE) should be noted. Its introduction was strongly supported by both the Confederation of British Industry and the Trades Union Congress (TUC), and it was designed especially for those sixth-formers who may not wish to sit for the Advanced Level (academic) examinations.

Funding levels for these programmes were as follows (£1 = $1.35, approximately):

Industrial Training Boards, 1981–82	£117 million
Youth Training Scheme, 1983–84	£845 million
Technical Vocational Training Initiative, 1983–84	£ 7 million

(MSC, *Annual Report 82/83*, cited in Ryan, 1984, p. 33).

Summary   Two main characteristics distinguish business/industry involvement in the education and training of young people in Britain: active encouragement of local firms' participation by the national voluntary organizations of employers and local collaboration of individual firms with schools and LEAs.

Legislation and initiatives of government agencies have been important in setting out the guidelines for these activities, revising the organizational frameworks necessary, and providing financial incentives for companies to increase job training opportunities.

In the course of developments over the past decade, the traditional separation of academic general education from vocational training has narrowed. Business/industry has contributed to new thinking and practice in general education, has expanded its training activities, and has participated in revisions of examinations and proposals to introduce new credentials and new forms of assessment.

Business/industry involvement over all aspects of education and training is of recent date, and has been growing rapidly. The series of new initiatives and the blurring of the distinctions between academic and vocational education has led to anxiety over what is regarded as vocationalization of the school curriculum, and rising tension between the Manpower Services Commission and the Department of Education and Science. As a memorandum submitted to a House of Commons committee by Imperial Chemical Industries noted: 'the national organizational relationships between MSC and DES undoubtedly have within them the potential to generate unsatisfactory local competition which can only in the end act to the disadvantage of the young people themselves' (Great Britain, House of Commons, 1983, p. 218).

□   **France**

In France most pre-service vocational training is undertaken full-time in the schools as part of general education. Moreover, as a consequence of the Haby Reforms of 1975, all 12–16-year-old students receive an introduction to manual and technical subjects, as part of a common, comprehensive curriculum at the lower secondary stage.

For most pre-vocational training, the Ministry of Education promulgates curricula, sets standards, and provides staff, finance and facilities. However, for the purposes of academic organization and educational provision, France is divided into 25 so-called *académies*. Nineteen *commissions professionelles consultatives* (CPC) (vocational consultative commissions), one for each major economic sector, advise the Minister on such matters as the establishment of training courses and diplomas, curricula and the number of training places to be financed. The membership of the CPCs is representative of the major interested parties: government, employers, chambers of commerce and trades, workers, teachers, parents and experts (*Le Monde de l'Education*, May 1982, p. 17).

Firms have only recently begun to play an active and direct role in pre-service training; previously, business/industry involvement was virtually entirely confined to contractually-based apprenticeships. Employers influence initial vocational preparation in the schools through local arrangements and are involved nationally with the school system through participation in the councils that govern the *lycées techniques* (technical *lycées*), and on the examination boards of the *LEPs* (vocational education *lycées*). Representatives of the skilled trades sit with education officials and teachers on boards of examiners. They will often participate in instruction in the vocational schools, and help define the curricula and examination regulations (T. Malan, private communication, April 1985).

Business/industry is formally involved in educational matters through national organizations of employers, workers and the specialized trade- and craft-based chambers. In each of the 25 *académies*, a Ministry of Education nominee is responsible for coordinating all in-service training activities. This official presides over the regional centre for the training of advisers working with firms to establish their in-service training needs, and with schools, *collèges* and *lycées* to establish the arrangements to meet those needs. Instructional staff who provide in-service training receive supplemental pay financed from the proceeds of a payroll tax. Business/industry in France has been acknowledged as a 'social partner' (together with unions) of the public authorities for the continuing education of school-leavers and young workers. This is organized within a legislative framework established in 1970–71 (the National Inter-Trade Agreement of 9 July 1970, for vocational and continuing education, signed by employers' and employees' organizations: and the Law of 16 July 1971, for continuing vocational education). However, this legislation was passed during a period of vigorous economic expansion and shortages of skilled labour, circumstances that have since changed.

The major national organizations of employers involved with educational policy are the *Confédération Générale des Petites et Moyennes Entreprises* (Confederation of Small and Middle-Sized Enterprises) and the *Conseil National du Patronat Français* (National Council of French Employers). In addition, there are three national chambers which include employer members and which discharge important education and training functions for companies: the *Chambres de Commerce et d'Industrie* (Chambers of Commerce and Industry), the *Chambres de Métiers* (Chambers of Manual Crafts) and the *Chambres d'Agriculture* (Chambers of Agriculture). These chambers provide an organizational framework for employer participation in training, establishing training facilities, supplying instructional staff and setting standards for qualification in their respective occupations.

The appointment of the Bloch Commission in October 1984 underscored French governmental interest in promoting closer collaboration between education and business/industry, with the aim of improving both sectors of society. The Commission included education system administrators, higher education officers, and representatives of business organizations and trade unions. They were charged with the task of reviewing conditions and making recommendations regarding overall educational policy and practice, and they were also asked to consider specific ways in which regional and local initiatives might be promoted, particularly in the form of joint school–enterprise consultation and activities. The eventual report, entitled *Mission Education-Entreprises: Rapport et Recommandations*, May 1985, set out a programme for tying education and the economic sector more closely together. Representatives of the national employers' organizations cited above participated in formulating the report and in the public discussions that took place after its appearance. An important outcome of the Bloch Commission's work has been the legitimation of participation by associations of employers and organized labour in the policy and practice of general education and vocational training.

The major source of funds for full-time apprenticeship education is the payroll tax levied on most firms (*Centre International d'Etudes Pedagogiques*, 1984, p. 24). Since 1975, a *taxe d'apprentissage*, amounting now to just over one-half of one per cent of their payroll, has been levied on French employers, who have the option of paying the proceeds directly to a secondary or higher education institution of their choice, rather than to the Paris Treasury. In 1971, a further tax, the *taxe de formation continue* (continued training tax) was introduced. This tax amounts to 1.1 per cent (minimum) of payroll. It is payable by firms employing 10 or more workers, and the proceeds are used to support both general and vocational recurrent education, either in courses run by the firms themselves, or in those given in other establishments. In 1982 for firms in France as a whole, the training tax contribution amounted to 1.96 per cent of payroll, substantially more than the compulsory minimum (CEDEFOP, 1984, p. 222). It is estimated that in 1981–82 about 6.5 per cent of the working population (1.5 million out of a total of 23 million) participated in the in-service training organized and provided at *lycées* and *collèges*, and financed by these levies.

In addition to formal financial involvement of employers with education, their national organizations have undertaken campaigns of information and consciousness-raising, to alert the general public about the importance of the business world, and to try to correct what it considers to be ignorance or misunderstanding among members of the general public. In 1984, an inventory of Chamber of Commerce and Industry activities along these lines identified a wide range of such public relations initiatives.

Government efforts to involve individual firms and organizations in a variety of educational activities as 'social partners' has been a progressive development for about two decades. The Chairman of the National Chambers of Commerce and Industry has observed:

> The extremely positive results (from these partnerships) have for some years now resulted in public authorities increasing the number of pro-grammes that bring the schools closer to the economy: educational programmes, internships for teachers. These have led today to ... twinning of *lycées* and *collèges* with enterprises. (*Assemblée Permanente des Chambres de Commerce et d'Industrie*, n.d. 1)

Encouragement of local and regional collaboration between schools and business/industry is a distinguishing feature of these initiatives, which have different emphases: the provision of opportunities for work ex-perience; the joining of business/industry and the schools for collaborative research and design in development and/or training; the involvement of firms in providing schools with materials and equipment; facilitating the membership of business/industry personnel on the schools' examination boards and informational and consciousness-raising activities, mostly directed at young people.

Summary France has had a strongly developed system of vocational training in the regular school system, alongside a relatively limited system of apprenticeship training. On the initiative of the Ministry of Education, employers' groups were involved in establishing the curricular outlines and content of this vocational preparation, but they were excluded from participation in school-based training as well as from involvement in academic education in the schools.

This exclusionary policy has been greatly modified in recent years, with a good deal of central government encouragement for business/industry to offer teachers and students information, counselling, work experience, tools, materials and opportunities for collaboration on specific production projects.

Other changes proposed to encourage business/industry participation in education and training have focused on simplifying the financial arrangements for reimbursing firms providing such facilities, and on adapting the content and organization of training programmes to the needs of small and medium-sized firms.

It is commonly assumed that the French administrative style calls for central control of every detail of local operations, in the interest of ensuring uniformity and equality across the entire country. However true this may be of school organization (and there are some doubts that it is indeed the case), it is decidedly not true with respect to involving employers with the school system and with training. Instead of detailed direction from the centre, the central authorities and the national organizations have chosen recently to promulgate general frameworks of law and encouragement, leaving the regional and local organizations to determine the extent and the form of their activities in detail. As a consequence, there are substantial differences in employers' involvement to be observed, both among the various geographical regions of France and, within the regions, from one economic sector to another.

☐   Germany

In Germany, business/industry prepares nearly 70 per cent of young people of secondary school age for employment. This dominant business/industry role is accomplished within the 'dual system', which provides for a division of responsibilities between the employers and government authorities. A further distinguishing mark of the German system is the decentralization of authority over school-based education and training to the 11 German *Länder*.

However, the general guidelines and specific content of training for each of the 439 occupations officially recognized (1983) are determined by Federal government agencies, employers and trade unions. Much of this is in the form of apprenticeship training, which takes place within firms, but with provision for apprentices to be released from work for one to one-and-a-half days a week to continue their general education in vocational schools. The programmes provided and implemented by individual companies are supervised by regional organizations with responsibility for maintaining standards and ensuring that Federal regulations are carried out. In this manner, vocational education is dominated by the firms and the associations of members of the major occupations. On the other hand, general education, whether full-time, or as a part-time component of vocational training, is determined by the *Länder*, with little direct input from either Federal authorities or business/industry.

The chambers of commerce and industry, crafts and professions (*Kammern*) are provided for by law in each *Land* and they are charged with providing and administering many types of programmes (including education and training programmes) in their respective economic sectors. Individuals (firms and masters) are legally required to be members. The functions of the *Kammern* include appointing the boards to examine apprentices at the end of their training, with the boards' membership drawn from among employers, trade union representatives and vocational school teachers. The *Kammern* thus exercise important influence over the implementation of vocational education, whether undertaken in the workplace or in vocational schools.

To the extent that employers dominate the training process and bear most of the immediate responsibility for training, 'the apprentices are thus primarily under the authority and control of the firms which give them their practical training' (Max Planck Institute for Human Development and Education, 1983, pp. 242–243). Though largely of a practical nature, this training may also include classroom instruction in vocational material and (occasionally) elements of further general education. As noted above, the *Land* education authorities provide in-school general and vocational education to apprentices on release time. In-school training is shared fairly evenly between further general education and theoretical aspects of the occupation. It is mostly classroom-based, but may include opportunities for practice in school workshops.

Virtually all the costs of in-company training are borne by the employers, while the *Land* authorities bear the costs of in-school education. It has been estimated that the total costs of vocational training (including in-company and in-school training) are shared in the ratio of approximately 40 per cent (*Länder*) and 60 per cent (employers) (Tanguy and Kieffer, 1982, p. 71). The average annual expenditure (1980) per apprentice across all occupations amounted to some DM17,000 (approximately $5600), of which trainees' allowances ('wages') averaged $1960, and the value of apprentices' output equalled $2240. Net 'instructional costs' thus amounted to about $1400 per apprentice *per annum* (National Economic Development Council, 1984, pp. 16–17). Gross costs of initial vocational and educational training in 1980 amounted to 1.68 per cent of Germany's GNP, a major commitment of the nation's resources.

A number of full-time vocational schools also prepare a relatively few students for entry into apprenticeship programmes. Other full-time schools extend the training given in firms, and/or provide training not otherwise available in release-time schools, or apprenticeships (Max Planck Institute for Human Development and Education, 1983, pp. 249–250). Although business/industry exercises the preponderate authority in its part of the dual system, it has little or no role in the other (school-based) segment of the dual system.

No doubt because employers in Germany are so heavily committed to the vocational education and training of young people in their transition from school to fully qualified employment, business/industry tends to play a sharply diminished role *vis-à-vis* the general education schools. This is reflected in the rarity of formal partnership activity and specific twinning arrangements linking firms with schools. However, business/industry activity outside the dual system is not entirely absent. For example, work experience opportunities are provided for *Hauptschule* teachers and school-children; there are some opportunities for immigrant youth to gain more knowledge of employment conditions and possibilities; business/industry provides information and instructional materials and resources to the schools; there are a few special programmes for the technical training of young women, and there is significant growth in the establishment of training consortia among groups of firms.

Summary   The long-standing and highly regulated participation of business/industry in training is an outstanding feature of the German system. It is characterized by clear definition of roles and responsibilities by the national government, specification of training content and standards by federal agencies (with business/industry participation), provision by employers, and supervision, evaluation and enforcement of regulations by regional and local employer-and-worker boards. The system reaches the majority of youth and enjoys high status. It exemplifies the adaptation of a traditional apprenticeship system to the requirements of a contemporary economy.

However, this intensive involvement of business/industry in work-related training is not matched with respect to school-based education and training, though a few isolated examples of firms' involvement can be identified. In any event, the contrast between the elaborate organization of the dual system and the reliance upon individual and local initiatives with respect to the secondary schools is marked.

■ Comparative discussion and findings

While collaboration between business/industry and the schools is widely supported rhetorically, it has not proved to be easy to install and maintain in practice. By tradition, business/industry has been excluded from direct participation in general education in the secondary schools, and the schools continue to maintain a certain degree of defensiveness against what they view as 'outside interference' in their work. At the same time, business/industry continues to feel that it has a special expertise and interest in vocational training, and should be its main provider.

This exclusion of business/industry from general education has been modified somewhat in recent years, as schools have recognized that they need to improve collaboration with the world of work. It is increasingly conceded that educators need to become better informed about employers' wishes; that, as education becomes more costly, it can profit from the material and political support the business sector can provide; and that the schools need access to the work-place in order to bring a greater degree of realism and sense of immediacy to their curricula. Also, as the general education component in vocational education curricula has grown, the distinction between general and vocational education has become less well defined. Finally, as secondary schooling has become less exclusively a preparation for university entrance, its significance for the economic welfare of the nation has been enhanced, and business/industry's role as a 'social partner' in the definition of secondary schooling has become more legitimized. In all three nations, the new conditions of transition have brought with them additional pressures for business/industry to become involved, and an increased willingness on the part of business/industry to do so.

☐   **Tensions and pressures**

In Britain, as the jurisdictional boundaries between the educational authorities' schools and the employers' training arrangements have blurred, uncertainties about the eventual limits of change have grown. This is evidenced in fears that current plans of the politically and financially well-supported Manpower Services Commission to extend the Youth Training Scheme from a one-year to a two-year programme of employment, education and training will undercut the Department of Education and Science, which is also trying to make school curricula more relevant to employment and more attractive to young people. The British worry especially about what they see as an undue vocationalization of the school curriculum. In France, too, the government is concerned that new transition programmes might empty the LEPs and, as it is committed to maintaining a variety of educational and training arrangements (traditional *lycées*, LEPs, apprenticeships and apprenticeship centres), it has tried to move forward on a broad front, first providing financial and political support to the LEPs, then to apprenticeship arrangements, then to the traditional *lycées*, all the while encouraging extension of business/industry involvement in schooling.

Germany's long-standing practice of having employers participate in the transition of youngsters from school to work, via the offer and operation of formal apprenticeships, has meant that Germany has not had so far to go as the other two countries in expanding the involvement of employers. Consequently, Germany has not experienced the wrenching adjustments that the introduction of new transition arrangements has brought about in Britain, and even to some extent in France.

Indeed, in Germany, if there has been change in the demarcation of responsibilities for transition education, it has been in a direction opposite from that of Britain and France. The tendency in Germany, especially under Social Democratic governments, had been to strengthen the school-based modes of training while faulting the traditional apprenticeship arrangements on at least three grounds. Specifically, the dual system has been charged with being overly and narrowly craft-based, and for that reason unresponsive to the needs of modern technologically-advanced industry; crudely exploitative of the cheap labour of young apprentices, in the interest of higher profits, and inherently incapable of meeting the quantitative demand for training places. However, attacks on the dual system along these lines have not gone unanswered (Lutz, 1981, p. 85), and the return to power of a Christian Democratic government at the Federal level has encouraged business/industry organizations to become more active than ever in support of a continued, and even expanded, role for employers in both defining the content of education and in providing young people with opportunities for the transition to work.

In France there has been a fairly clear and highly developed school-based system for equipping young people with academic and vocational knowledge; and in Germany the dual system also has been very clearly defined across all the *Länder*. Because of the absence of a uniform, central direction of their system of schooling and transition, the British may well have experienced unusual tension and difficulty in the process of adjusting the connections among schooling, training and work. The British had left school matters largely in the hands of local authorities, and training matters in the hands of professionals and industrial organizations. The result has been a hodge-podge of *ad hoc* arrangements, satisfactory-to-excellent in some areas (for example, advanced skill training of a relatively few young people), but only fair-to-poor for the majority entering lower skilled employment.

As concerns the impact of changes in transition education on administrative arrangements for providing education and training to young persons, Germany had a relatively easy task, given its long tradition of business/industry involvement. Britain, on the other hand, has had to create new mechanisms for incorporating business/industry organizations in educational planning and practice. In a somewhat startling paradox, the poor economic record of Britain in the past decade has led a Conservative government, inclined towards a *laissez-faire* rhetoric on most social and economic matters, to adopt an interventionist tone in educational policy, with the goal of providing radically altered transition arrangements for young people into work. Alongside an official policy of encouraging collaboration between firms and education authorities at the local level, the central government's Manpower Services Commission has become the chosen instrument for defining and executing education and training policy. The justification for this accretion of responsibility on a national scale has been largely in terms of the MSC's (alleged) keener appreciation of the skill requirements of the British economy as a whole, and of business/industry in particular.

While the British have been moving quite rapidly away from their traditional mode of decentralization, in France more responsibility for both the organization and funding of programmes of transition education has been recently assigned to the localities, perhaps as a reaction to the traditional practice of initiative and control from the centre (Jallade, 1985, pp. 178–179).

□   **The state of the economy**

Apart from adjustments in the traditional machinery of government and the financial arrangements governing firms' training efforts, economic conditions are likely to be a crucial factor shaping the nature and extent of business/industry participation in education and training. All three countries have experienced economic recession – France and Britain quite severely, and Germany noticeably, but more moderately.

The effect of economic downturn on business/industry efforts in education and training is likely to be somewhat ambiguous. Faced with a relatively abundant labour supply, firms will tend to curtail training, because they do not need to offer training opportunities as an additional recruitment incentive. They also have an incentive to call for more vocational training in the schools, in order to shift training costs to the public purse. But, working in the opposite direction, a slacker labour market implies less labour mobility. This means that firms do not have to fear quite as much the loss of newly-trained labour to competitors, thus giving them some incentive to maintain their training efforts.

In contrast to these ambiguities, government policies in all three countries have been strongly directed at promoting more business/industry involvement in education and training. This seems to have been prompted by two considerations. First, governments in Britain and France have now accepted the responsibility (long recognized in Germany) for providing a systematic, national approach to preparing young people for entry into work. Second, each nation views itself as being in severe economic competition with other industrialized and trading nations, and believes that success in that competition will depend importantly on the skills and adaptability of the labour force. Both considerations have argued strongly in favour of an enhanced role for business/industry in education and training. Thus, Britain, with the poorest economic record of the three, has witnessed the most change in government activity aimed at increasing such involvement; Germany, with the best economic and employment record (and also the most business/industry involvement already), has seen the least. France lies somewhere between these two extremes.

☐   **Findings and conclusion**

The major findings of the present study may be summarized as follows:

(1) Employers in all three nations make similar criticisms of the schools. These include: lack of connection of school curricula with the world of work, the schools' preoccupation with academic study and credentials, inadequacy of basic skill training, and the consequent unpreparedness of school-leavers for work.

(2) Their recommendations for change, aimed at repairing these deficiencies, are also very similar. They want a more 'practical' curriculum, greater knowledge and appreciation of the world of work on the part of both teachers and students, and more efficient management of the schools.

(3) Business/industry participation is organized in substantially different ways in each of the three countries, though specific types of activities tend to be repeated.

(4) The three nations represent three different models of transition education and training: school-based (France), firm-based (Germany) and a mixed model (England).

(5) There is considerable variation in the extent to which business/industry is involved in secondary transition education, from extensive (Germany) to relatively low (France).

(6) In Germany, there has been little change over the last few years in either the extent or the structure of business/industry involvement in education and training. This is in sharp contrast to both France and Britain (the latter, particularly), where the trend of government policies has made remarkable shifts. These shifts have, in turn, produced substantial tension between the traditional authorities governing education and the newly created ones.

(7) In Germany, employers bear a large proportion of the costs of training, recouping much of this by utilizing the relatively cheap labour of apprentices; in Britain, the wage costs of trainees are rather high for employers, and government tries to reduce these by

offering employment and training subsidies. In France, too, the combination of a secondary school-based vocational and technical training and a payroll training tax implies that a large fraction of total education and training costs are covered either directly or indirectly by public funds.

(8) There is no evidence from these three cases that any particular mode of financing (by State, employer or trainee) or administration (local or central) is to be preferred as a way of involving business/industry, though presumably the greater the reliance on public funding, the greater the risk that changes in government budget priorities will adversely affect business/industry involvement in the future.

(9) Business/industry continues to have an important if not dominant role in vocational training. In spite of the sizeable increase in business/industry interest in secondary education, the base from which it began was extremely small, and its involvement, therefore, remains limited and sporadic, especially as regards the general education system.

(10) If business/industry involvement in general education is to be successful, and even expand, careful attention has to be given to establishing the conditions and appropriate institutional arrangements for collaboration between business/industry and the schools. Some progress toward this in France and Britain is noted; in Germany the dual system has for long provided these conditions for vocational and technical training, though relatively little has been done to expand collaboration with respect to general education.

In Britain, business/industry involvement with education is shaped primarily by the national voluntary organizations of business and by local initiatives, nowadays with substantial governmental encouragement. The result has been an assortment of *ad hoc* arrangements, hardly amounting to a system of transition education and business/industry involvement in general education, though there is a good deal of agreement that it is precisely such a system that is needed. In France, government encouragement (and rhetoric) for business/industry to get involved is also quite strong, but the major locus of change remains the schools, with relatively little willingness to accord business/industry more than a supplementary specialized role in preparing young people for work. In Germany, not only is there little substantial change to be seen in the traditional ways of involving business/industry with the education and training of youth, but even the governmental rhetoric is muted. By and large, Germany is satisfied not only that it has come a long way in involving business/industry in the preparation of young people for work (certainly much further than all of the European countries, other than perhaps Austria and Switzerland), but that the nation has already encompassed the changes that both the British and the French are seeking to make. Under the circumstances, it is not surprising that both Britain and France look to Germany as a model of transition to work in which they find much to admire. However, a common set of challenges has produced noticeably different responses in each country, and it is likely that each nation's institutions will continue to respond in its own characteristic way.

References

Assemblée Permanente des Chambres de Commerce et d'Industrie (n.d.1) 'Allocution de M. le President Netter ...'. Press release, Paris (mimeo).
Assemblée Permanente des Chambres de Commerce et d'Industrie (n.d.2) 'Mission "Education-Entreprises": Conclusions du groupe de travail sur le thème "L'information économique aux divers niveaux de l'enseignement" '. Paris (mimeo).
Association of British Chambers of Commerce (1984) *Business and the School Curriculum* (London: Association of British Chambers of Commerce).
Cans, R. and Coutty, M. (1982) 'S'adapter à la réalité du travail'. *Le Monde de l'Education*, May.
CEDEFOP (1984) *Vocational Training Systems in the Member States of the European Community* (Luxembourg: Office for Official Publications of the European Communities).
Centre International d'Etudes Pedagogiques (1984) *An Outline of the French Education System* (Sèvres: CIEP) (mimeo).
Charte des Apprentissages Professionels (1984) (Paris: Assemblée Permanente des Chambres de Commerce et d'Industrie).
Confederation of British Industry (1981) Memorandum, Great Britain, House of Commons, Education, Science and Arts Committee (session 1981–82). *The Secondary School Curriculum and Examinations: with Special Reference to the 14 to 16 Year Old Age Group*, Vol. II.
Confederation of British Industry (1984) Memorandum, House of Lords Sub-Committee C (Education, Employment and Social Affairs). (London: CBI) v.28 (mimeo).
Confederation of British Industry (1985) Private communication, Feb.
Goebel, U. (1980) 'Wirtschaft als Partner der Schule', in Goebel, U. and Schlaffke, W. (eds), *Berichte zur Bildungspolitik 1980/81 des Instituts der deutschen Wirtschaft* (Köln: Deutscher Instituts-Verlag).
Goebel, U. (1984) 'Das Bildungskonzept der neunziger Jahre – Plaedoyer für ein begabungsorientiertes, flexibles und effizientes Bildungssystem', in Goebel, U. and Schlaffke, W. (eds), *Berichte zur Bildungspolitik 1984/85 des Instituts der deutschen Wirtschaft* (Köln: Deutscher Instituts-Verlag).
Great Britain, House of Commons (1983) Education, Science and Arts Committee (session 1982–83). *Education and Training, 14–19 year olds. Minutes of Evidence together with Appendices* (London: HMSO).
Jallade, J.-P. (1985) 'The transition from school to work revisited'. *European Journal of Education*, Vol. 20, No. 2–3.

Jamieson, I. and Lightfoot, M. (1982) *Schools and Industry* (London: Methuen).

Le Monde de l'Education (April 1982; May 1982; Sept. 1983; Feb. 1984).

Lutz, B. (1981) 'Education and employment: contrasting evidence from France and the Federal Republic of Germany'. *European Journal of Education*, Vol. 16, No. 1.

Malan, T. (1985) Private communication, April.

Max Planck Institute for Human Development and Education (1983) *Between Elite and Mass Education* (Albany: State University of New York Press).

Mission Education-Entreprises (1985) *Rapport et recommandations* (Paris).

National Economic Development Council (1984) *Competence and Competition: Training and Education in the Federal Republic of Germany, the United States, and Japan* (London: National Economic Development Office).

OECD (1984) *Youth Unemployment in France: Recent Strategies* (Paris: Organization for Economic Co-operation and Development).

Ryan, P. (1984) 'The New Training Initiative after two years'. *Lloyds Bank review*, 152.

Tanguy, L. and Kieffer, A. (1982) *L'école et l'entreprise: l'expérience des deux Allemagne.* (Paris: La Documentation française).

'Technical change triggers new discussion on education content' (1984) *Bildung und Wissenschaft*, 5/6.

Times Educational Supplement (12 Oct. 1984; 3 Jan. 1986).

Chapter 5

Education and Training

R. Dearden

From time to time an important shift takes place in how our social arrangements are conceived. Whereas formerly they were thought of under one description or category, now they are thought of under another. For example, nursery provision for very young children used to be thought of under the medical category, whereas now it is seen more in educational terms. Certain offences, even political dissent, may be shifted from the criminal to the medical category. One might be led by this reflection to ask whether the same thing is happening with respect to education and vocational training. Are we witnessing, perhaps even assisting in, a shift in the way in which institutional learning is seen from education to training?

There are many signs that this change is indeed happening. Greater practical relevance is urged for both the primary and the secondary school curricula. There is expanding provision for the Technical and Vocational Education Initiative (TVEI). There is a craze for information technology, which can indeed assist traditional educational purposes but which derives its main impetus from the vocational significance of the computer. Beyond schooling, there is the Youth Training Scheme (YTS) and the shift that universities are being required to make from the arts to science and engineering. There is also the passage of control over certain aspects of education from the Department of Education and Science, and now also local authorities to the Manpower Services Commission. The government white paper, *Training for Jobs*, summarizes these trends.

Sometimes training is explicitly contrasted with education and a revised comparative evaluation is advocated which will accord more with the 'real world'. More usually the shift is effected by running together education and training as if they were as inseparable as fish and chips, or bacon and eggs. It is even implied that there is no real difference between

Source: Dearden, R. (1984) 'Education and training', *Westminster Studies in Education*, Vol. 7, pp. 57–66, Carfax Publishing Co., Oxford.

the two, or none of sufficient importance to give us pause in conflating them. All that is being threatened is 'clutter', and who would want to keep that? We can see this conflation actually at work in the following passage taken from the DES publication *Education and training for 16–18 year olds*:

> For many years, the terms 'training' and 'education' have been commonly used as a rough and ready means of distinguishing learning to perform specific vocational tasks (training) and the general development of knowledge, moral values and understanding required in all walks of life (education). (DES, 1979).

Such a traditional distinction might both seem to be accurate and be thought to have much to be said for it. However, 'such definitions have obvious shortcomings' we are told.

There is a systematic ambiguity in much of this thinking and one which provides a convenient bolthole for anyone caught too openly in reducing education to training. It consists in trading on wider and narrower interpretations of some key term. There is first of all the automatic coupling of education and training. This coupling can at one and the same time serve to cover an important shift in arrangements while also providing a degree of soothing reassurance that education is in no way being threatened. Secondly, there is 'relevance'. Relevance, we are told, means 'that the curriculum should contain an adequate practical element and promote practical capability ... that the technical and vocational aspect of school-learning should have its proper place.'[1] But if challenged on this, it is possible to retreat to a wider sense of relevance which relates to the whole world of the child's experience. Similar shifts are evident with 'clutter'.

A comparatively generous view of all this would be to see it as just one-eyed determination to improve our national economic performance, though that way of looking at it has its plausibility diminished by the fact that all this training does nothing to increase the number of job vacancies, or to escape the fact that many school leavers will be unemployed no matter how much training they have. These are consequences simply of the mismatch between the numbers of vacancies and those looking for work. A less generous view of vocational training is that it is not primarily, or even at all, about preparation for work but is about bringing young people to believe that if they are unemployed then that is their own fault: they have not trained enough. Additionally, training may be seen as being about keeping youth off our potentially riotous streets, or driving down the wage costs of young people, or disguising the real extent of unemployment. No doubt politicians' motives are mixed in this connection, as they typically are in every connection, since they are the ones who have to effect the ultimate reconciliation and adjudication of conflicting interests in a society.

However, it is not part of my purpose to speculate about politicians' motives. The truth-tests for such attributions are in any case often unclear, or else are impossible to apply. By contrast, it is my intention to engage in a mainly conceptual inquiry into how education and training are to be characterized and what relations may hold between them. Clearly, they are both related to learning, but are they so related in quite the same way? Is there a difference between them of sufficient importance to lead one to resist the current tendency to conflate the two? To anticipate, I shall argue that there is a difference, and an important one which we do well to keep in view, but that in some circumstances the same learning sequence may satisfy the criteria for both. They are different but not necessarily mutually exclusive.

Training typically involves instruction and practice aimed at reaching a particular level of competence or operative efficiency. As a result of training we are able to respond adequately and appropriately to some expected and typical situation. Often training addresses itself to improving performance in direct dealings with things. Thus it is necessary to train drivers and pilots, carpenters and surgeons, electricians and computer programmers. Other sorts of training are more concerned with dealing with people, as with training in sales techniques, training for supervisory positions or assertiveness training for women. Yet other kinds of training are more indirectly concerned with changing or controlling people or things, such as training to be an architect, lawyer or administrator. But in every case what is aimed at is an improved level of performance or operative efficiency brought about by learning.

The most obvious ingredient in training is the development of skill. The skilled person knows how to do something, not in the sense that he can give a propositional description of how it is done but in the practical sense that he has mastered, through experience, the required procedure, tactic, strategy or technique. Indeed a skilled person may be unable to give a propositional account of how something is done, which is one reason why skilled performers do not themselves necessarily make very good trainers. Conversely, someone may be able to give a good description of how something is done, and even be a good trainer of others, but not know how to do it in the practical sense himself, for example an athletics coach who trains pole-vaulters to world standards. Many skilled performances are learned by almost everyone and at a very early age, for example, how to drink without spillage, how to fasten your clothes and how to walk without falling or bumping into people. Such skills are products of our early social training, which is usually given by our parents.

But training is not only a matter of skill acquisition. Some training calls instead, or additionally, for the development of strength and endurance. Athletes and workers with physically arduous jobs, such as navvies, have to build up their bodies in ways which may not enhance skills. Emotional steadiness may also be called for. A nurse who faints at the sight of blood, a fireman who panics when he sees the blazing oil terminal or a soldier who flees at the first enemy fire are not to be regarded as well trained in their callings. Thus a variety of resources is available to the trained person, the criterion of their unity being their relevance to operative efficiency in some expected and typical situation.

Yet a further ingredient in training is attitude. Consider the role that might be played in a TVEI scheme by 'clocking on'. Regarded simply as a procedure this is so simple that it is learned as soon as it is explained, in my own factory experience taking about five seconds. Surely this is an example of something that is so easy to learn that it requires no training at all, and thus to include it in a school as part of vocational training might seem a spurious form of 'realism'. Of course, understanding the deeper implications or considering the point of this practice might well take rather longer, but then that would not be training since improved performance is not what one would then be aiming at. The more likely explanation for including this practice is to produce a certain attitude: one of habitual compliance with the requirements of industrial discipline, in this case particularly in connection with punctuality and the distinction between free time and bought labour time. The practice would also be making its contribution towards acceptance of certain authority relations. Thus there could be more in an apparently simple procedure like clocking on than first meets the eye, and this more could well have a bearing on the relationship between training and education. But more of that later.

The connection between training and a typical situation means that the investment of time and resources in training gives hostages to fortune, since what was trained for may not come about, or not in the way that was expected. Particularly where jobs are concerned, they disappear, diminish in number, change in their nature or are replaced by new ones. There is point in the *Punch* cartoon in which a man says to a child: What are you going to retrain as when you grow up? The same point can be made in terms of Popper's argument to show that you cannot predict the course of history (Popper, 1960). Popper argues that the course of history is greatly influenced by scientific discovery. This is obvious enough as soon as one considers those scientific discoveries which have led to the many medical and technological innovations of modern times: health care, control over fertility, microelectronics, electricity, the internal combustion engine and so on. But one cannot predict scientific discoveries (one would already have made them in that case and so they would not have to be predicted). Therefore one cannot predict the course of history. And part of that history is the jobs which call for people to be trained in various ways: they too cannot be accurately predicted, at least in the detail that training requires.

One apparent escape from this vulnerability of training to change is to seek for so-called 'generic' skills. The idea is that if we can devise forms of training which are not so specifically tied to particular jobs, but are relevant to whole ranges of jobs, then the trainees will have more likelihood of finding employment for their trained capacities. There is an ambiguity in this project which needs to be noticed at once. What might be looked for here is skills which more than one employer would find useful. But such skills might still be very specific, for example, the skills possessed by those who have been trained in switchboard operation, operating a lathe, or office practice. In terms of specificity, such skills could be just as specific as those which are needed by very few or even by only one employer (firework making, perhaps). Truly generic skills would be useful not simply to many employers (who all wanted much the same specific competences) but in a diverse range of jobs. Possible examples of such generic skills might be decision-making, problem-solving, planning your work, improvising and communicating.

However, there must be a doubt in this connection as to whether such skills are truly general, or whether they are classes of separate skills each specific to some area of content. For example, simply because good judgement can be exercised in both the stockmarket and in landing a hot air balloon, it does not follow that there is some general skill of 'good judgement' which is common to both and in which we could be trained free from any particular context. The circumstances of the particular fields in which judgement is exercised here are too diverse for anything of much importance to be in common between them. Not surprisingly, there are neither 'O' nor 'A' levels, neither BEC nor TEC, in a generic skill of good judgement. Nevertheless, the same might not be true in every one of the cases mentioned earlier. Perhaps there really is something common and substantive that could be called problem-solving skill, or skill in decision-making (the idea of an orderly procedure of collecting information for sub-decisions which lead up to the main decision, for example). Each case would need to be considered on its merits, though what is more certain is that no such generic skill could ever by itself be sufficient.[2]

In the light of the foregoing account of training we may now ask whether any reasonably clear distinctions can be maintained between training and education. The fact that the two are nowadays habitually run together, and the fact that 'vocational education' and 'vocational training' are frequently used quite indiscriminately, are interesting points but they may well be best explained in the way that I indicated at the outset, namely as a rhetorical device for soothing any anxieties that may be felt over the making of an important transition in our arrangements for institutionalized learning. These facts also serve to remind us of the pitfalls of resting a distinction too closely on linguistic usage rather than on considered judgement.

The sense in which I am concerned with education is an evaluative one. From that point of view the possibility of there being a distinction between education and training is illuminated by a version of G. E.

Moore's 'open question argument' (Moore, 1903). Moore himself, of course, used this argument to insist on a distinction between 'good' and any naturalistic property, such as 'being more evolved'. Accordingly we might ask of any training programme: Has it any educational value? And if it is claimed to have such value, we might then go on to ask in what way it has that value. It seems to me very clear that the answer to the first question might well be that a particular training programme had no educational value whatever, without on that account alone necessarily ceasing to be training. It therefore follows that the two must be conceptually distinct. Of course, granted a certain curiosity and reflectiveness on the part of a person, probably any experience whatsoever could be educational, especially if the person has already been educated to a considerable extent. To refer back to a previous point, even clocking on *might* trigger a dawning realization of many aspects of industrial life. But at least in terms of intended result, such training contributes little if anything to a person's education. Think of bayonet practice for the ordinary soldier, or learning to apply the DHSS rules on supplementary benefit, or the training given to a filing clerk as fields typically rich in their educational harvest.

As preparation for teaching itself comes to be more and more narrowly conceived in terms just of trained skills, so aspects of preparation which gave it greater breadth of perspective, and which were accordingly educational, are being squeezed out. More ominously still, it is from a training perspective that we hear of people being 'over-educated', something which from a purely educational perspective would seem to be impossible. People are 'over-educated' when they possess knowledge and understanding going beyond what is called for by some particular role performance. This excess causes two sorts of anxiety. First, from an economic point of view something is seen as having been paid for which is not needed, since resources will have been consumed without benefit to employment. Secondly, there may be some anxiety that these 'over-educated' persons will be dissatisfied in their mentally cramping jobs and that they may even be sources of political unrest.[3] My concern is not to allay that anxiety but to point out that it presupposes a conceptual distinction between education and training. To the more fully explicit clarification of the concept of educational value we must now turn.[4]

An apparently simple and no-nonsense way to give an account of what education is would be to look at what goes on in educational institutions, such as schools and colleges. But that would be too simple. On any defensible account of education some things which happen in those institutions have no educational value (calling the register, making purchases from the school tuck shop), while other things which happen outside such institutions are educational (certain holiday trips or television programmes). Furthermore, the no-nonsense approach is circular in that it assumes that we already know which are the educational institutions in the first place. But how are they identified? How are they distinguished from churches, restaurants, prisons or leisure centres? Furthermore, to equate an educational institution with any institution that calls itself such would preclude the possibility of criticism for failing to do anything much of educational value. Here we would do well to heed Illich's warning that powerful interests constantly try to define some human good in terms of what they actually provide. We need some way of assessing the legitimacy of any such claim.

A possible alternative approach with some topical interest might be to consider institutions which purport to be educational and to assess whether the learning that they provide has the requisite quality. Quality, however, is a very ambiguous notion when applied to learning. In searching for quality we might want more pupils to come up to a standard already achieved by some, or some pupils to reach a standard hitherto achieved by none. When Sir Keith Joseph set as an objective 80–90 per cent of pupils reaching at least the present CSE grade 4, together with more achieving GCE grade C, he was searching for improved quality in the first sense. But either way, these are qualitative judgements of product. Schools might also be judged for quality in terms of the degree to which they have successfully transformed pupils. A school might rate more highly in this respect, even though it reaches a lower absolute standard than another school, if its initial intake was very much lower and hence it had had to effect a much greater change. This distinction leads to a perception of schools' published examination results as a very unfair way of comparing their quality. Yet a further and for us much more important ambiguity in quality applied to institutionalized learning is that between the kinds of standards that may be aimed at. Nothing that has been said so far in this paragraph distinguishes between learning which is appropriately seen as of educational value and learning which is most appropriately viewed as training, especially vocational training. That distinction remains yet to be made.[5]

Probably the clearest if not the only criterion of educational value, I suppose, is that the learning in question contributes to the development of knowledge and understanding, in both breadth and depth. This is, of course, a matter of degree. Education is not a matter of acquiring discrete information, isolated knacks, rules of thumb, or unexplained habits, and it goes beyond the simpler and less sophisticated kinds of understanding. Thus it is very much a matter of conceptual insight, explanatory principle, justificatory or interpretative framework and revealing comparison. It also involves a degree of critical reflectiveness and hence autonomy of judgement, since it will need to consider the distinction between true knowledge and what may only pass for knowledge, and between true understanding and misconception.

Being concerned with understanding does not exclude from education any concern for feeling and desire, attitude, action or activity, but they will not be fostered apart from understanding. However, a necessary condition may not in every case be the most important condition. Moral education, for example, will be concerned with developing insight into moral notions, such as courage, kindness and justice. At the same time, and to the extent that they harmonize with this understanding, it will be concerned with the encouragement of corresponding feeling and action. A necessary condition of understanding many things is participation in them or experience of them. Education is not a purely intellectual affair.

While the traditional academic subjects provide very suitable vehicles for learning which has educational value, this criterion might be met by quite other patterns of curricular organization, for example with a focus of interest on the community, on personal relationships, on health or on the problems of women. Yet other patterns might subordinate content to some overarching political, moral or religious ideal. Not all education is classical liberal education. Conceptions of education are various, especially in a pluralist society, all of which has implications for teacher training and current assumptions that such training should address itself to the (one) best practice.

Understanding has its own internal standards which have to be satisfied if learning is to be educational. These standards must be violated neither by the teacher not by the intrusion of extrinsic doctrinal factors. But this does not mean that what is understood must be worthwhile in itself if there is to be educational value in understanding it. It is arguable that R. S. Peters gets himself into difficulties over this point when he says that engineering and cookery can be educational, but on condition that they are viewed under the aspect of the worthwhile in itself. But bridges and cakes are eminently useful products and their point lies in their utility. Abandoned sections of elegant city motorway, which have no use at all, are not the normal case. That intrinsic standards have to be satisfied, even intrinsic standards of understanding, does not mean that the overall project must be worthwhile in itself. This point has important implications for the possible relationship between education and training.

The understanding which is conferred upon us by education thus involves breadth and depth, a degree of critical reflectiveness and corresponding autonomy of judgement, and its own internal standards of truth and adequacy. As a result of being educated in some degree, our eyes are opened and we see the thing both in its wider relations and more fully in its nature. New dimensions are disclosed to us so that our experience is enriched. As well as gaining a broadened outlook and a more adequate conception, feeling and attitude are refined and become more discriminating. All of this is especially true if what we have in mind is general education, general in the sense which contrasts with specialized. General education is not confined in its interest to people as future functionaries in some job but has a bearing on, or a relevance to, their future as a whole: as husbands, wives and parents; as consumers of goods and services; as dealers with various institutions and bureaucracies; as travellers; as recipients of messages from the media; as political citizens and of course as contributors to society through the work that they do. And in this, general education is also concerned with us as individual persons with something to make of our lives. From this point of view it is hard to see how anyone could be 'over-educated'. In practice, a more likely difficulty would be to tap sources of interest and motivation necessary to becoming more educated.

What I am suggesting, then, is that the educational value of some learning is primarily to be assessed in terms of its contribution to the development of knowledge and understanding in breadth and depth, this development also involving a degree of critical reflectiveness and corresponding autonomy of judgement. A 'purely educational' argument or consideration is one which refers only to such development. But of course, nothing is said in this as to what is worth understanding, and a fully articulated conception of education must declare itself on that point. This will involve values other than the purely educational, such as moral, political, economic or religious values. 'Liberal' education might be called purely educational in the stronger sense that it concerns itself with the free development of understanding along lines which have historically turned out to be the most intrinsically rewarding. The more determinate articulation of educational value with which I have been concerned is that of general education, understood as the preparation of the generality of pupils for life in a general way, and certainly not just as workers. In an informal way, this general education continues throughout our lives, but schools are concerned with those aspects of it which are keys to other aspects and which are accordingly basic in some sense, or which if not done at school will very likely not be done at all. But what is still not clear from this is whether such an education is compatible with vocational training. Are the two mutually exclusive, or conterminous, or permissive of some degree of overlap, or much the same thing in practice, or what? To this final question we must now turn.

Education has its own internal kinds of training, for example training in laboratory procedures and mathematical algorithms, in artistic technique and instrumental competence. Sometimes education can be sharply contrasted with training, as when R. S. Peters draws our attention to the contrast between moral education and character training, physical education and physical training, training colleges and colleges of education, or sex education and sex training (Peters, 1966). In each of these cases, the educational member of the pair particularly emphasizes the importance of understanding as opposed to some specific kind of performance. Sometimes training within education subverts that enterprise altogether, as when preparation for some examination becomes the mastering of a set of tricks without any comprehension of the reason why. 'If it is in miles per hour, multiply by 22 over 15 and you have got it in feet per second'. Such a rigmarole is a kind of training, aimed at an operative efficiency, though not in some job but in the examination room.

The point of learning considered under the aspect of vocational training is to secure an operative efficiency: the person will be able to operate the word processor, give first aid, administer the injection, or run the shop. The point of learning under the aspect of education is to secure breadth and depth of understanding, a degree of critical reflectiveness and corresponding autonomy of judgement. Are the two compatible? There would seem to be no *a priori* reasons why they should not be. A process of training could be liberally conceived in such a way as to explore relevant aspects of understanding, and in a way which satisfies the internal standards of truth and adequacy. Training for the liberal professions is often like this. Training for teaching, at least until recently, fulfilled educational functions in ways which were, according to R. S. Peters, the reasons why training colleges came to be called by Robbins colleges of education.

But training can be, and often is, very illiberally conceived, and then it may not merely be uneducational but even be anti-educational. As an example of the uneducational, one might mention the recent controversy over whether trainees in the YTS should be given any opportunity to consider the social significance of work as part of their 'off-the-job' provision. Ministerial opposition was expressed to this and one could well see employers being opposed to it if only because it does not contribute directly to improved performance. The example of 'clocking on' given earlier could be an example of training being anti-educational, since pupils are being habituated to acceptance of certain kinds of authority relations without any reflection on the necessity or possible alternative forms of that. They are, in an important way, being indoctrinated. That is not to say that if they were led to reflect on this situation they would necessarily draw different conclusions about the nature of industrial discipline, but it is to say that critical reflection and autonomy of judgement are absent. Pupils are, at least in that perhaps minor phase of that particular version of TVEI, not being educated at all.

One obvious meaning that might be given to the phrase 'vocational education' is vocational training that is liberally conceived, as was discussed above. But another meaning that might be given to it is learning about the nature of work, discussing its forms and contexts: a version of careers education in fact. Work is an extremely important part of the lives of those who have work to do. It not only provides material rewards; it also structures time, choice and activity. It modifies the worker in all sorts of ways: in his skills and sensitivities, in his knowledge and attitudes, and in his self-concept. It confers a status. A general education which failed to find any place to consider something of such importance would be importantly defective. One currently popular way of doing this is to arrange some work experience for pupils. While this is unrealistic in that there is no pay, no submission to the full disciplines of work, no possibility of experiencing work that requires previous training and none of the implications of full commitment, still it is better than nothing in conveying some impression of working life. Back in the classroom alternative possible structures could be discussed, such as job enlargement, job rotation, working on whole processes not finely specialized ones, flexitime, staff development and equality of opportunity. Such an interpretation of vocational education would fully justify its claim to have educational value.

General education, quite apart from such an explicitly vocational component, can have much bearing on future vocational training. Most obviously this is true where the subjects or topics that are studied have content which constitutes a prerequisite of training success. The so-called 'basic subjects' are an example of this, since arithmetic and elementary physics, reading and writing, enter into very many forms of work. Training also presupposes a general context of understanding if it is to be possible at all, and this is provided by general education together with the more informally gained understanding which derives from everyday experience in a given society. To be trained as a policeman you already need some understanding of law and its enforcement. The typical purposes and activities of people in a society have to be understood as a backcloth to training programmes. Indeed, granted this, many jobs can be done with little or no training at all. The great variety of tasks successfully undertaken by students in vacations testifies to this, while in the home much use is made of microelectronics without benefit of any training: in operating a videotape recorder, or taking a course in washing machine studies. In this sense, general education could be the richest source of the supposed 'generic skills' mentioned earlier as the objective of training programme organizers.

I began by commenting on the shifts which take place in our social arrangements when something is moved from one category to another, and I asked whether we might not be witnessing such a shift in our institutionalized learning arrangements away from education towards vocational training. At the same time, the regular and automatic coupling of education and training could serve to facilitate such a transition without stirring anybody into a realization that something of importance might be in process of being lost. Against that whole drift I have argued for a clear conceptual distinction between education and training, even though they may often overlap in practice. I have given some reminders of the nature and function of general education and pointed to ways in which it could have bearings on vocational training without being conflated with it. Finally, I have suggested that vocational training itself could well be supplemented, or rather liberalized, by some attention to possible complementary educational studies. In that way, vocational training might be safeguarded not only from being uneducational but even from being anti-educational.

Notes

1. Quoted from Sir Keith Joseph's North of England Conference speech as reported in *The Times Educational Supplement*, 13 January 1984, p. 4.
2. For a more extended discussion of general skills, see Dearden, R. F. (1984) *Theory and Practice in Education*, Ch. 6 (London: Routledge & Kegan Paul).
3. For an interesting example of looking at eduation in just such an economic way, see Hayek, F. A. (1960) *The Constitution of Liberty*, Ch. 24, Sect. 4 (London: Routledge & Kegan Paul).
4. In what follows I am greatly indebted to the work of Richard Peters, though I do not follow or agree with him on every point of his analysis of the concept of education.
5. For a fuller discussion of quality in education, and one to which I am indebted, see Peters, R. S. (1977) *Education and the Education of Teachers*, Ch. 2 (London: Routledge & Kegan Paul) and Cooper, D. E. (1980) *Illusions of Equality*, Ch. 3 (London: Routledge & Kegan Paul).

References

DES (1979) *Education and Training for 16–18 Year Olds*, para. 26 (London: HMSO).

Moore, G. E. (1903) *Principia Ethica*, ch. 1 (Cambridge: Cambridge University Press).

Peters, R. S. (1966) *Ethics and Education*, pp. 32–34 (London: Unwin).

Popper, K. R. (1960) *The Poverty of Historicism*, Preface to 2nd edition (London: Routledge & Kegan Paul).

Chapter 6

The Present Economic Sea Changes and the Corresponding Consequences for Education

R. A. Brosio

The USA, and most of the world's other economies, ahve undergone basic, structural changes which have been profoundly disruptive since *circa* 1970. The economic, political, and military crises caused in part by the erosion of the *Pax Americana* – and by the changed conditions necessary to maintain US corporate world hegemony – have had, and continue to have, serious domestic consequences. The tactical and strategic responses to the threat to the world order, which has developed during the aftermath of World War II (1945–70), have constituted a broad and complicated front. The educational communities in the USA, and throughout the West, have become important sectors of that broad frontal tactic/strategy. Although correspondence between substructure and superstructure is not iron-clad in deterministic causality, this writer will argue that fundamental sea changes in the economy do in fact influence, and bring powerful pressures to bear upon, institutions and persons throughout society. The educational communities within the USA are no exception. The model of analysis used in this paper is based upon the assumption that because there are no iron-clad deterministic laws which govern the economy and society, men and

Source: Brosio, R. A. (1988) 'The present economic sea changes and the corresponding consequences for education', *Teacher Education Quarterly*, Vol. 15, No. 1, pp. 4–37 and *Educational Foundations*, No. 3, pp. 4–38, Caddo Gap Press, Ann Arbor MI.

women can act efficaciously in order to influence public events; however, they do not act under conditions of their own choosing (Brosio, 1985, pp. 73–83). As Lukacs has said, social activity is made up of individuals' actions, '. . . and no matter how decisive the economic basis may be in these decisions, its effects are felt only "in the long run", ... This means that there is always a concrete area of free choice for the individual, which does not conflict with the fact that history has its general and necessary trends of development. . . .' (Lukacs, 1973, pp. 261–262). The economic sea changes have been mainly caused by the actions of specific men who have exercised power within: corporations, technological centres, banks, the military, and the governments. These actions occurred within a certain context of historical and institutional reality, and within a series of relationships with persons and groups who did not possess enough power to resist the decisions which caused the sea changes, and their widely experienced consequences, since 1970. The economic sea changes have brought intense pressures[1] to bear upon less powerful, and dependent, institutions such as schools, colleges, and universities. These pressures have been directed at convincing, cajoling, or forcing the educational communities to march correspondingly along the path that those who are mainly responsible for the sea changes have chosen. These pressures have, of course, been resisted; however, much time and energy have had to be spent in order to contest such powerful pressures.[2]

Professors, and other practising intellectuals, who have been trained in the social foundations of education, are uniquely equipped with the analytical tools, concepts, traditions, interests, and motives with which to explain what pressures have been brought to bear upon the educational communities by those who control hegemonic multinational corporations, along with their allies in government and in other institutions. Social foundations professors who work in colleges of education, or other teacher education contexts, are in crucially key positions to educate their students about the contemporary threat to turn much of education and schooling into whatever may be in the short-term interest of those who make corporate policies in the USA, and globally. This writer realizes that the struggle between those who sought progressive outcomes and preparation for democratic empowerment through schooling have been fighting a long – and losing – battle with those who sought to turn education into instrumental and vocational goals. The current problems caused by the economic sea changes of the 1970s are only the most recent manifestations in an unremitting struggle (Wirth, 1983).

We foundations teachers and scholars have the advantage of having historically monitored and analysed the various attempts to gain dominant power in schools by those who do not view schooling and education as the systematic attempt to uncover and understand the very assumptions upon which a particular *status quo* rests. Our audiences are comprised of: (1) teachers in training (undergraduates), (2) in-service (graduate) students,

(3) K-12 teachers in the field, (4) doctoral students in social foundations programmes, (5) colleagues throughout the higher education community, (6) and finally, the larger public. Foundations scholars have developed useful insights in the realities of power, and its relationships to education and schooling. As a result of our strengths, we are uniquely qualified to bring our students, colleagues, and fellow-citizens the world, in terms of pointing out what the sea changes in the international economy mean, and their corresponding relationships to education and schooling.

Logic compels us to turn our attention in Part I to a general description of the sea changes which have occurred since *circa* 1970. Part II will seek to establish an interpretation of the term correspondence which is non-deterministic, and which is useful in explaining the relationships between the economic changes, and education. Part III will describe some of the corresponding changes in education since the pressures from the economic sea changes were brought to bear on education. The focus will be on the national reports of the early 1980s, and the reforms enacted by various state governments. Finally, a sketch will be provided which shows what the 'reforms' did not address nor accomplish.

■ Part I

Robert Heilbroner has explained, in *Marxism For and Against*, that capitalism is inherently anarchic. The historical record demonstrates that the capitalist system has always featured patterns of economic expansion, interruptions, malfunctions, recessions, and depressions. Sea changes have occurred periodically in many economic systems, and certainly within the capitalist system before 1970. These dynamic, but disruptive, ups and downs derive from the lack of any long-term trustworthy mechanism which is capable of bringing the private aims of capital into equilibrium and accord with the social needs of the community as a whole. The celebrated allocative function of the market has been at the root of the anarchic characteristics just described. According to Heilbroner: '... these anarchic properties of capitalism, follow from the deepest social and historical properties of the system, and not from circumstantial accidents' (Heilbroner, 1980, p. 132). Many observers whose analysis teaches them that capitalism's social effects are anarchic also see intrinsic conflict between the horizontal tendencies of democracy and egalitarianism, and the vertical hierarchical realities of contemporary capitalism. Heilbroner has said: 'In social life it [the radical view] sees strains that result from the continuous restructuring of daily life as the side effect of economic "growth"' (Heilbroner, 1981, pp. 38–39). Mainstream economists tend to obscure the deep political – even ethical – nature of most economic questions. Under conditions of advanced capitalism the state must interfere in the workings of a 'market system', which consistently causes social problems considered to be intolerable in a *de jure* representative democratic system. However, governmental interference in the economy – most often on terms favourable to corporate interests – must be camouflaged in order to preserve the myth of the independent and naturally functioning market. The state often acts as a partner of powerful private interests who are structurally uninterested in the broad social consequences and implications of their actions (Keller, 1972).

The anarchic nature of capitalism and its fundamentally non-democratic nature have given rise to corporate power which in many cases acts as a private government. The current form of corporate power most responsible for the economic sea changes is the multinational corporation. The internationalization of capital has gone on for a very long time. The movement towards expansion was first translated into the building of large domestic corporations; whereas today's multinational, or transnational, corporation is the fullest, most logical development of capitalism's impetus. The anarchic features of this international development are obvious to all who bother to study the situation of capital's penetration into new markets and countries. Technology and capital are introduced into pre-industrial countries and zones without regard for the needs and desires of the majority of citizens in the new market areas. Indigenous peoples are attracted to, or forced, into new occupations, often with little regard for their health, security, or self-esteem. All factors are subservient to the requirements of capital – as represented by the multinational corporation. Governments of countries penetrated by Western or Japanese multination-als are pressured to adopt policies which answer to the imperative of economic 'efficiency'. The power of the multinationals also profoundly affects the governments of the host countries as well – most of which are *de jure* democracies. In fact, the multinationals are able to avoid national jurisdiction – obviously there is no international jurisdiction – because they are powerful, operate within the capitalist zones, and are based in many different countries. In the early 1970s it has been said that the top eight industrial corporations – seven of them being American – ranked among the top 47 nations whose GNP exceeded $8 billion (Edwards *et al.*, 1978, p. 479). The driving force behind the internationalization of capital is 'bottom line' profitability. Heilbroner connects the first two points in Part I of this paper, namely, the anarchic nature of capitalism, and the role played by multinational corporations. Our experience is to live in

> a world continuously in imbalance – monetary … trade … resource … developmental imbalance[s]. And this imbalance will continue – despite the best efforts of governments to patch up or offset its more dangerous manifestations – as long as the economic unfolding of world history is left to the stimulus of private accumulation. That is the anarchy of capital today … (Heilbroner, 1980, p. 134).

Manuel Castells believes that we are living in an economic crisis whose causes are social. The social relations underlying the pattern of capital accumulation had been seriously altered by 1970 because of contradictions within the capitalist system, and specifically by the disruptions and challenges visited upon that system during the 1960s. As we know, the upheavals of the 1960s did not lead to a general breakdown of the system itself; however, the result has been a structural crisis of world capitalism. A structural crisis is one where it becomes impossible to expand or reproduce the system without a transformation or reorganization of the basic characteristics of production, distribution, and management, and their translation into different kinds of social organizations (Castells, 1980, p. 8). The structural crisis has caused profound alterations in economic and social forms, as we shall see.

□   **Deterioration of hegemony**

The late 1960s and early 1970s were a time of the deterioration of US hegemony in economic, political, and social terms. The defeat in Vietnam is only a spectacular manifestation of the erosion of a hegemony which was importantly a result of the American role played in World War II and its immediate aftermath. There were many reasons for the weakening of US hegemony; let us consider the following ones: the growing competition of other capitalist powers; the dramatic emergence of OPEC power with resultant sky-rocketing petroleum prices; the growing deficit and balance of payments problem; all of this, plus the crisis of the dollar. The emerging parity of Soviet military power exacerbated the crisis for the West. In addition to Vietnam, we have witnessed mounting resistance by oppressed people around the world. The present crisis in Central America is an example of such resistance, as is the great movement of black power in institutionally racist South Africa. In addition to problems abroad, it appeared for a time that Western capitalist democratic societies had lost a good deal of control over, and allegiance of, members of their own societies. The radical, if not revolutionary, action by US, French, and Italian youth in the late 1960s frightened the establishments in those countries. These characteristics of the structural crisis are all signs of the '... putting into question ... the absolute supremacy held by American capital and its state since the Second World War' (Castells, 1980, p. 255). Robert Kuttner has zeroed in on the cause of the US's hegemonic erosion: growth 'expired' because the huge economic spending boom which was fuelled by World War II, and then by European recovery, mass consumer spending, and the automobile age finally played themselves out. A combination of saturated consumer spending on the demand side, plus heightened global competition on the supply side, have been the main causes of the stagnation beginning in the 1970s (Kuttner, 1984, p. 270).

The political right has assigned other reasons for the troubles. The following are some of those reasons: the cost of the 'welfare state', an uncooperative, lazy, and incompetent workforce, and finally the high cost of the gains made by popular forces since the Great Depression.

The economic sea change that is being described is characterized by the erosion of US hegemony, as we have just seen, and by a tearing apart of the pact between labour and management, which had been established during the 1930s and 1940s. Charles Berquist has written that up until the early 1970s, a pact or compromise between popular forces and capitalists created conditions which caused a virtual explosion of growth, one that seemed to have eliminated class conflict in the developed societies of the northern hemisphere. The 'end of ideology' intellectuals, professors, journalits, and commentators interpreted this brief period of expansionist harmony as permanent; whereas it was a temporary compromise in the historic contestation of terrain (Edwards, 1979). The accommodating and hegemonic intellectuals (Aronowitz and Giroux, 1985) seemed to believe that a comparative respite in the long historical battle between the popular forces and those who exercised hegemony over them was in fact the dawning of a new world order – an order within which the prospects for capitalist expansion seemed limitless and where the left no longer posed a realistic threat (Berquist, 1984, p. 13).

☐   **Popular forces and capital**

The pact between popular forces and capital in the developed core countries, including the USA, featured a significant redistribution of wealth, power, and access, all of which were importantly caused by a weakening of the disciplinary power within worker–boss relations. The social welfare institutions which were put into place during the structural world crisis of the 1930s were kept in place – and even improved upon – during and after World War II (Piven and Cloward, 1982). One might say that capital was forced to validate and sanction in law the gains achieved by labour in the workplace. However, it is not the case that capital has ever accepted US labour as a co-determining partner in formulating economic macro-policy. Capital has always been too strong, and labour too weak to achieve anything like partnership. Andrew Martin has explained what would have to occur if such co-determination were to occur in a country like the USA. In his essay titled 'Is democratic control of capitalist economies possible?', Martin argues that

> ... the entrenched power of business in a market capitalist economy can be counterbalanced only if several conditions are present: a strong, ideologically coherent labor movement; a very high voting participation by wage

earners; and a labor or social-democratic party that is the party of
government most of the time (Kuttner, 1984, p. 268).

In spite of gains made by labour and popular forces, capital has been able
to exercise hegemony throughout most of the industrialized societies of the
West, or the so-called Free World, since 1945 – this has been especially
true in the USA.

In spite of this fact, capital was responsible for precipitating the crisis
which began *circa* 1970 as it declared war on the gains so painstakingly
achieved by popular forces. By the time of Thatcher's victory in Britain,
and Reagan's taking the presidency in 1980, we witnessed a new class war,
one launched by capital and its allies against the achievements that have
been commonly called the welfare state (Piven and Cloward, 1982).
Capital developed the multinational corporation, as has been mentioned
earlier, in order to get around – to outflank – the restrictions imposed upon
business, profit, and bossism by the achievements of labour, popular
forces, and the left. Berquist thinks that it was in order to protect and
develop the activities of the multinational corporations – for the
transnational investment of capital on an unprecedented scale – that the
whole political, military, monetary, and financial superstructure of the
post-war capitalist order was created. The multinational corporation was a
product of domestic class struggle that had been forced upon capitalists by
the victory of labour, popular forces, and the left during, and after, the
Great Depression structural crisis of the 1930s (Berquist, 1984, p. 9). The
equilibrium established in the world after the Depression and World War
II remained in effect from 1945 to around 1970. Domestic peace in the
USA rested importantly upon a foundation of steady economic growth,
and upon government transfer payments which grew in absolute terms and
as a percentage of the national budget. These transfer payments, chief
among them being Social Security, enhanced working-class and middle-
class security. As long as no one asked for more than a little security and a
little more income each year, the political system could respond without
basic changes in structure and authority. Questions concerning equitable
distribution of wealth, income, and power were not part of the agenda –
except for a few old, or new, leftists, and mainly during the 1960s. There
was little opposition to the intensification of transferring of capital abroad
in search of new markets, lower labour costs, and higher profits (Farr,
1982, p. 40). There are important political consequences resulting from
this transfer: '. . . the wealthy of the world have a strong interest in
internationalism in order to preserve their position. Freedom to inter-
mingle and compete in the world capital market allows them to diversify
their holdings and escape supervision of national governments' (Edwards
et al., 1978, p. 497). The US people have increasingly been told since the
crisis of the 1970s became apparent, that our entry into the world economy
is both inevitable and good for everyone – or at least for those with talent

and energy. Although it is admitted that many persons and firms might suffer during the so-called transition to high-tech internationalism, there has been too little discussion about the non-democratic decision-making and how this may have been the chief cause of the crisis. The establishment of an integrated world economy along capitalist lines has required the internationalization of political power. This has occurred, especially under President Reagan's administrations, and during the USA's re-adoption of the role of world gendarme.

☐   A general picture

Let us look back to the period before the coming of Reaganism in order to focus upon a general picture of the sea changes. As Robert Reich has said, in the quarter century after World War II the US economy performed well with Keynesian demand management. This period demonstrated the crucial nature of governmental intervention with regards to prosperity, and a rough drive toward a modicum of social justice to accompany prosperity.

> Since 1970 . . . [the] liberal promise [of steady economic improvement and growth] has been broken. Our economy is now [1981] in decline, largely because of America's worsening international competitive position. During the past decade [1971–81] nearly a million manufacturing jobs have been lost in a region stretching from the factories of Baltimore to the auto plants of St. Louis, and another million in the rest of the country. The share of the world market claimed by US manufactured goods has fallen by 23 per cent. Thirty per cent of our autos are now made abroad; 15 per cent of our steel, compared to 9 per cent in 1970; over 50 per cent of our consumer electronic products, compared to 10 per cent in 1970. The list goes on . . . . Ten years ago productivity – real output per hour of work – rose at an annual rate of 2.9 per cent; since 1977 productivity has declined 0.4 per cent a year. In the face of this precipitous decline liberalism has been all but silent. It has been replaced by another ideology that promises prosperity, but not social justice . . . (Reich, 1981, p. 20).

The 1970s were a time of deepening conflicts between state capitalist interest and human needs. Much of the malaise experienced during the 1970s, and up until the present, can be said to result from systems of production having fallen out of harmony with the larger economic order. In the 1970s the mass production economy broke down; and this threw the whole system into disequilibrium. The 1945–70 pact had been based upon the high wages and security of the workers in the mass production industries – in conjunction with high profits and capital's right to control work according to management priorities. After 1970, the system began to experience crucial structural problems. Floating exchange rates undermined the stability and predictability that mass production requires.

Globalization of production undermined the labour mechanisms which had balanced purchasing power and supply. Job markets began to divide into high-paid unionized workers and low-paid non-union workers. The corporate response – more multinationals, more conglomerates, more pressures to lower wages – failed to solve the system imbalance between supply and demand. 'Despite the emerging technologies, governments have not devised a new, sustainable macroeconomic order that will translate industrial breakthroughs into broad prosperity' (Kuttner, 1985a, p. 30).

What has occurred during the 1970s, in part because there has been an absence of democratic alternatives, is the emergence of a new kind of accumulation which Mike Davis calls 'overconsumptionism' (Davis, 1986, p. 211). Davis refers to the steady political subsidization of a sub-bourgeoisie – a mass layer of managers, professionals, new entrepreneurs, and rentiers, who, faced with the rapidly declining ability of the working-class (including the working poor, the unemployed, and the minorities) to defend themselves during the 1970s, have been overwhelmingly successful in profiting from both inflation, and specifically targeted state expenditures. These trends have continued and have been strengthened since the election of Reagan. At the same time that this overconsumption was being made possible, many other Americans had to be satisfied with low-wage jobs without union protection.

As Emma Rothschild has said, structural changes have taken place in the US economy in the 1970s. From 1973 to 1979 almost 13 million new nonagriculture jobs were created, of which almost 11 million were in the private economy. However, the new American jobs were concentrated in two sectors of the private economy – services and retail trade. By 1979, 43 per cent of all Americans employed in the private non-agricultural economy worked in services and retail trade. The two sectors together provided more than 70 per cent of all new private jobs created from 1973 to the summer of 1980. Growth in employment was further concentrated within the two aforementioned sectors. According to Rothschild:

> Three industries provided more than a million new jobs during the 1972–1979 period: 'eating and drinking places', including fast food restaurants; 'health services', including private hospitals, nursing homes, and doctors' and dentists' offices; and 'business services', including personnel supply services, data processing services ... and the quaintly named 'services to buildings' (Rothschild, 1981, p. 12).

This transformation to a service economy has profound consequences for the organization of US society. In the first place, they mostly provide employment for women. Secondly, the jobs in the big three industries of the 1970s offer short hours. Third, the hourly pay is very low. Fourth, the new positions are mostly dead-end jobs. Fifth, these new service jobs with their short hours, temporary and part-time employment, and women workers, are less protected by union agreements and benefits than those in the old manufacturing industries (Rothschild, 1981, pp. 12– 13). This sea change in employment is toward the non-productive sectors of work: retail trade and services have been marked by the lowest productivity. Many of the new jobs are subsumed under the frivolous consumer mart of advanced decadent capitalism. These jobs support the fundamental assertion of contemporary advanced capitalism that the primary requirement for individual self-fulfilment and happiness is the possession and consumption of consumer goods. Furthermore, these new jobs make a mockery of the contention within our civilization that human beings develop their personhood through authentic work – through the individual and collective transformation of recalcitrant matter into harmony and human usefulness.

☐   **Rise in supervisory labour**

Despite the much publicized 'white-collar blues', and managerial retrench- ments in certain industries, there has occurred a spectacular rise in supervisory labour. Mike Davis has said that although blue-collar employment has fallen by 12 per cent since the onset of the 1980 recession, by December of 1982 there were nearly 9 per cent more managers and administrators working in the US economy (Davis, 1986, p. 213). One could argue that an important consequence of the creation of an overconsumptionist group and more supervisors is the shoring up of corporate domination and hegemony in this country. Paul Goodman, Harry Braverman *et al.* have pointed out that white-collar and/or supervisory work under conditions of contemporary capitalism do not necessarily mean autonomy in decision-making, or even interesting work. In fact, the failure to view work as authentically educative and socially useful has been one important reason why many educators and others have naively looked upon 'high-tech' jobs as 'exciting', and even as a panacea for our economic woes. As we know, these jobs are seldom creative, the pay is low, the benefits inadequate, and the managers can, and do, move the jobs from US Silicone Valleys to East Asian ones (Goss, 1985, pp. 26– 32). It has been estimated that at present high-tech comprises *circa* 3 per cent of the workforce, and that a third of these jobs are for scientists, engineers, and technicians. Most of the jobs are for the low-paid operators and supervisors.

Many observers have sounded the alarm that the movement towards middle-class status has been stopped in the US, and that we are seeing the emergence of a split-level economy or society. It could be said that we are moving towards three rather distinct societies. The first could be characterized by comfortable suburbs occupied by the rich, middle-classes, and elements of the highly skilled (mostly) white workers. The second society would consist of ghettos, barrios, and places where deskilled, *declassé* white workers and their families live. According to Davis, this second society would possess

> ... 'citizen' rights to a minimal social safety net [and] this enlarged low-wage working class would remain politically divided and disenfranchised, as unions continue to be destroyed and the influence of labor and minorities within the political system declines. With fading hopes of entry into the norm of consumption defined by the boutique lifestyles of the ... 'secure' employment status of the shrunken core workforces of the great corporations, this [second] sector of the nation will increasingly encounter social degradation and relative impoverishment ... (Davis, 1986, p. 304).

The third society would consist of irregularly employed workers without citizen rights or access to the political system at all – a society of illegal aliens, or *gastarbeiter*. Inside the materially comfortable confines of the first society of yuppie comfort and professional management values, an enlightened psychologically oriented, management of human relations will prevail; whereas, a more authoritative environment will prevail in the second society. The third society may well become a free-fire zone. Those fortunate persons in the first society may even more resolutely gear-up to defend their advantage against those who have been cast-out from the luxuries of consumer capitalism in the USA.

This 'bunkered' favoured class may continue to gear-up to protect their privileges against the members of societies two and three; moreover, they may favour policies which seek to crush revolutions abroad that seem to threaten the privileges enjoyed by the first society. The Reagan administration has demonstrated how important 'defense' is viewed by those who have the power to make decisions in this country. The single most important sectoral investment trend in the economy is for national defence. Predictably, the current version of the arms race has been the most important impetus in the recovery of certain manufacturing sections. It has been estimated that defence expenditures at the beginning of Reagan's second term will eventually have an economic impact comparable to the Vietnam War at its height.

Military spending lies at the heart of the US economy in the 1970s and 1980s. Military spending may be highly compatible with the purposes of contemporary capitalism because it doesn't interfere with existing areas of profit making. Furthermore, it doesn't challenge the class structure, nor does it seriously affect income redistribution possibilities. Social spending would have a powerful effect upon all of these things, and that may be why we do not have it. Massive military expenditures saved the depression economies of the capitalist democracies in the 1940s. Defence spending helps 'high-tech' corporations today. Weapons become obsolete; the layperson knows little about sophisticated systems; and there is little cost accountability. Reliance on weapons leads to an 'all power to the experts' condition, which further weakens democratic participation. No one knows how much defence is enough. The average citizen doesn't want to gamble. Emma Rothschild has written:

> The ... military expansion seems organized to maximize the costs of defence and to minimize its economic benefits. It ... favour[s] nuclear missile 'systems', submarines, planes, and other 'big ticket' items (Rothschild, 1981, p. 15).

Lester Thurow has argued that when so much increased expenditure and production goes into defence, it drains skilled workers and professionals from the civilian sector. 'Would the typical engineer rather work on designing a new missile with a laser guidance system or on designing a new toaster?' (Thurow, 1981, p. 6). But, the USA cannot afford to destroy the competitive strength of its already weakened domestic economy.

Finally, we come to a specific look at the Reagan administration's contributions to the sea changes in the US, and world economies. James Tobin has written of the attempted Reagan counterrevolution,

> The economic program of the Reagan administration ... manifests a counter-revolution in the theory, ideology, and practice of economic policy. The aim of counterrevolution is to shrink the economic influence of the government, especially the central government, relative to that of private enterprise and free markets (Tobin, 1981, p. 12).

The present administration has made it clear all along that the problem of inequality is no longer a concern of the federal government. it has accomplished a redistribution of wealth upwards. There has occurred a drive by the *nouveaux riches*, under the auspices of Reaganism, to increase social and economic inequality. More specifically, the drive has been to expand low-wage jobs, reduce tax overheads for the rich (and becoming rich), and to provide a 'union-free' environment. Although the rhetoric of the Reagan alliance is anti-statist, the real goal has been to bring the state even more solidly on the side of capital – and to remove its support from the left coalition and the welfare state (Piven and Cloward, 1982). Instead of a diminution of state spending, there has occurred a restructuring of it toward defence (as we have seen), and in order to expand the frontiers of entrepreneurship and rentier opportunity. The Reagan Administration, and its allies in Congress, have made possible huge profits and salary increases for those who command the heights of corporate power.

As collective bargained wages were increasing at less than three per cent *per annum*, a leading firm of management consultants ... was reporting that the average salary of corporate CEOs had skyrocketed forty per cent since 1980, from $552,000 to $775,000. Similarly ... the share of management in the national income had increased from 16.5 per cent in 1979 to almost 20 per cent in 1983 (Davis, 1986, p. 234).

These facts either reflect a tremendous increase in merit, or a riot of hoggishness. The percentage of personal income derived from interest has nearly doubled in the 1980s – rising 24 per cent in the first years of the Reagan presidency alone. In the USA a new middle-class of professionals, salaried managers, and credentialled technicians already comprised 23.8 per cent of the labour force. This 23.8 per cent was higher than in any other country except Sweden. Because the US state sector is not larger than in other major capitalist countries, it is important to realize what the special characteristics of our private economy are which support such an enlarged middle strata.

☐ Reaction by the haves

An important part of the economic sea changes has been the effective reaction by the haves in America against the real, and perceived, gains by the minorities, union members, working poor etc. Reaction by the haves moved from mere defence of socio-economic inequalities to shrewd strategies for upward redistribution of power and income through shifting tax burdens, and by removing obstacles to the exploitation of cheap labour. Overrepresentation at the electoral level is in rough correspondence to overconsumption at the economic level (Edsall, 1984).

In 1982 Emma Rothschild tried to describe what the philosophy of Reaganism really meant. She writes that what Reagan called 'the people's tax cut' was in fact a cut for savers and for earners of capital income.

> The Gotha Program [major guidelines for the united German Social-Democratic Party in 1875, which Marx critiqued] of the conservatives is reduced in the end, to a less complex philosophy: redistributive income to people with a high propensity to save – who happen to be rich people – and hope that their high spirits or their thrift will in some manner inspire economic growth (Rothschild, 1982, p. 25).

The Reagan administration judged that the federal government exceeded its legitimate functions, of which the most important are to correct market failures, and to involve itself in the provision of public goods. This judgement rests on the political definition of what constitutes a public good – or a market failure. Reaganites seem to have judged that while defence is a true public good, education is a good that could be private. The Reagan administration certainly represents a radical change in the policies of all the presidents since Franklin Roosevelt – including Nixon. Rothschild zeroes in on what she believes Reaganism really to be.

> What remains after this expedition through economic premises and political considerations, political premises, and economic conclusions of the Reagan administration's bold explanation for the economic crisis of the 1970s and 1980s? ... They amount to little more than a macroeconomic veil of modesty for the administration's political objectives: to redistribute income and well-being toward the rich and away from the poor; to redistribute health and education and security toward much the same people who could have enjoyed them before the Second World War, or before the New Deal, or before the [new conservative] Gotha Program (Rothschild, 1982, p. 28).

In summary, we have seen in Part I an explanation of the sea changes in the economic picture since *circa* 1970. Our description and analysis have focused upon: the anarchic characteristics of capitalism; the role of multinational corporations; the social and structural nature of crisis; the deterioration of US hegemony; the weakness of organized labour, and management's assault on its old pact with labour; capital's reaction to earlier (before 1970) victories by labour and popular forces; the emergence of a corporate-defined new internationalism; the emergence of a new kind of accumulation and a sub-bourgeoisie; the predominance of low-wage jobs among those which were generated since 1970; the key role of defence spending in US economics; and, finally, Reaganism. Part II will seek to establish an interpretation of the term 'correspondence' which is non-deterministic, and which is useful in explaining the relationships between the economic sea changes and education.

■ Part II

If the principle of correspondence does not work in a fashion believed by iron-clad determinists, the fact remains that the power of the economy at this time in history can be said to exercise a singularly most important influence upon the rest of the culture. There are powerful carry-overs from the dynamic economy to institutions which are not as powerful – institutions which are part of the superstructure. Although it is true that various sectors of contemporary culture in the USA, and in other developed countries, are relatively autonomous and have a dialectical relationship with each other and the economy, it is *not* true that these sectors, and the actors within them, can operate as though those who control the command heights of the economy are not in charge of the rules by which the interaction occurs. There does exist contested terrain upon which non-determined historical actors struggle against one another, but the advantage in capitalist systems has been on the side of capital. While there is no determined guaranteed outcome, there is causation. There do exist correspondence and some forms of causality between what occurs at the economic (substructural) level, and the other sectors of this complex culture (superstructure). I do not think that it is crucial to be definitive concerning the exact relationship between the brute power of the economy and principal economic decision-makers *vis-à-vis* the other cultural sectors. What is crucial is to recognize theoretically what is clear to almost everyone who bothers to study, or notice, what occurs in the modern world. What *is* clear is that:

> Authority in a capitalist system typically resides in two realms: state and market. Of these, the coercive power of the market is more indirect and elusive than that of the state. Despite its ostensibly private character, however, it must be understood as a dominant political factor. For the logic of capitalism as an economic system spills over into far-flung social and cultural spheres, subjecting even non-economic relationships to the utilitarian criteria and social discipline of commodity and exchange. 'The market needs a place', wrote the late liberal economist Arthur Okun, 'and the market needs to be kept in its place'. But ... [as Robert Heilbroner has said] the essence of capitalism is that the market *won't* stay in its place (Kuttner, 1985b, p. 43.4).

Robert Kuttner asks his readers to pay attention to the annoying commercialization of everything from sports to art – a phenomenon which strikes most people as a casualty of modern times '... but which the Marxian method understands as a quite logical systemic imperative known as "commodification"' (Kuttner, 1985b, p. 45).

☐   Concept of correspondence

As I develop a workable concept of correspondence – one that is not mechanically deterministic – let us reconsider Edmund Wilson's chapter on the dialectic from his *To The Finland Station* (1940). Wilson informs us that Engels, as an old man, admitted that he and Marx were partly responsible for the fact that their disciples sometimes put more weight upon the economic factor than it deserved. But, 'We were compelled to emphasize its central character in opposition to our opponents who denied it, and there wasn't always time, place and occasion to do justice to the other factors in the reciprocal interactions of the historical process' (Wilson, 1940, p. 183). Let us see how Engels envisioned these so-called reciprocal relations. The image that comes to mind is that of a tree whose roots are the method of production. The trunk is the social relations; whereas the branches, or superstructure, are law, politics, philosophy, religion, art, education etc., whose relationship to the trunk and roots is concealed by 'ideological leaves'. Engels claimed that neither he, nor Marx, regarded the superstructure merely as a reflection of the economic base. 'Each of the higher departments of the superstructure – law, politics … etc. – is always struggling to set itself free from its tether in economic interest' (Wilson, 1940, p. 183).

Michael Apple has written in his *Ideology and Curriculum* (1979), that there exists a version of determination – and correspondence – which views these terms as a complex nexus of relationships that, in their final moment, are economically rooted but exerting pressures and setting limits on cultural practice, including schools. Therefore, the cultural sphere is not a 'mere reflection' of economic practices. Instead, the influence, the 'reflection', or determination, is highly mediated by forms of human action. 'It is mediated by the specific activities, contradictions, and relationships among real men and women – as they go about their day-to-day lives in the institutions which organize their lives' (Apple, 1979, p. 4). While granting the point that schools are part of a semi-autonomous sector in an advanced society like the USA, Martin Carnoy and Henry Levin state in their *Schooling and Work in the Democratic State* (1985), that both the structure and content of certain contemporary educational reform '… tend to correspond to particular changes in the workplace, and that some are more likely to be adopted than others' (Carnoy and Levin, 1985, p. 217). Carnoy and Levin '… reject both a mechanistic correspondence between work [as shaped by capitalist conditions] and school and a clear separation of the two' (Carnoy and Levin, 1985, p. 4).

Michael Apple, in his review of Carnoy and Levin's *Schooling and Work in the Democratic State* claims that they return to the economic problematic of the 1970s, and that it is warranted, especially in view of the real economic crisis of today. Apple tells us that he is not falling into the reductionist trap when he recognizes that there exist general priorities and interests which provide an historical centre of gravity (Apple, 1986a, p. 403). Apple claims that Carnoy and Levin's analysis '… privileges economic "causes" over others' (Apple, 1986a, p. 406). The current discourse, carried on by those who see schools and education in relational terms, is a discourse framed in economic language and concepts. Because of the enormous radical sea changes which have occurred in the economy, those of us who think relationally about education are warranted to place economic considerations at centre stage. Many of the cultural claims concerning the relative autonomy of actors in autonomous, or quasi-autonomous, contexts must be critically reviewed as a result of the enormous consequences experienced by persons within these superstructural contexts. The arguments which seek to establish the autonomy, or

partial autonomy, of actors within the interstices of what many had thought
was a one-dimensional society may have to be studied more rigorously
during a time when these so-called interstices seem very narrow indeed
(Marcuse, 1964). We cannot, must not, go back to mechanistic concepts of
deterministic causality with regard to our views on correspondence. The
scholarship already done concerning how hegemony must be continuously
re-imposed upon resisting agents is crucial to understanding how anti-
democratic forces continue to make the democratic potential non-
realizable in countries like the USA. However, the fact that this hegemony
is mainly still in place is due importantly to the reality of the correspondence principle. The advantage lies with those who make the macroeconomic decisions. The contesting parties do not fight on equal ground,
nor with equal power. We are witnessing the brute manifestations of this
unequal contestation since *circa* 1970 in the capitalist West. The economic
sea changes within the substructure have had corresponding consequences
upon superstructural institutions, like the schools.

As we know, Samuel Bowles and Herbert Gintis's *Schooling in
Capitalist America* (1976) has given rise to much analysis whose main
purpose was to point out the mechanistic determinist underpinning of that
landmark book. Scholars in education feared that Bowles and Gintis
presented us with a 'black box' within which capitalists simply reproduced
persons useful to capitalism. There seemed to be little that teachers,
democrats, critical progressives etc. could do about the iron-clad determinism of the box. Some of the reaction and analysis to *Schooling in
Capitalist America* may have been inaccurate and overwrought. A whole
industry emerged – one that was made up of thinkers and scholars who
warned us about Bowles and Gintis's overemphasis on economic tilt in
Marx and Marxist tradition. As stated earlier, this reaction to Bowles and
Gintis was warranted, and many of us tried to stake-out a claim for agency,
or the historical actor(s) (Brosio, 1985). But, when one has studied and re-
studied *Schooling in Capitalist America*, one realizes that there are many
ideas within it which are not as deterministic as critics have claimed. There
is a call for a mass-based democratic party at the end of the book.[3]
Furthermore, there exists the sophistication of the following concepts
which speak to the idea of correspondence being developed within Part II
of this work.

> The day-to-day operations of . . . pluralist forces – the 'free market' choices
> of students, the school bond-issue referenda, the deliberations of elected
> school boards and the like – reinforce the image of an educational system
> whose open and decentralized structure defies control or even significant
> influence by an elite. Indeed, it is absolutely essential for the school system
> to appear to be democratically controlled if it is successfully to contribute to
> the legitimation and reproduction of the US capitalist order. What is less
> often noted is that the accommodation by the educational system to

changing economic reality, however pluralistic, is, in essence, a process led by a changing structure of production ... [furthermore] the evolution of the structure of production is governed by the pursuit of profit and class privilege by a small minority of capitalists and managers who dominate the dynamic sectors of the economy. The process of pluralist accommodation thus operates within an economic framework determined almost entirely outside of the democratic political arena (Bowles and Gintis, 1976, p. 237).

Bowles and Gintis's central contention lies at the heart of the Marxist tradition, which is the belief that changes in the structure of production have preceded, and are mainly responsible for, corresponding changes in superstructural sectors and institutions like schools. Such parallelism or correspondence establishes a strong *prima facie* case for the '... causal importance of economic structure as a major determinant of educational structure' (Bowles and Gintis, 1976, p. 224).

☐ **Not democratically answerable**

The historical actors do in fact act, contest terrain, become mediated by their gender, ethnic, racial, nationality membership; however, this occurs within an arena most importantly established by an economic system which is fundamentally not democratically answerable. The state in the USA, and throughout the West, is more answerable to popular democratic forces than is the economy. The school lies within the state sector and is answerable to popular democratic pressures. The relationship between the state and the capitalist economy is complex, and beyond the scope of this analysis. The literature from Antonio Gramsci through Carnoy and Levin's *Schooling and Work in the Democratic State* is an increasingly important corpus of work on this relationship. This literature has always accepted the fundamental central importance of the primacy of the economic substructure. In spite of dialectical interaction and complexity between substructure and superstructure, the left has in general terms supported the view that the capitalist economy has been more dynamic than superstructural sectors and institutions like education. Bowles and Gintis think that, as the economy moves, the school falls out of correspondence with it, then the schol sees to it that it must 'modernize', 'become relevant', and catch-up. Schools and other institutions in a pluralist society seek to accommodate themselves to economic change – economic change which is made by a few with profit as a motive (Bowles and Gintis, 1976, pp. 236–7). Those who have historically been in control of the capitalist economy have had the power to fight with crucially important advantages against popular and democratic forces, so that reproduction and correspondence do occur in the superstructural sectors and institutions. This is not deterministic in the sense of non-human forces dictating to men and women. Instead, it is the age-old story of certain persons exerting their wills for their own 'bottom line' interests, instead of *pro bono publico*, or for the good and welfare of the whole public.

Carnoy and Levin consider the imperfect correspondence between (1) the capitalist dominated economy, including its work relations, and (2) the school system to be a paradox. They believe that a crucial task for the late 1980s is to explain how the public school can be both an institution that reproduces unequal class relations of capitalism, and an institution which is more democratic and equal than the workplace. Their dialectical position on education and work is summed up by: 'We reject both a mechanistic correspondence between work and school and a clear separation of the two' (Carnoy and Levin, 1985, p. 4). For Carnoy and Levin, both the structure and content of certain educational reforms advocated in the 1980s '... tend to correspond to particular changes in the workplace ... [although] some are more likely to be adopted than others' (Carnoy and Levin, 1985, p. 217). One key thesis in *Schooling and Work in the Democratic State* is that the major struggle within US schooling has historically featured: (1) education, which provides opportunity, equality, and democratic participation, *vs* (2) education or training (reproduction), which presses for appropriately efficient docile workers within the proper skills, attitudes, and behaviour useful to capitalist production and accumulations. This struggle is carried out within – or is framed by – the larger struggle '... taking place between the pressures for a more efficient workforce and those for a more egalitarian and democratic educational process' (Carnoy and Levin, 1985, p. 231). Carnoy and Levin assert that basic changes within the schools have followed changes in the workplace. Bowles and Gintis do not disagree with this view in their *Schooling in Capitalist America*. Their agreement can be seen in the following passage from *Schooling and Work in the Democratic State*.

> The educational thrust of the 1950s and 1960s was toward equality, but the economic crisis of the late 1970s and early 1980s served to shift the momentum to the efficient production of a work force that would respond to the needs of employers (Carnoy and Levin, 1985, p. 259).

It has been argued in Part II that the correspondence principle is still a useful one which enables us to understand the link between what occurs in the substructural economy, and the superstructural school. Specifically, a non-mechanistic or deterministic version of correspondence allows us to understand the educational or school ramifications of the powerful economic sea changes that have occurred since *circa* 1970. Recent scholarship has established that superstructural institutions like schools do exercise significant autonomy. We know that schools are contested sites. Historical actors do in fact act. There does exist empirical evidence of agency so that determination is properly discredited; however, 'We should remember that these resistances occur on terrain established by capital . . .' (Apple, 1982, p. 25).

■ Part III

In this final section we shall turn to a description and analysis of the corresponding consequences for education – consequences caused by the economic sea changes. The focus in this section will be on the years after 1970, but more specifically the talk about, and actual, reforms since 1980. The profound economic changes beginning in the early 1970s had a continuing impact upon education and schooling from the outset; however, the specific educational response became most evident by the time of the famous national education reports in the 1980s. Our description and analysis begin with attention to the national 'blue-ribbon' commission reports. This will be followed by an examination of what the various states have proposed in terms of educational changes. Some attention will also be given to local developments.

In the early 1980s, national attention was given to the supposed need for educational reform. The discourse of this reform was marked by terms like educational excellence; higher academic standards; harder work; back to basics; emphasis on science, math, and technology; ability to compete internationally; teacher competency; etc. This discourse was documented by a number of policy reports released in 1983, all of which called for reforms which were presented as being able to improve the quality of US education.[4] An overview of the policy reports includes the following: (1) the need to combat students' abandonment of the core curriculum, (2) warnings against lowered graduation requirements, (3) dangerous grade inflation, (4) disastrous decline of scholastic aptitude scores, (5) poor US comparisons with students from other industrial nations, (6) some 25 million US adults who are thought to be functionally illiterate, (7) about 13 per cent of US 17 year olds being functionally illiterate – with the rate jumping to 40 per cent among minority youth, (8) business and military leaders complaining that they have been required to spend millions of dollars on remedial education and training. The reports' underlying structure appears to be based upon the fear that the USA is being overtaken by other nations in commerce, industry, science, and technology (Ornstein and Levine, 1984, pp. 464–5). The reports emphasize tougher curricular standards and courses. They propose more rigorous grading, testing, homework, and discipline. All of these recommendations are seen against an atmosphere of 'emergency', 'urgency', 'risk', 'global competition', 'unilateral disarmament', etc.

All of the reports are concerned that the schools are pressed to play too many social roles, that schools cannot meet all these expectations, and that they are in danger of losing sight of their key role of teaching basic skills and the core academic subjects (math, science, English, foreign language, and history or civics), new skills for computer use, and high-level skills for the world of work and technology. The reports consider the restoration of academic excellence to be the overriding national aim (Ornstein and Levine, 1984, p. 468).

In general, the skills which are accentuated in the reports are geared to industrial, business, technocratic, and military needs. Furthermore, some reports advocate that industrial and business leaders participate with school personnel, and especially administrators, for the purpose of school planning, budgeting, etc., and that courses be conducted 'realistically' about the world of work. Finally, to quote from the report by the National Commission on Excellence in Education, *A Nation at Risk*:

'If an unfriendly foreign power had attempted to impose on America the mediocre educational performance that exists today, we might well have viewed it as an act of war'. We have in effect, 'been committing an act of unthinkable, unilateral educational disarmament' (Ornstein and Levine, 1984, p. 471).

These reports reflect the shift from an earlier commitment to equity, for the economically disadvantaged, bilingual, handicapped, and racially discriminated-against youth, to an emphasis upon those who can be easily helped to become the 'qualified' elite needed for the new business order of contemporary international competition, and the disciplining of labour. According to Carnoy and Levin:

The educational response to the economic crisis was to reject the pattern of equality and democratization of education that had characterized the three previous decades in favor of shifting support to private schools and to more advantaged students who were preparing themselves for college careers (Carnoy and Levin, 1985, p. 260).

In the late 1970s and early 80s, we can easily understand the attempts to reform education so that it will provide labour requirements of the emerging production system – one which capital hopes will feature stable patterns of labour–management relations. The structure and content of the reforms tend to *correspond* to particular changes in the contemporary workplace (Carnoy and Levin, 1985, p. 217).

☐   A crisis of ideology

Michael Apple has written that the nature of the crisis the reports have been responding to is most importantly an economic crisis, but looming behind the economic lies a crisis in authority relations and of ideology. Apple, as always, warns against being 'reductive'. He asserts once more that schools and contemporary educational reports cannot be interpreted as unmediated needs of capital and the state; however, '... since the reports *are* so self-consciously directed at current economic conditions it is crucially important to place the documents within these conditions' (Apple, 1986b, p. 176). For the authors of the reports, economic problems are those defined by business and industry. The corporate sector, which has come to dominate US society since the mid-nineteenth century, and which has pushed the logic of commodification, 'bottom line-ism', instrumentalism, rationalization, de-skilling, and subtle domination to new heights, is curiously left off the hook for the monumental problems sketched for us by the reports. The current economic crisis is structural, and the most serious since the 1930s, and in order to solve it, in an advantageous way for capital and other dominant interests, the eduational sector must help prepare the conditions for capital accumulation. The gains made by popular and democratic forces must be rescinded. Americans must be educated into seeing that these former gains are 'too expensive', both economically and ideologically. We must be made to see that current 'realities' do not allow the preference for democratic and personal rights over capital, property and profit.

Andrew Hacker has written that the reports have in common a lack of emphasis that learning may be pursued for its own sake, or that the 'cultivated mind' is worthy of esteem. A nation at risk, or in peril, has no time for such luxuries. 'Excellence' comes to mean the upgrading of the design and delivery of educational products (Hacker, 1984, p. 35). Michael Apple thinks that we are undergoing the creation of an expansive capital-intensive curriculum, and that this process makes the public schools more serviceable to, and an agent of, the capitalist state and industry (Apple, 1986b, p. 174). There is occurring a commodification of education, and the reports' recommendations aid in that development. Good curricula become those which have easily testable results. Good learning becomes the accumulation of atomistic, discrete skills and facts which can be evaluated by 'objective' tests. This is a victory for technique. Apple is correct in judging these trends as favourable to the children of those who make the most important decisions in our country.

Edward Berman believes that the current educational reform proposals give little or no attention to how the improved schools will serve the interests of individual students. This omission is attributable to the weakened position of the individual (in spite of his/her celebration by mass media and entertainers) within our evolving system of state capitalism. Berman is convinced that US public schools '... have lost any semblance of a coherent philosophy, common purpose, or shared direction' (Berman, 1986, p. 2). Not one of the educational reports offers the possibility of an emancipatory, democratic, empowering education for students. The proposed reforms seem to hitch students to the purposes of the corporations and state, with very little intellectual encouragement to think beyond the one-dimensional (albeit rich in consumer and 'experience' choices) society. Many students will benefit career-wise from the implementation of the 'blue-ribbon' reform proposals, but that may be merely incidental to the underlying purpose. Many critics of the proposed reforms see them as a stabilization of the present *status quo* – in that sense they are reactionary. They have been developed in reaction to the victories by popular and democratic forces within the school and society. In plain and simple terms, US schools are being asked to concentrate more attention and resources on 'gifted' youngsters and to encourage them to excel in math, science, and technology, so that US capitalists can re-establish their economic hegemony. Berman, and others, are convinced that the search for 'gifted' students will exacerbate the stratification of schools according to social class, race, ethnicity, gender, region, etc. In fact, 'The schools' role in reproducing the existing inequitable economic and social order will hardly be challenged as the reform juggernaut moves apace' (Berman, 1986, p. 5).

☐   Human capital theory

Stanley Aronowitz and Henry Giroux see the national reports as attempts by the so-called reformers to lock schools and students into the narrow confines of human capital theory. The proposed reforms, according to Carnoy and Levin, are direct attempts to make the educational system more responsive to the immediate needs of the capitalist-dominated workplace (Carnoy and Levin, 1985, p. 223). Students are to be delivered to the labour market possessing the skills that employers require. For example, the widespread concentration on computer use and 'computer literacy' is only part of the larger shift proposed by conservatives in this country. This conservative agenda or discourse has argued for a school atmosphere which emulates so-called market conditions. Schools are to present a Darwinian jungle picture to students so that they come to realize the cruciality of social Darwinistic feelings and views. The fit will survive, and fitness shall be determined by the curricula proposed by the national reports. According to Aronowitz and Giroux (1985, p. 191), the emerging school is saying, 'If you don't learn, "we" the school will not punish you, *life* will'.

   As we know, the concept called hegemony allows us to understand that domination in advanced societies is seldom achieved by the use of overt or naked force. The dominant groups and their allies represent what is in their own self interest in terms of what is 'natural', or good for all. The dominant groups in contemporary America have succeeded in integrating, under the aegis of their discourse, the perspectives and aspirations of the many. For example, the codes of the old middle-classes, which feature control, individual achievement, morality, etc., are placed into congruence with codes of the new middle-class, with their emphasis upon getting ahead, technique, efficiency, etc. These codes are subsumed under the dominant economic discourse sponsored by capital which stresses commodification, labour discipline, huge profits, some privatization, corporate consumerism, militarization, some competition, and the fuelling of a non-democratically directed technology (Apple, 1986b, p. 187). Many critics of the national reports believe that the reports have not been reflectively nor critically aware of how their agenda is made easily useful to capital. Various groups have sponsored components of educational reform which can be judged as ultimately useful to capital's strategic purpose.

> By framing nearly all important questions around the logic of standardiza-tion, production, and accumulation, capital is able to accommodate these groups within its own slogan system. The vision of the economy in the reports may be unequal and wrong, but there is little doubt that they have had considerable success in moving the debate onto capital's terrain (Apple, 1986b, p. 186).

Many persons, professionals, organizations, etc. have seemingly uncritically forwarded their own agendas without realizing the possibilities of how their priorities end up strengthening the strategic agenda of capital. Apple has explained this very well when he writes that capital has allies in conducting its current offence on the educational system.

> Often, other groups are ... instrumental both in sponsoring capital's requirements and setting limits on them so that these groups' own needs are met as well .... For example, the continuing growth of power ... [of] those with administrative expertise, behaviorally oriented curriculum specialists ... will account for some of the reasons that such pressures are generated and how they will be taken up in the form they are. As holders of ... technical/administrative knowledge, these groups ... will have their own relatively autonomous interests in maintaining and enhancing their positions and paths to upward mobility .. the reports will signify a 'settlement' ... among .. [various] groups, not only between factions of capital and the 'populist' groups that support the New Right's program. The result will be a compromise, but one decidedly *within* the limits imposed by the tightening relationship between the State and the economy (Apple, 1986b, p. 184).

Educational reform, as proposed in the 1980s, is not simply meeting capital's needs during this crisis. The reports *do* speak the language of varied social groups and interests. As Svi Shapiro has said, it is not surprising, because it is what is meant when we refer to hegemony.

Hegemony entails the construction of a climate, a context, a discourse which appears to articulate the concerns and agenda of the majority of the society. The members of the national commissions represent many social and professional points of view. The crucial question is to discern which points, which agendas *are* finally represented in the reports – and which ones *are not*. According to Shapiro:

> Finding evidence in the reports of diverse, or even oppositional statements concerning what is required in education is not ... [the] issue here. Such evidence does not refute my claim that the real significance of the educational reports has to do with attempting to remedy the capitalist crisis of falling productivity and the decline of US capital in the world.... (Shapiro, 1987, p. 77) [...]

☐   **Crisis in schooling**

Lawrence Stedman has argued that the national reports were as much a response to the basic crisis in schooling as to a crisis in US capitalism. According to Stedman, from the middle 1970s parents and local school officials have tried to address and repair what they felt to be a deteriorating school situation. They originated many of the reforms which finally found their way to the national reports and then state action (Stedman, 1987, p. 70). Stedman admits, though, that the suggested reforms do not suggest basic changes in curriculum, pedagogy, or the structure of schooling. The 1980s reform agenda for education and schools '... failed to rise above the prevailing ideological climate characterized by the back-to-basics movement and the threat of Far East global economic competition, they [the reports] certainly did not challenge the power of dominant social groups or explore what role schools could play in building a new social order' (Stedman, 1987, p. 84). The reports, and corollary state actions, must be understood as promotions of agenda, discourses, and reforms which are congruent with the priorities of capital, and of the Reagan administration. The fact that there does exist popular support for some of the reforms does not allow us to equate popular with authentic democracy, nor with authentically progressive reform. Students of education and society are aware of populism of the right, and of how those who fight to maintain hegemonic control are often successful at converting legitimate grassroots issues into what is best for the maintenance of the *status quo*.

Because the current crisis of global monopoly capitalism has been primarily responsible for the present economic sea changes, the educational reforms proposed and enacted have corresponded to the economic crisis as defined by capital and its conscious or seemingly unaware hegemonic allies and minions. Had the present economic crisis been defined by other social classes, groups, and alliances – those using other discourses – then the pressure on the educational system would have been different from what we have witnessed. Whether or not the reforms of the 1980s will get the school back in sync with the needs of capital remains to be seen. What is clear is that there is much that the reports, and state/local reforms, do not address nor seek to solve. The rightist agenda for school reform has no programme for democratic empowerment, only one for providing human capital for the current needs of business and industry. As we have seen, this is not surprising because the schools are defined mainly by those interests capable of mounting a systematic and sustained campaign to determine their shape and direction. Berman has said: 'The efforts of the corporations and financial sectors, in league with representatives of the state, are unambiguous in this regard' (Berman, 1986, p. 5).

☐   Critical citizenship

The current spate of reforms does not take critical citizenship education seriously. Nor is the possible role of the school as a place which must be protected from the juggernaut comprised of technocracy, commodification, positivism, reductionism, consumerism, narrow vocationalism, etc. appreciated by the reports and so-called reformers. There is no honest talk about encouraging teachers to become the kind of critical intellectuals who understand what the underlying assumptions of this *status quo* are, nor about the teachers' commitment to educate their students about what they have discovered. The current reforms speak about fixing-up certain losers in the American Darwinian race, but there is no mention of the unfairness of the race itself. All of the reforms are ones that the secure middle- and upper-classes can live with and profit from. The programmes proposed and enacted will surely allow the sons and daughters of the privileged – those who have money, power, and access – to increase their lead over those who have been victimized by social-class, racial, ethnic, and gender inequities. The reforms do not send supplies to those who wish to encourage democratic empowerment and the civic courage to establish such participation. The participation suggested and spoken of by the current reforms speak of inclusion in the credentials race, the one-ups-manship race, and the right to score well in the merchandise and investment markets of capitalism. It does not speak of the kind of participation that would allow *de jure* democratic power to become *de facto* by its necessary intrusion into the economic realm – a realm which continues to be mainly controlled by capital and its allies in the state and elsewhere.

For those who care systematically and carefully to investigate the problems of school and society, it seems clear that at the greatest sea depth there lies the non-democratically answerable power of monopoly, transnational, consumer capitalism. It is true that superstructural institutions, like the schools, are able to exercise some autonomy *vis-à-vis* the substructure. The pressures emanating from those who control, and most greatly benefit from, capital are mediated through complex institutions before they have an impact upon you and me, but they do affect us mightily day after day. Persons do resist the power and blandishments of capitalism while in the schools, factories, neighborhoods, organizations, etc.; however, it should be clear by now that it is not being resisted on terrain which is owned by popular democratic forces. More often than not, the resistance is unsuccessful. Those of us who seek genuine democratic humanistic authentic reform must focus our attention upon the economy and the power of capital. If we are to resist, if we are to be *contra* anti-democratic forces and persons in the schools and the larger society, we must see, as Marx did, that capitalism must be replaced before an agenda which is *pro bono publico* can be seriously considered.

■ Conclusion

In the introduction to this work, it was claimed that professors within the social foundations of education area and disciplines are uniquely qualified and motivated to explain what occurs, and fails to occur, in schooling and education *vis-à-vis* the larger social, economic, and political context. Hopefully, this description and analysis have shed some more light upon the relationship between the sea changes in economics and education in the USA. The references within this work allow one to go beyond this analysis and get into a broader literature – some of it being foundational. The school's responses to the specifics of the crisis, which were explained in Part I, are not in specific correspondence to the demands raised by economic disequilibrium. The claim instead has been that there does exist a higher congruence, or correspondence, between the imperatives of the capitalist-directed economy and the responses made by those who make school and educational policies. This lack of specific, point-by-point correspondence allows some observers to miss the higher congruence.

I hope that this work contributes to the ongoing attempt to discern just how correspondence works. The most recent trend toward softening the principle of correspondence to a point of meaninglessness, because of the need to defend the concept of agency, should be halted. The current massive brute intrusions of capital's imperatives into nearly every facet of superstructural institutions should alert us to the need for using the explanatory power of the correspondence principle.

As we have seen, the educational reforms of the early 1980s are not the result of direct orders by capital, but can be understood in terms of the crisis exemplified by economic sea changes. The reforms can be interpreted as a result of the continued domination of the economy and the society by capital and its allies. Otherwise the flurry of activity within education can be seen as periodic occurrences which 'just seem to happen'. As we now know, the popular democratic forces have not been strong enough to resist the hegemonic atmosphere which allowed the discourse which resulted in the national reports and the educational legislation enacted in the various states. At bottom, the crisis described and analysed here is the crisis in US democracy itself (Brosio, 1986, p. 3).

Notes

1.   The kind of pressures being discussed can best be understood within the meaning of hegemony as used by Antonio Gramsci, 'The bourgeois civilization which controlled the workers, and other subaltern classes [Italy in the early twentieth century], could do so because its leaders controlled the very definitions of what was considered real, commonsensical, good, etc. Bourgeois hegemony meant [and still means] that a class could rule a highly developed society without the flagrant, or regular use of force ... hegemony ... consists of a group or class creating a state of affairs in which their leadership and privileged positions seem natural. It consists too of ways of living, thinking, speaking, habits, hopes, fears, and underlying assumptions'. From Brosio, R. A. (1983) 'Essay on Antonio Gramsci', in Devine, E. *et al.* (eds), *Thinkers of the Twentieth Century*, p. 22 (Detroit, Mich.: Gale Research Company).

2.   For an explanatory model of dialectically related contestants who struggle over specific work terrains, see Edwards, R. C. (1979) *Contested Terrain: The Transformation of the Workplace in the Twentieth Century* (New York: Basic Books).

3.   Although it has been argued that the call for this mass-based party at book's end seems like a *deus ex machina*, that is a conclusion unsupported by what preceded it.

4.   The five national reports on education published in 1983 were: (1) *Academic preparation for college* (The College Board), (2) *Making the grade* (Twentieth Century Fund), (3) *Educating Americans for the 21st century* (National Science Foundation), (4) *Action for excellence* (Education Commission of the States), (5) *A nation at risk* (The National Commission on Excellence in Education).

References

Apple, M. W. (1979) *Ideology and Curriculum* (London: Routledge & Kegan Paul).

Apple, M. W. (1982) *Education and Power* (Boston: Routledge & Kegan Paul).

Apple, M. W. (1986a) 'Review article – bringing the economy back into educational theory' (review of Carnoy, M. and Levin, H., *Schooling and Work in the Democratic State. Educational Theory*, Vol. 36, No. 4 (Fall)).

Apple, M. W. (1986b) 'National reports and the construction of inequality'. *British Journal of Sociology of Education*, Vol. 7, No. 2.

Aronowitz, S. and Giroux, H. A. (1985) *Education Under Siege*, ch. 2 (South Hadley, Mass.: Bergin & Garvey).

Berman, E. H. (1986) 'The improbability of meaningful educational reform'. *The Education Digest*, Vol. LII, No. 2 (October).

Berquist, C. (ed.) (1984) *Labor in the Capitalist World Economy* (Beverly Hills, Calif.: Sage Publications).

Bowles, S. and Gintis, H. (1976) *Schooling in Capitalist America* (New York: Basic Books).

Brosio, R. A. (1985) 'One Marx, and the centrality of the historical actor(s)'. *Educational Theory*, Vol. 35, No. 1 (Winter).

Brosio, R. (1986) 'The current industrial economic crisis and the weakness of American democracy'. *The Labor Beacon*, Vol. 36, No. 6 (December).

Carnoy, M. and Levin, H. (1985) *Schooling and Work in the Democratic State* (Stanford, Calif.: Stanford University Press).

Castells, M. (1980) *The Economic Crisis and American Society* (Princeton University Press).

Davis, M. (1986) *Prisoners of the American Dream* (London: Verso).

Edsall, T. B. (1984) *The New Politics of Inequality* (New York: W. W. Norton).

Edwards, R. C. (1979) *Contested Terrain: The Transformation of the Workplace in the Twentieth Century* (New York: Basic Books).

Edwards, R. C., Reich, M. and Weisskopf, T. E. (eds) (1978) *The Capitalist System*, 2nd edn (Englewood Cliffs, N.J.: Prentice-Hall). Also, see all of chapter 13.

Farr, T. J. (1982) 'The making of Reaganism'. *The New York Review of Books*, Vol. XXVIII, Nos 21 & 22 (January 21).

Goss, M. (1985) 'Smokestacks revisited: the future of high-tech'. *Management Review*, Vol. 74, No. 5 (May).

Hacker, A. (1984) 'The schools flunk out'. *The New York Review of Books*, Vol. XXXI, No. 6 (12 April).

Heilbroner, R. L. (1980) *Marxism For and Against* (New York: W. W. Norton).

Heilbroner, R. L. (1981) 'The demand for the supply side'. *The New York Review of Books*, Vol. XXVIII, No. 10 (11 June).

Keller, E. (1972) 'Social priorities, economic policy, and the state', in Howe, I. and Harrington, M. (eds), *The Seventies* (New York: Harper Colophon Books).

Kuttner, R. (1984) *The Economic Illusion: False Choices between Prosperity and Social Justice* (Boston: Houghton Mifflin).

Kuttner, R. (1985a) 'The shape of things to come' (review of Priore, M. J. and Sable, C. F., *The Second Industrial Divide: Possibilities for Prosperity*). *New Republic*, Vol. 192, Nos 28 & 29 (7 & 14 January).

Kuttner, R. (1985b) 'High Marx' (review of Heilbroner, R. L., *The Nature and Logic of Capitalism*). *New Republic*, Vol. 193, No. 18 (28 October).

Lukacs, G. (1973) *Marxism and Human Liberation* (New York: A Delta Book).

Marcuse, H. (1964) *One-Dimensional Man* (Boston: Beacon Press).

Ornstein, A. C. and Levine, D. U. (1984) *An Introduction to the Foundations of Education*, 3rd edn (Boston: Houghton Mifflin).

Piven, F. F. and Cloward, R. A. (1982) *The New Class War: Reagan's Attack on the Welfare State and its Consequences*, ch. 4 especially (New York: Pantheon Books).

Reich, R. (1981) 'The liberal promise of prosperity'. *New Republic*, Vol. 184, No. 8 (21 February).

Rothschild, E. (1981) 'Reagan and the real America'. *The New York Review of Books*, Vol. XXVIII, No. 1 (5 February).

Rothschild, E. (1982) 'The philosophy of Reaganism'. *The New York Review of Books*, Vol. XXIX, No. 6 (15 April).

Shapiro, S. (1987) 'Reply to Stedman'. *Educational Theory*, Vol. 37, No. 1 (Winter).

Stedman, L. C. (1987) 'The political economy of recent education reform reports'. *Educational Theory*, Vol. 37, No. 1 (Winter).

Thurow, L. (1981) 'How to wreck the economy'. *The New York Review of Books*, Vol. XXVIII, No. 8 (14 May).

Tobin, J. (1981) 'Reaganomics and economics'. *The New York Review of Books*, Vol. XXVIII, No. 19 (3 December).

Wilson, E. (1940) *To the Finland Station* (Garden City, N.Y.: Doubleday & Company).

Wirth, A. (1983) *Productive Work – In Industry and Schools*, ch. 4 (Lanham, Md: University Press of America).

Chapter 7

The Compliant–Creative Worker: The Ideological Reconstruction of the School Leaver

H. E. Cathcart and G. M. Esland

Our purpose in this chapter is to examine some of the more recent developments in the education of 14–16 year olds, and in particular certain curriculum initiatives in the areas of industrial awareness and preparation for work. We shall be concerned both with the ideological substance of these initiatives and with the centralist–corporatist political structures which are being brought into play to legitimate and strengthen their adoption, recognizing that they represent a major departure from what had previously been regarded as the constitutional basis on which the state, LEAs and teaching profession had co-existed (Lawton, 1980; Kogan, 1983). We recognize, too, that the commitment of the present Thatcher government to an authoritarian mode of curriculum regulation at all levels of education and its expanding use of the apparatus of the state for this purpose should caution us against being over-sanguine about the capacity of teachers and educational administrators to debate and confront the implications of these new developments. The use of expenditure cuts in education to create space for political intervention in the internal activities of educational institutions, as, for example, in the case of the Technical and Vocational Education Initiative (TVEI) and the transfer from the

Source: Cathcart, H. E. and Esland, G. M. (1985) 'The compliant–creative worker: the ideological reconstruction of the school leaver', in Barton, L. and Walker, S. (eds), *Education and Social Change*, Croom Helm, Beckenham, pp. 173–192.

LEAs to the MSC of 25 per cent of the funding for non-advanced further education have shown that the Thatcher administration feels little necessity for restraint in the setting up of machinery for extending its political control over educational policy. Combined with the creation of the NAB and the Council for the Accreditation of Teacher Education, which is to review the balance and content of teacher education, and with the movement towards national and local corporatism in curriculum planning, this policy has tightened by several notches the ratchets of political control and ideological pressure on educational practice.

It would be mistaken to assume that these and other assaults on existing educational structures will generate anything like a unified reaction, either from teacher organizations or from the various consumer groups within education.[1] Intrerests around specific issues are inevitably fragmented and usually give rise only to limited and disparate forms of resistance. One of the clear sources of this fragmentation is the disjunction which exists between resource issues ('fighting the cuts') and ideological issues relating to the implementation of policy. As Cawson and Saunders (1983) have pointed out, local resistance in particular tends to be characterized by the competitive politics of consumerist interest groups which may not necessarily coalesce on other issues. These groups are often middle class and tend to mobilize most readily around questions of resource provision (hospitals, schools, transport etc.). On these grounds, of course, there is strong likelihood of convergence with professional interests, but on ideological issues relating, for instance, to the relevance of technical and vocational curricula, political reactions are likely to be less uniform. This is further underlined by the ambivalence and separation of identity which exists within teacher organizations between their functions as professional associations and as trade unions. As recent political events have demonstrated, it is this ambivalence and diffusion of focus which has rendered them ineffective in the forming of a collective response to the curricular and training initiatives taken by the state in the transition from school to work.

Another important conditioner of professional and consumer responses is the depoliticization of issues which might be expected to generate resistance. It is clear that the ideological parameters which prefigure and legitimate many of the initiatives currently being taken have been so thoroughly prepared, constructed and transmitted during the past decade that they effectively depoliticize the content which is prescribed within them. A significant feature of the Conservative administration since 1979 has, for example, been its relative success in sustaining the depoliticization of its economic policy. Such a statement, of course, ought to be a contradiction in terms but it is the case that in spite of the depth of the recession, the deindustrialization of manufacturing centres and the massive increase in youth unemployment, the Thatcher administration has managed to sustain the belief among a substantial proportion of the electorate that structural changes in the economy on the scale which we have witnessed are not only inevitable but in some senses desirable, and only insignificantly connected with political choices. As Hall has argued, the durability of the government's economic policy ultimately rests on its apparent success in making sense of the perceptions and material conditions of large sections of the working class (Hall, 1983). The view that the processes of industrial decline and recomposition are the unpalatable but necessary preconditions for industrial revival ultimately has to win acceptance from those who have most to lose by it. That it has done so for the past five years is due in no small measure to the proclaiming of economic and political nationalism and to the mobilization of a large-scale and broad-fronted ideological onslaught on the social democratic, liberal humanist philosophies which had underpinned social policy since 1945.

Using Gramsci's distinction between the 'organic' and the 'conjunctural' elements of crisis, Stuart Hall has argued that the move to the right in Britain constitutes 'an "organic" phenomenon', in which efforts by the right to conserve and defend the existing economic and political structure

> cannot be merely defensive. They will be *formative*: aiming at a new balance of forces, the emergence of new elements, the attempt to put together a new 'historic bloc', new political configurations and 'philosophies', a profound restructuring of the state and the ideological discourses which construct the crisis and represent it as it is 'lived' as a practical reality: new programmes and policies, pointing to a new result, a new sort of 'settlement' .... Political and ideological work is required to disarticulate old formations, and to rework their elements into new ones (Hall, 1983).

Education has borne as much of the brunt of this disarticulation and restructuring as any other area of national policy. The message by now is familiar: Britain's economic decline and uncompetitiveness are due on the one hand to the efficiency and innovativeness of other national economies, which are reducing Britain's share of world markets, and, on the other, to the legacy of social democratic consensus politics and labour practices, which have led to British industry becoming overmanned and burdened with restrictive practices. Add to this the putative failure of the British education system to give support to the 'wealth-creation' process, and to produce adequately-prepared school leavers and graduates, and almost the entire case is seen to rest on the lack of national resolve, the narrow self-interest of the unionized working class, the perpetuation of outworn practices and institutions and the self-indulgence of an education system which over-values its academic and liberal humanist traditions. Thus, the restoration of the interests of capital and the conditions of expanded accumulation are represented in a form which scapegoats the trade unions, the education system and the public service sector generally, while the consequences of monetarist policies and political choices favouring defence, law and order, privatization and the free movement of capital are ignored. By screening off these and similar issues and by substantially moving the terrain of debate from the social democratic position which had prevailed since the 1950s, this ideological package has, in Hall's phrase, 'shifted the parameters of common sense', and now constitutes the framework within which new agendas for policy are constructed (Hall, 1982).

As far as educational policy is concerned, this shift has led to fundamental reappraisals by the state both of the purpose and content of education as well as of the political structures through which resources for education are 'delivered'. Ideologies of educational content and practice have become increasingly fashioned around the view that the liberal humanist emphasis of British education has somehow failed the nation. A recent influence in this development has been Martin Weiner's book *English Culture and the Decline of the Industrial Spirit* which has been much quoted in business and political circles (Weiner, 1981). Weiner's argument that the tradition of liberal education in Britain has played a significant part in the creation of negative attitudes towards industrial capitalism has been cited by many as evidence for the need for a major shift in national values towards a greater recognition and support of 'enterprise'. As part of the belief that liberal education has promoted anti- or non-capitalist attitudes, it is claimed that it does little for the average and lower achiever in providing a relevant basis for work, and for higher achievers it provides a curriculum which is too academically specialized and, therefore, inappropriate for industrial regeneration. This is in spite of the fact that substantial numbers of large employers persist in favouring academic over applied degrees, and university graduates over polytechnic graduates (Boys, 1984). The conclusion is unmistakable that through a variety of interventions, the Thatcher government has set out to destabilize the curriculum and the teaching profession and to further the delegitimation of liberal education, while promoting a curriculum whose concerns are instrumental and skill-led and predicated on 'capability' and 'enterprise' rather than on critical understanding.

What we are witnessing is, in Wexler's terms, a process of 'deschooling by default' in which curriculum subjects are 'decomposed' into skills, and alternative (non-school) sources of education and training are increasingly looked upon as providing the appropriate models of learning. Although the extensive cuts in resources experienced by education fall ostensibly within the government's policy for the control of the money supply, they also betoken a political resolve to weaken the capacity which liberal education has for promoting social and political dissent and intellectual critique. The problem for the New Right lies, in Wexler's terms, in education's potential for 'truth-seeking': 'Teaching in the name of truth may include critical evaluation of the capitalist version of reality, or even the demand and right to realise possibilities that capitalism would deny' (Wexler *et al.*, 1981). The growing emphasis in teacher education on subject specialism and the downgrading of educational theory, the repeated searches for and accusations of 'Marxist bias' in higher education, and the vociferous attack from the right on peace studies are merely the most obvious manifestations of a political project which has as its objective the political and moral transformation of education.

The attack on liberal education from the New Right is in some senses a mirror image of the critique mounted by the left during the mid-seventies. At the heart of that critique was the concern that liberal humanist ideology while proclaiming the importance of individual self-development was lending legitimacy to the requirement of the capitalist economy for a stratified and attitudinally attuned labour force. What this critique underestimated was the degree to which the curricular and pedagogical reforms of the late sixties and early seventies had actually led to the creation of an educational agenda which could be represented by the right as undermining the nation's economic future. The compromises within liberal humanist education which for the left could be portrayed as inadequately facing up to the capitalist reality underlying it could be attacked by the right for promoting values antithetical to industry and the national economy and to the standards required of young people. Thus, in spite of the rapid rise in youth unemployment since 1976, the right has succeeded in retaining the offensive against liberal education, has continued to promulgate the myth that young people (and their teachers) are responsible for their own unemployment, and, largely through the invoking of economic survival, has begun the process of decomposition of elements of liberal education.

This process draws much of its impetus from a revival of economic nationalism and a rampant technological determinism, in which the main burden of responsibility for industrial decline in the past and economic regeneration in the future is laid on institutions of education and training. The other potential partners in this undertaking are on the whole sleeping ones, immutable within the monetarist ideological universe: the export of capital and the transfer by multinationals to overseas sites of production, the favoured treatment of agriculture and the dominance of defence contracts within the electronics industry are typically set aside, as is the responsibility of high interest rates and crippling exchange rates between 1979 and 1982 for Britain's unprecedented deindustrialization. In a political economy where these factors are seen as imperatives, the liberal humanist goals of social justice and personal development have been severely attenuated in favour of those emphasizing vocational preparation and a technically-oriented curriculum. The pressure on education to deliver technical competences, skills and respect for workplace disciplines has, outwardly at least, transformed professional concerns and vocabularies as can be seen from the current range of DES in-service and ESRC research priorities. Clearly, for liberal humanism is being substituted a version of social and economic Darwinism where enterprise and the possession of skills for 'technological capability' have become the dominant values.

This reappraisal of the nature, purpose and content of education has, of course, been fuelled by the dilemmas of educators facing disappearing employment opportunities for their school leavers. But, more significantly, the reappraisal has drawn some of its strength from a readiness in some (largely Conservative) quarters to exploit the unresolved contradictions which lay behind the comprehensivization settlement during the 1960s. Throughout the development of the comprehensive school policy, the concern has been largely with the *form* of comprehensivization rather than its substance. The primary issue has always been one of access to educational resources and the location of the individual pupil in an ostensibly non-selective system rather than the class–cultural basis of the curriculum and examination system which have continued to perpetuate the class divisions of the tripartite system. The disguised nature of the selection process in the comprehensive school was, of course, at the heart of the attack on reformist policies by the so-called 'new' sociology of education of the early 1970s, but recognition of this contradiction has re-emerged in the education policy of the Conservative government in quite a new guise. We now find that the 'irrelevance' of education for the lower-achieving 40 per cent of school leavers is used to legitimate the *strengthening* of selection and the allocation of this band of young people of a more 'relevant' technical and vocationally-oriented curriculum. In view of the continuing low probability of employment for this group of school leavers it is difficult to escape Gleeson's conclusion that

> the plethora of curriculum guidelines emanating from the MSC and the DES at the present time may obscure a related and perhaps more pressing political problem: namely the effect a fall in demand for labour has on the principles of authority and discipline in society. Work preparation for non-existent jobs, therefore, takes on a 'new' connotation; one less concerned with training for particular technical skills and one more concerned with 'educating' young people for the social order (Gleeson, 1983).

That this policy has not produced the wholehearted condemnation from the liberal wing of the educational community that might have been expected is a measure both of the ambivalence towards educational ends which currently prevails and of the difficulty which liberal educators have in defending comprehensives against the charge of failing the low achievers. Perhaps the clearest demonstration of this has been the public commitment of a number of prominent 'liberal' members of the educational establishment to the RSA's project 'Education for capability' with its very clear espousal of technical values.

Although schools have yet to move some way before this technicist ideology becomes practice, the revival of an aggressive form of technological determinism within the state departments responsible for industry and employment has led to the clear prescription for education to service the technological future rather than to engage critically with it. This applies particularly to further education, where social education has been largely displaced by courses in social and life skills (Moore, 1983), and to some extent to higher education where the hostility shown to sociology and the attempts to reduce the social science input to teacher education give fairly convincing indications of the wish to curtail the critical study of policy and social institutions. Predictably, in much of the literature available for 'awareness of industry' courses in schools, it is an idealized view of industry which is presented. Teachers are enjoined to foster an understanding (that is, an acceptance) of the 'wealth creation' process and a recognition that industrial growth, consumerism and new technology are synonymous with progress. In outlining the education and training aims of his Department to the House of Lords Select Committee on Science and Technology, the Chief Engineer and Scientist at the Department of Trade and Industry made the statement that

> These aims reflect the two sides of the education process: first getting youngsters to see education as a preparation for a productive life contributing to the wealth on which our Society [sic] and its values depend; and second to try and match the content of education to the future needs of employers so that it lays the foundation of understanding on which specific skills can be built through occupational training and the continuing education which will be an increasing feature of working life (House of Lords Select Committee on Science and Technology, 1984).

The Industry–Education Unit at the DTI which was established in 1978 sets out to promote and fund a range of activities in the education system which embody the aims outlined above. These include the Micro Electronics Project, the SATROs – Science and Technology Regional Organisations – the Information Technology Centres and the CNC equipment in further education college programmes.

The unproblematized view of industry which the DTI takes as part of its aim of changing the attitudes and culture of young people can be seen in the booklet entitled 'Industry in perspective' (BP et al., 1983). Published in conjunction with a number of large companies, it is intended as a briefing document for teachers and senior pupils. Although there is a passing mention of some of the social costs associated with industrialization, it is most striking that almost all of the problematic issues are ignored. In an important sense, the fostering of an unproblematic 'awareness of industry' as understood by the protagonists of this view is a serious political intervention in the curriculum but one which is largely unrecognized as such. So 'naturalized' has this view of industrial capitalism become that any questioning of it would in all probability be attacked as 'Marxist bias'. That it has survived with relatively little debate is an indication of the hegemonic power of the current wave of economic nationalism and the technological determinism which goes with it.

After James Callaghan's Ruskin College speech in October 1976 had launched the so-called 'Great Debate', a number of initiatives were begun which attempted to implement the new commitment to developing in schools a positive view of industry. One of the more well-known was the Schools Council Industry Project (SCIP) which had originated in 1975 with an approach to the Schools Council by the TUC requesting curricular materials which would counter the negative attitudes of school leavers to trade unions. But the Schools Council felt that there were advantages in including the CBI in a wider scheme to improve young people's understanding of industry, and it was on this basis that the 'Industry project' was planned. The SCIP was the only initiative to emerge during the late 1970s which formally built in a trade union perspective. Others such as the CBI-sponsored *Understanding British Industry*, *Project Trident*, *Young Enterprise*, *Understanding Industry*, and the Industrial Society's *Challenge of Industry* Conferences identified specific tasks and modes of operation and became part of the repertoire available to the Schools Industry Liaison Officers who were appointed in increasing numbers by LEAs from the late 1970s onwards. The main concern shared by each of them was the development of a greater awareness of industrial processes and practice. Some UBI schemes, for example, have concentrated on promoting teacher secondments into industry. *Project Trident*'s school–industry work is concerned with the development of work experience schemes for young people, and the *Young Enterprise* Scheme provides encouragement to sixth-formers to set up and run their own 'scale-model' companies on commercial lines with their own working capital and management structures.

For the six-year period after the start of the Great Debate, 'awareness of industry' curricula in schools were extremely variable and dependent on the energies and availability of staff attached to the various national projects. Since the introduction of TVEI in November 1982, the piecemeal nature of this provision has begun to give way to more coherent strategies within LEAs in which industrial practice is seen in relation to systematic programmes of technical and vocational education.

A new feature in this development and a direct outcome of New Right ideology is a growing emphasis on 'education for enterprise'. This encouragement of school leavers to consider setting up their own businesses, ostensibly promoted as a means of creating jobs, also clearly carries within it the essence of competitiveness and possessive in-dividualism. A particularly notable example of the importance currently attached to 'education for enterprise' is a discussion paper from the Society of Education Officers which takes as its starting point the view that

The economic, cultural and social future of the United Kingdom rests on our ability to exploit the new technologies in competition with other advanced nations. Without the contribution of education in developing the attitudes and skills which make up technological capability, the economic future must be in serious doubt. The slow response in this country to opportunities which have already appeared and been lost can be attributed in a large part to deeply inbuilt social forces and to the shortcomings of education itself. Weaknesses in technological capability point inevitably to a decline in material standards and, in important respects, in the quality of life (Society of Education Officers, 1983).

In order to overcome what the SEO identifies as the shortcomings of education in this regard, the paper proposes that the

long-term objectives of the education service ought to include the following:
1. To emphasize publicly the value of a systematic approach to teaching the individual and collective skills and attitudes which are associated with enterprise; such teaching to be through the existing curricular structures wherever possible, in business-related contexts and at all stages of education – beginning at the most general level in primary schools and stretching through advanced academic research.

2. To encourage a more closely co-ordinated national strategy towards Education for Enterprise.

3. To reorient and co-ordinate the use of project work in secondary schools, further and higher education, such as to draw more effectively on opportunities for commercially viable service or product innovation and development.

4. To examine the contribution of further and higher education in meeting the special needs of small businesses and to encourage a more effective use of the resources available in education (Society of Education Officers, 1983).

The arguments adduced for the strategies proposed are predicated on a vision of the new industrialism in which information technology becomes the 'meta-technology' which is 'energizing a new phase in the economy and culture'. It subscribes to a computer utopianism with global implications and, ironically, draws the conclusion that 'Education must be much more strongly oriented towards giving individuals the capacity to be autonomous, self-supporting and self-directing'. What is absent from arguments such as these is any concept of education doing anything other than passively accepting this process with all its implications for deskilled and fragmented work roles and the concentration of control in the hands of companies and organizations whose task is to manage information. The notion that one of the major purposes of education is to permit the critical understanding and evaluation of social futures is entirely absent.

The new educational principles being called for to support the new industrialism are epitomized in the concept of the compliant–creative worker. Constructed during the course of the attack on progressive education in the 1970s by the right in Britain, this concept encapsulates much that has followed in education and training policy since that time. The apparently contradictory characteristics it implies are highly functional to the working experience which has given rise to it and consistent with much of the criticism which has been made of the preparedness of school leavers for work and the unsatisfactory nature of the transition from school to work. In short, it defines the ideal worker of the future.

The creativity envisaged bears little relationship, of course, to the concept of creativity which flourished in the educational theories of the 1960s. That creativity which drew its sustenance from the psychological theories of Piaget and existential philosophy was founded on an open-ended concept of cognition and an expanding consciousness in which the concrete and the abstract were seen in a continued dialectical relationship. The ideal pedagogical mode, in the phrase of the time, was 'learning by discovery'. By contrast, the innovation, initiative and enterprise called for in the current discourse are entirely instrumental. They are directed at practical or technical rather than intellectual development, at information rather than knowledge, at syncretism rather than criticism and at skills rather than understanding. Above all, the initiative and enterprise thought to be needed by current conditions of work are not expected to be directed towards those conditions themselves. The expectation is that workers will be creative in the furthering of capitalist goals but compliant towards the social relations and structures they find in the workplace, including the need to adapt to the consequences of the introduction of new technology.

Wexler et al. have argued that schools are now being asked to satisfy fundamentally contradictory demands of the production process:

> When the skills needed for job performance come to include the ability to understand and respond creatively to the changing needs of the overall process and to participate actively in coordination and innovation, then it is more difficult to maintain the attitudes and dispositions necessary for a willing submission to an hierarchical organisation of that production process .... The concrete expression of these contradictions is the simultaneous demand for workers who have broad general competencies (smart workers) but who have also internalized the model of hierarchical social relations as personal dispositions (docile workers). Without these general competencies, the competitive, adaptive development of production is inhibited. But if they are in fact developed, they threaten to disrupt the existing social relations of production (Wexler, et al., 1981).

Wexler et al. go on to suggest that to achieve this contradiction, curriculum subjects are undergoing 'decomposition' – English into communication skills, social education into social and life skills – thereby reducing their potential for promoting critical understanding. This point is also made by Moore in his analysis of further education curricula in Britain, in which he argues that the emphasis on skills within the FE curriculum

> effectively cuts young people off from bodies of abstract theoretical knowledge through which they could elaborate structural and collective understandings of their situation (Moore, 1983).

In tandem with this ideological attack on liberal education has been a substantial shift within the political structures used in the delivery of these new curricula. The hitherto decentralized nature of the British education system and teacher autonomy have represented a fairly substantial buttress against political control of the curriculum. In Kogan's term, the 'socio-technology of education' makes it inherently impossible for the state to control the curriculum in any direct sense. And further, as he points out, the current international consensus is that the top-down strategies of curriculum change do not generally work because teachers' attitudes to the cumulative impact of such innovation are unfavourable. For this reason, he suggests that even where there are strong policy directives from the centre, they 'have probably generally been followed by empirical–rational strategies of information, dissemination and training' (Kogan, 1983). Citing the growth of progressive education as an example, he argues that 'the most important changes in British education have been bottom-up' and that 'on the larger social objectives endorsed and pushed by central government, such as ... education as a way to economic change, there has been virtually complete failure' (Kogan, 1983). The failure of the top-down model of educational innovation is also a factor in the development of the Schools Council Industry Project which is discussed below.

But if we look at the actual operation of the policy to strengthen the industrial orientation of schools, the picture is considerably more complex than Kogan's analysis would imply. The two state departments most conspicuously involved in this activity – the MSC and the Department of Industry – combine a top-down policy of selective funding and ultimate control of content with the exploitation of locally-generated curricula and pedagogical approaches. Quite clearly, since the start of the Great Debate there has been a considerable extension of the role of the state in curriculum regulation at all levels of education.

It is openly acknowledged by the Departments of Industry and of Education that the Industry–Education Unit of the DOI was set up in 1978 to facilitate the influence of industry on the education system and to provide direct funding of school–industry initiatives in a way in which the DES was constitutionally unable to do. The primacy of the DES within education has, of course, been further substantially diminished by the large-scale involvement of the MSC in education and training – most recently in the setting up of the TVEI. Part of the response of the DES can be seen in the increasingly directive stance of HMI with regard to vocationally-relevant curricula both within schools and initial teacher training. A recently published HMI Discussion Paper entitled *Teacher training and preparation for working life* contains the recommendation that

> No student preparing for secondary school teaching should complete a course of initial training without a clear idea of how to help pupils prepare for their adult working life. This idea should include some specific understanding of the needs of industry; the personal as well as academic qualities needed for the school leaver; some knowledge of careers education, and the channels of information open to young people in their choice of career or, increasingly, their search for alternatives to immediate employment (DES/HMI, 1982).

The existence of two state departments in this field as well as the MSC, each with a distinct budget, constitutional status, ideological stance and mode of operation underlines the necessity for a disaggregated theory of the state in the empirical investigation of this policy area. It is also necessary to recognize both the corporatist and pluralist tendencies which are apparent in the operations of state departments in interactions with their interest groups. As a recent article by Streeck has argued, neither corporatist nor pluralist theories are adequate in themselves for explaining the complexities of such relationships, and he suggests that they should be seen in combination (Streeck, 1983). The Department of Industry's role, for example, in promoting industry–education liaison demonstrates elements of both corporatism and pluralism. Its main function is to act as financial provider for the approved activities of a wide range of interest groups, such as the Science and Technology Regional Organizations (SATROs), the 'Opening windows on engineering' Project and the Microelectronics Project, which determine their own agendas and forms of local practice but also constitute part of the consultative process operated by the Department.

The MSC, on the other hand, can be seen as a more thoroughgoing corporatist structure with a composition at national, regional and, in the case of TVEI, local levels, which includes unions, employers, representatives from education and departmental staff. Perhaps the most significant aspect of this in the case of the TVEI is that it uses financial provision to allow the formal involvement of non-educational bodies in the determination of LEA policy. As Streeck has argued, the price of incorporation in a corporatist structure is the requirement for self-regulation in the implementation of policy outcomes, and the control of dissent among rank and file members. The trade-off of advantage to the participating group is very finely balanced. The ambivalence of the TUC and its member unions towards the introduction of the YTS scheme is a clear example of the tension which can arise between the leadership and rank and file in a corporatist context.

The Schools Council Industry Project (SCIP) which has been one of the principal recent initiatives in school–industry collaboration exemplifies corporatism at both national and local levels. The Project took as its starting point the view that there was little to be gained from the provision of centrally-prepared teaching materials. 'The Council's experience has led it towards the view that locally-based curriculum development was markedly more effective than what is known in the jargon as "centre-periphery" models . . .' (SCIP, 1979). The Project chose rather to adopt a localized mode of operation in which SCIP co-ordinators in five contrasting LEAs were 'to work with the teachers in the process of forging links with the local employment environment in order to develop the curriculum' (Jamieson and Lightfoot, 1982). Local groups of teachers, employers and trade unionists were asked to draw up proposals for introducing 'industrial awareness' into the curriculum, with a strong emphasis being placed on the use of 'adults other than teachers' in educational roles, non-vocational work experience for pupils, as well as problem-solving techniques, group work, simulation and role playing.

The corporatism which characterized the initiation of the Project by the TUC and CBI therefore came to be superseded by a form of 'local' corporatism. Although the central organizations of both the TUC and CBI had envisaged the Project in terms of a top-down, centralized provision of materials, the Project team decided to opt for a bottom-up model – a devolved pattern of development which relied almost wholly on local collaboration. In this it can be contrasted with the mode of operation adopted by the MSC and DOI in which, as was argued above, locally-generated curricula are used within a top-down model ensuring ultimate control.

This reliance on local collaboration, and its attendant emphasis on *processes*, means that responsibility for *content* has been left to local decision-making. The implications of this policy for the content of industrial awareness initiatives in schools have been documented by Jamieson and Lightfoot in their account of the first phase of the SCIP Project. They argue that because the imprimatur of the CBI and TUC as joint partners in the project was thought by teachers to ensure balance, teaching material on the subject of industry and society was almost always seen as uncontroversial. They point out that teachers tend not to handle many of the fundamental issues which tend to be controversial (the distribution of rewards in society, the causes of unemployment, ownership and control of industry) although they add that 'There was considerable treatment of what might be called "lower level" controversy (strikes, media coverage, picketing)' (Jamieson and Lightfoot, 1982). Teachers tended to concentrate on the reactions of individuals to economic processes rather than on the causes of those processes and to transmit essentially technical information about industry. In the light of this it is not surprising to find the statement that 'it is difficult to find many examples of employers indicating displeasure at syllabus content on the grounds that it did not show industry in a good light' (Jamieson and Lightfoot, 1982).

The involvement of adults other than teachers in the classroom also increases the likelihood of depoliticization, as there is an imbalance between the involvement of employers and trade unionists in industrial awareness activity in schools. It appears that employers and industrial managers argue for the inclusion of their contributions across a broad range of the curriculum, while trade unionists habitually take a narrower view, restricting themselves to such areas as health and safety at work. Schools mirror these judgements, calling on employers and managers to fulfil a number of functions while viewing trade unionists as having a narrower brief. Although this imbalance has become apparent to those within the project, it is difficult to see how it could be remedied with such an extensively devolved system.

The Schools Council Industry Project is important for a number of reasons. It demonstrates how a bottom-up model of educational innovation can result in the depoliticization of contentious material through its own organizational structure. In addition, its supposedly liberative pedagogy, in the use of adults other than teachers, can be seen as a strengthening of hegemonic control and 'commonsense attitudes', particularly when this is reinforced by a local corporatist structure. This local corporatism is legitimating intervention by industrialists in curriculum planning in ways which until recently were seen as inappropriate by industrialists themselves, and which are still not wholly espoused in formal statements by employers. This is a significant extension of the long-standing role of companies in producing subject-based curriculum materials for use in schools. Employer participation characterizes most of the local committees which have come into being in the industry–education area, but it is particularly significant in the case of SCIP which presents itself as liberative pedagogy offering a non-partisan view of industrial practice. It is partly because of this status that SCIP local projects have been able to provide the blueprint, in pedagogy, subject matter and use of personnel, for a number of TVEI schemes.

We have attempted in this paper to review the ideological substance of educational initiatives taken for the social and political education of 14–16 year olds, particularly under the Conservative government since 1979. We have also considered some of the political structures created to secure changes in the behaviour and attitudes of teachers, which have been characterized by an emphasis on national and local corporatism, the use of adults other than teachers in the educational process, and the mobilization of local resources for the development of relevant curricula. But this appears to have taken place in a way which has squeezed out the trade union contribution and perspective and offered an inherently conservative and non-critical view of industry. We would argue that the content of this industrially-oriented curricula requires fuller discussion in the context of a more rigorous and less biased social and political education.

Note

1.　A possible exception to this is the rejection by a number of parent groups of proposals for a return to grammar schools which some Conservative-led education committees have put forward. See Simon (1984).

References

Boys, C. (1984) 'Are employers making the most of higher education?' *Personnel Management*, August.

BP *et al*. (1983) *Industry in Perspective* (published by a consortium of companies with the support of the DOI).

Cawson, A. and Saunders, P. (1983) 'Corporatism, competitive politics and class struggle', in King, R. (ed.), *Capital and Politics* (Routledge: London).

DES/HMI (1982) *Teacher Training and Preparation for Working Life: an HMI Discussion Paper* (London: HMSO).

Gleeson, D. (1983) 'General introduction', in Gleeson, D. (ed.), *Youth Training and the Search for Work* (London: Routledge).

Hall, S. (1982) 'The battle for Socialist ideas in the 1980s', in *The Socialist Register 1982* (London: Merlin).

Hall, S. (1983) 'The great moving right show', in Hall, S. and Jacques, M. (eds), *The Politics of Thatcherism* (London: Lawrence and Wishart).

House of Lords Select Committee on Science and Technology (1984) *Minutes of Evidence taken 16th February, 1984*. Department of Trade and Industry (London: HMSO).

Jamieson, I. and Lightfoot, M. (1982) *Schools and Industry: Derivations from the Schools Council Industry Project*. Schools Council Working Paper 73 (London: Methuen).

Kogan, M. (1983) 'The case of education', in Young, K. (ed.), *National Interests and Local Government* (London: Heinemann).

Lawton, D. (1980) *The Politics of the School Curriculum* (London: Routledge).

Moore, R. (1983) 'Further education, pedagogy and production', in Gleeson, D. (ed.), *Youth Training and the Search for Work* (London: Routledge).

SCIP (1979) *Interim Report* (London: Schools Council).

Simon, B. (1984) 'Breaking school rules', in *Marxism Today*, September.

Society of Education Officers (1983) *Key Issues for Industry and Education*. Society of Education Officers Occasional Paper, No. 3.

Streeck, W. (1983) 'Between pluralism and corporatism: German business associations and the state'. *Journal of Public Policy*, Vol. 3, No. 3.

Weiner, M. J. (1981) *English Culture and the Decline of the Industrial Spirit 1850– 1980* (Cambridge: Cambridge University Press).

Wexler, P., Whitson, T. and Moskowitz, E. J. (1981) 'Deschooling by default: The changing social functions of public schooling'. *Interchange*, Vol. 12, Nos 2–3.

Chapter 8

Satisfying the Needs of Industry: Vocationalism, Corporate Culture and Education

P. Watkins

During the last twelve months (1987–88) there have been renewed calls to maximize the potential for the development of more efficient links between the corporate industrial and educational sectors of society. Both schools and tertiary institutions have been called on to develop closer links with the business world so that students might develop attitudes and skills appropriate to the needs of business.

In the Federal sphere of politics both the Minister for Industry, Technology and Commerce, Senator Button, and the Minister for Employment, Education and Training, Mr Dawkins, have lent their support to tighten the nexus between education and industry. At the time of taking over his new super ministry, Mr Dawkins is reported as suggesting that in future more children will be trained for jobs rather than for higher studies (*Herald*, 24/7/87).

Likewise with the tertiary sector, in the recently published *Higher Education: a Policy Discussion Paper* (1987), Mr Dawkins proposed closer interaction between tertiary institutions and industry. In the instrumental, 'human capital' rhetoric of the paper, tertiary education is conceived in terms of an economic investment to rectify the worsening world economic position in which Australia finds itself. A well educated workforce is seen as the solution to the difficulties 'in a world in which the times have turned

Source: Watkins, P. (1988) 'Satisfying the needs of industry: vocationalism, corporate culture and education', *Unicorn*, Vol. 14, No. 2, pp. 69–76, Australian College of Education, Turkin.

sharply against us' (Dawkins, 1987, p. 2). Moreover 'our narrow export base and the volatility of world resource prices has meant that on a number of occasions the economy has had to shoulder a substantial adjustment burden' (Dawkins, 1987, p. 8). To decrease our reliance on such a narrow export base it is considered imperative to expand the manufacturing and service sectors, which, it is suggested, will require 'a more highly skilled and better educated workforce'. Consequently, 'as the prime source of higher-level skills for the labour market, the higher education system has a critical role to play in restructuring the Australian economy' (Dawkins, 1987, p. 8). In this fashion, education is presented in an instrumental and technicist way as a means of improving Australia's economic position and regaining her rightful place in the world.

A similar position was adopted by the now former Minister for Education in Victoria, Mr Cathie. He has suggested the setting up of a new tripartite body representing unions, industry and educational bodies to develop closer cooperation between the bodies. Mr Cathie is reported as stating that educationalists must give greater emphasis to economic priorities and accept a role in industry restructuring (*Herald*, 23/7/87). Underlying this approach is the instrumental belief that industry will become more efficient if students entering particular companies have the required attitudes and skills. But such sentiments are not new. As Blackmore has clearly shown in her discussion of vocational education in Victoria between 1935 and 1960, 'twentieth-century educational rhetoric in Australia assumed the human capital argument that schools could and should produce skilled employees capable of meeting the demands of an increasingly complex and technologically advanced workplace' (Blackmore, 1987, p. 31).

This paper firstly critically looks at the vocational orientation of education in light of the changing skill requirements for industry. Secondly the paper examines the attempts of industry to resolve the contradictions arising between the employment of skilled workers and the technological changes in the workplace which give rise to problems of alienation through the fostering of corporate cultures. Lastly the paper sums up by discussing the implications for education.

■ Vocationalism, efficiency and skill

Comparing the responses to youth unemployment in the 1930s and 1980s, Holbrook and Bessant (1987) have recently highlighted the startling similarities which existed between the two periods. In particular, during both times of economic difficulty there emerged calls for vocational forms of education to slot young people more easily into the labour market and 'for the efficient conduct of industry and agriculture' (Holbrook and Bessant, 1987, p. 45).

Indeed, vocational education reflects a concern for social efficiency which while perhaps more overt in the 1930s still manifests itself in reports calling for efficiency and effectiveness. Embedded within the advocacy of vocational education is the concern that resources are being underutilized. As Holbrook and Bessant suggest:

> In the thirties as in the eighties it evoked demands for more efficient use of human resources. In the thirties national efficiency was the catchcry. The need to be more competitive on international markets extended to the education system where it was reflected in the much quoted phrase of the time, 'education for efficiency'. The phrase is no longer in fashion but the extention remains (Holbrook and Bessant, 1987, p. 43).

The call for vocational education meeting the needs of industry implies that the more efficient use of individuals within society will lead to a more efficient nation. But to decide how the individual would most efficiently fit into the spectrum of vocations available a system of testing was needed. A need which seems to have its parallels in the present period with calls for national testing in Australia and the implementation of national testing in Great Britain.

Earlier this century, intelligence testing provided the means for supposedly revealing the segment in the labour force in which the individual could most efficiently operate. Through these tests individuals could be 'objectively' differentiated from each other. These tests were developed by Binet in France and were later brought to the English speaking world by such people as Terman at Stanford. Binet stated quite clearly that the aims of the intelligence tests were to not only distinguish an individual from others but also to deduce particular habits and faculties (Rose, 1979, p. 8). Such principles were easily applied in the recruitment of young people in the workplace. Issues relating to the suitability of young people to a particular occupation, their fitness with regard to specific work situations and their suitability for training came under the umbrella of psychological testing. Myers, for example, argued that:

> The psychological factors involved in purely muscular fatigue are now fast becoming negligible, compared with the effects of mental and nervous fatigue, monotony, want of interest, suspicion, hostility, etc. The psycho-logical factor must therefore be the main consideration of industry and commerce in the future (Myers, 1920, pp. v–vi).

In this scenario, schooling can be viewed as a vehicle for social control operating to fit students most efficiently into the industrial and corporate sector while maintaining order through discovering a student's capacity and then moulding him/her, to fit in harmoniously with the needs of a satisfied labour market.

Violas sums up the movement toward vocational education in the first half of this century by pointing out that:

> The vocational guidance movement reflected the general direction of liberal social philosophy in moving away from coercion to more subtle and effective kinds of social control. Rather than impose industry's will by command or exhortation, the new techniques relied upon the internalization of goals and ideals which had been previously selected by experts. At times, individuals were even allowed to choose their own goals – if these were acceptable to the professionals (Violas, 1978, p. 216).

Thus if we are to take heed of the assertions of employers and politicians that vocational education is required to satisfy the needs of society, we must ask whose needs are being satisfied. Firstly the need for greater profit can be achieved by the transfer of much of the cost of on-the-job training to the education system. Secondly the basic questions on the way work is organized and the choices involved are unanswered as students are socialized and trained for a workplace which is seen as unproblematic (Watkins, 1987). Thirdly the position the student attains within the labour market with its inequalities of status and reward is seen as a reflection on the individual abilities of the student.

The benefits of vocational education should be considered in ideological terms because in terms of students achieving the goal of acquiring jobs for which they have been trained, the evidence suggests that vocational education is a failure. For as Kantor and Tyack have written in a recent important book, *Work, Youth, and Schooling: Historical Perspectives on Vocationalism in American Education* (1982)

> During the last fifty years, major evaluations of vocational programs have repeatedly questioned the benefits of vocational training. Although some studies have found that vocational graduates have lower unemployment and receive higher wages than other comparable students, the majority of studies have concluded that there is little economic advantage to vocational training as opposed to non-vocational, at the high school level (Kantos and Tyack, 1982, p. 2).

Meyer and Wise's research (1982) supports the general argument put forward by Kantor and Tyack. They found that there was 'no measure of high school vocational or industrial training that was significantly related to employment or wage rates after graduation' (Meyer and Wise, 1982,

p. 307). While the rhetoric and ideology of efficiency has influenced educators to link vocational programmes to the ability to move easily into the workforce and to be 'trained for job' more proficiently, Meyer and Wise found that this was not the case. Instead their research suggested that vocational training in high schools would seem to bear no relationship to the jobs students eventually obtain and the wage rates which they are paid.

This confusion between ideology and what occurs in the workplace can be observed in the call to train young people for the new high technology industries. While many young people may see vocational training leading to work in high technology as a solution to their future job problems, the reality is that high technology industry requires only a small percentage of high technology occupations.

Rumberger (1986) illustrates that in the USA high technology occupations represent only about 4 per cent of the overall labour market. While, naturally, high technology industries have the dominant share of high technology occupations, even in these industries only 15 per cent are of the high technology variety (Rumberger, 1986, p. 11). The majority of the jobs are relatively low paid, assembly-line occupations. Studies of Silicon Valley (Howard, 1981; Rogers and Larsen, 1984) support the evidence that many of the jobs in high technology industries are repetitive, routine assembly-line jobs which highlight a distinct segmentation in the high technology labour market (Watkins, 1986). While the primary sector contains highly paid researchers, technicians and managerial staff, the secondary sector, comprising the bulk of the workers, is made up of women and minorities. For these employees, work in high technology industries means low wage, dead-end jobs, unskilled tedious work, and exposure to some of the most dangerous occupational health hazards in all of US industry (Howard, 1981, p. 22).

Rumberger in the USA and Sweet (1987) in Australia have challenged the proposition that directing young people into high technology vocational training will prove the salvation of youth unemployment and the elimination of mundane, repetitive occupations. Such a proposition seems oblivious to numerous studies which indicate that the general trend in the workplace is to deskill occupations. While students are leaving the education system better educated and more highly qualified than ever before in the workplace, 'the pattern of change over a twenty year period does not support a view that the long term trend in jobs held by teenagers has been an increasing demand for skills' (Sweet, 1987, p. 20). This situation illustrates the paradox occurring within society where young people seek higher and higher credentials in order to enter the labour market while industry strives for greater financial efficiency by rationalizing and automating the workplace to minimize the human factor. In particular, in Australia, Ford (1983) has noted that the use of scientific management as developed by Taylor with its stress on efficiency through the rationalization of work and the separation of conception from execution is 'readily apparent in the way employment has developed in the computer related occupations in the service sector. The production line techniques of the industrial world are being moved into offices' (Ford, 1983, p. 171).

The underutilization of skills in a high technology industry has been recently exemplified by the study of the US Bell companies by Tsang (1984). The empirical results of Tsang's research supported the proposition that underutilization of educational skills does occur and that a firm which does not fully utilize the educational skills of its workers suffers a loss in output (Tsang, 1984, p. 15). But, in addition, the underutilization of skills is likely to cause a high degree of worker dissatisfaction with the structure of work leading to a likely consequence of psychological strain and a sense of alienation.

Ford has suggested that the Anglo–American preoccupation with scientific management techniques which rationalize, degrade and deskill the labour process might be rectified by emulating German and particularly Japanese approaches to management (Ford, 1982, p. 452). These include such techniques as quality circles and generally humanizing the workplace. However, recent studies of Japanese industry have emphasized the part scientific management still plays in the organization of work (Schonberger, 1982; Greenwood and Ross, 1982; Dohse, et al., 1985). The fact that Japanese factories can be as dehumanizing and alienating as any in Australia has been illustrated by Kamata's *Japan in the Passing Lane* (1983). Similarly Schonberger (1982, p. 198) after studying quality circles in Japan concluded:

> I have been astounded by statements I have heard from some American 'authorities' to the effect that the Japanese reject Taylorism, supposedly in favour of a more humanistic approach. Frederick W. Taylor, an American, is the father of IE/Work study (industrial engineering) *circa* 1900, but the Japanese out-Taylor us all – including putting Taylor to good use in QC circles or small group improvement activities.

Indeed, the highly structured nature of Japanese organizations was found to produce results which were consistent with 'bureaucratic alienation' (Lincoln and Kalleberg, 1985, p. 757). Consequently, in light of such studies, it would seem wise to treat the Japanese model with a degree of caution.

The contradictory effects of introducing sophisticated technology basically designed to increase managerial control but which in reality underutilizes the abilities and skills of employees producing alienation and discontent, as illustrated by the Bell research, are at the basis of the attempts to employ the concept of culture in the workplace. Companies are now seeking to foster a corporate culture in an effort to extract greater commitment and productivity from their workers.

However, it should be stressed that the main thrust is from industrial psychologists representing management interests, who seek through on-the-job education to change the subjective state of the individual worker. Essentially, the basis of this exercise is not the doing-away of the objective reality through which work is alienated. Instead the eradication of the workers' awareness of this alienated reality is the focus of the attention of these human relations and motivation experts (see Watkins, 1986).

■ Organizational culture: educating employees on the integration of work and corporate values

The recognition that worker alienation is a significant factor which is likely to lead to decreased productivity and consequently reduced profits has led to the increased interest in the fostering of a work culture where the beliefs and goals engendered within an organization can be internalized by the employees. This has been exemplified by the common concern for the culture of work in a number of popular books by Ouchi (1981), Pascale and Athos (1982), Deal and Kennedy (1982) and Peters and Waterman (1982), while in academic and professional journals there has been a flood of papers examining work and organizational culture. Some recent examples of these would be those by Malinconico (1984), Schein (1984) and Wilkins (1984). With regard to education, Bates (1986) has critically discussed the implications of the cultural approach in educational administration.

The current concern with organizational culture is not to gain an understanding of the culture which exists in the workplace but to use it as a managerial tool so that management values and criteria of acceptable behaviour in the workplace are communicated and reinforced (Malinconico, 1984). Deal and Kennedy (1982) argue that acceptance of such values and their transformation into a taken-for-granted form takes both time and money. But in the final analysis they claim that the adoption of the right approach will pay off for the firm as:

> companies that have cultivated their individual identities by shaping values, making heroes, spelling out rites and rituals and acknowledging the cultural network have an edge. These corporations have values and beliefs to pass along – not just products. They have stories to tell – not just profits to make. They have heroes whom managers can emulate – not just faceless bureaucrats. In short, they are human institutions that provide practical meaning for people, both on and off the job (Deal and Kennedy, 1982, p. 15).

It should be realized though that the values, beliefs, stories and heroes have been fostered by management and represent a top-down perspective of work. Wilkins (1984) indicates that the management of a number of the leading companies considered as the foremost examples in developing organizational culture have presented an overarching theme for their company. This theme or vague idea is then frequently reinforced by stories of the 'great men' who have led the organization. Peters and Waterman (1982) suggest that the ability to direct attention and focus through such stories is the most powerful and subtle control which top management can assert over their workers. In such a situation where employees have internalized the values of the company, the requirement for overt surveillance is drastically reduced. For 'value leads to a behaviour, and ... the value gradually is transformed into underlying assumption about how things really are. As the assumption is increasingly taken for granted, it drops out of awareness' (Schein, 1984, p. 4).

Management not only endeavours to foster a taken-for-granted cultural ethos, but also overtly rewards those workers who accede to the values espoused by the company. Wilkins (1984) illustrates this point through a study of Hewlett-Packard:

> At HP they conduct a 'personnel audit' each year as they review a company division to determine whether the division general manager and staff have consistently followed the HP way. They sample 20 or 30 employees from the division and conduct in-depth interviews to make their determination. The results of these interviews are put in the division general manager's file and figure heavily in his performance (Wilkins, 1984, p. 58).

Through this evaluation process, employees who have not absorbed the values of the company through myths and stories are quickly set straight about the relationship between top management values and their work practices. If there is a gap between company values and the way they work, then they leave the company.

The concern to find and cultivate an appropriate technique of using stories or myths to control workers neglects the interpretive and critical dimensions of culture (Habermas, 1972). Habermas advocates the use of the critical dimension to closely question the taken-for-granted assumptions underlying the making of decisions. A critical perspective is also useful in the unmasking of the veil which frequently hides the inequalities of power and rewards present in the workplace. A critical examination of work, on this basis Habermas claims, would lead to the emancipation of all human beings which would result in the betterment of human society.

The present interest in work and culture is clearly related to a technical dimension and not concerned with the emancipation of those working in the organization. Rather, the emphasis is on how culture can be fostered to meet the needs of the company. The focus has been on the ways top management can use culture to manipulate and control workers in the company. The essence of this approach has been outlined by Peters (1978) who suggests to top management in his paper that the use of symbols and cultural patterns might be of greater value than conventional managerial approaches which seem to be relatively unsuccessful. In this context Peters suggests that:

> managing the daily stream of activities might be said to consist of the manipulation of symbols, the creation of patterns of activity, and the staging of occasions for interaction (Peters, 1978, p. 9).

For Peters, culture, and its various facets, symbols, myths and stories, are powerful tools which can be used to facilitate management's ability to control and direct the focus of people working in the organization. The senior executive can 'grasp control of the signalling system' and by 'adroitly managing agenda, he can nudge the day-to-day decision-making system, thus simultaneously imparting new preferences and teaching new initiatives' (Peters, 1978, p. 22). The use of culture in this fashion merely reinforces and even perhaps enhances the unequal power structure of work while clearly ignoring any critical, emancipatory potential which organization culture might have. The current literature on culture and work, in general seems to suffer from 'managementcentric bases' (Gregory, 1983) with the emphasis on manipulation and control. In particular, the major preoccupation of much of the research and the theoretical literature in the administration field is 'how to mold and shape internal culture in particular ways and how to change culture, consistent with managerial purposes' (Smircich, 1983, p. 346).

A critical approach in the study of culture in organizations is provided by the recent work of Michael Rosen (1985). Rosen has explored the symbols, style, rituals and language during a business breakfast in an advertising agency. He examines the way in which culture is able to illustrate the unequal power and control which can exist in organizations. The basic concern of his research is to examine 'culture as a template with social ramifications for domination' (Rosen, 1985, p. 259). In pursuing this theme, Rosen attempts to uncover the implicit power relations which underly the organizational process of work in an advertising agency. To do this he treats the breakfast as a social drama. Here 'symbolic forms are manipulated in social drama by asymmetrical groups, in which the subsequent evocation of meaning, though contested, probably aids in the reproduction of the basic dominance structures of the bureaucratic form, and hence of capital control' (Rosen, 1985, p. 259). Rosen's research findings indicate that although management attempts to use culture in its interests, it is not without a struggle. In particular, his data revealed that the creative department of the advertising agency clearly resisted the attempts to impose alien values on their work practices. Such findings reinforce Gidden's (1982) theoretical proposition of the dialectic of control, for the forms which work take are never subject to a simple functionalist explanation, where people are slotted into appropriate jobs, but are the result of ongoing human interaction.

■ Summation – implications for education

Much of the literature on vocational education and the changing patterns of the structure of work would seem to indicate that training of young people by schools in specific skills is of limited value to the students. As Blackmore in her study of vocational education in the form of commercial education for girls shows, 'this form of schooling largely constrained the work options and life chances of girls by encouraging them "to make curriculum choices" within the limited number of occupational positions and societal roles regarded as suitable for women' (Blackmore, 1987, p. 46). Not only is gender differentiation exacerbated but also class differences in society seem to be emphasized by vocational education. This form of education, it has been claimed, has been developed in the name of efficiency to fit young people into 'the unjust nature of corporate–industrial society . . . and to teach working-class youth their proper place', within the structure of society (Kantor and Tyack, 1982, p. 3).

In addition, vocational education does not broach the problematic nature of the workplace. There is an inherent deterministic flavour that work can only take on one particular form and that changes are inevitable and beyond human involvement. Education about work in schools should emphasize rather, that the patterns of work in society can be comprehended as capable of taking a number of different forms. These forms are not the outcome of some predetermined course but are a reflection of the predelictions, whims, intelligence and creative abilities of human beings. When placed within its historical and social context, the structure of work can frequently be seen to merely represent a particular ideological position of certain groups within society.

If education about work adopts a critical stance which develops a problematic view about the structuring of the workplace and terms like efficiency and effectiveness, then students will come to realize that they themselves have the ability to shape how work is structured. A start in this direction has been made by the important Curriculum and the World of Work Program in which a number of the monographs set out to inform students and teachers about work and how work and technology have been socially shaped. (Details of the programme can be obtained from J. Cummings, CDC, Canberra.) Education should not merely comply with the needs of industry but should take on an educative stance through which students come to question the taken for granted needs which they are asked to satisfy.

References

Blackmore, J. (1987) 'Schooling for work: gender differentiation in commercial education in Victoria 1935–1960'. *History of Education Review*, Vol. 16, No. 1, pp. 31–50.

Dawkins, J. S. (1987) *Higher Education: A Policy Discussion Paper* (Canberra).

Deal, T. E. and Kennedy, A. (1982) *Corporate Cultures: The Rites and Rituals of Corporate Life* (Reading, Mass.: Addison-Wesley).

Dohse, K., Jurgens, U. and Malsch, T. (1985) 'From "Fordism" to "Toyotism"? The social organization of the labor process in the Japanese automobile industry'. *Politics and Society*, Vol. 14, No. 2, pp. 115–146.

Ford, G. W. (1982) 'Human resource development in Australia and the balance of skills'. *The Journal of Industrial Relations*, September, 443–453.

Ford, G. W. (1983) 'Technology, women and employment: the need for new concepts and criteria for policy formation', in R. Chapman (ed.), *The Future: Fantasy, Fatalism or Fact?* Public Policy Monograph (University of Tasmania).

Giddens, A. (1982) *Profiles and Critiques in Social Theory* (Macmillan: London).

Greenwood, R. G. and Ross, R. H. (1982) 'Early American influence on Japanese management philosophy: the scientific management movement in Japan', in Lee, S. M. and Schwediman, G. (eds), *Management by Japanese systems* (New York: Praeger).

Gregory, K. L. (1983) 'Native-view paradigms: multiple cultures and culture conflicts in organizations'. *Administrative Science Quarterly*, Vol. 28, pp. 359–376.

Habermas, J. (1972) *Knowledge and Human Interest* (Boston: Beacon Press).

Holbrook, A. and Bessant, B. (1987) 'Responses to youth unemployment in the 1930s and 1980s'. *Unicorn*, Vol. 13, No. 1, pp. 40–50.

Howard, R. (1981) 'Second class in Silicon Valley'. *Working Papers*, Vol. 8, pp. 21–31.

Kamata, S. (1983) *Japan in the Passing Lane* (Sydney: George Allen & Unwin).

Kantor, H. and Tyack, D. (eds) (1982) *Work, Youth and Schooling: Historical Perspectives on Vocationalism in American Education* (Stanford University Press).

Lincoln, J. R. and Kalleberg, A. L. (1985) 'Work organization and employment commitment: a study of plants and employees in the U.S. and Japan'. *American Sociological Review*, Vol. 50, pp. 738–760.

Malinconico, S. M. (1984) 'Managing organizational culture'. *Library Journal*, Vol. 109, No. 7, pp. 791–793.

Meyer, R. H. and Wise, D. A. (1982) 'High school preparation and early labor force experience', in Freeman, R. B. and Wise, D. A. (eds), *The Youth Labor Market Problem* (University of Chicago Press).

Myers, C. S. (1920) *Mind and Work* (London University Press).

Ouchi, W. (1981) *Theory Z* (Reading, Mass.: Addison-Wesley).

Pascale, R. and Athos, A. (1982) *The Art of Japanese Management* (Penguin: Harmondsworth).

Peters, T. J. (1978) 'Symbols, patterns and settings: an optimistic case for getting things done'. *Organisational Dynamics*, Vol. 7, Autumn, pp. 3–23.

Peters, T. J. and Waterman, R. H. (1982) *In Search of Excellence* (New York: Harper and Row).

Rogers, E. M. and Larsen, J. K. (1984) *Silicon Valley Fever: Growth of High Technology Culture* (New York: Basic Books).

Rose, N. (1979) 'The psychological complex: mental measurement and social administration'. *Ideology and Consensus*, Spring, pp. 5–68.

Rosen, M. (1985) 'The reproduction of hegemony: an analysis of bureaucratic control'. *Research in Political Economy*, Vol. 8, pp. 257–289.

Rumberger, R. W. (1986) *The Changing Industrial Structure of the U.S. Economy: Its Impact on Employment, Earnings and the Educational Requirements of Jobs* (Project Report no. 86 – SEP 1–8). Stanford Education Policy Institute, School of Education (Stanford University).

Schein, E. H. (1984) 'Coming to an awareness of organizational culture'. *Sloan Management Review*, Vol. 25, No. 2, pp. 3–16.

Schonberger, R. J. (1982) *Japanese Manufacturing Techniques: Nine Hidden Lessons in Simplicity* (New York: The Free Press).

Smircich, L. (1983) 'Concepts of culture and organizational analysis'. *Administrative Science Quarterly*, Vol. 28, pp. 335–339.

Sweet, R. (1987) *The Youth Labour Market: A Twenty Year Perspective* (Canberra: CDC).

Tsang, M. C. (1984) *The Impact of Overeducation on Productivity: A Case Study of Skill Underutilization of the U.S. Bell Companies* (Program Report no. 84 – B10). Institute for Research on Educational Finance and Governance, School of Education (Stanford University).

Violas, P. C. (1978) *The Training of the Urban Working Class* (Chicago: Rand McNally).

Watkins, P. E. (1986) *High Tech, Low Tech and Education* (Geelong: Deakin University Press).

Watkins, P. E. (1987) *An Analysis of the History of Work* (CDC, Canberra: CDC).

Wilkins, A. L. (1984) 'The creation of company cultures'. *Human Resource Management*, Vol. 23, No. 1, pp. 41–60.

Chapter 9

Education, Vocationalism and Economic Recovery: The Case against Witchcraft[1]

I. Stronach

Watch out Japan. Here comes Tracy Logan. Tracy Logan is a typical British sixteen year old, leaving school this year. But to Japan, and our other international competitors, she's a big threat .... That's because this year she'll be starting 2 years' paid skill training on the new YTS.... Tracy will be spending the next two years learning how to take trade away from them for a change.

(MSC advertisement for the new 2-year YTS, *Guardian*, 28.1.86)

... the initiand begins as a person on whom no-one depends, and through the course of initiation becames one on whom the welfare of the entire cosmos hinges. Every time a woman is initiated, the world is saved from chaos, for the fundamental power of creativity is renewed in her being.
('Emerging from the chrysalis. Studies in rituals of women's initiation' (B. Lincoln, 1987, p. 107)

On the one hand Tracy Logan: on the other the Navajo Indian. In each case, cosmos out of chaos, and a personal transformation that carries within it the promise of a general recovery. One purpose of this chapter will be to reduce the distance between these two figures in transition, and to obscure the polarities of modern/archaic and rational/ritual that appear to divide them. For which is the more mythic character? In the context of

Source: Stronach, I. (1989) 'Education, vocationalism and economic recovery: the case against witchcraft', *British Journal of Education and Work*, Vol. 2, No. 1, pp. 5–31. Copyright © Trentham Books Ltd.

vocationalist ideologies in the UK in the 1970s and 1980s, we cannot be sure.

If we are to bring these two figures together, then we must first set other things apart. Above all we must question the means/ends, cause/ effect assumptions that relate the 'modern' education and training of the individual to broad moral and economic outcomes. It will be argued that behind these 'rational' connections lies a sleight of hand. To take the vivid example of Tracy, she is invested with a magical agency concerning an economic problem. The means/ends rationale is clearly unbelievable in itself – and so there is a 'reminder' of the meaning of that message to be explained if it is to be plausible at all. The 'remainder' contains an elision, in that the parts that stand for the whole (Tracy, skills, certificate, training) are taken to cause the whole (economic recovery, overtaking foreign competition). 'Standing for' becomes confused with 'causing', and so synecdoche masquerades as explanation. I will argue that such a rhetorical device also characterizes government policy statements, as well as 'economic' analyses by academic commentators. This raises a second problem: how can such a rhetorical trick possibly persuade the reader that schoolchildren are the cause of economic decline? After all, attempts to blame a military defeat on indiscipline in the Brownies would be discounted. The explanation of vocationalism offered here will rest on the nature of ritual rather than rationality, and on the way that certain rituals of induction 'stand for' reaffirmed adult values, and address an adult 'congregation' (Rappaport, 1968, p. 1) rather more than the youthful participants:

> The individuals are, to this extent, objects used in the ritual, rather than its central focus through which the ritual is to be explained. Initiation rituals cannot be understood simply as a means of changing the status of individuals (La Fontaine, 1985, p. 104).

In short, I will argue that vocationalism can be interpreted as a kind of contemporary magic, a form of reassurance as well as a 'rational' response to economic problems.

Of course, that sketch of an interpretation so far relates to a 'mere' advertisement, but the following analysis of the 1986 White Paper on Education and Training (Cmnd. 9823) will try to show that the same kind of rhetorical relation of agent-and-effect (Burke, 1962) is powerfully present in that document, and that it is possible to offer an interpretation in terms of ritual that is not mere anachronism. A first purpose of this paper, therefore, will be to examine the rationale of official discourses in the area of vocationalist transition – from school to work or training or adulthood. I hope to show that these discourses have their own limitations, gaps, or irrationalities (in their own terms), and that the extent to which these are unacknowledged or denied opens up new ground for analysis.

The first of these discussions is expressed in the 1986 White Paper 'Working Together – Education and Training', and it is to be a consideration of its rationale that we turn.

■ The White Paper

The White Paper is a remarkably succinct justification for prevocational and vocational education. Essentially, it offers a view of vocational education nested within a psychological theory, which in turn is contained within an economic argument.

The economic argument is this. Britain has serious economic problems because of a lack of competitiveness. The reasons do not involve investment or resources – 'The same machines and equipment are available to all'. (1.3) Therefore the problem is one of people. People lack motivation and training. In turn, that problem breaks down into the three issues of 'climate', motivation and skills: 'There must be a climate in which people can be motivated, and in which their potential can be harnessed.' (1.4) Climate means incentives '... in which learning is rewarded and is seen to lead to progress for individuals and companies.' (1.4) Thus the economic problem boils down to national deficiencies in personal attitudes and skills: 'We live in a world of determined, educated, trained and strongly motivated competitors. The competition they offer has taken more and more of our markets.' (1.1) The economic remedy is to promote higher 'standards of performance, of reliability and quality. It is these which will make the critical difference to the design of British products and services, their delivery, after-sales services, customer relations and marketing and, not least, management.' (5.37)

The heart of the solution is psychological: 'Motivation is all important so that attitudes change and people acquire the design to learn, the habit of learning, and the skills that learning brings.' (1.4) Motivation can be built on a climate of incentive, and will involve a 'change of attitude towards learning.' (2.9)

Given that psychological climate, the vocational outcomes become possible. These are 'the three essential elements of preparation for competence in any field of employment: skills; knowledge and understanding; and practical application.' (2.11) The outcomes depend on effective learning which is relevant to employer needs. Such learning emphasizes active and practical methods, and stretches each individual. It broadens the curriculum while preparing young people for working life – as TVEI does: 'the provision of technical and vocational education in a way which will widen and enrich the curriculum, and prepare young people for adult and working life.' (3.1) In this prescription, several definitions of education are proposed. All qualifications 'will need to be practical and relevant to employment' (2.10) within an education designed to enable 'people to progress to the limit of their creativity and potential.' (2.12) Such an education will aim 'to give to every pupil a capability which makes them versatile and sufficiently adaptable for the technological challenges of employment.' (2.2) (The Report is jointly authored by the DoE and the DES and at times reads as if they took turns to write each sentence.)

It is worth examining some of the rhetorical features of this nested vocational–motivational–economic rationale and the extent to which they recur in the general education–economy debates.

☐   **Juvenalize and personalize the problem**

The White Paper's case rests on an economic assumption that recovery depends on improved motivation and skills among – principally – the young. This kind of 'regeneration' is axiomatic across the debate, whether in the media or in more academic analyses. '. . . most children could do better – and . . . the country urgently requires them to do better because as a nation we survive on our brains and our skills' (Maureen O'Connor in the *Guardian*, 7.10.86); 'Mr Lawson said that one of the most long-standing problems in Britain was the failure to prepare school leavers adequately for work' (*Guardian*, 20.3.85). Prais argues that there is an intermediate 'skill gap', and that education is failing the less able in comparison to Maths achievement levels in Germany and Japan (Prais, 1981, 1985, 1987). Cantor argues for more basic skills in core subjects (Cantor, 1985). The 'most serious issue', according to Sanderson, is the 'failure in the twentieth century to develop a technical education for teenagers of school age' (Sanderson, 1988, p. 38), while Critchfield concludes 'What's wrong? Everybody gives an outsider the same reply: education' (Critchfield, 1988, p. 10).

Thus many fingers point accusingly at the qualities and experiences of the young in order to explain economic failure. Governments – both Labour and Tory – have been responsive to this definition of the problem. Currently the government is spending £1.14 billion in TVEI initiatives, while City Technology Colleges and the Education Reform Act promise yet more change directed towards the promotion of these ends.

In addition, both the problem and the solution are personalized by the White Paper in terms of the individual attributes that young people lack. Indeed, personification extends to rival countries as well – 'determined', 'educated', 'trained', 'strongly motivated' (1.1). Presented in these terms, the person is invested with a tremendous agency in terms of the nation. She is responsible, and all the mediations of natural resources, investment policies, class, gender, racism, organizational structures, and historical legacy, fall away. There is a similar tendency towards personification in academic debates on the connections between the economy and education – except it is the qualities and attitudes of the 'worker' that are excoriated (Nichols, 1986; Senker, 1986):

> Again and again instances are to be found where important facets of social structure are referred to, but not situated in their context, where certain leads are followed up with alacrity and others not, a superficial and in some respects misleading understanding being fostered as a consequence of this – misleading because it fails to make plain where 'attitudes' *come from*. (Nichols, 1986, p. 115) (his stress)

The recourse to 'attitudes' (or other individual characteristics) in both the blaming of the worker and of the young is part of the reductive synecdoche with which this article began – the 'Tracy' effect.

□   Assert the certainty of the problem and its solution

The White Paper maintains that a successful economy is based on high productivity, which is the result of the good quality and right mix of education and training for the young. Prais refers to the many decades of this problem, while Russell comments: '... we have always known what to do; therefore, there must be very deep reasons why the problems persist' (Peston, 1985, p. 76). And indeed Wellens' prescription (Wellens, 1963) retains a contemporary feel: a 'bridging occupational training of a general kind between school and work, the abolition of apprenticeship and its replacement with a competence-based system, emphasis on learning rather than teaching situations, an end to gender discrimination, greater mobility across the training tracks, and the need for industry to value and invest in training for workers and management. As the *Economist* wearily noted of the 1984 NEDO report: 'The recommendations are boringly familiar; firms should invest more in their human capital; governments should have a strategy for training (and provide money to match); education should prepare young people for working life. Even the contradictions are predictable – reports usually combine a paean to the German system of vocational training (where the state plays a major role) with support for the US one (where it doesn't)' (*Economist*, 8.9.84).

□   Privilege the reality of work

As many have noted, the idea of education as preparation for work has become rooted in contemporary debate (Abbs, 1981, 1986, 1987; Bates *et al.*, 1984; Dale, 1985; Dearden, 1984). It is seen to be economically essential – 'the urgency of raising *general* schooling attainments at early schooling ages in Britain cannot be over-emphasized' (Prais, 1987, p. 51). Adequate preparation for work is also often thought to be never quite realized, never sufficiently privileged, and thus failing because of 'liberal' or 'elitist' sabotage. Thus, even in 1989, after massive investments in a whole alphabet soup of initiatives, the education correspondent of the *Observer* can still write as if she were firing the first shots in the Great Debate of 1976: 'Any suggestion that school would be more attractive to more children if their studies were more closely related to the world of work is decried. Vocationalism is a dirty word' (Judith Judd, *Observer*, 28.5.89). In curricular terms, the rise of Work Experience is an icon of this concern. Whether 'real' or 'simulated', it becomes a major strategy, as in contemporary TVEI initiatives, YTS provision, or European Community projects ('School-industry pilots light the way ahead', *Times Educational Supplement*, 8.4.88). Work is projected as a paramount reality – and education becomes an initiation into that 'truth' (Stronach, 1984).

☐   Understate more parsimonious causes, or, find a scapegoat

Within education–economy debates there are, of course, discrepant voices. Quite apart from Marxist and neo-Marxist critique (Bowles and Gintis, 1976; Willis, 1977; Bates *et al.*, 1984; Dale, 1985) and philosophical opposition (Abbs, 1981, 1986, 1987; Dearden, 1984) there is a large body of contradictory empirical data belonging to the same paradigm of enquiry as the conventional economic discourse. Lying around in often less well-publicized corners, there are criticisms of management, investment, company training, technical expertise, union traditions and structures, national culture, and, of course, government policy in general. To understand the extent to which the 'problem' of the economy is reduced to the 'problem' of the education of the young, we need to register something of that neglect of alternative interpretations.

Let's start with management. The Handy Report argues the case against the quality of British management (only 12.5 per cent of managers with degrees), while the 1985 MSC survey pointed to the very low investment in training by British industry – 0.15 per cent of annual turnover invested in training (Handy, 1987; Huhne, 1987; Taylor, 1987). Nichols' review of the field led him to conclude that 'British management may be as deficient in its organisation – in the work of coordination, in planning, and in its functional integration – as it tends to be in some respects on the technical side' (Nichols, 1986, p. 168). Daly *et al.*, comparing a sample of British and German firms, claimed that the key problem was a 'lack of technical expertise and training' and bemoaned British industry's flight from craft training in the 1980s – 'very puzzling to anyone taking a long view of the future of British manufacturing' (Daly *et al.*, 1985, p. 60). Robert Taylor concluded: 'The lack of interest in the training of their own workers [by management] is one of the mysteries of our society' (Taylor, 1987). Benyon quotes a management expert's comments on the likely effects of the 1982 Employment and Training Act – which abolished most of the Training Boards: 'We'll run out of skilled labour about the same time as we run out of oil' (Benyon, 1987, p. 254). In an equally depressing vein, Birley reported recently that a comparative study of the 'new entrepreneurs' in the UK and the US showed the familiar pattern of high educational and technical qualifications among the US sample, and low qualifications in the British sample (Rodgers, 1988).

Blame the management, or blame the workers. In an ailing economy, such scapegoating is inevitable, and probably has as much to do with class antagonisms as with rational explanation. Criticisms of the British worker are not hard to find, and Nichols shows what a long and recurrent litany they represent – the 'go-easy' worker was the focus for prolonged complaints in the *Times* in 1901–2, while Webbs pointed out that 'complaints as to diminished quality or energy at work, and of the tacit conspiracy to discourage individual exertion, occur with curiously exact iteration in every decade of the last hundred years at least' (Nichols, 1986, p. 5). Current criticisms recur around the themes of restrictive trade union practices (Crafts, 1988), 'overpriced' labour, and a lack of incentive for workers to aspire to skilled grades or to technician status (Prais and Wagner, 1988). This chapter will later try to explain that there is nothing curious about these 'iterations' and the reasons for their recurrence point towards their ritualistic nature.

In addition, it may be equally wrong to restrict criticism to the factors of labour – at whatever level of involvement – since it is claimed that manufacturing investment in the UK in 1987 was still 19 per cent below 1979 levels (Keegan, 1987), and since there is considerable controversy over the reality of the Thatcher 'economic miracle', Wynne Godley regarding such claims as a 'gigantic con-trick' (Godley, 1988). Nolan also rejects the 'miracle' claim, finding that increases in productivity, while real enough, reflect increases in work effort and changed working practices after the 'shake-out' of the early 1980s, but that these improvements are short-term and do nothing to change Britain from a low labour cost/low productivity economy into a 'virtuous circle of high productivity and high levels of remuneration' (Nolan, 1989, p. 84) – 'For one of the most striking features of the Thatcher years is the extent of the decline in new investment: in physical capital; research and development; and education and training.' (Nolan, 1989, p. 85).

The above diagnoses are parsimonious in that they attribute industrial decline to factors directly involved in industrial production, and emphasize the role of management or workforce skills as determinant. They stand in contrast, therefore, to theories that locate the causes of poor performance in the school, the home, or the national culture. Nichols argues that these industrially-located explanations have been under-researched and under-reported: 'In retrospect it is quite clear that a good deal was wrong on the management side, and that we did not hear about it

– certainly not in any detail – because those who conducted this research either did not look and see, or having seen did not tell' (Nolan, 1989, pp. 213–14). This kind of research coyness has also been a feature of the evaluation of recent vocational initiatives in the educational sector, and is a long-standing problem in evaluation. A further problem, and an equally old one, has been the difficulty of persuading managers (of whatever sector) to listen to critical research findings, as Whyte found in his human relations research in the US in the 1950s (Whyte, 1987; for a minor TVEI example see Stronach, 1988).

Blame management, blame the workers, or blame everything – the national culture. Peston, among many others, has argued for a much more radical understanding of the education and training aspects of the problem – recognizing the role of public schools, Oxbridge, the examination system, and the educational culture (Peston, 1985; see also Weiner, 1981).

Thus, there are plenty alternative explanations for economic decline available, but none of them have achieved as high a political sponsorship, and apparently fundamental status, as the 'problem' of the qualities of the young. In passing, it is ironic that the government now claims a fundamental economy turn-around, despite the fact that none of its educational training 'solutions' have had time to take economic effect. It might be asked: if that was the correct pathology, how come the cure happened before the treatment?

What *is* the case for regarding school reform as the focus for economic redemption? Raffe argues that the government has hold of the wrong end of the stick in terms of anticipated economic outcomes: 'the relative employment rates of young people leaving different education or training programmes should be seen as constraints upon, rather than indicators of, the programmes' relative success and development' (Raffe, 1988). His later study of broad TVEI outcome indicators was generally negative about the impact of the programme, as was Fitzgibbon's earlier study (Raffe, 1989; Fitzgibbon *et al.*, 1988). Senker's review of the potential relevance of TVEI changes for economic performance was also pessimistic. Like Nichols, he argued that comparisons between the UK and elsewhere suggested deficiencies located in management rather than in the workforce, and that bad habits were learned after leaving school: 'Deficiencies in management education and training seem more significant than any "disease" curable by TVEI' (Senker, 1986, p. 298).

What can we conclude? The vocationalist rationale draws on a very narrow and partial version of the economic 'problem', expressed in terms of the deficient pupil, the school, and of the individual 'worker'. On *a priori* grounds, it seems that the least parsimonious attributions are among the most favoured. The problems defined in the White Paper concern industrial design, service, marketing, and management (5.37), yet the solutions invoke highly mediated and controversial linkages between the education of the young and the economic productivity of the adult population. It is noteworthy that the government offers an exogenous critique of British industry in terms of British schooling, but an endogenous critique of state schooling – in terms of poor teaching, wrong attitudes, inadequate performance, inappropriate subjects, and low expectations. Neither the logics nor the empirics of that case are compelling.

☐ **Cast aside methodological doubt**

The equation at the heart of the discourse is this:

> *good education/training = higher worker productivity = economic success*

Yet the gaps and uncertainties in these linkages are legion. First, the economic science behind these connections is hopelessly fragmented between monetarist, neo-Keynesian, and neo-classical paradigms. Economics is in well-publicized disarray. Thus state intervention in training is either necessary and effective (as the White Paper argues) or unproven – as Peston seemed to conclude in summing up the joint conference of NIESR/PSI/RIIA: 'no systematic evidence had been offered to link British deficiencies in training to economic performance' (Peston, 1985, p. 91).

Second, the 'logic of enquiry' (Nichols, 1986, p. 41) is fundamentally partial. Nichols points out how economic explanations tend to explain what they can in economic terms (like investment etc.) and then to attribute remaining discrepancies to an unexplained set of 'residual differences'. In so doing they neglect the social production of all economic activity. That residual becomes the X factor, and is attributed to 'attitudes' and 'spirit'. I take that to be the same rhetorical device that was evident in the 'Tracy' advertisement of the MSC, and in the White Paper. Synecdoche masquerades as explanation: the 'young' are made to stand for economic recovery; and individual qualities are held to be a first cause both of decline and recovery.

Third, quantitative evaluations of the relation of education/training to economic growth – such as Becker's human capital theory, and 'growth accountancy', are controversial and imprecise (Dean, 1984). Davis and Morrall (1974, p. 74) concluded: 'We are still at a loss to explain the real dynamics of economic growth, and the specter of an uncomfortably large residual persists.' The decline of the 'residual' (that part of growth unattributable to other factors of production and so ascribed to education) after 1973 tended to suggest that other factors (baby boom, oil prices, recession) were responsible (Mincer, 1984). Roderick and Stephens offer a suitable warning against the comparison of single factors in different contexts: 'The links between the education system and the rest of the social structure are peculiar to the society concerned. Separate analysis of the economy and education, therefore, if used to explain differential levels of economic performance, may lead to over-simplified accounts and optimistic hopes, through quick changes in educational policy, of rapid alleviation of malfunction, the roots of which lie in complex interrelationships between a wide range of social institutions whose characteristic quality may depend on the apparent vagaries of historical development' (Roderick and Stephens, 1981, p. 63).

Fourth, evaluation conclusions from programmes that try to connect education to economic outcome, such as the War on Poverty programme in the US, are indecisive (Davis and Morrall, 1974). Their conclusions are often sceptical – short-lived gains, effects on opportunities rather than skills, and no increase in subsequent earnings.

Thus the methodologies behind these confident assertions of deficiency and remedy suggest an uncertain science of weak and highly mediated correlations between factors which do not necessarily make much sense as separate variables, and whose national 'cases' are neither comparable nor independent of each other. Yet the debate is dominated by those sorts of single-factor comparisons – see particularly Prais's work, and its impact on policy-makers and media commentators.

■ Reading the economic discourse

Weber offered this criterion for rationality: 'methodical attainment of a definitely given and practical end by the use of an increasingly precise calculation of adequate means' (Gerth and Mills, 1948, p. 293). The definition, at heart, is progressive. But the features of the economic discourse are recurrent rather than progressive, and persistently divergent rather than convergent. It might be possible to think of the discourse as itself an epiphenomena of economic cycles. At any rate, it does not offer rational paths in terms of Weber's criterion of rationality. Nor is recurrence simply an outsider's charge; it is widely acknowledged within the discourse – the problem is held to be why the problem is never solved (Russell, Prais, Judd etc.). It is known, understood, constantly addressed, but never redressed – rather like debates on crime and punishment. (It will later be argued that the analogy is more than coincidental.)

Secondly, the White Paper is typical in that it offers an intense personification of the problem, both at individual and national level. The direct mediation between individual attributes and national destinies sets up a simple logic locating responsiblity in the attributes of an aggregate of individuals – a highly voluntaristic and individualistic theory of development, in which groups are no more than the aggregate of individuals.

Thirdly, the personification of problem and solution sets up two polarities – the first is between the 'real' individual and the 'ideal' person, that is to say, between what anthropologists have called notions of individual selfhood and 'sociocultural personhood' (Poole, 1982, p. 103); the second is between the implied polarities of the adjectives – strong/ weak, competitive/non-competitive, motivated/unmotivated. These polarities carry very simply explanations of the 'problem' at their negative poles, and prescribe 'solutions' at the positive poles. They are the discursive structures on which much vocationalist rhetoric rests (Stronach, 1989).

Fourthly, the personalizing of economic competitiveness (be motivated, get skilled) offers both an economics of recovery and a metonymics of blame (if you were trained and motivated we wouldn't be where we are today). Thus the rhetoric explains youth unemployment while prescribing economic success, aligning both these phenomena on the simple polarities we have outlined. The possibility that youth unemployment may be a consequence rather than a cause becomes hard to envisage in the schema.

Finally, these features of the economic discourse are held within a historical period (1977–present) when vocationalism at least partly became a way of not talking about disastrous levels of youth unemployment and the near collapse of craft training.

The historical evolution of the 'case' of youth unemployment bears repeating. Eleven years ago, when Callaghan was addressing the schools– industry divide, the Holland Committee began to inquire into youth unemployment. How could the 'personal needs' of the young unemployed be met? They sensibly concluded that young people were not to blame for their unemployment: '... getting a job is often a matter of luck and frequently determined by factors well beyond the control or achievement of the individual such as the state of the national economy, the local industrial structure or the kind of preparation for work available at school' (Holland, 1977, p. 33). A major effect – perhaps even purpose – of the ensuing vocational debate has been to bury that insight, leaving only the last phrase sticking out of the ground. The national economy, it was later claimed, is not to be blamed for youth unemployment. Indeed, inadequately trained and motivated young people are a basic cause of the economic malaise. The blame is thus shifted from the economic arena to the personal, or to the educational. The problem of unemployment becomes the problem of training. This alchemy was already evident in the 1982 MSC Youth Task Group Report – 'This report is about providing a permanent bridge between school and work. It is not about youth unemployment' (MSC, 1982, para. 1.1). Instead YTS was to be 'a historic step which marks a turning point in the industrial history of this country and a decisive break with the past so far as education and training of young people are concerned' (MSC, 1982, para. 3.8).

By 1986 it was no longer necessary to mention unemployment: the White Paper makes only a passing reference to unemployment in terms of the Youth Guarantee of training opportunities (4.7). But because the notion of training is hiding the fact of unemployment, the vocationalist drive intensifies as youth unemployment (the 'policy-off' version) continues to grow. The more unemployment grows, the more training must be needed. The more training is needed, the more it must be the fault of the young, or of their teachers. In more polemic mood, I concluded that 'what we have uncovered, of course, is Young's Law of Vocational Absurdity: that vocational preparation expands in inverse proportion to the likelihood of jobs' (Stronach, 1987). But others have reached similar conclusions: 'In the event the original aims of the Youth Opportunities Programme were drowned by the rising tide of youth unemployment. Remarkably, this led not to a renewed search for policies to deal with youth unemployment, but to an increased emphasis on education and training' (Raffe, 1984, p. 8).

Thus we can see that the recurrent, personifying, blaming and redeeming discourse of vocationalism was rooted in a context of crisis, unemployment, and 'youth surplus'. But the story does not end there. Let Norman Fowler have the last word on this conflation of youth unemployment and economic recovery:

> I feel that with the establishment of two-year YTS we have seen the end of youth unemployment in this country' (*Observer*, 2.8.87).

Indeed, it has come to pass: a recent newspaper report confirmed the end of youth unemployment as an official concern: 'The official unemployment count will be reduced by about 100,000 this autumn because a change in Government rules effectively disbars anyone under 18 from being counted as jobless' (*Guardian*, 16.7.88).

But there is a more potent shift taking place than Fowler's creative accountancy – one that government ministers have identified recently as a 'demographic timebomb': the 'youth' population is about to drop by almost 30 per cent, and so the talk now has to be about recruiting more labour into the workforce, the increase in part-time work by women, the need for employment-funded crèches etc. (*Guardian*, 22.12.88). No sooner was the corpse of youth unemployment buried by Dr Jekyll, than Mr Hyde – in the form of Mr Baker – had to dig it up again. Surplus was becoming scarcity; the whole archipelago of vocational this-and-that had to be re-appraised. Standards of conventional schooling had to be raised – more young workers were needed with the basic qualifications for entry to various levels of work. It is early days, of course, for such an analysis, but the underlying demographic change may help to explain the ebbing of the vocational tide that the National Curriculum and Assessment arrangements bring in their wake. In this light, we might view TVEI, and the like, as the last spring tide of the vocational response to the 'youth surplus' of the 1970s and 1980s. The new youth 'economy' based on scarcity rather than on surplus is likely to demand different initiatives.

Thus far, we have tried to understand the discourse constructed between the economy and the education system. The next task will be to understand the curricular and pedagogical aspects of that bridge – to look at the educational prescription that addressed this 'problem'. Meanwhile, we may conclude that the complexities of economic decline and recovery received a remarkable simplification, focusing on the young rather than on the old, on the individual rather than on the group, and on labour rather than on the other factors of production. In the final section of this chapter, it will be argued that there are elements of ritual reassurance in this reduction – and that we may echo the wonder Frazer expressed in the *Golden Bough* about the old European fire-festivals that sought to prevent disease and bring good crops:

> But we naturally ask, How did it come about that benefits so great and manifold were supposed to be attained by means so simple? In what way did people imagine that they could procure so many goods or avoid so many ills by the application of fire and smoke, of embers and ashes? (Frazer, 1913, p. 329).

■ The educational rationale

This section examines the rationality of the educational as opposed to the economic discourse that the White Paper represents, posing the central question: is it really educational? It will be argued that the 'educational' discourse of vocationalism is a much more broadly-based theory of social productivity, both in its origins and in nature.

First, what is the educational discourse associated with vocationalism? Its detailed history cannot concern us here (see McCulloch, 1987), although the foundations were clearly laid by the MSC, and especially by the FEU, in the late 1970s. Others, such as the ITRU and IMS, contributed to its procedures and rationale. Perhaps 'Trainee-centred Reviewing' and 'A Basis for Choice' were among its earliest influential tracts. Current development is perhaps most active in the 14–18 sector, particularly in schools and further education colleges, where TVEI, TRIST, and TVEI Extension activities have been considerable, and this analysis will focus on these developments.

TVEI debates on changes in learning styles have come to dominate discussion, particularly in the TVEI Extension phase: they centre on the following notions:

- *relevance and reality (such as work, technological change, enterprise, the self)*
- *ownership (such as student learning, innovation, teacher development, LEA implementation of national policy)*

- *negotiation (such as teaching/learning styles, institutional change, assessment, curriculum)*

- *active learning (such as for students, teachers, projects, LEAs)*

- *delivery (such as learning outcomes, INSET, project outcomes, LEA policies in national priority areas)*

(These concepts, and the accompanying 'equation' – see below – are derived from a variety of sources, including materials submitted to the 'TVEI Working Papers', a scrutiny of the preoccupations of TVEI publications such as 'TVEI Insight – a forum for shared experience' (MSC/TC/TA, 1984–89), and a review of LEA publications in the TRIST/TVEI area.)

Perhaps the central equation of the educational discourse is this:

$$change = collaboration + negotiation + contracting$$

This educational equation is variously interpreted, according to the political orientation of the LEA contractors, the project personnel, or the individual schools and teachers. 'Left-vocationalists' hope that they are in the business of emancipation, empowerment and education (for example, Sheffield); 'Right-vocationalists' speak a language of reality, enterprise and employability (for example, Norfolk). But 'ownership' seems to be the unifying characteristic in reports on TVEI developments. It is 'crucial' (Hinckley, 1987, p. 9). It is also central in the reporting of Nixon (1987), Jamieson (1987) and Barnes *et al.* (1987). What is most interesting about this concept is that, like the others, it contains a multiple reference – applying to student learning, teacher development, institutional change strategies, and LEA policy development. The bid/negotiate/contract prescription turns up in classrooms, as part of learning strategies and profiling; it exists at teacher level as teacher-focused, needs-based INSET; it reappears within educational management as school-focused INSET, and also characterizes the new categorical and competitive funding arrangements that link central government agencies like the MSC with LEAs. It is, therefore, a generic strategy. What are the implications?

When Jamieson raises the issue of 'corporate hegemony or pedagogic liberation' in relation to the schools–industry movement, he is right to reject the notion in the terms in which he raises it: industry does not typically impose on schools in those sorts of liaison – more usually it is difficult to get industry to stay involved (Jamieson, 1985). But the corporate tendency may be internalized by the education system itself (Cockburn, 1977), as part of a more general managerial paradigm. If so, what are these generic strategies of owning, negotiating, and contracting? Are they managerial theories of education, or educational theories of management? Perhaps that is a better question. It is one to which we now turn.

The five central notions of 'process' in the discourse are associated with a whole gamut of roles and procedures: the enabler, the facilitator, the resource manager, the networker; identifying needs, self-assessing/ appraising, contracting, learning collaboratively, sharing experience, raising awareness; problem-solving, transferable skills, experiential learning, and so on. This constellation of roles and processes is increasingly portrayed as the 'domestication' of the cruder vocationalist ambitions of the MSC and the government by the local education service – who claim to have educated MSC during the four years of TVEI pilot, a charge that MSC happily concede. TVEI is now (1989) essentially an enlightened pedagogy; it stands for effective learning. Part of this switch from technology and resources to pedagogy is a simple consequence of different funding levels for TVEI Pilot and TVEI Extension. The latter is much less generously funded (£80 per student as opposed to a maximum of £2000 in Pilot – Norfolk estimates), and so the switch from technology to pedagogy is partly inevitable. Nevertheless, the September 1987 TVEI conference at Jordanhill College, Glasgow, was not alone in claiming that these processes were 'classic' educational reform goals (Jordanhill, 1987, document b1). The response to TVEI Extension from the LEAs seems to be: it's what we wanted to do anyway – can't we just drop the TVEI label? Thus the new pedagogy meets with general favour as an educational strategy. More than that, TVEI is now portrayed as an educational ally in the struggle against the latest dragon, the National Curriculum.

But what is the educational nature of the 'new pedagogy', this *esperanto* for learning and development at all levels?

■ The 'new pedagogy'

The most comprehensive account of TVEI pedagogy is Brandes and Ginnis's, *A guide to student-centred learning* (1986). Citing Carl Rogers in the Preface, they define student-centred learning as involving ownership, participation and potential for growth, and identify the role of the enabler and the facilitator. They offer an equation for development: 'possession + responsibility = ownership' (Brandes and Ginnis, 1986, p. 26). They integrate the cognitive and the affective in the 'confluent', and describe the new pedagogy in terms of facilitation, choice, participation, discovery, self-evaluation, and responsibility (Brandes and Ginnis, 1986, p. 12). In TVEI debates these learning processes are often taken to lie at the heart of the educational definition (or reappropriation) of TVEI. They are not instrumental, not about training, nor are they preparation for industry – they are good practice in education and self-development, and they promote the forms of critical reflection that philosophers might demand from an educational process (Dearden, 1984).

It is possible to criticize these ideas from the point of view of educational philosophy (and TVEI has been open season in this respect) but the intention here is to locate these ideas sociologically rather than philosophically. This is important because the 'new pedagogy' is not confined to vocational preparation or prevocational education. 'Owner-ship', 'negotiation', 'collaborative groups', and 'participation' are central to the more humanistic branches of organizational theory, as are 'facilitators' and 'enablers' (McGregor, 1960; Tichy and Nisberg, 1980). They are found in places as various as branches of the sociology of work, social work counselling models, industrial management, and even in prescriptions for 'sexual healing' where the needs/awareness/ownership/celebration cycle is also invoked as a change mechanism in human behaviour (Ballinger, 1988, p. 2). Essentially, these ideas all seem to be posited as theories for more productive transitions, at the level of organizations, groups or individuals, theories which all assume that '... increases in worker participation are positively correlated with increases in productivity' (Whyte, 1987, p. 496). [...]

The underlying theories are eclectic – based on life stages, person–environment fields, or organizational contexts or cultures – with Rogers, Maslow, Erikson, Argyris and Lewin commonly cited in support. But despite these epistemological differences, the procedural level seems strangely coherent, giving the impression that something like a generic theory of social productivity can be identified, at least at the level of labelling:

Management role	Task descriptor	Process description
enabler	ownership	participative
facilitator	autonomy	supporting
resource person	needs-based	learning to learn
partner	consensus	sharing
	holism	integrating
	enrichment	problem-solving
	enlargement	decision-making
		realizing

[...]

Thus the pedagogy of TVEI stresses growth, ownership, participation, facilitation, and resource management. So does 'socio-technical' reform in industry, and various forms of 'human resource' management. Socio-technical theory claimed that the '... fundamental flaw of technical efficiency is that [such experts] insist on seeking purely technical solutions to systems that are, in fact, socio-technical .... The technical efficiency models are out of touch with the personal, subjective, and creative aspects

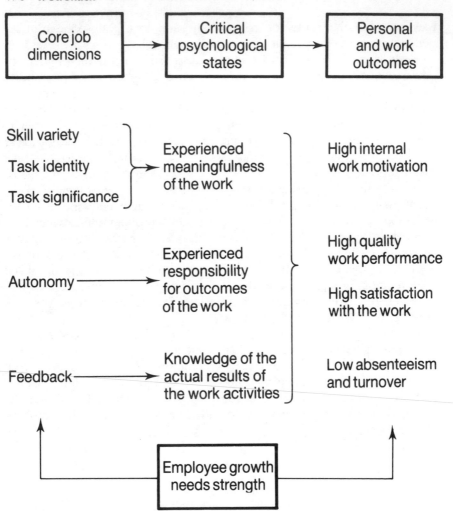

Figure 9.1   Job enrichment strategies. (*Source*: Hackman and Suttle, 1977, p. 129.)

of human reality' (Wirth, 1981, p. 1). Greater productivity is therefore achieved by integrating the technological with the 'human resource system' (Heller, 1988). Management literature sometimes supplies euphoric examples of this kind of productive humanism: 'I can only describe the experience as a moment of communion, of a feeling of unity and wholeness of the sort that Rosebeth Kanter observed in utopian communes' (Ouchi, 1981, p. 201). Brandes and Ginnis called this 'confluence', it will be recalled, and such an affective and cognitive integration characterizes forms of client involvement, and especially job enrichment strategies, as Figure 9.1 suggests.

To give two further examples, Walton (1977) and Thorsrud (1980) both envisage reforms in the scope of industrial jobs, and a change in the power relations within them. Thus work structuring tries to 'build an "internally consistent work culture", to increase the workers' skills, the "identification with the product", and to promote their sense of dignity and self-worth' (Warner, 1984, p. 82). Thorsrud stresses the need to shift job structure towards holism, variety, adaptive technology, and decentralized and less hierarchical patterns of authority and reporting (Thorsrud, 1980). The imperatives for these changes are held to lie in mass education, and changing attitudes in the young, as well as in the demands of new technology.

It is not suggested that the new pedagogy derives directly from these industrial and social work contexts, only that it fits them in terms of its key concepts and procedures. It seems to be part of a general and contemporary transition theory concerned with social productivity of one kind or another, usually involving adaptation to external changes, and one which crosses many areas of human activity (like crisis counselling, industrial participation, organizational psychology, preparation for retirement courses, bereavement counselling, school to work transitions, sales management, and social work).

There are interesting contradictions in these intersections, particularly between the economic and the educational discourses about the competence of youth. While Callaghan was arguing that education must catch up and fit the needs of industry, others – including Bullock – were making an opposite appeal. Industry must catch up with democracy and its effects on education. The Bullock Report (1977) said: 'The coming of an age of democracy is a process that inevitably affects the whole of people's lives; it cannot be excluded from the workplace' (Warner, 1984, p. 68). Education was no longer authoritarian, pupils and society were no longer 'deferential' (Bullock, 1977, p. 22), and the educational qualifications of entrants to industry were rising. Warner concluded: '... the issue of industrial democracy will not go away and we shall see experimentation continue over the coming years. There is a growing demand by employees for greater influence over their working lives, and as educational levels rise this will increase further' (Warner, 1984, p. 106). In this version of the 'problem', industry had to catch up with education – by increasing motivation and productivity through participative management, restructured work, job enlargement, holistic task definition, Quality of Working Life innovations, Quality Circles, and so on. Adding to the discursive confusion, the 'work progressives' tended to hold, and want to respond to, inaccurately perceived participative notions of what went on in schools: 'we have educated them to regard themselves as mature adults ... then we offer them no choice in our overorganized industrial units' (Gyllenhammer, 1977, cited in Wirth, 1981, p. 2). Meanwhile the vocational progressives (such as FEU, ITRU, CPVE, TVEI) responded to patterns of industrial work organization that had seldom been implemented in the UK (see, for example, Heller, 1988). Myth called to myth across the industrial and educational discourses.

Thus the first level of contradiction concerned the relations between democracy, education, and economic organization. How could the values and skills of an educated democracy be maximized in terms of productivity? The second level of contradiction concerned roles and procedures. Callaghan had cast doubt on 'informal methods' and promoted a back-to-the-basics movement concerned with the relevance of education to prosperity. Ten years later, TVEI had reclaimed these informal methods (student-centred, experiential, project-based, continuously assessed procedures) and connected them to economic relevance. They were no longer the problem: they were the solution. They were how industry did (or should do) things. They were the key to the flexible, problem-solving, self-reliant work force of the future. But industry didn't do these things (Senker, 1986). The socio-technical approaches to the organization of work that the Tavistock Institute had promoted since the late 1940s were largely spurned by British management. Warner pointed out how lukewarm British managements had been – 'only been moderate interest on the part of practising managers' (Warner, 1984, p. 56). And as Heller recently noted, the UK prophets of socio-technical approaches are in exile – Trist and van Beinum in Canada, Emery in Australia (Heller, 1988). The second version of this level of contradiction, then, was that education promoted ideas on the organization of work, and on worker qualities and competencies, that were at odds with British practices in industry. 'Hi-tech, hi-touch' may or may not be a 'Megatrend' for the future (Naisbitt, 1984), but it is not a current reality in British industry. Indeed, it seems that the 'new realism' of the 1980s was more rather than less authoritarian – managers must manage etc. (Nolan, 1989). We can now pose this second level of contradiction in the form of a question: are our new and relevant vocational pedagogies more at odds with British realities of work than old-fashioned, disciplinary schooling?

The third level of contradiction concerns the educational nature of these rhetorics of social productivity. Within vocationalist debates the 'new pedagogy' of student-centred learning, negotiation, and so on, is taken to be the most educational feature of the initiative, proof that education did not sell out to training, that the 'real' education of the primary school is at last spreading to the secondary. But it could be argued that the 'new pedagogy' is the least educational feature of vocationalism – it turns up everywhere as a form of management for change, a recipe for adaptation to continuous change, a nostrum for contemporary crises. What seems to be a theory of education turns out to be a theory of productivity for troubled times.

Are such theories of productivity necessarily non-educational? Of course, they may not be, but the sorts of definition that are given to the 'self' – to the qualities and attitudes an individual ought to have, and to the nature of 'centredness' (Stronach, 1989), suggest that they usually involve a subtle or not so subtle alienation from the self. Again, a theory of productivity has by definition an uneducational assumption (that we ought to produce X), making it the more unlikely that such approaches could develop the critical reflectiveness to ask questions such as 'why produce?' and 'with what effects on whom?' Finally, a traiing curriculum is instrumental – it has an end in view, 'operative efficiency' in some task (Dearden, 1984, p. 59). For that reason it is vulnerable: no end, no justification. Witness the despair about declining YOP 'placement' rates, and the subsequent changing and renaming of the programme. But a theory of social productivity is not restricted to competence at work because it deals with the universal figure of the 'client': student, worker, citizen, partner. In its ambition or potential to offer an administration of whole areas of personal, social and productive life, it can become a way of Being, and find an ominous justification in 'process' itself – the circular and open prison of the 'process' curriculum?

'In this approach, the key concept is that of the image. By bringing it to the fore, one can turn the subject around, get him to accept responsibility for expertise, since it is he who reveals his own, get him at the same time to accept what he was refusing to hear, to see, to do, since it no longer has to do with morality, laws or merits, with the possible or the impossible; it involves his own being, his relational equilibrium, his psychical and sexual fulfilment' (Donzelot, 1979, p. 213).

■ Rationality and ritual

This article began with Tracy, and her personal transformation that stood for a more general economic recovery. That kind of personification was also found in the kinds of economic–educational accounts expressed in the 1986 White Paper. An extreme reductionism related personal and individual qualities and skills to national redemption. It was argued that such a discourse served to do the following:

(1) juvenalize and personalize the problem
(2) assert the certainty of the problem and its solution
(3) privilege the reality of work
(4) understate more parsimonious causes
(5) cast out methodological doubts
(6) equate simplistically education and economic success
(7) deflect attention from youth unemployment

In terms of rationality, the policy outlined in the White Paper did not appear to make sufficient sense. The economic warrant for the argument was unconvincing in itself, and the case against the 'qualities' of youth and for vocationalism highly selective – there was a 'remainder' left over that could be attributed to error, ideology, or . . . it was signalled but not argued . . . ritual.

The second discourse to be examined was the educational one that lay within vocationalist initiatives in schooling. It was argued here that the 'new pedagogy' – far from being an essentially educational domestication of 'vocationalism' – was an unproven generic theory of productivity, neither limited to the educational arena, nor originating in it, nor, indeed, ever implemented and evaluated in any systematic way. This discourse was contradictory in the principal sense that two rather mythic notions of education and of industrial organization were trying to catch up with each other.

Thus the coupling of education and economics ends in a voca-tionalism that may not either be educationally or economically productive, even in its own terms. As with Tracy's advertisement, Nichols's critique of economic productivity debates, and human capital's notion of a 'residual', we are left with a 'remainder' of meaning. We are left, once again, with Frazer's sense of wonder – '. . . that benefits so great and manifold were supposed to be attained by means so simple . . .'

The approach in this final section of the article will be to explore the notion of 'ritual' as an explanation for vocationalism, as an interpretive framework within which we might locate the economic and educational discourses.

This is not such a bizarre project. The notion that ritual and magical thinking are a vital aspect of modern cultures is not original. Lane has written of ritual creation and management in the USSR (Lane, 1981). Erikson points out that we cannot see our own ritualizations just because that is what they are: '. . . ritualization is an aspect of everyday life which is more clearly seen in a different culture or class or even family than in our own, where, in fact, ritualization is more often than not experienced simply as the only proper way to do things . . .' (Erikson, 1978, p. 80). More significant to the kind of analysis that will be given here, Hobsbawn and Ranger argue that modern Britain has developed a 'heritage' view of its history. In that mythicization of history we find 'invented tradition': '. . . a set of practices, normally governed by overtly or tacitly accepted rules of a ritual or symbolic nature, which seek to inculcate certain values and norms of behaviour by repetition, which automatically implies continuity with the past' (Hobsbawm and Ranger, 1983, p. 1). And Eliade, despite his separation of archaic and modern, argues that the kind of history that the primitive celebrated – mythic, regenerative, and circular – is perhaps a notion of history to which modern man is returning – in terror of the history he has known (Eliade, 1954). Finally, ritual analysis of contem-porary schooling is not unknown (McLaren, 1986).

Thus it seems reasonable to argue that the notion of ritual is not necessarily anachronistic in its possible application to 'modern' societies.[2]

A second question: if vocationalism is (or is also) a ritual, what kind of ritual is it? Obviously, an initiation ritual of some sort – since vocationalist rhetorics shepherd our youth through training and educational stages. La Fontaine lists typical features of such rituals: initiation is like a play, with some idea of the 'ideal' usually involved: it is highly symbolic, and can have many layers of meaning. Unlike a play, however, it is purposeful, 'it aims to affect the world'. Nor is the first audience of a ritual necessarily the novices themselves: they may be the occasion rather than the purpose (La Fontaine, 1985, p. 184). Rappaport offers a similar notion of 'congregation' – 'aggregates of individuals who regard their collective well-being to be dependent upon a common body of ritual performances' (Rappaport, 1968, p. 1).

There is a final point to be made about the importance of context to ritual. Sometimes change is not contained in the life-stages of the individual or his or her age-cohort. Sometimes it is a result of political and economic change. Ritual can be a reaction to external crisis. Hobsbawn points out that 'we should expect it [invented tradition] to occur when a rapid transformation of society weakens or destroys the social patterns from which "old" tradition had been designed' (Hobsbawm and Ranger, 1983, p. 4). [. . .]

Thus there does seem a case for concentrating on some of the ritual practices that address the problems of initiation and social incorporation in the face of external changes and crises in 'modern' societies.

A third question: how can the rationales of vocationalism be understood in terms of ritual? The answer to that question will involve relating specific aspects of the structure of vocationalist discourse to the complex nature of ritual as symbolic, value-laden, role-based and 'telic' – 'its design as a system of ends and means' (Turner, 1981, p. 3). It will first be argued that features such as personal transformation and universal salvation are connected in ways characteristic of ritual accounts; that there is also a close analogy in the play of opposites and the moulding of attitudes; and that the notions of recurrence and a return to eternal values add to the case for interpreting vocationalism as ritual. Finally, the logical structure of the vocationalist discourse will be compared with the structure of ritual explanations, in order to bring out certain parallels.

□ **Individual transformation and universal salvation**

As we have seen in the case of Tracy, and of the White Paper, individual and general outcomes are distinctively related in vocationalism. Personification is the typical metaphor, and it is used to make individual young people responsible for general recovery. Individual qualities are asserted as the determinants of success (for example, PM Thatcher, BBC TV, 14.5.88: 'thrift', 'self-reliance', 'enterprise', etc.). Exemplary individuals are held up to illustrate this process, and it is no coincidence that the re-issue of Samuel Smiles' *Self-Help* had an introduction written by Sir Keith Joseph (Smiles, 1986). The pattern of exemplary individuals is similar to the vocational strategies of the Victorian period, when *Boyhoods of Great Men* (Edgar, *c*.1850) typified the instructive convention.

The pattern is similar to that found in many rituals: 'The ritual remedy thus invoked itself possesses a form similar to the whole process of crisis and redress. It originates in trouble, proceeds through the symbolization of trouble and feelings associated with it, and concludes in an atmosphere of re-achieved amity and cooperativeness, with the hope of restored health, prosperity and fertility' (Turner, 1981, p. 52). Just as in some forms of vocational profiling, the ritual moves the individual from 'experiental selfhood' to 'social personhood' (Harris, 1978, p. 63; Poole, 1982), creating an archetype of the young citizen/worker in a series of idealized personal qualities (self-reliant, enterprising, thrifty, problem-solving, reliable etc.). Eliade termed this process 'the transformation of man into archetype through repetition' (Eliade, 1954, p. 37). At the same time, ritual typically associates a personal with a cosmic pole, round which prosperity, morality and civilization are clustered – and against which disorder and chaos are arraigned. So too did the MSC advertisement, and the White Paper.

☐   The play of opposites and the moulding of attitudes

The logic of the archetype is to create poles of negative and positive attributes. Thus, for example, profiling offers this sort of range, as we have already seen (Stronach *et al.*, 1982, p. 34):

> ... the Ideal Worker, the Celestial Citizen. Or their negative shadows ...

• self reliant	• with guidance, can understand consequences of actions
• quick and accurate at complex calculations	
• adept at most kinds of verbal encounter	• has to be given simple instructions
• can independently derive, implement and evaluate solutions	• speed well below industrial requirements
	• makes little effort
• copes sensibly with moral dilemmas	• ordinarily obedient complying by habit
• sensitive to others perceptions	• is aware of own personality and situation

The focus is personal – the 'egocentric interpretation of misfortune', as Clyde Mitchell put it in discussing the discourse of witchcraft. Such simple and stark dichotomies are common in ritual explanations. 'Litima' (personality, motivation) is opposed by 'bunyali' (competence and ability); 'kutama' (the worthwhile and desirable in life) by 'kuwla' (La Fontaine, 1985). And for the Navajo, the 'Blessingway' opposes the 'Enemyway':

Blessingway	*Enemyway*
propriety	chaos
safety	monsters
civilisation	masturbation
cosmos	
sexual maturity	

(Lincoln, 1981, p. 95)

The notion of moulding and shaping is also common to both ritual and vocationalist accounts. In vocationalist ritual as in 'archaic' practice, the novice has to learn to define and shape the self against an ideal – 'the presentation of the self to the self' (Harris, 1978, p. 146). A Navajo informant told Lincoln:

'The woman moulds the girl to press her into a good figure and shape her body. At that time and period she is soft and can be pressed into certain forms. You shape her so she will have a good figure. If it is not done, she will probably have a belly like a nanny-goat's'.

Lincoln goes on to quote Frisbie: 'The girl is moulded so she will be beautiful. Being beautiful in this case, however, implies more than having a good figure. It means the girl will be strong, ambitious, and capable of enduring much. The moulding affects the girl's personality as well as her body. It implies that she will be friendly, unselfish, and cheerful; it means she will be a kind mother and a responsible housekeeper. A "beautiful" girl, therefore, is not only physically appealing, she is also "good" and "useful" ' (Lincoln, 1981, pp. 94–5).

In that account, the synecdoche is vivid: minor physical actions stand for great changes at different levels, from the personal to the cosmic. Again, there is a parallel with the economic 'beauty' of Tracy and the abstract individuals of the White Paper on the one hand, and the cosmic outcomes envisaged as a consequence of the ritual – economic recovery, the envy of the world, the triumph of virtue. This may help to explain both the great size of the rationality gaps between means and envisaged ends, and the fact that they are so little remarked upon and so culturally unexceptionable.

☐   **The symbolic Centre, recurrence, and return to eternal values**

In the first section of this article, the 'privileging' of the reality of work was pointed out. In mini-companies, Work Experience, curriculum design and pedagogical strategy, the 'reality' of work determined the nature of education and training. The emergence of work as a 'paramount reality' to be experienced, as well as learned about, echoes the 'Sacred Centre' of ritual – the mountain or temple wherein the sacred is the outstanding reality. In this sense, we might see Work Experience as a kind of pilgrimage to the 'real world of work':

> '. . . To the center of the world you have taken me and showed the goodness and the beauty and the strangeness of the greening earth, the only mother . . . At the center of this sacred hoop you have said that I should make the tree to bloom . . .' (Black Elk, cited by Kehoe, 1989, p. 51)

But the paramount reality of Work Experience is symbolic rather than 'really real' – it is not more real than other curriculum events or life experiences. Indeed, Work Experience and mini-companies do not even offer windows or doors into the real world of work, although they must claim to do so. Instead, they enact condensed ideological dramas of that reality, sometimes 'scripted' through a catalogue of objectives or 'things to do', and very often versions bearing little resemblance to the experience of 'being a worker' or 'running a business'. But that does not mean that we should criticize them for being 'unreal'. Their reality, like ritual reality, is significant because it is exemplary; it stands for a truth but is not itself that truth. It points to what is culturally important, rather than economically necessary, or educationally essential. Eliade indicates the importance of seeing this kind of ritual as a place where reality is enacted and internalized, and where the boundary between the meaningful and the meaningless can be drawn:

> 'Thus reality is acquired solely through repetition or participation; everything that lacks an exemplary model is "meaningless", that is it lacks reality.' (Eliade, 1954, p. 34)

The importance of the economy to our cultural concerns mirrors this centrality. The economy is personified in media presentations (sick man of Europe, the British disease, Britain proud again, the ailing pound etc). The metaphors of disease and recovery are applied to the economic 'body' (well/sick;   deteriorate/strengthen;   ailing/healthy;   crisis/regeneration). Media bulletins are issued on the rate of exchange, as if it reflected a vital national pulse. The centrality of economic 'health' to a sense of cultural well-being cannot be doubted in these discourses, and it is this 'sacred centre' round which education and training debates have spun. Work Experience, and vocationalism more generally, reflect the reality of this cultural concern, rather than the existential realities of 'working'.

Recurrence – often around the 'symbolic centre' of work – is the dominant feature of vocationalist initiatives. The problem, as the economists noted, recurs. Attempts to address it recur – in SCIP and TVEI Extension and CPVE. Within initiatives, reforms recur – the TVEI initiative is really more than 100 projects, each of them working more or less independently on similar changes like IT, Work Experience, student-centred learning, and profiling. Indeed, the notion of recurrence is written into the rhetoric of the Initiative, belonging to the logic of 'ownership' – part of that generic strategy earlier noted. So recurrence is also part of the constituting metaphor. These attempts to define and solve the problem do not build on each other in any obvious way (eg in terms of a Weberian rationality) and reflect something of what Kundera called an 'organised forgetting' of previous definitions and attempted solutions (Kundera, 1982, p. 235). These innovations whose urgency is recurrent, whose solutions never seem to materialize, and whose failure never seems to register on any policy review, are not restricted to vocationalism – as the Director of the Prison Trust noted (Shaw, Guardian 2.9.87) with regard to the recent rise and fall of the 'short, sharp shock' Detention Centre strategy (see also Pressman and Wildavsky on the perennial lack of success in the implementation of government funded projects in the US – 'Particular facts may vary but the general story is the same: a sensational announcement from Washington on page 1, temporary local jubilation, permanent difficulties, and, perhaps years later, a small blurb on the back page signaling the end'. (Pressman and Wildavsky, 1979, p. 135)

Pressman and Wildavsky see these recurrent phenomena as a failure of innovation that can be remedied. But it is hard to explain the recurrent and cyclical nature of these innovations, and the apparent amnesia and acceptance that surrounds their failure and later revival – for the system seems to offer a kind of institutionalization of failure in terms of innovation. Perhaps Foucault offers a better understanding when he argues that recognition of weaknesses, failures to reform, and defective institutional practices ought to be seen as part of the same governing strategy. The reforming impulse is a condition of stability rather than of change, and we should regard the whole cycle of deficiency and remedy as 'utopian duplication' (Foucault, 1977).

The notion of ritual allows us to give these recurrent failures a positive reading. As responses, they address, and are seen to address, the problem. In ritual terms, recurrence is necessary for success: the re-enactment is as logical as it is to put on a play more than once. It is the performance and not the outcome that is important, and the audience rather than the actors. In this account, our vocational initiatives are also contemporary dramas that ritually involve young people in enacting solutions to economic decline. The root values they invoke are traditional and nostalgic: the Protestant work ethic is reinvoked; they undertake the repetition of the cosmogony. The Great Time, the Golden Age, and the First People are recalled. Their values are reasserted, their actions recreated: '... what is primordial is the idea of regeneration, that is, of repetition of the Creation'. (Eliade, 1954, p. 64) The 'heritage' industry, Hobsbawm's critique of 'invented tradition' in the UK, the invocations of Samuel Smiles and mythicized Victorian values may all be interpreted as part of this ritual of regeneration wherein Britain can once more, in the words of the White Paper, become 'the envy of the world'. (1.7) As in 'archaic' society, '... there is nothing that does not, in one way or another, find its explanation in the transcendent, in the divine economy'. (Eliade, 1954, p. 100)

□ **The rationality of rationality**

Personification in metaphor makes for circularity in logic. The first principle of the circularity is that objections to the basic theory can be met one by one, since an aggregate theory of individuals is proposed. That is to say, each individual will succeed or fail according to the degree to which she holds the appropriate qualities: the notion that individuals are one of a class (young, female, black, northern), and may fail for those sorts of reasons, is suppressed.

The second principle is that contradictory evidence can always be met by extending the circle of the theory. Thus lack of employability in the late 1970s rested on poor attitudes in the young, and a lack of experience of the disciplines and realities of work. Programmes of correction were set up, but the problem grew more extensive. Longer programmes were introduced in order to provide the necessary skills and qualities. It was then felt that training was necessary, first one year, then two years. At the same time, the criticisms of school grew, and prevocational initiatives entered the schools in order to remedy the problem at its source. Social and Life Skills, CGLI, RSA, Social and Vocational Studies, Certificate of Prevocational education, and Technical and Vocational Education Initiatives followed. Each expansion of the circle – Polanyi calls it epicyclical elaboration – confirms the original diagnosis, while conceding that the problem is more profound than first thought. Thus the debate threatens to melt down into the structures of schooling itself, as the privatization of schools follows the vocationalizing of the curriculum.

The third principle is that the basic synecdoche at the heart of the discourse does not allow any other explanations in its own terms. Once the idea of individual qualities is set up to 'stand for' economic prosperity, there are few alternatives within the logic of the discourse. Thus the welter of other possible explanations offered by economists and educationalists are unrepresented in the debate, and either ignored or treated as separate issues.

Polanyi discusses the effects of such logics: 'Circularity, combined with a readily available reserve of epicyclical elaborations and the consequent suppression in the germ of any rival conceptual development, leads to a degree of stability to a conceptual framework which he may describe as its completeness'. (Polanyi, 1958, pp. 286–294). His discussion is based on an analysis of Zande witchcraft belief, but the same sorts of self-fulfilling rhetorics are evident in vocationalism. There is, therefore, nothing bizarre about the claim that the logics of witchcraft and the structures of ritual invest vocationalist discourse, although their presence should not reassure us.

☐ Vocationalist ritual: a vessel for meanings

The relation of rationality to ritual is more complicated than the above discussion would suggest. Ritual does not set out to be rational, and yet that is how it was evaluated above – as a deficient rationality. But the point about ritual is its power to make things come true whether or not they are held to be true on other grounds – that is, to convince. It sets out, as La Fontaine argued, to enact a moral code, to dramatize, to give purpose, to test, to be open to a range of symbolic meanings and audiences, to express regeneration or change to a new status. Its force is metaphorical and dramaturgical, and that is why the synecdoche, the personification, the reduction and intensification of the problem and solution, are so prevalent in vocationalist discourse.

It is also a powerful reason why the vocationalist experiments of the last decade are often so loosely and cursorily evaluated. The evaluation process is neither independent nor critical: it is part of an apparently technocratic legitimation of the ritual (LEA evaluations of TRIST and TVEI may turn out to be the best illustration of that kind of evaluation role). In this kind of perspective, evaluation is much more than merely 'bureaucratic', in MacDonald's terminology (MacDonald, 1976), because its 'capture' is a necessary part both of the confirmation of the innovation and, in turn, of the functioning of the system which it purports to reform; that is, an aspect of 'utopian duplication'. We might summarize the point thus: to the extent that vocationalism is ritual, critical evaluation is blasphemy.

But that does not mean that we confront ritual and only ritual. Rationality, ideology and ritual are all present: each has its own space and purpose. Economic rationality addresses decline, its means are better skills and attitudes in the young, and its end is economic prosperity. The socially productive rationality addresses motivation, its means are participative management procedures at all levels, and its end is individual adaptation to change. Ritual addresses crisis, its means are rhetorics, rationales, projects and vocational rites, and its end is reassurance. That reassurance is especially addressed to the managers rather than the managed. Like the 'chingsu' rituals reported by Richards (Richards, 1957), it perhaps offers more to the old who carry out the rituals than to the young who are its formal object. In this, it is not a conventional ideology at all – it seeks to reassure the powerful as much as it seeks to mystify the powerless, and that allows us to interpret vocationalist initiatives of the last decade in a rather different light. Marxist critiques which see in these events only mystification and manipulation of the young miss an important set of meanings; and by failing to recognize the ritual for what it is, they participate in it (through oppositional accounts such as these). The difference is important. In the end, the polemical contrast between the points of view of ideology and ritual about the role of the powerful is this: ideology believes that they are clever and they are out to deceive us; ritual believes that they are stupid and they are out to deceive themselves.

There are also implications for how we see the rationality of modern society. Habermas argues that the fundamentally different practical and technical discourses have been made indistinguishable by 'scientification' (Habermas, 1974, p. 255). Science comes to dominate all theories: '. . . the formalization of one sole relevance to life, namely, the experience of success as feedback control, built into the systems of social labor and already realised in every successful performance of labor' (Habermas, 1974, p. 264). But the apparently technocratic rationality of vocationalism shows scant regard for scientific procedure or feedback controls (the relation of the outcomes of the TVEI 'experiments' to any rewriting of the vocationalist discourse, for example, is far from clear) and elements of its structure are highly ritualistic. Absurdity, fantasy, and magic (even as defined from the point of view of a technocratic consciousness) are as much part of that discourse as technology.

In those discourses, with their mixture of rational processes and ritual responses, their interweaving of economic, social, political and educational themes, their cyclical ebb and flow of crisis and response, there is no possibility of singularity – of a vocationalism to be 'found out' amongst a range of possibilities: centralization, mystification, recovery, ritual, hegemony, a new 'discipline' of and for youth, or even contemporary magical thinking. Instead, we have to see vocationalism as something that has to be understood in terms of its range of meanings rather than in terms of once-and-for-all definition.

Thus we should not judge too quickly whether vocationalism is 'modern' – standing for technological progress and rationality – or whether it is 'archaic' and offers a more cyclic and ritualistic recovery: '. . . the complex symbolism of periodic regeneration (. . .) [which] has its foundation in lunar mysticism' (Eliade, 1954, p. 64). The tin plates of TVEI may also turn out to be the 'fingernails of the moon':

'The old men in the village remember when first they saw some "Malay" hunters after birds of paradise who travelled south of the village but did not come into it: they came from the west (...) They carried guns and showed the Gnau salt (the Gnau mistook it for their semen), matches and tin plates which, to the Gnau, shone like the moon and they called them "fingernails of the moon".'

(Lewis, 1980, 'Day of Shining Red', p. 200)

Notes

1.   An earlier version of this paper appears as a chapter in Stronach, I., 'Transition Learning: a reflexive approach to education and politics in a new age' unpubl. Ph.D., CARE, University of East Anglia, 1989. A condensed version of the 'ritual' section of the paper appears in eds Brown, S. & Wake, R. 'Education in Transition. What role for research? A collection of papers to mark the 60th anniversary of the founding of The Scottish Council for Research in Education', SCRE, Edinburgh, 1988.

2.   A more detailed argument for the appropriateness of 'ritual' as a contemporary social construct appears in Stronach, I. (1989), see note (1).

References

Abbs, P. (1981) 'Promoting new first principles', *THES*, 28.8.81; 'The poisoning of the Socratic ideal', *Guardian*, 13.1.86; 'Training spells the death of education', *Guardian*, 5.1.87.

Ballinger, L. (1988) 'Sexual healing. One woman's experience of the basic sexuality group at Spectrum'. *Human Potential*, Autumn 1988.

Barnes, D. *et al.* (1987) *The TVEI Curriculum 14–16. An Interim Report Based on Case Studies in 12 Schools.* School of Education, Univ. of Leeds.

Bates, I., Clarke, J., Cohen, P., Finn, D., Moore, R., Willis, P. (1984) *Schooling for the dole: The New Vocationalism* (London: Macmillan).

Benyon, H. (1987) 'Dealing with icebergs: organisation, production and motivation in the 1990s'. *Work, employment and society* 1, 2, pp. 247–259.

Blaug, M. (1985) 'Comment', in Worswick, G. D. N. (ed.), *Education and Economic Performance*. Joint Studies in Public Policy 9, National Institute of Economic and Social Research/Policy Studies Institute/Royal Institute of International Affairs (Aldershot: Gower).

Bowles, S. & Gintis, H. (1976) *Schooling in Capitalist America* (London: Routledge & Kegan Paul).

Brandes, D. & Ginnis, P. (1986) *A Guide to Student-centred Learning* (London: Blackwell).

(Bullock Report, The) (1977) *Report of the Committee of Inquiry on Industrial Democracy. Presented to Parliament by the Secretary of State for Trade.* HMSO, January, Cmnd. 6706.

Burke, K. (1962) *A Grammar of Motives and a Rhetoric of Motives*. (Cleveland: World Publishing Co).

Cantor, L. (1985) 'A coherent approach to the education and training of the 16–19 age group', in Worswick, G. D. N. (ed.), *Education and Economic Performance*. Joint Studies in Public Policy 9, National Institute of Economic and Social Research/Policy Studies Institute/Royal Institute of International Affairs (Aldershot: Gower).

Carter, C. (1985) 'Implications for policy and research', in Worswick, G. D. N. (ed.), *Education and Economic Performance*. Joint Studies in Public Policy 9, National Institute of Economic and Social Research/Policy Studies Institute/ Royal Institute of International Affairs (Aldershot: Gower).

Cockburn, C. (1977) *The Local State. Management of Cities and People* (London: Pluto).

Crafts, N. (1988) 'The Assessment: British economic growth over the long run'. *Oxford Review of Economic Policy*, 4, 1, pp. i–xxi.

Critchfield, R. (1988) 'A visitor's view. A survey of Britain'. *Economist*, 21.2.88.

Dale, R. (ed.) (1985) *Education, Training and Employment* (Oxford: Pergamon).

Daly, A., Hitchens, D. M., Wagner, K. (1985) 'Productivity, machinery and skills in a sample of British and German manufacturing plants: results of a pilot inquiry'. *National Institute Economic Review*, pp. 48–61, Feb.

Davis, J. R. & Morrall, J. F. (1974) *Evaluating Educational Investment* (Lexington: D. C. Heath).

Dean, E. (ed.) (1984) *Education and Economic Productivity* (Cambridge, Mass.: Ballinger).

Dearden, R. (1984) 'Education and Training'. *Westminster Studies in Education*, 7, pp. 57–66.

Donzelot, J. (1979) *The Policing of Families. Welfare versus the State* (tr. Hurley, R.) (London: Hutchinson).

Edgar, J. G. (c.1850) *The Boyhood of Great Men Intended As An Example To Youth* (London: Routledge & Sons).

Eliade, M. (1954) *The Myth of the Eternal Return* (translated by Trask, W.) (New York: Pantheon).

Erikson, E. (1978) *Toys and Reasons. Stages in the Ritualization of Experience* (London: Marion Boyars).

Fitzgibbon, C. T., Hazelwood, R. D., Tymms, P. B. and McCabe, C. (1988) 'Performance indicators and the TVEI pilot'. *Evaluation and Research in Education 2*, 2, pp. 49–60.

Foucault, M. (1977) *Discipline and Punishment: the Birth of the Prison* (translated by Sheridan Smith, A.) (Harmondsworth: Penguin).

Frazer, J. G. (1913) *The Golden Bough: A Study in Magic and Religion. Pt 7 Balder the Beautiful*, Vol. 1 (London: Macmillan).

Gerth, H. and Mills, C. W. (eds) (1948) *For Max Weber. Essays in Sociology* (New York: Macmillan).

Godley, W. (1988) 'Why I won't apologise'. *Observer*, 18.9.88.

Gyllenhammer, P. G. (1977) *People at Work* (Reading: Addison-Wesley).

Habermas, J. (1974) *Theory and Practice* (translated by McCarthy, J.) (London: Heinemann).

Handy Report (1987) *The Making of Managers: a Report on Management Education Training and Development in the USA, West Germany, France,*

Japan and the UK (London: NEDC).

Harris, G. G. (1978) *Casting out Anger. Religion among the Tanta of Kenya* (Cambridge: CUP).

Heller, F. A. (1988) 'Working models after Taylor on the shop floor'. *THES*, 20.1.88.

Hinckley, S. (1987) *The TVEI Experience Views from Teachers and Students* (Slough: NFER).

Hobsbawm, E. and Ranger, T. (1983) *The Invention of Tradition* (Cambridge: CUP).

Holland, G./MSC (The Holland Report) (1977) *Young People at Work. Report on the Feasibility of a New Programme of Opportunities for Unemployed People* (London: MSC).

Huhne, C. (1987) 'Is industry aware there is a skill gap?' *Observer*, 29.4.87.

Keegan, V. (1987) 'Now it is up to Reagan'. *Guardian*, 26.10.87.

Kehoe, A. B. (1989) *The Ghost Dance. Ethnohistory and Revitalization* (Holt Rinehart Winston: New York).

Jamieson, I. (1985) 'Corporate Hegemony or Pedagogic Liberation? The Schools–Industry Movement in England and Wales', in Dale, R. (ed.), *Education, Training and Employment: towards a new vocationalism* (Oxford: Pergamon).

Jamieson, I. (1987) *TVEI. The Wiltshire Scheme*. Second Report of the external evaluator (School of Education, University of Bath).

Jordanhill College of Education (1987) *TVEI conference for Scotland* (conference documentation) (Glasgow: INSET Division).

Kundera, M. (1982) *The Book of Laughter and Forgetting* (translated by Heim, M. H.) (Harmondsworth: Penguin).

La Fontaine, J. (1985) *Initiation* (Harmondsworth: Penguin).

Lane, C. (1981) *The Rites of Rulers. Ritual in Industrial Society – the Soviet Case* (Cambridge: CUP).

Lewis, G. (1980) *Day of Shining Red. An Essay on Understanding Ritual* (Cambridge: CUP).

Lincoln, B. (1981) *Emerging from the Chrysalis. Studies in Rituals of Women's Initiation* (Cambridge: Harvard U.P.).

McCulloch, G. (1987) 'History and policy. The politics of the TVEI', in Gleeson, D. (ed.), *TVEI and Secondary Education: A Critical Appraisal* (Milton Keynes: Open University Press).

McGregor, D. (1960) *The Human Side of Enterprise* (New York: McGraw-Hill).

MacDonald, B. (1976) 'Evaluation and the control of education', in Tawney, D. (ed.), *Curriculum Evaluation Today: Trends and Implications*, pp. 125–36. (London: Macmillan).

McLaren, P. (1986) *Schooling as a Ritual Performance. Towards a Political Economy of Educational Symbols and Gestures* (London: RKP).

Mincer, J. (1984) 'Comment: overeducation or undereducation?', in Dean, E. (ed.), *Education and Economic Productivity* (Cambridge, Mass.: Ballinger).

MSC (Manpower Services Commission) (1982) *Youth Task Group Report* (London: MSC).

MSC/TC/TA (Manpower Services Commission) (1984–89) *Insight. The Journal of the Technical and Vocational Initiative*, MSC/TC/TA, Nos. 1–15.

Naisbitt, J. (1984) *Ten New Directions Transforming Our Lives* (London: MacDonald).

Nichols, J. (1986) *The British Worker Question: a New Look at Workers and Productivity in Manufacturing* (London: RKP).

Nixon, J. (ed.) (1987) 'Curriculum change: the Sheffield experience'. *USDE Papers in Education* (University of Sheffield).

Nolan, P. (1989) 'walking on water? Performance and industrial relations under Thatcher'. *Industrial Relations Journal*, Vol. 20, No. 2, pp. 81–92.

Ouchi, W. G. (1981) *How American Business Can Meet the Japanese Challenge* (Reading, Mass.: Addison-Wesley).

Peston, M. (1985) 'Comments', in Worswick, E. D. N. (ed.), *Education and Economic Performance*. Joint studies in Public Policy 9, National Institute of Economic and Social Research/Policy Studies Institute/Royal Institute of International Affairs (Aldershot: Gower).

Polanyi, M. (1958) *Personal Knowledge* (Chicago: Chicago U.P.).

Poole, F. J. P. (1982) 'The ritual forging of identity: aspects of person and self in Bimin–Kuskusminmale initiation', in Herdt, G. H. and Keesing, R. M., *Rituals of Manhood. Male Initiation in Papua New Guinea*. (Berkeley: University of California).

Prais, S. J. (1981) 'Vocational qualifications of the labour force in Britain and Germany'. *National Institute Economic Review*, 98, pp. 47–59.

Prais, S. J. (1985) 'What can we learn from the German system of education and vocational training?', in Worswick, G. D. N. (ed.), *Education and Economic Performance*. Joint Studies in Public Policy 9. National Institute of Economic and Social Research/Policy Studies Institute/Royal Institute of International Affairs (Aldershot: Gower).

Prais, S. J. (1987) 'Education for productivity: comparisons of Japanese and English schooling and vocational preparation'. *National Institute Economic Review*, 119, pp. 40–56.

Prais, S. J. and Wagner, K. (1988) 'Productivity and management: the training of foremen in Britain and Germany'. *National Institute Economic Review*, 123, pp. 32–40, Feb.

Pressman, J. L. and Wildavsky, A. (1979) *Implementation* (Berkeley: University of California).

Raffe, D. (ed.) (1984) *Fourteen to Eighteen. The Changing Pattern of Schooling in Scotland* (Aberdeen: Aberdeen U.P.).

Raffe, D. (1988) 'Going with the grain: youth training in transition', in Brown, S. and Wake, R. (eds) *Education in Transition*, pp. 110–23 (Edinburgh: Scottish Council for Research in Education).

Raffe, D. (1989) 'Making the gift horse jump the hurdles: The impact of the TVEI Pilot on the first Scottish cohort'. *British Journal of Education and Work*, Vol. 3, No. 2, pp. 5–15.

Rappaport, R. A. (1968) *Pigs for Ancestors. Ritual in the Ecology of a New Guinea People* (New Haven: Yale U.P.).

Richards, A. I. (1957) *Chisungu: a Girls' Initiation Ceremony among the Bemba of Northern Rhodesia* (London: Faber & Faber).

Roderick, G. and Stephens, M. (1981) *Where Did We Go Wrong? Industrial*

Performance, Education and the Economy in Victorian Britain (Lewes: Falmer).

Sanderson, M. (1988) 'Technical education and economic decline: 1890–1980s'. *Oxford Review of Economic Policy*, Vol. 4, No. 1, pp. i–xxi.

Senker, P. (1986) 'The technical and vocational education initiative and economic performance in the United Kingdom: an initial assessment'. *Journal of Educational Policy*, Vol. 4, No. 1, pp. 293–303.

Smiles, S. (1986) *Self-help* (Harmondsworth: Penguin).

Stronach, I. *et al.* (1982) *Assessment in Youth Training: Made-to-measure?* (Glasgow: Scottish Vocational Preparation Unit, Jordanhill College).

Stronach, I. (1984) 'Work experience: the sacred anvil', in Vaughan, C., *Rethinking Transition: Educational Innovation and the Transition to Adult Life* (Lewes: Falmer).

Stronach, I. (1987) 'Ten years on'. *Forum*, Vol. 29, No. 3, pp. 64–66.

Stronach, I. (1988) *Parts One and Two of the Final Report of the Local Independent Evaluation of Norfolk TVEI* (University of East Anglia: CARE).

Stronach, I. (1989) 'A critique of the new assessment: from currency to carnival?', in Simon, H. and Elliott, J., *Rethinking Assessment and Appraisal* (Milton Keynes: Open University Press).

Taylor, R. (1987) 'The thick man of Europe'. *Observer*, 12.4.87.

Thorsrud, E. (1980) 'The changing structure of work organisation', in Kanawaty, G. (ed.), *Developing New Forms of Work Organisation* (Geneva: International Labour Organization).

Tichy, N. M. with Nisberg, J. N. (1980) 'Restructuring work', in Etzioni, A. and Lehman, E. W. (eds), *A Sociology Reader on Complex Organisations*, 3rd edn (New York: Holt, Rhinehart and Winston).

Turner, L. W. (1981) *The Drums of Affliction. A Study of Religious Process among the Ndembu of Zambia* (London: International African Institute/ Hutchinson).

Walton, G. (1977) 'Successful practices for diffusing work innovations'. *Journal of Contemporary Business*, 6, pp. 1–22.

Warner, M. (1984) *Organisations and Experiments. Designing New Ways of Managing Work* (Chichester: Wiley).

Weiner, M. J. (1981) *English Culture and the Decline of the Industrial Spirit 1850– 1980* (Cambridge: CUP).

Wellens, J. (1963) *The Training Revolution: from Shop-floor to Board-room* (London: Evans).

Whyte, W. F. (1987) 'From human relations to organizational behavior: reflections on the changing scene'. *Industrial and Labor Relations Review*, Vol. 4, No. 4, pp. 487–500.

Willis, P. (1977) *Learning to Labour: How Working Class Kids Get Working Class Jobs* (Farnborough: Saxon House).

Wirth, A. G. (1981) *Alternative Philosophies of Work: Implications for Vocational Educational Research and Development.* Occ. Paper no. 78, Nov. (NCRVE, Ohio State University).

Chapter 10

Corporate Hegemony or Pedagogic Liberation? The Schools–Industry Movement in England and Wales

I. Jamieson

■ Introduction

It has probably always been the case that employers operating in a market economy are dissatisfied in one way or another with the performance of their employees. The reasons for this go beyond the scope of this chapter, but are related to such factors as the difficulties in assessing the work capacity of individual workers at the time of selection (compared with the purchase of machinery), and the difficulties inherent in the employers' attempts to harness the talents and capacities of autonomous human beings for their own ends.

In seeking to account for the poor, or at least variable, performance of their workers, employers seek scapegoats. If we took the population of workers in general, then the list of potential scapegoats is very long. We would soon be into such popular territory as 'national culture' and other 'explanations' that have been made so popular by writers like Weiner (1981). If we narrowed our scope, however, and concentrated on young workers – first time entrants to employment – then the explanations become altogether firmer.

Source: Jamieson, I. (1985) 'Corporate hegemony or pedagogic liberation? The schools–industry movement in England and Wales', in Dale, R. (ed.), *Education, Training and Employment: Towards a new Vocationalism*, Pergamon, Oxford, in association with the Open University, pp. 23–38.

School-leavers are an important part of the labour force. Over 57 per cent of 1983/84 16-year-olds were available for work, some 1.6 million young people. For the majority of employers this is the largest group of employees that they take on in any one year. Not only are they the largest group of employees for many employers, but they traditionally make less 'good employees' than other groups. There are many reasons for this: their position in the life cycle gives them fewer responsibilities and cares compared with other workers; their set of 'working skills', both technical and social, tend to be less well developed than other employees; they are still at the stage of establishing some sort of 'fit' between their identity as individuals and the demands of particular occupations and/or employers. These factors, which have always been present, produce a characteristic pattern of young worker behaviour. This is marked by frequent job changes (unless prevented by very high unemployment rates), and by noticeably higher absenteeism, accident and lateness records. In short, such workers are, in employers' terms, less responsible than many other groups of employees.

Although we have argued that there are certain characteristic features of the work performance of young people that are endemic to this form of labour, employers are rarely either brought into contact with such arguments, or impressed with them when they do encounter them. Employers react in a number of different ways to the 'problem'. Some try to substitute other forms of labour which they believe to be more pliant and reliable, for example married women workers. When the labour market allows it, some employers expend more effort on the selection process in order to try to make sure that their employees are of better quality than those of their competitors.

One feature of the school-leaver labour market which many employers observe, and which appears to damage the analysis of the 'young worker syndrome' that we have outlined above, is the fact that the 'problem' seems to vary over time. Sometimes the cohort of school-leavers appears better adapted to the world of work than others. There are a number of quite straightforward explanations of this phenomenon. In the first place it is true that the quality of 16 year-olds available for work has declined over the recent past. This is because more and more able students have either stayed on at school, or have gone on to further or higher education. Employers who have stuck with recruiting this age group are thus recruiting from a significantly different range of ability. Our second explanation, by contrast, produces a rise in the quality of recruits. The slackening in the demand for all labour from the early 1970s has meant that the pool of workers from which employers can choose has grown. This has allowed employers to become more selective about their young recruits and to choose those who appear to have mastered certain basic skills, and who have an appropriate set of 'attitudes'.

■ Let's blame education

We have spent some time analysing the problems that employers have with young workers, because it is this phenomenon that is at the heart of the schools–industry movement. As we shall show, the movement that was reborn in the 1970s is composed of a wide variety of different groups, organized in different ways and with different goals and interests, but we must never forget that it is primarily driven by the recruitment problems of employers.

Of course employers recognize that their young worker problems are unlikely to be fundamental to the success of the business, although such 'soft' factors as the general attitude or culture of the work force might be (compare Peters and Waterman, 1982). Poor economic performance at either the level of the firm or the economy must entail a consideration of a wider set of factors. It is important to realize this fact because the schools–industry movement that arose from the ashes of previous similar movements must also be placed in the context of the wider debate about the performance of the British economy.

The British economy has been declining steadily since its heyday in the 1850s. At each new turn in the crisis the debate about the causes of the decline has intensified. The social fabric of the society has been earnestly scrutinized in an attempt to see which elements of it were not congruent with the needs of the economy. The fortunes of education have varied. In the late 1950s and 1960s there was a view that 'in a modern economy the quality and efficiency of the working population very largely depend on the educational system' (Floud, 1961). The restructuring of schools along comprehensive lines was begun, at least partly, because it was believed that such a system would make better use of the 'pool of ability', and thus ultimately benefit the economy.

In the 1970s the faith in education as a contributor to economic well-being quickly ebbed away. The oil crisis of 1973/74 helped to usher in a new economic analysis that saw education, alongside other state services, as part of a policy of social engineering that was syphoning off wealth from the economic heart of the society. It was at this time that the macroeconomic analysis of economists and politicians of the political right was brought together with the microanalysis of employers. Together they erected the ideological stage on which that great show, the Great Debate, could be performed.

The employers focused on their problems with young employees. Although several social institutions were implicated in the problem, for example family life and the mass media, it was the schools that were directly in the firing line. After all, weren't the schools directly responsible for the fact that 'children these days couldn't add up and spell?' and weren't employers justified in expecting the schools to educate for employment? – after all, they were paying for them via taxation and rates. These local cries of anguish contributed significantly to the growing mood of disillusionment with education. The Black Papers[1] had attempted to give a veneer of respectability to the view that standards were falling. Some economists argued that education was assisting in the shift of resources away from the wealth-creating private manufacturing sector towards the non-productive sector (Bacon and Eltis, 1976). This was happening both because of the enormous cost of the education system, and because teachers were not encouraging able young people to go into industry as a career, particularly manufacturing industry. All this presaged a scrutiny of the great secret garden of education – the curriculum.

■ The Great Debate

The Great Debate – a public dialogue about the system of education in England and Wales – was formally opened by the then Prime Minister, James Callaghan, at a speech at Ruskin College, Oxford in 1976. One of the major themes of the speech, and of the series of regional conferences that were subsequently held, was the lack of relationship between industry and education. It should be clear from the foregoing analysis that the Ruskin speech did not conjure up the schools–industry debate out of thin air; rather it gave a focus and added legitimacy to many existing complaints about the education system.

The charges that Callaghan levelled against the education system were ones with which many people, both inside and outside education, had some sympathy. Indeed several organizations and projects had been launched before the Ruskin speech in order to try and remedy some of the alleged deficiencies. These included the Schools Council Industry Project – a tripartite CBI/TUC/Schools Council venture; Understanding British Industry – a CBI initiative; Project Trident – an organization dedicated to widening the experiences of young people, especially in the work area; the Standing Conference on School Science and Technology, and many more. The Great Debate was not a tightly focused challenge to the education system; it contained a myriad of elements. It could be described in much the same way as political journalists are apt to describe Chancellors' budgets – there was something in it for everybody.

■ The schools–industry movement in the 1980s

It is difficult to describe the schools–industry movement. There are two major difficulties. First, it doesn't stand still. The number of groups, organizations and government agencies constantly grows. Secondly, it has no one focus of attention, save that it wants to change the education system in one way or another. The agenda of the movement changes with the vicissitudes of the economy, and as emphasis and money are placed on different facets. Like many other movements dependent on financial donations from government and industry, it is subject to fashion and political whim. In summary, the movement can be described as a diverse collection of employer and trade union groupings; specially constructed educational or quasi-educational 'projects'; government agencies and government statements and exhortations – all designed to put pressure on the education system to change the content of what is taught, how it is taught, and how it is assessed and examined. Its focus is largely on secondary education, and within that primarily on the 14–19 age group.

■ Skills, attitudes and knowledge

Although the schools–industry movement is difficult to describe, it is possible to provide a crude analytical map of some of its major interests by delineating some of the skills, attitudes and knowledge that it tries to promote inside the school system.

Of the three elements, the skills component is the most difficult to describe. This is because many of the things described as skills by the schools–industry lobby are not skills at all, but either attitudes or knowledge. The second difficulty is that it is in this area that the greatest shifts of emphasis have taken place.

In the beginning there were 'basic skills'. Basic skills meant literacy (later extended to communication skills) and numeracy. The main protagonists of basic skills were local employers who claimed in the mid 1970s that their school-leaver recruits couldn't add up or spell. This lobby received powerful support from the Black Paper movement.

Numeracy and literacy weren't the only problems of employers. Their complaints were soon extended to encompass the 'fact' that school-leavers were poor at being interviewed; listening to and following instructions; social and interpersonal skills at the workplace – in short, a wide range of skills which it was alleged every competent adult needed at the workplace. This rather heterogeneous collection of skills soon came to be dubbed 'social and life skills'.

The other strand of the skills component is more difficult to grasp. Its roots lie in the relatively low status accorded to the 'practical' professions in England and Wales – particularly engineering. When this is extended to schools, it becomes a concern that teachers unconsciously, or sometimes even consciously, dissuade young people from considering careers in technological occupations. The scope for studying technological subjects at school, particularly for girls, is generally assessed as poor. One outcome of this state of affairs is a shortage of technicians and technologists, particularly in the electronics field, one of the few industrial sectors to hold up during the economic depression. Employers have seized on this shortage as yet more evidence of the shortcomings of the education system.

Yet the malaise is thought to be wider than mere technological inadequacy in the schools. It is that our schools are not producing young people who are 'practically capable' in the modern world. Significantly, it is argued, we even have difficulty in expressing the deficiency, and adherents of this view fall back on the French word *métier* or the German *technik*. In England it finds its expression in the Education for Capability movement. This alliance of educationalists and industrialists wishes to make 'knowing how' at least as important as 'knowing that' in the school system.

If skills are not the traditional fare of the school curriculum, then attitudes have an even less legitimate place, at least in the formal curriculum. Of course most teachers are aware that schools are one institutional part of the process of attitude formation among young people, but they are apt to shift the blame for dysfunctional attitudes on to those other powerful socializing agencies, the family and the mass media.

In many ways the 'attitude problem' is regarded by many members of the schools–industry movement as the key problem. This is certainly true for the employer community. At the end of the day most employers believe that they can remedy deficiencies in basic skills among their new recruits, and they can train youngsters in technical skills. These are only issues for employers because they believe that the schools should be doing a better job in these two respects. The attitude of young people towards work, employment, the reward structure of industry – even the system of private enterprise itself – gives them much more cause for concern.

Attitude change is a sensitive issue for most teachers. Whereas the inculcation of knowledge or skills is regarded as legitimate, attitudes lie in a dangerous border region. Over that border lies the infamous land of propaganda. Is this the reason why much of the concern about the attitudes of young people towards work is obfuscated by referring to them as skills? A cynic might indeed be tempted to conclude that the emphasis on social and life skills is no more than a modern version of the nineteenth-century worry about the attitudes of the labouring classes, and might be confirmed in this view on discovering that in practice the only young people who receive such training are those destined for working class jobs, or unemployment (Atkinson *et al.*, 1982).

The traditional curriculum arena for schools in England and Wales is not skills or attitudes, it is knowledge. While it is generally accepted that there is a distinction between knowledge and skills (between knowing that, and knowing how – although the distinction is not nearly so clear cut as most imagine), many in the schools–industry field have a naive view about the relationship between knowledge and attitudes. At its most simplistic, it is the view that if only the children knew and understood some basic facts about the industrial world then their attitudes would change. Such a view is held as strongly in the trade union movement, which is worried about young people's attitude towards the trade unions as well as their reluctance to join, as it is among employers, who are worried about their view of industrial careers, and of the nature of industrial and commercial life. Both groups have good cause for concern (Jamieson and Lightfoot, 1982).

The knowledge strand of the schools–industry movement takes many forms. Curiously, it informs much of the experience-based learning that is characteristic of schools–industry work, that is, the practice that places many young people in real or realistic work situations. Such a practice emanates from the belief, in both industry and the trade unions, not only that they are misunderstood by school students, but that if those students came into greater contact with 'real' industrialists and trade unionists, then they would form a more favourable view. Such a position is perfectly legitimate if somewhat optimistic (compare Jamieson and Lightfoot, 1982).

A more traditional view is that much of the problem stems from a fundamental misunderstanding of some basic facts of economic life. This line was perhaps most clearly articulated by Sir Keith Joseph, the former Secretary of State for Education, who in a written parliamentary answer, subsequently sent to all Chief Education Officers in England and Wales, declared that:

> Schools and businesses need to understand each other better. Business should be helped to appreciate the aims of the schools and the context in which these seek to achieve them. Conversely, schools and pupils need to be helped to understand how the nation earns its living in the world. This involves helping pupils to understand how industry and commerce are organized; the relationship of producers and consumers; the process of wealth creation; the role played by choice, competition and profit; and the traditional liberal view of the interdependence of political and economic freedom, as well as rival theories of how production and distribution should be organized and the moral basis commonly adduced by those theories (Joseph, 1982).

Thus, if pupils understand the process of wealth creation then it is believed that more would be attracted to careers in industry and commerce, particularly the more able, and would be better motivated to work.

■ The analysis of change

The analysis that we have offered of the schools–industry movement, describing it by reference to the skills, attitudes and knowledge which it wishes to promote in schools, shows something of the diversity of the movement. That diversity is also a function of the large number of different organizations and pressure groups trying to bring about change in the school system.

The process of educational change in England and Wales is often a great puzzle to foreign observers. The problem is that while we have a national system of education it is organized locally, and the Local Education Authorities and their schools have enormous discretion. Indeed, in terms of the curriculum, the discretion is almost total. The most important consequence of the devolved system of organization is that for change to take place it becomes necessary to convince education authorities and the schools of the need for change. It is also necessary to point out that there is no mechanism which automatically adjusts the education system to the 'needs of the economy' or to the needs of employers, even supposing it was clear what the needs of the economy were, or that employers spoke clearly and with one voice about their own requirements.

To describe the agencies of change operating in the schools–industry field is then to describe the organization of pressure on schools exerted by outside organizations. We can identify three main areas of pressure on the schools. The first comes from central government; the second from local employers; the third from *ad hoc* projects and organizations specifically designed to change some elements of schooling.

The main arm of central government that deals with the school system is the Department of Education and Science. The DES has issued a stream of documents urging LEAs and their schools to draw closer to industry and to make their curricula more relevant to the needs of industry and commerce. The Department was responsible for the Education (Work Experience) Act, 1973. This important piece of enabling legislation opened the doors to work experience for school pupils, a central schools–industry activity. The Inspectorate (HMI) have also devoted considerable time and energy to schools–industry matters. They have offered specific advice to schools within their general curriculum documents, and they have published case studies of practice (HMI, 1981). The HMI have also urged teacher-training establishments to include 'preparation for working life' in their pre-service courses (HMI, 1982).

The DES and Her Majesty's Inspectors of Schools have not however, been the most influential arm of government in schools–industry matters. This is because their stock in trade is advice and exhortation, a commodity in considerable oversupply in the schools system. By contrast, money is a commodity that is conspicuously short in the system and it is by their control of such a resource that two other arms of government, the Department of Trade and Industry (DTI) and the Manpower Services Commission (MSC), have become important agencies for change. The DTI has from its budget of £2 million per year (excluding the micro-electronics programme) financed important developments in school science and technology, but most significantly has helped LEAs set up local change agents – the network of Schools–Industry Liaison Officers (SILOS). The MSC launched a five-year major curriculum programme in 1983, the Technical and Vocational Education Initiative (TVEI), at an annual cost of over £25 million. The SILO programme is discussed in more detail later in this chapter [. . .].

The second source of pressure on schools is employers. In terms of their importance for schools, it is *local* employers that are significant. They are significant in two ways. First, they can exert pressure on the schools just because they are local. As businessmen or councillors they may sit on the governing body of schools; as parents they can exert pressure through the PTA or other similar bodies. As significant members of the local community they have access to the local media – in the middle 1970s many local papers carried employer broadsides against schools for not achieving basic levels of competence among their pupils. The second source of local business influence resides in their role as local employers of labour. Most young people who leave school at 16 and get a job find employment locally. Local employers are thus the direct recipients of the schools' output. Discrimination against the products of one school, or public denunciation of a particular school's ability in a certain curriculum area, can therefore be particularly powerful.

Also on the local stage are employer groupings like local chambers of commerce, or organizations like Rotary which are largely composed of business people. These often act as facilitating agencies when schools wish to arrange something which involves employers, but they rarely act as pressure groups.

One or two organizations and some very large companies are active on the national stage. Firms like BP, Unilever, and ICI; organizations like the CBI and TUC; the Bank Information Service, the Engineering Industry Training Board and several others, are prominent at this level. These organizations play several important roles in schools–industry work. In the first place they provide individuals to sit on the wide range of committees, project-steering groups, and advisory panels that preside over various schools–industry activities. Secondly, they try to energize their local 'branches' to participate actively in local schools–industry matters. Finally, the commercial organizations channel significant funds into the schools–industry movement, largely but not solely, through the established schools–industry projects like Trident, Understanding British Industry, Understanding Industry and, to a lesser extent, the Schools Council Industry Project.

The last source of pressure on the schools comes from a curiously British educational phenomenon – the project. Because each school is more or less allowed to decide its own curriculum, then curriculum change comes about by what often amounts to a sales campaign mounted by various agencies.

Schools–industry work in England and Wales is marked by the existence of a large number of national and local projects all trying to persuade schools to change some existing practice, or adopt a new programme. The unpublished Cooper Report commissioned by the DES to chart the area found fourteen major projects working in the nation's schools, and innumerable local endeavours. These national projects were spending £2.9 million annually (1981 prices).

The majority of these projects are single-purpose projects, in business to try to persuade schools to adopt one particular educational programme or idea. Some of the best known projects include Project Trident, whose major activity is to organize work experience for pupils; Young Enterprise, which arranges for students to set up their own business enterprises; Understanding Industry, which arranges for industrialists to give talks to schoolchildren. There are two large multi-purpose organizations whose remit is much wider. Understanding British Industry (UBI) is a CBI project whose activities include in-service training for teachers and general help and advice for LEAs. The largest organization is the School Curriculum Industry Project, formerly the Schools Council Industry Project (SCIP). An LEA has formally to join this organization, whose aim is to promote curriculum development in the schools–industry field. Over half of the LEAs in England and Wales belong to SCIP. It is distinctive in at least two respects: (1) it is the only organization whose money comes out of public funds, all the rest competing for funds from private industry; (2) it is the only organization formally supported by the TUC, and as such is the major vehicle for trade union involvement in the schools–industry field.

■ The environment of change

The schools–industry movement does not operate in a social, economic and political vacuum. Effectively there are two environments, one at the national level, the other at the local authority level. All the leading projects, the government agencies, the TUC and CBI, and the major firms are influenced by the 'national environment'. Discussions at this level concern themselves with both economic and educational questions. Thus Britain's GNP and the balance of payments problem join with youth unemployment and national systems of examining and profiling as areas of study and concern. The national environment is considerably influenced by the attitude of central government and some of the larger firms, simply because they provide the major financial backing for the schools–industry movement. Two examples illustrate the pattern of influence. In the late 1970s the schools–industry movement was dominated by central government's view that Britain's survival as a nation depended on the success of her traditional manufacturing sector. Industry meant manufacturing industry. During this period projects which did not share this view, and companies and organizations operating outside of this sector, took a low profile. As the government view has mellowed, the banks, building societies, and the whole of the service sector of the economy have risen to take on a key role in the movement. In a slightly similar fashion we can chart the growth in the importance of the small business sector. The rise in the esteem of this sector has led the schools–industry movement to embrace 'enterprise' as a key theme in its work. It has been estimated that almost one-fifth of all secondary schools now run business enterprises for some of their pupils (Jamieson, 1984).

The local environment for schools–industry work is naturally much more varied. The worries of Whitehall, or the CBI or even the TUC, do not necessarily intrude on life in schools. The startling fact that Britain is now running a deficit on its balance of trade in manufactured goods for the first time in its history, for example, does not impinge on the organization and curriculum of schools, save in those exceptional cases where the head teacher interprets this fact as having implications for the school.

What matters much more than national politics and economics is the local environment of the school. As we have argued, the local economic community can bring pressure to bear on schools through its influence on local councils and governing bodies, and through its control of employment opportunities. Surveying variations in schools–industry work in the nation's schools, it is certainly possible to make a case which suggests that both its amount and type are influenced by the socio-economic characteristics of the local area.

The urban north, for example, displays the greatest amount of schools–industry activity. The traditional industrial communities (places like Barnsley and Wakefield) have a sense of community and of ownership of their schools. Industrial capital *and* labour are strong local forces in these areas, and this is reflected in both business and the trade unions being prominent in the work. The suburban ring round the big cities, for example the outer London boroughs, also see schools–industry work flourishing. The sense of community is not as strong, but there is a lot of industrial and commercial activity in these areas on which the schools can draw. The amount of trade union involvement tends to reflect the political character of the area. In the inner city most people report that schools–industry work has an uphill task. There is precious little industry and commerce in much of the inner city, and the decay and disorganization of many of these areas present schools with many problems which are judged to be more important than drawing schools closer toward the industrial community. Although schools–industry work is bipartisan in political terms, it is true that Labour councillors do tend to be less committed – quite rightly they see the trade unions as poor relations to business in the majority of schools–industry activities. The Shire counties occupy a midpoint between the inner cities and the urban north in the schools–industry world. Town schools naturally find a greater range of opportunities than their more isolated rural counterparts. Although rural schools are surrounded by what is claimed to be Britain's most efficient industry, agriculture, it is interesting that schools–industry work has almost completely neglected this sector.

■ Unemployment

No description of the environment of schools would be complete without a recognition of the importance of the employment environment. The relationship between high levels of youth unemployment and the schools–industry movement is a complex one. Many commentators are surprised that the movement has not withered away with the collapse of large sections of Britain's manufacturing industry, and with it the job market for school-leavers. The impact of youth unemployment is marked by substantial local variations, and the position is masked by the variety and scope of the schemes designed to train or retrain prospective young workers. The effect of this, plus the widely reported reaction of teachers and students that 'unemployment is something that happens to somebody else', is to dilute the potential effect of unemployment on the schools. Many schools, even in areas of substantial youth unemployment, still cling to the traditional school-to-work scenario, and are happy to use the schools–industry organizations and projects to help their students become more competitive in job seeking.

We must also realize that the schools–industry movement as we have described it is a diverse movement. Not every group or organization working within its framework has been concerned with preparing young people for work. For example, those organizations who see their task in terms of explaining certain industrial and economic 'facts of life' to young people have been spurred on by unemployment. Such topics clearly need a lot of 'explaining' to young people. Furthermore, the organizations have, in general, adapted to the changing educational and economic scenario. Many of those who found themselves unhappily aboard the 'transition from school to working life' ship, have jumped ships and are now happily aboard the 'transition from school to adult life' boat, having made the happy 'discovery' that the qualities necessary for a well-adjusted adult life are more or less the same as those required in working life. A remarkable piece of seamanship by any standards.

■ Environment management – the role of the schools–industry liaison officer

We have argued that in order to understand the schools–industry movement it is necessary to understand the heterogeneous nature of the

various organizations which make up its 'membership', and the environments in which it operates. Our model is one of a variety of salesmen and
persuaders trying to influence the schools. The schools 'buy' both what
they feel they cannot avoid, and those 'goods' which they feel will be
attractive and useful for their pupils.

One of the most significant developments in this model, and hence
in the schools–industry movement, has been the rise of an intermediary
between the schools and the environment. The schools–industry liaison
officer (SILO), nearly always an employee of the Local Education
Authority, acts as a broker, adviser and facilitator, both to the schools and
the schools–industry organizations. The rise of the SILO has been
dramatic. The first recorded post was in 1966 (Wood, 1983); by 1985 three-
quarters of all LEAs had one. Their rise was fostered by the two big
national projects, SCIP and UBI (over three-quarters of all the SILOs
belong to the SCIP organization); by advice from the DES which
recommended, 'that wherever practicable, one member of the CEO's staff
should be given full-time responsibility for the promotion of schools–
industry links' (DES, 1983); and finally, and most significantly, by funding
from the Industry/Education Unit of the Department of Trade and
Industry.

The schools–industry liaison officers are nearly all ex- or seconded
teachers. This gives a strong clue to their major brief, which is to foster
curriculum change in schools (or at least facilitate such change), so that the
curriculum is more relevant to the needs of the pupils *and* the economy.
Such a statement is fraught with difficulties and open to a large number of
different interpretations. Different SILOs interpret their brief in very
different ways. They are influenced by the policies of the LEA; the type
and amount of local industry; the strength of the local trade union
movement; the desires and interests of the local schools; and, not least,
their affiliations to the various schools–industry organizations, particularly
SCIP. Perhaps the most significant feature of the SILOs is that they are
gradually dispensing with the services of the various national projects and
running activities themselves. This is especially notable in the areas of
work experience and the so-called mini-enterprises.

■ Corporate hegemony?

One of the great fears that teachers have about schools drawing closer to
the industrial world is that the curriculum, and maybe even the ethos and
organization of schools, will come to be dominated by business interests.

Most teachers are surprised to learn that there are those who believe that business, or more properly the system of private enterprise, already dominates the education system (Bowles and Gintis, 1976).

Whether one believes these fears to be justified or not depends a great deal on the perspective adopted. At the level of the system it is possible to make a case, although rather a weak one in our view, to suggest that employers find the organization, curriculum and assessment system of schooling useful for their purposes. This is not of course to say either that education consciously organizes it in this way, or that employers are satisfied with the 'goodness of fit' between the two systems.

It is also possible to assemble some evidence to suggest that in the last few years many schools have moved closer to satisfying the needs of employers. Much of the evidence for this statement has been contained in the previous part of this chapter. It could be argued that the pressure exerted by the schools–industry movement, particularly perhaps the adoption by so many LEAs of schools–industry liaison officers, is evidence enough of the system's desires to appease industrial criticism. In addition we might also note the rapid growth of prevocational and vocational courses in the schools, many of which require activities like work experience, and strongly recommend cooperation with local employers. Interestingly, many of these new courses are run and assessed not by the traditional university-dominated examining boards, but by bodies like the RSA, the City and Guilds, and the Business and Technician Education Council (BTEC), which pride themselves on the fact that they are dominated by industrial and business interests. There have also been developments in pupil assessment which could be interpreted as in the interests of the business community. It is argued, for example, that criterion referencing rather than norm referencing will be much more helpful for industrial selectors. Pupil profiling, when it becomes a national system, might well help employers to make ever finer selections among prospective employees.

Despite this evidence, the view that the schools–industry movement represents some form of corporate hegemony is unconvincing, not least because it has not managed to make substantial changes in most secondary schools. The reason for this is that schools are relatively autonomous institutions, well used to resisting pressure from a wide variety of outside groupings. 'Academic freedom' and 'professional autonomy' have until now proved to be reasonably effective slogans with which to combat the demands of 'industrial relevance'.

A detailed observation of what happens 'on the ground' in schools–industry affairs is instructive. In the first place the employers are often divided among themselves: at the tactical level the needs and interests of different industrial sectors are not the same; big business is interested in a different range of problems from small business; banking has different interests from manufacturing industry, etc. We must also not forget the role of trade unions; although they are often poor relations, in practice they do offer some sort of check on the dominance of capital.

When the industrial world meets the schools it is argued that it often has divisions within its own ranks. We must also remember that the debate nearly always takes place on education's territory. The agenda is, 'How should the schools change?' Education displays all the normal advantages of 'home teams' by having a vastly superior knowledge of its own territory.

The result of all these 'disadvantages' is that very often employers become 'incorporated' into the educational world. We have described elsewhere the characteristic stages of schools–industry work (Jamieson and Lightfoot, 1982), whereby the suspicions and criticisms of employers are gradually transformed into qualified support for the system. This happens at all levels of schools–industry work: an interesting example is how the education/industry officers of some of the major companies, themselves usually ex-teachers, gradually become incorporated into the stage army of education. Many of them end up as apologists for the schools to their industrial and commercial colleagues.

■   Pedagogic liberation?

It is one thing to cast doubt on the corporate hegemony thesis in schools–industry work, but quite another to claim that it is a potential source of pedagogic liberation. And yet this thesis looks at least as convincing as its corporate counterpart. The radical case rests on the following arguments. First, that the schools–industry movement underlines the important pedagogic fact that learning can and does take place outside of schools. After all, it was the deschooler Illich who proclaimed that: 'Access to reality constitutes a fundamental alternative in education to a system which only purports to teach *about* it' (Illich, 1973).

As part of its attempt to break down barriers between school and the outside world, the schools–industry advocates encourage schools to involve industrialists and trade unionists in the educational process. These 'adults other than teachers', as they are usually called, are rarely used in didactic teaching situations, at which they are often unskilled. Instead they are used in learning situations which make good use of their experience, and which place pupils in an active learning mode. Examples of this experiential learning include role plays, games and simulations, as well as work experience.

One of the effects of the schools–industry movement then is to crack the edifice of didacticism in some schools. Another challenge is presented to an even more secure construction – the organization of learning within traditional academic subjects. Here radical teachers join with industrialists in claiming that 'real world' problems do not fall neatly into academic subject divisions. Some unlikely schools–industry activities have been heralded by radical teachers as 'breakthroughs'. While school–business enterprises can be used by Young Enterprise to give 'young people from all walks of life an idea of how business is organised and run in the Free World' (Bray, 1983), they can equally be used to give young people an opportunity to cooperate with each other, and to work things out for themselves without being constantly dominated by teachers (Jamieson, 1984).

Finally, we should note that even in the area of assessment, radical teachers can embrace many of the changes which are supported by industry. Pupil profiling is a good example. The industrialists believe that with more information about the young person, especially her skills and attitudes, the selection process will be eased. Many teachers welcome profiles because they see a chance of breaking out of the present system of 'graduated failure'. In a profile, pupils will be able to record their *achievements*, both in and out of school.

■ Conclusion

We have argued that, despite the pressure exerted by the schools–industry movement on the schools, there has not been a radical move toward the 'industrial curriculum' in most secondary schools. We have explained this in terms of the power of the system to resist change, and its 'incorporation' of many industrial interests.

Before the advent of the TVEI initiative (the manner of whose introduction indicates that the government has learned a lot about changing the system) the schools–industry movement bore all the marks of what we might describe as the English model of curriculum change. Change depended on the ability of government and exemplars produced by various projects to convince educational professionals that change was necessary. Certainly there was more pressure, more projects, and certainly more money in this curriculum initiative than in most others. There was also evidence that, *compared with other curriculum movements*, the schools–industry initiative was pretty successful. It must be stressed that such success was not purely a function of a good sales campaign, but was also because many schools did genuinely want to make their curriculum more vocationally oriented, closer to the industrial world, more experience based – in short, what many of the schools and the schools–industry practitioners would describe as more 'relevant' to the modern world. In the schools–industry case, demand has been at least as important as supply.

The success of the schools–industry movement has clearly not been sufficient for the government. The Technical and Vocational Education Initiative represents an altogether different approach to changing the curriculum. And however it is sold to the LEAs and the schools (there has been no shortage of takers), it looks to many like the first step on the road to government control of the curriculum. If this does turn out to be the case, it will not surprise many people that the dam was breached by a programme which wished to draw the schools nearer to the world of industry.

Note

1.   The Black Papers were five papers published between 1969 and 1977 that attacked aspects of what they called 'progressive' or 'socially motivated' developments in the educational system (see Cox and Dyson, 1969).

References

Atkinson, P., Rees, T. L., Shone, D. and Williamson, H. (1982) 'Social and life skills: the case of compensatory education', in Rees, T. L. and Atkinson, P. (eds), *Youth Unemployment and State Intervention* (London: Routledge & Kegan Paul).

Bacon, R. and Eltis, W. (1976) *Britain's Economic Problem: Too Few Producers* (London: Macmillan).

Bowles, S. and Gintis, H. (1976) *Schooling in Capitalist America* (London: Routledge & Kegan Paul).

Bray, E. (1983) 'Mini-Co's in schools', in Watts, A. G. (ed.), *Work Experience in Schools* (London: Heinemann).

Cox, C. B. and Dyson, A. E. (eds) (1969) *A Black Paper* (London: The Critical Quarterly Society).

DES (Department of Education and Science) (1983) Schools/industry liaison, letter to Chief Education Officers, SS/5/19/0127D (London: DES).

Floud, J. (1961) 'Social class factors in educational achievement', in Halsey, A. H. (ed.), *Ability and Educational Opportunity* (Paris: OECD).

HM Inspectors of Schools (1981) *Schools and Working Life* (London: DES).

HM Inspectors of Schools (1982) *Teacher Training and Preparation for Working Life* (London: DES).

Illich, I. (1973) 'The deschooled society', in Buckman, P. (ed.), *Education without Schools* (London: Souvenir Press).

Jamieson, I. M. (1984) 'Schools and enterprise', in Watts, A. G. and Moran, P. (eds), *Education for Enterprise* (Cambridge: CRAC).

Jamieson, I. M. and Lightfoot, M. (1982) *Schools and Industry* (London: Methuen).

Joseph, Sir Keith (1983) Written parliamentary answer, 29 July 1982, contained in DES Circular letter SS 5/19/0127D, 15 March.

Peters, T. J. and Waterman, R. H. Jr (1982) *In Search of Excellence: Lessons from America's Best Run Companies* (New York: Harper and Row).

Weiner, M. (1981) *English Culture and the Decline of Industrial Spirit* (Cambridge: Cambridge University Press).

Wood, B. (1983) 'Schools Industry Liaison: The Development of Policy and the Role of the Schools Industry Officer', Unpublished M.Ed. Thesis, Worcester College of Higher Education.

Chapter 11

The Curriculum and the New Vocationalism

R. Pring

■ Ten years on

It was ten years ago that the then Prime Minister, James Callaghan, made his speech at Ruskin College, Oxford, chiding the educational system for its irrelevance to working life. Of course, that speech was the culmination of several years of criticism of schools and colleges for their apparent failure to serve society and the economy in the way that they should. People, particularly employers, were concerned about standards, about attitudes to industry, about the values being (or not being) promoted, about lack of basic skills. Much of this criticism was ill-founded, and was indeed shortly to be contradicted by the evidence of the most thorough educational surveys that this country had ever seen, those undertaken by the Assessment of Performance Unit and by Her Majesty's Inspectorate. Nonetheless, people, even intelligent people who should know better, are not on the whole affected by evidence or argument, for criticisms of education often stem from anxieties that have little to do with standards, as they are *currently* measured. Worries expressed are usually about more fundamental matters, although they may not be recognized as such: about the values that underpin education and about the relevance of the curriculum to what others (parents, employers, politicians) see to be a main purpose of schooling. It was as though teachers and educational administrators had been given too much autonomy to pursue goals and to promote values within a major public service which paid little regard to the public it was meant to serve. The source of those anxieties were captured in

Source: Pring, R. (1989) 'The curriculum and the new vocationalism', *British Journal of Education and Work*, Vol. 1, No. 3, pp. 133–148. Copyright © Trentham Books Ltd.

the Prime Minister's address, which questioned some of the most cherished assumptions of educational practice. And indeed one can understand many of the changes that have subsequently taken place as a footnote to that speech.

'Preparing future generations for life' was the explicit theme of Mr Callaghan's address. There was nothing profound in what was said (and indeed it would not today seem particularly exceptional) but it did ten years ago pose a challenge to those who would wish, under the banner of liberal education, to disconnect education from economic or industrial needs. To such people, education was of intrinsic worth whose aims derived, not from an analysis of adult needs or of work-related skills, but from the academic traditions through which children were put in touch with the 'very best that has been thought and said'. It was that assumption that the Prime Minister challenged.

Four reasons behind Mr Callaghan's emphasis upon the need to prepare future generations for life were: first, 'new recruits from the schools sometimes do not have the basic tools to do the job that is required'; secondly, there is an anti-industrial spirit especially among the most able; thirdly, students were ill-equipped technologically in a society dominated by new technologies; and, fourthly, students were not developing those qualities that equip them for making a living. Hence, when he said:

> '... the goals of our education ... are clear enough – they are to equip children to the best of their ability for a lively, constructive place in society and also to fit them to do a job of work' (Callaghan, 1976).

he seemed to have in mind the following:

(1) skills or knowledge that industry needs (for example, the practical grasp of mathematical concepts or manipulative skills, or the ability to estimate measurements of various kinds);

(2) the industrial spirit which, in the Victorian era, had enabled Britain to lead the world in technology, commerce, and industry, but which subsequently had been in decline;

(3) technological understanding;

(4) personal qualities such as initiative, cooperativeness, flexibility, sense of responsibility.

Admittedly, such a list of desirable educational changes was rather general. There was scope, as we shall see, for a range of interpretations. Nonetheless, it set the tone for the debate in which the curriculum, so it was claimed, should become more relevant and indeed more vocational. Looking back upon this period one high ranking Treasury official felt able to say:

We took a strong view that education could play a much better role in improving industrial performance. The service is inefficient, rather un-productive and does not concentrate scarce resources in the areas that matter most. The economic climate and imperatives are clear; the task is to adjust education to them (quoted in Ranson, 1984, p. 223).

But how exactly education was to adjust to the economic climate and imperatives became, quite understandably, a matter of debate. Different interests were involved – teachers of subjects that might thereby be threatened, Examination Boards that defined standards in quite different terms, employers who hoped to get better prepared employees for industry's needs (if only these could be identified), politicians and administrators who tried to predict long-term manpower surpluses or shortages. Translating the aspirations of the Prime Minister ten years ago into organizational and curriculum terms could not be other than a highly charged, indeed political, matter. For much was at stake – the very values and aims of education itself, the definition of standards by which performance is to be judged (and in which so many vested interests lie); the most effective and fruitful ways in which pupils can be motivated to learn; the kind of person that should be shaped for society *or* indeed the kind of society that should be shaped by the young persons, empowered by a reformed curriculum.

These are the profound educational questions that are currently being addressed and that are reflected in the organizational upheaval, the fudged boundaries between training and education, the uneasy alliances between Government departments and between Government and Local Authorities, the changing responsibilities in the rapidly changing examina-tion structure, the radical shifts in curriculum content and processes.

■ Context

The social and economic background to this growing disenchantment with the education service, and to the demand for it to become more closely related to adult and industrial needs, might be summarized as follows:

☐ Qualified workforce

Despite unemployment, there are evidently vacancies in key industrial areas, because of lack of suitably qualified applicants. A recent report from the Department of Trade and Industry to the European Commission shows, region after region, a shortage of qualified people. In some instances that shortage arises from under-investment in apprenticeships; in others; as in the South West, from a lack of those personal skills and qualities necessary for a thriving tourist industry. The point is that the industrial base of our society is changing, and there is a need for a much more sophisticated and highly trained workforce. In the last five years, one million unskilled jobs have been lost from the economy. In the next ten years it is predicted that a further million will go. Traditional craft-based industries – for example, the small cutlery firms that contributed so much to the wealth of Sheffield – have largely been replaced by technician-based industries requiring fewer people to operate them – and, then, only those who have reached a higher standard of education and training. The decline in manufacturing industry is mainly offset by the growth of service industries (retailing, selling, banking, etc.) which require different personal qualities and know-how. The kind of employment, therefore, that will be available is very different from that which young people have traditionally entered – making different demands on qualities and skills, and attitudes required in the preparation for work.

☐   Attitudes to industry

There are two aspects to this dearth of suitably qualified personnel. First, potential employees do not have the appropriate skills or knowledge. Secondly, however, irrespective of whether or not they have those skills or knowledge, they may lack the appropriate attitude. Indeed, the two may well be related. People may lack the appropriate skills because their attitude to industry is such that they do not seek to be qualified in that way. According to a recent UCCA report on University applications, there were 5000 applications for medicine, 4000 for law, but only 800 for engineering.

The anti-industrial attitude has been well charted by Martin Weiner in his book *English Culture and the Decline of the Industrial Spirit* (Weiner, 1981) and by Correlli Barnett in *The Audit of War* (Barnett, 1986). Both point to the deeply rooted cultural weakness behind Britain's industrial and economic decline – a weakness embodied in the nineteenth century public school and Oxbridge disdain for industry and commerce. A gulf was established between an educated elite and the practical man of business or of invention. This disdain for the practical, for the entre- preneural spirit, for invention and indeed for science, became, too, the model of the grammar schools when introduced into the public system of education by the 1902 Education Act – and from which very few recovered. This anti-industrial spirit has been summed up by Lord Annan as follows:

> ... one common assumption shared by most Englishmen of letters in this century was 'that the career of money-making, industry, business, profits, or efficiency is a despicable life, in which no sane and enlightened person should be engaged; and that indeed such people are unworthy of a novelist's

attention'. But this assumption went across the whole spectrum of opinion-makers, where the life of industry and business was denigrated [quoted in Weiner (1981), p. 131].

☐   **Unemployment or intermittent employment**

The rapid decline of certain industries, the changing pattern of employment and its regional variation, the increased mobility that is expected of people in work, and the widespread unemployment are further factors that affect the relevance of school to subsequent opportunities and to the quality of life. There are not the secure and traditional routes into jobs that their parents had. Unemployment in Britain is (1986) somewhere between three and four million. Regionally there are enormous variations. For example within the catchment area of one large community school in an inner city, unemployment among school leavers is 85 per cent. Among the working population as a whole in that area it is 80 per cent. In parts of Liverpool, hardly anyone under the age of 25 has experienced regular employment. These admittedly are the extremes, but there are several extreme examples, as old industries decay and new ones, not so labour-intensive, start elsewhere.

Nonetheless, it is not just a matter of employment or unemployment. In 1982 six million jobs changed hands – requiring personal qualities and flexibility of purpose in coping with change and in seeking fresh opportunities.

☐   **Postponement of employment to 18**

Whereas a decade ago two-thirds of young people entered employment straight from school at the age of 16, now it is about 10 per cent. Why? Well, partly there are no longer jobs for early school-leavers to go to. Furthermore, it now seems part of Government intention that few should be in employment until the age of 18. That is not to say that they will be unemployed. There are alternative provisions, particularly youth training schemes. But the normal route through which most young people did, until recently, establish their identity as adults, and gain some measure of independence, has been postponed for two years. As many teachers point out, the deleterious effect of this upon motivation and sense of relevance further down the school is now evident.

☐   **Longer education, earlier maturity**

This gradual extension of education coincides with the earlier maturation of young people. We are, because of the nature of our extended education and training, prolonging childhood while physically and emotionally (and thus in what they require of relationships with adults) they are children for a much shorter period. This quite clearly affects their expectations of education and how they tolerate, or don't tolerate, the authority of the teacher. The average youngster at the turn of the century spent five years in employment before the onset of puberty. Now the position is reversed. Our young people are often physically and sexually mature four or five years before we 'release them from childhood'.

These then are some of the factors that should persuade us to reappraise how we are preparing young people for life after school, particularly working life: a more qualified and differently qualified workforce; a changed attitude towards the wealth-producing areas of our social life; coping with unemployment or intermittent employment; and prolonged education at the same time as earlier maturity. But already we can detect interesting differences between the *kinds* of reasons for advocating a more relevant, and vocational, curriculum. And these different reasons, when explored further, reflect different traditions, values, and educational aims. The burden of this paper is to make these differences and conflicts explicit, and see at what level they can, if at all, be reconciled.

■ Meeting the needs of society

On the one hand, there is the view that schools and colleges should be more closely related to the needs of society as these are perceived by politicians, manpower planners, and employers. Professional educators are seen to have failed to teach the skills, the knowledge, and the attitudes that a healthy economy requires. As one senior Civil Servant is quoted as saying:

> Education has been too isolated and independent of the country's economic needs, and in future the output of schools will have to be keyed more tightly to employment needs.

And therefore, according to Geoffrey Holland of the Manpower Services Commission:

> the country must build a new system based on the assumption that the skills, knowledge, experience, and competence of people can create jobs.

We need, however, to pause a while and to reflect, even here, upon the different interpretations of the theme 'meeting the needs of the economy'. On the one hand, there is what one might see as 'demand led training and education' – the provision of those qualities and skills that industry is clearly wanting. On the other hand, as in Holland's statement, what is suggested is an interesting reversal of Keynes – a supply-led economic revival where the very existence of surplus skills will produce the need for them.

Again, there are interesting differences concerning the specific level at which one should prepare for jobs in what is a very imprecise science of manpower planning. At what level should one pitch the objectives of job-related qualities and skills for 16, 17, or 18 year olds? When the White Paper *Education and Training for Young People* stated that:

> Young people in the UK are not provided with as good a foundation for the continuing education and training in adult life which must be an increasingly important feature of modern economics (HMSO, 1985)

it is necessary to work out in some detail what the foundation should be, and how it connects up with the future needs of the individual and of society.

Put crudely, it is argued, now by the Government but previously by employers, that the educational system has let the economy down by producing students with inadequate or irrelevant skills and, above all, with the wrong attitudes towards the wealth-creating basis of society. And it is argued that, with a change of attitude and with the development of the right kind of qualities and skills, we shall be better able to respond to changing market forces as well as be able to stimulate economic growth. But within this position as stated, there are many different angles: from that which presses for an improvement of general education as the best base for creating an intelligent, adaptable, and personable workforce, to that which wants a more direct drive, even at school, upon basic vocational skills and upon attitudes that will cast industry in a more favourable light.

■ Meeting the needs of students

There is, on the other hand, a different rationale for the reform of education emerging from the changing context as I have outlined it – namely, the need to help young people to cope psychologically as well as economically with changed employment patterns and possibilities and above all with the blocking off of secure and traditional routes into an adult form of life that *they* recognize and want. The need to extend the period of education and training to 18 arises as much from the importance of keeping otherwise idle youngsters gainfully occupied as it does from the need for a fully-skilled workforce to meet the needs of industry. I am not convinced that *educationally* it is desirable that young people prepare for adult life through extended schooling – adults with L plates, as one local authority referred to them. There is something rather arrogant about this attitude. Until recently most people have become adults without special courses or educational help – transition learning, as it is called – simply by living and working alongside other adults.

However, the fact remains that youngsters cannot get jobs; they do need to learn how to deal effectively with an unpredictable future; and it is the teacher's job to pick up the bits and to make educational sense of problems that are not of education's making. Furthermore, the economic and social problems that youngsters are now facing simply highlight the defects in the curriculum that many teachers are aware of.

This is the problem we need to tackle – the formation of a system of education, on the one hand, that will fit young people for the hoped-for regeneration of the economy (and thus the emphasis upon acquiring employment-related skills); and a system of education, on the other hand, that concentrates, not so much on skills, but upon those personal qualities and personal guidance needed by young people who are being denied the normal routes through which they would otherwise develop and reach maturity. It is not easy to reconcile in curriculum terms these two separate demands. And the problems become particularly acute, as we shall see, in the focus upon personal development which seems central to the different initiatives, but which means something different within the different traditions that are currently shaping this 'preparation for life' which Mr Callaghan spoke about.

■ Courses

The response to the changing context that I have outlined has been a quite radical shift, not only in the shape and content of courses, but also in the financial and political control over them. I shall, therefore, very briefly, sketch out the framework of these changes – indicating the different ways in which such preparation for life is being interpreted, and the complex, indeed contradictory messages that teachers are having to absorb and implement.

Certainly very different patterns are emerging, representing the different emphases identified in the last section. On the one hand, the emphases upon preparation for work conceived either narrowly (for example, job specific skills) or broadly (for example, generic skills or personal effectiveness) and, on the other hand, the emphases upon meeting the personal and social needs of young people, frequently disillusioned, as they face an insecure future. And behind these different emphases, despite the similarity of language in which the curriculum is described, are philosophical differences (about educational aims, about developments as a person, about social relevance, about learning), which are increasingly hard to reconcile. Hence, the current confusion over examinations, the overlapping of qualifications, the inequality of Government support for different initiatives, the uncertainty prevailing over the continued life of certain courses, the barrier of public ignorance in the absence of adequate publicity.

Before identifying more closely these differences, underlying the language of vocational and pre-vocational education, let me outline the ways in which the structure of secondary and tertiary stages of education are changing.

☐   Pre-vocational education

Traditionally, and very simplistically, further education colleges had catered for two groups of students – those who, either full-time or part-time, aimed at vocational qualification at operative, craft or technical level, and, increasingly, those who chose to go to Further Education (FE) for 'A' level studies (or repeat 'O' levels). But in the mid-1970s a different group was appearing in the colleges, namely students who were either unwilling or unable to engage in further academic study but who could not decide what vocational direction to take, or for whom vocational opportunities were disappearing as local industries, and thus courses, closed. Therefore, there was the gradual establishment of 'pre-vocational courses', which aimed to continue the general education of young people but to do so in the context of work experience and general vocational studies which could help them to make more considered choices.

In 1979, the Further Education Unit at the Department of Education and Science produced its own model of pre-vocational education in a document significantly entitled *A Basis for Choice* (FEU, 1979). This describes the general shape of pre-vocational courses and the criteria to which they should conform. The general idea was that, unlike the curriculum as it is traditionally conceived, that is, as an aggregate of quite distinct and unrelated subjects, the new courses should provide an integrated educational experience that, for the sake of analysis, would contain three elements:

(1) A Common Core of general education (60 per cent)

(2) Vocational Studies (20 per cent)

(3) Job specific experience.

The Common Core was defined in terms of aims and objectives that bore only passing resemblance to traditional school subjects, and arose from an analysis of what young people aged 16 or 17 were thought to need. The aims focused in large measure upon issues of personal concern, though with one eye the whole time on preparing students both psychologically and socially for entering eventually into vocationally specific studies. The aims included, for example, among the total number of twelve:

Aim 1:   To bring about an informed perspective as to the role of and status of a young person in an adult society and the world of work;

Aim 4:   To bring about an ability to develop satisfactory personal relationships with others;

Aim 5:   To provide a basis on which the young person acquires a set of moral values applicable to issues in contemporary society.

The objectives would spell out in greater detail what these aims signified and what experiences it would be desirable for the young people to have.

A *Basis for Choice* became the model upon which the DES based its new Certificate of Pre-Vocational Education. The CPVE, under the Joint Secretariat of the CGLI and BTEC, was then awarded to those completing one year of full-time education post 16. The Core Curriculum of this Certificate, integrated as much as possible with vocational studies, was described

> ... in terms of a range of experience and competencies ... which are essential to the students' chances of making a success in adult life including work (Joint Board, 1985).

These core competencies, though broadly based, look very different from the usual statement of curriculum content associated with subjects. They include personal and career development, information technology, practical skills, problem solving – not as subjects but as competencies that should characterize the learning, even when vocationally oriented, of each student.

CPVE is post 16. But here, as elsewhere, these principles of pre-vocationalism were seen to be relevant to pre-16 – and, desirably, to characterize the learning from 14 upwards. Therefore, CGLI and BTEC are presently piloting and will, from September 1987 onwards, be offering a certificated pre-vocational course from the 14–16 age range. We are therefore seeing the quick development of very different kinds of education aims: emphasizing the practical, personal initiative and respons-ibility, problem solving, communication, experiential learning, and in-tegration; which are shaping the curriculum from 14 upwards to make it, so it is claimed, more relevant to the adult world the young people are about to enter.

But beware. Already there are interesting paradoxes and discrepancies between this and other educational goals and, indeed, within the pre-vocational programme. First, the integrated experience of pre-vocational courses sits uncomfortably alongside the subject-based programmes of the new GCSE. Secondly, the more open-ended, negotiated curriculum of CPVE and pre-vocational 14–16 is often expressed in terms of precise objectives reminiscent of a teacher-centred programme. See, for example, the checklist of skills in the City and Guilds profiling matrix – a left-over, maybe, from the vocationally specific ethos of Further Education. Thirdly, rivals are appearing on the scene that jeopardize the viability of the progressively developed curriculum 14–17. BTEC has recently announced the new First Certificate which, in the area of business studies, would clearly become the most efficient route into BTEC national certificate course, thus torpedoing the efforts of the schools and colleges to launch the CPVE.

□   **Training initiatives**

A different pattern of response to the changing economic social conditions emerges, not from the world of education, but from that of manpower planning and training. Remember the reference earlier to the distrust of education – its failure in the eyes of some to prepare youngsters adequately for the world of work. Lord Young, formerly chairman of the MSC, spoke at the Industrial Society Conference in May 1985 about the aim of vocational education to break down the *artificial* distinction between education and training. Employers had to go into schools and 'directly shape the content of courses', and, again:

> examination boards should be helped by employers to refine the content of public examination to reflect the modern work place.

This, then, has a quite different flavour from the educational initiatives. Once the distinction between training and education is removed, and schools are to prepare students for the world of work, then they are vulnerable to a more specifically directed form of vocationalism.

Two initiatives by the MSC are of particular concern. First, obviously, is the Youth Training Scheme, now extended to two years. The other is the Technical and Vocational Education Initiative. YTS includes off-the-job education and training, planned work experience, occupational training, and personal guidance and assessment. It provides training opportunities for all youngsters between 16 and 18, whether or not they are in employment. In one sense, it at long last fulfils the aim of the 1918

Education Act which stipulated further education and training for all young people up to 18, including day release, but which never materialized – except in one local authority, namely, Rugby.

The details of the YTS scheme are well known but certain features ought to be picked out for mention. First, it claims to be 'a permanent bridge from school to work'. Secondly, the bridge, including the 'off-the-job training', is increasingly being taken from the responsibility of the education service and put into the hands of employers and private agencies. The 'bridge', sets out to blur the distinction between training and education. Thirdly, it competes on unfair terms with full-time education in the sense that (a) trainees but not full-time students receive a grant, and (b) the scheme is, in effect, the necessary route into certain occupations, such as hairdressing or engineering, because of agreements with various Training Boards.

Already then one can see how training initiatives, aimed at helping future generations prepare for life, particularly working life, could be at odds with educational traditions supported by a different Department of State both in theory, a very different concept of education and of personal development, and in practice, making CPVE a non-viable option in many cases because of its particular ground rules.

One key feature of any training programme, with ambitions of YTS, must be skills-based accreditation. Following the de Ville Report *Review of Vocational Qualifications* (de Ville, 1986), the Government has established a National Council for Vocational Qualifications, under which there will be a coherent and comprehensive system of vocational qualifications, at four levels, which will fix standards of assessment of skills and knowledge based upon employers' needs. 'Coherence', 'progression', 'clear standards', 'relevance' – these are the watch words. These are summed up in the words of the White Paper *Training for Jobs*:

> a coherent system of training standards and certificates of competence, covering achievement in vocational education and training, both initially and through working life (DES, 1984).

Connections will have to be made with GCSE and CPVE, but how such objectives-led assessment will fit with the pre-vocational stress upon negotiations and learning processes is less and less easy to understand.

□   **TVEI**

Finally, we have TVEI – the Technical and Vocational Education Initiative, announced by MSC in 1982, launched in 14 pilot schemes in September 1983, through which consortia of schools and colleges mount a progressively developed curriculum from 14 to 18 that would meet certain general criteria, namely a greater technical and vocational emphasis; the pursuit of more equal opportunities; links between school and college and the world of work; personal qualities such as initiative and responsibility; regular assessment through profiling; and so on. In the last three years, over 100 TVEI schemes have been established, and for the first time we have major course developments in schools that are not financed by or ultimately responsible to the normal education authorities.

At the University of Exeter we are evaluating four of these schemes, and, in one, we have just produced the most thorough evaluation of the first three years of any scheme that has yet been achieved. Part of our evaluation has been the interviewing of every student for a half hour each – nearly 1000 interviews over three years. We have systematically observed many classrooms and workshops, interviewed teachers – in fact lived and breathed the scheme for a considerable time. That provides a massive amount of data on possibly the most significant attempt to bridge education and training, school and the world of work, liberal and vocational education.

Generally speaking, the students are very satisfied. They enjoy the more practical basis of education, the more relaxed relations between student and teacher, the greater responsibility for their own learning, the use of modern technology. Real changes in teaching and learning styles have clearly been made. But not all is rosy. There are serious problems, despite the eulogies of official reports about TVEI that we so often hear. And these arise mainly from those inner contradictions that I have referred to.

First, the more practical, assignment-led, group work ill-fits an examination system whose national criteria allow little scope for these characteristics. Try to convince an examination board of the certifiability of work submitted on the basis of group cooperation – yesterday that was called cheating. Secondly, a full-time four year course is incompatible with progression to a YTS scheme at 16 – and yet that is what is necessary if the students wish to enter into certain kinds of employment – catering, hairdressing, construction, engineering. Thirdly, there are mixed reports about the ability range. Unless we are careful, the scheme could become the basis of a vocationally divided system – at 14 the academic, single-subject route into higher education and the professions for the better motivated or more able, and the vocationally oriented skills-based and practical route for the rest. Already in one local authority a paper is circulating for selection of the majority at 14 for a vocational, as opposed to an academic, education.

These then are the major ways in which schools and colleges, aided or led by examination boards, are responding to the need for greater relevance to adult life and the world of work. In sum, we are witnessing, both full-time and part-time, a more self-conscious attempt to relate studies progressively to vocational preparation and qualification, across the part-time and full-time provision, from 14 upwards. But we can also see how, within and between these course structures, there are important differences over what that preparation should be like, who should be the beneficiary of it, and who ultimately should control it. Different bodies, Examination Boards, Government Departments, participate in different traditions, and old habits die hard, such as that of having an examination at 16.

What, then, in summary do we see to be happening? There is an attempt, in response to the changing context outlined earlier, to develop a coherent and interrelated package of education and training from 14 to 18, that aims to do the following:

(1) redirect the curriculum of schools more toward preparation for the world of work – and other aspects of adult life;

(2) establish greater central Government influence to ensure that this occurs;

(3) rationalize a system of assessment and accreditation that,
    (a)   is linked to agreed standards of performance at different levels and in different skill areas, and
    (b)   enables, through the acquisition of credits, progress to be made through full-time and part-time courses to more advanced education and training.

The problems of this more vocationalized and rationalized system are that the initiatives have come from different Government sources, based on different Government reports, with different views about the purpose of education and thus with different understandings of the problem.

■ Curriculum

Behind some of these initiatives are, as I have hinted, radical changes in curriculum thinking – expressed, for example, in the aims of the ABC Report or in the national criteria for TVEI, and demonstrated in the work that is being initiated in pre-vocational courses both pre and post 16.

A summary of these curriculum developments is as follows:

(1) *Continuity from 14 to 18* (although this is, as I have pointed out, confused by rivalry between different providers who lay down incompatible conditions).

(2) *Integration of the educational experience*, a core of interrelated

skills and experience that permeate the curriculum (although this is hard to reconcile with the subject specific nature of GCSE).

(3) *Changed styles of learning and teaching* reflected in the practice-based assignments, negotiated curriculum objectives, stress upon processes of learning rather than product or content (although the unpredictability and open-endedness of negotiated and experience-based learning lives uncomfortably with the pre-specification of objectives demanded by the tighter vocational traditions).

(4) *Use of technology*, especially as the means through which resources can be made available and practical work engaged in (although, in the emphasis upon process of learning rather than product, there seem few signs of that *progression* in technological understanding, which surely is needed).

(5) *Work-related*, not only in the experience of work that most fifth formers now enjoy, but also in the curriculum 'subjects of business, community services, and technology'.

(6) *Skills development* – 'basic skills' in numeracy, communication, physical manipulation, keyboard, personal effectiveness (although the concept of skill is used in such an elastic way as to confuse skills, knowledge, personal qualities and attitudes in a most alarming way; we see in the media the emptiness of *skilful* communication that has nothing of importance to communicate).

(7) *Person-centred*, reflected in the focus upon a more negotiated programme, upon the centrality of guidance and counselling, upon developmental group work, upon profiles and records of achievement through which the many positive qualities of each student might be demonstrated (although, as we shall see, there are major differences over what is to count as personal development).

(8) *Community-centred*, especially that part of the community represented by industry (although the problems of school–industry partnership lie as much in industry's ignorance of schools as they do in schools' ignorance of industry).

(9) *Equal opportunities*.

(10) *Communication*.

All this, of course, has far-reaching implications for the assessment and accreditation of young people, the ways in which what they can do gets recorded and recognized. How can we do justice to cooperative rather than individual work? How can we ensure the connection between what we assess or diagnose, and what or how we teach? How can we demonstrate the personal qualities and achievements without encroaching upon the privacy of students' lives? How can we accredit, through public certification, what is negotiated (as all good education should be) in the transactions between teacher and taught? How can those cross-curriculum competencies (problem-solving, initiative, personal effectiveness, communication etc.) have their due place in an examination system that traditionally has looked for facts, knowledge, or specific skills? It is significant that few GCSE examination boards have yet tackled these core competency areas, despite the increasing number of TVEI schemes that will be looking to them for validation.

More seriously, however, are the problems encountered in curriculum development within schools and colleges.

There are, as I am arguing in this chapter, different, and indeed hardly compatible, traditions through which the curriculum, as I have outlined it, might be interpreted and put into practice. And these different traditions, representing as they do different educational aims and values, different senses of what it means to develop as a person, different theories of student learning and motivation, are themselves reflected in such dichotomies as education *versus* training, liberal *versus* vocational, person-centred *versus* subject-centred, the processes of learning *versus* the product of (others') learning. The difficulty that teachers have lies in resolving these dichotomies in practice, in relating these different and competing traditions to the problems as they see them in the classroom and workshop. TVEI could be seen as a lump of money given to teachers, in cooperation with employers and other representatives of the community, to *devise* a progressively planned curriculum from 14 to 18, that answers the overall aim of preparing young people for life – the theme of Mr Callaghan's speech. TVEI is not itself a curriculum. It is the opportunity to create a curriculum. And the teachers, in doing this, have no ready made-formula, no accepted curriculum tradition upon which to draw. They are forced back to deeper, more significant questions about educational purposes, aims, and values. Hence, the need to examine more closely the different educational ideas which are entering into that thinking.

☐ The skills direction

First, there is the emphasis on, and thus the specification of, core skills, the acquisition of which will help young people prepare more effectively for the world of work. The MSC has supported research which will enable it to discover what these skills are. Remember that, at this pre-vocational stage, it is important not to teach skills that are peculiar to very specific vocational areas, because one of the difficulties is that of predicting the skills that future employees will need. Hence, there is the emphasis upon 'generic skills', which will provide a foundation for more specific vocational preparation later or, to use the jargon, will be transferable to new situations.

Recently, the MSC published its list of 103 basic or core skills in number work, communication, problem-solving and the practical (MSC, 1984). Further core skills have been identified in Computer and Information Technology. At a meeting with the MSC representatives who are developing the curriculum in the area of core skills, I produced a different list of 153 basic skills produced by the office of Career Development at the University of Illinois (Freeman, 1983). The point of introducing a different list was to show that what counts as a basic skill is not just an empirical matter. There is an infinite number of skills that could be identified, depending on the concepts and values through which you analyse what needs to be done.

But one can see the significance of this emphasis upon skills training within pre-vocational education. It is part of a view of education in which outsiders (employers, Government departments, course planners) establish in detail what *exactly* should be taught, what the behavioural outcomes should be, and how precisely these should be assessed. There is certainly an important place in schools for the teaching of skills that will enable students to do more effectively what they need or want to do. But the concept is, in my view, hopelessly overblown as a basis for curriculum planning. First, what constitutes a basic or generic skill is very confused. But secondly, and more dangerously, the whole skills-based approach to curriculum development represents a shift away from a curriculum as a set of transactions between teacher and taught, responding to the student needs as teachers sensitively identify them, towards a much more mechanical and externally controlled conception of what the curriculum is about.

□   **Person-centred direction**

Secondly, there is emerging a different kind of challenge to the traditional curriculum, one which takes seriously the problems of personal response to the social changes outlined earlier. How do we prepare young people psychologically for a future which is unpredictable in what it holds in store for them and in which there seems less stability, less certainty about those values which in the past have afforded a backcloth of security? As teachers, we are being asked to extend the period of schooling at the very time when the students are, in important respects, maturing earlier and thus less ready to accept the wisdom and the authority of the teacher. Furthermore, many of those students are on courses reluctantly and their experience of schooling will primarily be one of failure. As Hargreaves in his book *The Challenge for the Comprehensive School*, writes:

> ... our present secondary school system, largely through the hidden curriculum, exerts on many pupils, particularly but by no means exclusively

from the working class, a destruction of their dignity which is so massive and pervasive that few subsequently recover from it (Hargreaves, 1982).

Hargreaves' view is a devastating attack upon the pretensions of schools who claim to be fostering personal and social development, where the sense of personal worth is nearly destroyed through the constant experience of failure and through the lack of respect felt for those values which they, the pupils, prize more dearly and which they bring with them into the school. I say 'nearly destroyed' because Hargreaves points to the various ways in which youngsters do preserve a sense of dignity, often finding refuge in a shared opposition to what the school offers or in rebellion against authority, or in an assertion of *their* different cultural values – in their style, dress, language, music, and so on – the social world so aptly described by Paul Willis in *Learning to Labour* (Willis, 1977).

The more person-centred curriculum or programmes have created the most successful economic boon in textbooks on social and life skills. For no one would admit to personal developments being unimportant. Indeed, there is much evidence to show that employers are much more interested in personal qualities than in academic achievement. But the underlying concept of personal development is rarely made explicit. Here in particular we see the divergent paths being taken under the influence of very different traditions.

The mid 1970's Job Creation Programmes were very much concerned with 'socialization into the world of work' which seemed a reasonable aim. Young people who had been idle for a few months needed to develop habits of going to work, accepting the discipline of work, responding to the demands that work imposed. Gradually their aims became more explicit as the job creation programmes assumed the status of training schemes. 'Training' and 'skills' are closely related concepts, and in 1976 the MSC produced its *Instructional Guide to Social and Life Skills* – a taxonomy of specific behaviours which spelt out the otherwise general concept of socialization. In terms of *personal* development, these were often trivial: the use of directories, wiring a fuse; rather than, say, learning how to engage in political argument. Gradually, however, as the Work Experience Programmes and other preparatory courses developed, social and life skills were filled out with more general qualities such as self-awareness and confidence.

Note, how, there was here an underlying concept of personal development which saw the young people as somehow deficient *as persons*, in need of training to make them ready for the world which in itself was OK but for which they were not ready. These, of course, are the same kind of youngsters who, a generation ago, would have moved into this adult world without a social and life skills training programme.

There was, however, a different model of personal preparation which presupposed a rather different concept of being, and of developing as a person. Already Youth Schemes of one sort and another, and then schools under the influence of such people as Hamblin, Eileen Chandler, and Leslie Button, were introducing a counselling rather than training model of personal development that aimed at supporting and strengthening those qualities already there, empowering the person to 'be herself', to act in an autonomous way, to engage in the mutually beneficial transactions between student and student, and between student and teacher. Which model was to dominate in the more person-centred approach to learning – the transactional or the training?

Of course, even in the transaction model (stressing counselling rather than training, promoting the autonomy rather than dependence) there was recognized the need for guidance and help – not necessarily because of any personal inadequacy but because of the complex and often depressing world that the young person had to sort his way through. The consequence of the transactional model was a less objectives-based approach, a stress upon self-management and decision making, a significance attached to genuineness of feeling and of interpersonal trust and empathy.

Here, of course, is an important difference in our conception of what it is to be, and to develop as, a person and it has a profound effect upon curriculum and upon the control of education.

What is it to prepare *persons* for life? Is it to spell out exactly how they should behave, what particular thoughts they should have, what specific skills they should own, what precise values they should hold dear? Or is it to recognize that, as persons, they should be empowered to develop some *autonomy* of purpose, a *rational capacity* to think through issues of transition, *self-confidence* in their beliefs and relationships, a *sense of dignity* and personal worth even when the world seems against them, a worked out and defensible set of *moral principles*?

To *say* 'yes' to the latter is easy; but it is not easy to act upon. For one thing, it is dangerous and threatening. The students may be critical of, and may reject, what you want them to believe. It is less and less easy for parents to clone their children. How much more difficult for teachers. And, secondly, much needs to happen in schools and colleges to make sure that these are the personal qualities developed – the capacities to think, to make decisions, to be confident and proud of one's achievement, to take on responsibility, to be sensitive to others. These demand both curriculum and institutional changes.

And, indeed, we are seeing in *some* of the pre-vocational and TVEI schemes precisely these changes – muddled very often, delicately poised, not quite found favour among Examination Boards, regarded with suspicion by those who are hooked on more traditional definitions of standards, regarded as dangerous by those who fear the consequences of a more articulate, questioning, independent future generation. Did not the draft instructions from the Department of Employment for 'off-the-job trainers' forbid them to include matters relating to the 'organization and functioning of society', unless they are relevant to trainees' work experience (thus ruling out the political education packs produced by the British Youth Council with the encouragement of HMI and DES)? How different from FEU's booklet *Supporting YOP*:

> to provide a basis on which the young person acquires a set of moral values applicable to issues in contemporary society ... to bring about sufficient political and economic literacy to understand the social environment and to participate in it (FEU, 1979b).

Different Departments of State, different traditions, different conceptions of preparation for life, different ideas about 'development as a person'. These differences however have their wider social and political – not just economic – significance. In commenting on many of these changes, both those of course of organization and of curriculum development, senior administrators made some interesting observations when interviewed in recent research by Stuart Ranson. As one put it:

> There may be social unrest, but we can cope with the Toxteths. But if we have a highly educated and idle population we may possibly anticipate more serious social conflict. People must be educated once more to know their place (Ranson, 1984, p. 241).

And, therefore, (another high ranking official):

> There has to be selection because we are beginning to create aspirations which increasingly society cannot match. In some ways this points to the success of education in contrast to the public mythology which has been created (Ranson, 1984, p. 241).

Hence, so it is argued, the need for more central intervention in the curriculum:

> I see a return to centralization of a different kind with the centre seeking to determine what goes on in institutions. This is a more fundamental centralization that we have seen before (Ranson, 1984, p. 238).

And for what purpose? To quote from one chief education officer interviewed:

> to facilitate social control as much as encourage manpower planning.

Preparing future generations for life, which Mr Callaghan pointed to as an aim of education, included preparation for the world of work – and to that extent it should be vocational. But this can be interpreted generously – where social awareness includes the capacity for political argument and criticism, where communication skills do not ignore the richness of literature and of experience as a basis of something to communicate about, where teaching respects activity and practically based learning that we know pupils respond to. Or it can be narrowly interpreted where persons are subjects to be trained, where communication is limited to the safe and non-controversial, and where there is an over-emphasis on skills that derive from others' often mistaken view of what the economy needs.

The touchstone of an educationally acceptable interpretation of vocationalism lies in the arts. Where are they in the many new initiatives? And, where they are present, how are they understood – as one (among many) opportunities for leisure or as part of the serious business of living where the gulf between work and non-work is finally bridged?

■ Conclusion

What then is it to prepare the future generation for that rate and level of change that we are all beginning to experience? What qualities should we promote to help them achieve a sense of dignity and worth, when many of the props have been knocked from underneath them. What skills do they need in order to feel pride in what they can do in order that they may contribute to the regeneration of the economy and of their community?

There *must* be an educational response – that, I think, almost all recognize, although there are some interesting pockets of resistance. But *how* we should respond pushes us down to more fundamental questions of educational aims, of what it means to grow as persons, of the relationship between education and society. And in this chapter I have tried to show how there are different traditions, different values, different views of personal development vying with each other to write the educational agenda and to say what that response should be.

There, indeed, lies the most serious criticism of the new vocationalism, for, where it fudges the distinction between 'training' and 'education', or fastens on to the model of 'skills training', or maintains the erroneous separation of work from pleasure, or comprehends educational aims in terms of utility, the key educational (and vocational) task of developing youngsters as persons become submerged and the arts become an embarrassment – something for the less serious, leisure moments of one's life. But, to the contrary, the arts and the humanities should be central to education – to the development of that reflective state of mind in which one comes to understand what it is to be and to grow as 'a person' in all its facets, and vocational education should respect that growth as a person, and thus respect the arts and the humanities in the vocational preparation. Not to so respect entails a curtailment of growth, a narrowing of vision, an impoverishment of emotional life, and a barrier to critical judgement, which may provide an adequate vocational *training* for some aspects of industry, but hardly the vocational *education* that a healthy and democratically run society would require. And, indeed, it is a major task for the arts and humanities to re-examine their place in the new circumstances I have been talking about, and to explore the curriculum implications of giving the arts a central role in a more vocationally oriented education. Certainly, 'arts for leisure' won't do, because the artist is a serious person, not a playboy, and through the arts and humanities the values, which determine our notions of 'vocationalism', would be explored in all seriousness.

References

Barnett, C. (1986) *The Audit of War* (London: Macmillan).

Callaghan, J. (1976) 'Ruskin College Speech'. *Education*, 22 October.

DES (1984) *Training for Jobs* (London: HMSO).

De Ville, O. (1986) *Review of Vocational Qualifications, in England and Wales* (London: MSC/DES).

FEU (1979a) *A Basis for Choice* (London: FEU).

FEU (1979b) *Supporting YOP* (London: FEU).

Freeman, J. P. (1983) *Identification of Generalisable Skills in Secondary Vocational Education Programs* (Illinois: Illinois State Board of Education).

Hargreaves, D. (1982) *The Challenge for the Comprehensive School* (London: Routledge & Kegan Paul).

HMSO (1985) *Education and Training for Young People*, Cmnd 9482 (London: HMSO).

Joint Board for Pre-Vocational Education (1985) *The Certificate of Pre-Vocational Education Part B, Core Competencies and Vocational Module Specifications* (London: CGLI/BTECH).

MSC (1984) *Assessing Practical Skills* (London: MSC).

Ranson, S. (1984) 'Towards a tertiary tripartism', in Broadfoot, P., *Selection, Certification and Control* (Lewes: Falmer Press).

Weiner, M. J. (1981) *English Culture and the Decline of the Industrial Spirit 1850–1908* (Cambridge: Cambridge University Press).

Willis, P. (1977) *Learning to Labour* (Guildford: Saxon House).

Chapter 12

The Technical and Vocational Education Initiative

R. Dale

The Technical and Vocational Education Initiative (originally known as the N (New) TVEI) was announced by the Prime Minister, Margaret Thatcher, in the House of Commons on 12 November 1982. She announced that 'in response to growing concern about existing arrangements for technical and vocational education for young people expressed over many years, not least by the National Economic Development Council', she had asked 'the chairman of the Manpower Services Commission together with the Secretaries of State for Education and Science, for Employment, and for Wales, to develop a pilot scheme to start by September 1983, for new institutional arrangements for technical and vocational education for 14–18-year-olds, within existing financial resources, and, where possible, in association with local authorities.'

That announcement came like a bolt from the blue to all the most directly interested parties. Neither the DES, the local education authority associations, the teacher professional organizations, nor even the MSC, had been consulted before the announcement was made. It created an enormous furore not only by the manner of its delivery but also by what it appeared to threaten. The reference to 'new institutional arrangements', and to collaboration with local authorities 'where possible', gave rise to considerable fears that a new kind of institution was intended – or rather that something like the old technical school was to be revived. There were some grounds for these fears. David Young (then chairman of the MSC,

Source: Dale, R. (1989) *The State and Education Policy*, The Open University Press, Milton Keynes, chapter 9, pp. 148–164.

now a Cabinet Minister, and together with Sir Keith Joseph and Norman Tebbit credited with producing the original plan) made it clear that MSC was in the last resort (if local education authorities did not cooperate in the scheme) prepared to set up their own schools, which he thought might even be called 'Young' schools (*Education*, 26 November 1982).

However, local authority resistance crumbled very rapidly (though complaints about lack of consultation continued) and their collaboration in the scheme was assured with Mr Young's announcement that the membership of the National Steering Group to be set up to run the initiative 'would reflect the key part the education service would play in the pilot projects' (*Education*, 26 November 1982).

The TVEI scheme emerged as:

> a pilot scheme; within the education system; for young people of both sexes; across the ability range, voluntary. Each project must provide a full-time programme; offer a progressive four-year course combining general with technical and vocational education; commence at 14 years; be broadly based; include planned work experience; lead to nationally recognized qualifications. Each project and the initiative as a whole must be carefully monitored and evaluated. The purpose of the scheme is to explore and test ways of organizing and managing readily replicable programmes of technical and vocational education for young people across the ability range (MSC, 1984).

In his letter to all education authorities in England and Wales, inviting them to submit applications, David Young amplified this frame-work by indicating that the general objective was to 'widen and enrich the curriculum in a way that will help young people prepare for the world of work, and to develop skills and interests, including creative abilities, that will help them to lead a fuller life and to be able to contribute more to the life of the community'. Secondly, he suggested that 'we are in the business of helping students to "learn to learn". In a time of rapid technological change, the extent to which particular occupational skills are required will change. What is important about this initiative is that youngsters should receive an education which will enable them to adapt to the changing occupational environment.'

Sixty-six LEAs applied to be included in the project and 14 were chosen (the originally planned number was enlarged to ensure better geographical coverage). A central feature of the scheme is that these authorities then signed contracts with MSC for the delivery of the project outlined in their application. These projects were all drawn up to match the guidelines contained in David Young's letter, but they differed con-siderably from each other in philosophy, numbers of schools involved (though most schemes included between five and eight schools and colleges of further education) and the number of pupils to be involved (though the funding basis assumed five annual cohorts of 250 pupils per authority). Some of these differences and their implications are elaborated more fully below. Each local project is responsible to a local steering group made up of representatives of both sides of industry, educational interests, voluntary organizations and so on. The steering groups report to the TVEI Unit in the MSC and to the local authority.

Twice as many Conservative as Labour authorities applied. Labour authorities refused to submit bids on the grounds that the scheme would both be divisive by reintroducing some form of selection into comprehensive education, and have a narrowing, excessively vocationalizing effect on the curriculum. These have been the dominant criticisms of the TVEI scheme throughout its short history. At first, the pilot nature of the scheme received a great deal of emphasis. Critics in the House of Commons (where questions on TVEI were answered by both the Employment and Education ministers) and elsewhere were typically told not to become too anxious or worried about what was after all only a small pilot scheme. And yet, scarcely 3 months after the announcement of the first group of pilot LEAs and before the projects had started, it was announced that the scheme would be extended, with another £20 million in addition to the original £7 million available to bring in another 40 or so (in the end 44 more authorities were accepted) LEAs in September 1984. And then, in October 1984, a further extension of the scheme was announced to start in September 1985. The indications are that all those who apply in this round will be successful, leaving only a residue of Labour authorities opting out, on broadly the same grounds as they originally gave.

TVEI does not follow any of the three main routes of bringing about major educational change in Britain, either in the nature of its aims or in its methods. It is neither a programme drawn up by and in consultation with practising educators, aimed at improving the content and/or delivery of (parts of) the school curriculum (the Schools Council model); nor does it follow the Plowden Advisory Committee model, where representatives of a wide range of appropriate interests join with the 'great and the good' to scrutinize, and recommend a series of more or less major changes; nor does it follow the model of legislative change, which encouraged comprehensive schooling, for instance, or raised the school-leaving age. Rather, it might be argued, it follows a business or commercial model, moving resources into a new 'line' when the existing one is proving ineffective. At the centre of its aims is improving the service to a particular group of customers, clients and consumers – it does not seek to improve the service to those already seen as (too) well catered for. Its mode of operation is executive rather than legislative or advisory. And it is singularly unencumbered either by the professional experts, or by the 'great and the good' – there are no latter-day Lords Vaizey or (Michael) Young in TVEI.

TVEI, then, is a political intervention, in the sense that it was introduced into the educational system from outside, albeit with the acquiescence or even encouragement of the Secretary of State for Education (though without even the knowledge of his department officials, or any other part of the educational apparatus, national or local). Though in the end the cooperation of the majority of LEAs was secured – at least to the extent of making themselves contractually accountable for disposing of very large sums of money for specified purposes (though, as I shall show below it cannot be assumed that these purposes were necessarily inimical to them) – it is clear from David Young's comments quoted above that the scheme would have been introduced anyway (though whether it could have succeeded without the cooperation of the education service is a matter of fascinating, if now futile, debate).

Another crucial feature of TVEI is its size and scope. It now involves the majority of education authorities (though, not, of course, the majority of schools or pupils) in the country and provides unprecedentedly large amounts of money for those involved. Its objective is not merely the improvement or updating of a particular aspect of the school curriculum – although this is undoubtedly part of its intention – but the redirection and restructuring of the school experiences of a large proportion of pupils. This redirecting and restructuring is aimed at bringing schools into a closer relationship with the world outside them, especially, though not exclusively, 'the world of work'. This will involve making 'the vocational' rather than 'the academic' the central purpose and criterion of what a considerable proportion, if not all, children learn in school. In both these aspects, then, its extra-educational, political origins, and its funding and ambitions, TVEI is quite unlike any curriculum innovation we have seen in this country before.

TVEI also differs from what has gone before in the pattern, process and pace of curriculum change it involves. It represents an obvious and deliberate break with the essentially incremental, apparently haphazard, pattern which had typified educational change. It represents as much a break with, as continuity with, existing provision, seeking to renew or even replace it as much as building on it. Its size and its ambitions also push it towards being comprehensive rather than piecemeal.

The accepted pattern is challenged, too, through its operation at the margins of the school, both financially and educationally. That is to say, TVEI gains maximum 'bang for a buck' from all its funding being devoted to additional items, and none of it to the continuing basic cost of running the school, which accounts for nearly all the funding it receives, leaving very little available for 'development'. Educationally, its funding and the conditions attaching to it mean that, at least formally, the school has to adjust to the innovation rather than the other way round.

The process of change is not wholly dependent on persuasion and the marshalling of voluntary effort in the schools involved. LEAs and schools are contractually accountable for implementing the changes they propose to introduce. They must be able to demonstrate that the material and human resources they have bought with TVEI money are being used, at least preferentially, with the pupils, and for the purposes, specified in the contract. A second major difference is that formal authority for the direction of the project is vested not in the schools, the LEA or the MSC alone, but in the local steering group (on which, of course, all three parties are represented, along with both sides of industry). A third difference is that the projects are also monitored by members of an advisory team within the TVEI unit. All those appointed so far have had extensive experience within the education service, and they appear to see their role as supportive and advisory as much as evaluative.

Finally, it is clear from the timetable outlined above that the TVEI has been introduced at quite unprecedented speed. Scarcely 9 months after the first, entirely unheralded announcement, the scheme was operating in 14 LEAs, who had had 2 months to prepare their applications and who learned that they had been successful barely a term before the programmes had to start. The pace has hardly relaxed since then, certainly in the schools, as the implications of those very rapid decisions became transformed into timetable, resource, administrative and pedagogic problems, all requiring almost immediate responses.

■ The background to TVEI

Its unique, secret and personal origins make it difficult to point with any conviction of accuracy to the sources and diagnosis that lay behind the TVEI proposal. Nevertheless, it is possible to infer a good deal about that diagnosis. It has two main elements. One is that what is taught in schools has to be changed. The other is that the process of changing what is taught in schools has itself to be changed. Both these elements were, of course, central to the 'Great Debate' on education of 1977, and they remained important, though not exclusive, components of the diagnosis which 5 years later produced the TVEI.

The influence of the teaching profession over what went on in education had already begun to decline before the institution of the Great Debate, under the influence of falling school rolls (and consequent loss of union 'muscle'), the ideological onslaught on the alleged consequences of a teacher-dominated system, encapsulated in the Black Papers, and a general feeling of dissatisfaction that education had failed to deliver what it had promised, socially, politically and economically, and for which it had claimed ever-growing funds. In particular, the education system had at the very least done little to forestall or inhibit the country's economic decline. And this apparent failure of the education system was laid very much at the door of the teachers, especially following the William Tyndale affair, which led to teachers being identified as the major culprits in this situation. This was possible in large part because of the 'licensed autonomy' which gave them great influence over the kinds of changes that should take place in the education system [. . .].

A clear recognition of the perceived need to curtail 'teacher power' was inscribed in the very format of the Great Debate. As Bates (1984, p. 199) puts it:

> the Great Debate reflected a trend towards defining and limiting the boundaries of teacher autonomy. The very initiation of a public debate on education, involving the unprecedented consultation of industrial organizations and parents as well as educational organizations, served as an explicit reminder to the teaching profession that the curriculum was not solely their responsibility to determine . . . . Thus the Great Debate, irrespective of its content, simply as a means of intervening in education helped to change the political context in which educational issues were discussed.

That teachers' licensed autonomy affected not only the process of educational change, but also its content was, of course, a central theme of the Great Debate. A clear tension was discerned there between teachers' professional interest and the interests of the wider society, and especially of industry. This professional interest led to an over-emphasis on the academic and a matching neglect of the vocational aspect of schooling.

The argument that it is essential to change this emphasis, and the stress on the 'need' to bring education and industry closer together, to attach the former more closely to the needs of the latter has, of course, been the object of a 'recurrent debate' (Reeder, 1979) in English education over the course of this century. This is not the place to go through that debate (which is developed more fully in Reeder, 1979 and Esland and Cathcart, 1981, while useful accounts of US experience, which suggests that education is called in to solve a range of social and economic problems, are given in Grubb and Lazerson (1981) and McGowan and Cohen (1977)).

Beck has convincingly argued that through the second half of the 1970s, industry's contribution to this recurrent debate took a dual form. On the one hand, larger employers and, significantly, the Department of Industry were putting forward the criticism that the education system's longstanding academic bias 'had played a major part in creating and maintaining the situation in which wealth creation, the profit motive and engineering were accorded less status in Britain than in most other manufacturing countries' (Beck, 1983, p. 221). On the other hand, a campaign against alleged declining standards and discipline, generated mainly in the press, pointed to the negative consequences for pupils' attitudes to work and authority of progressive teaching methods, teacher autonomy and certain aspects of comprehensive reorganization.

However, it was quite clear that it was not enough merely to advise, counsel and tinker. Stripped of its academic bias, the education system would not automatically revert to some pristine 'economy-friendly' state; a positive alternative was required. This alternative, heavily implicit in the Great Debate, and explicit before and after it, remains vocational education.

The problem is that vocational education is a very slippery and ambiguous concept. This is because it is defined in opposition, or contrast, to what it is hoped it will supplant. Thus vocational education is called on in the Great Debate and Green Paper to save a system with an inappropriate curriculum bias, low standards, and insufficient and ineffective links with industry. Hence vocational education comes to be associated with three quite distinct purposes, making pupils more able to get jobs, making them better performers in jobs, and making them more aware of the world of work, and of the workings of the economy which awaits them.

The term 'vocational education', then, covers three different and separate – though not necessarily mutually incompatible – aspects of the diagnosis produced by the Great Debate. It is to counter: (a) the teacher-based progressive ideology which allegedly leads to a neglect of, or even contempt for, rigour and standards, and produces pupils with attitudes inimical to the disciplinary and moral requirements of many employers, who prefer therefore to offer jobs to older, more mature and more 'stable', if less qualified, people; (b) the fact that the things that pupils are taught at school are inappropriate, and often do not equip them to do the jobs they are offered; (c) the fact that they do not know enough about the world of work, and especially about the economic importance of industry. This applies almost as much to those who will enter other economic sectors as to those who will remain unemployed (see Moore, 1984). As an answer to all these shortcomings, a more vocationally-oriented education consequently becomes even more difficult to define and to prescribe in detail.

The diagnosis contained within or implied by the Great Debate does not, however, exhaust the diagnosis which underlies TVEI. There are at least two factors which led to the need for its supplementation. First of all, though the diagnosis was at least superficially clear, very little had happened between 1977 and 1982 to shift schools in the required direction; many of the criticisms contained in the Great Debate and Green Paper still held good. And, secondly, over that period there had been a quite dramatic increase in youth unemployment, as well as continuing expansion of 'high-tech' industry. Both these factors were incorporated into the diagnosis which we can infer underlay TVEI.

It is clear that the work that the MSC had done in response to youth unemployment influenced the thinking behind TVEI. (This is not to say that because TVEI is located in the MSC it automatically parallels MSC's policies for young people post-school in school. It is clear that TVEI is not 'YTS in the schools' – though many critics originally assumed that it would be.) Essentially, the recognition that youth unemployment was too important and, certainly in the wake of the Toxteth riots, too potentially dangerous to be left to the market, produced a dual response. On the one hand, it greatly intensified moves towards providing far more training. This was an original purpose of the MSC, which became less prominent during the period of the Youth Opportunities Programme, but resurfaced again very powerfully in the New Training Initiative and the Youth Training Scheme. This latter scheme was held by many (see Farley, 1985) to contain the seeds of the comprehensive training programme which it was held Britain, in contrast to its competitors, and especially West Germany, had never had. The possibility that this kind of training could be built into a single, coherent 14–18 scheme, certainly seems to underlie some TVEI projects.

The other part of the MSC response to youth unemployment is 'vocational preparation'. This consists of programmes aimed at attuning young people to the world of work, though they may never experience it directly themselves. It is a series of solutions to what Offe (1984, p. 99) calls 'the problem of institutional "storage" of the portion of the social volume of labour power which (because of conjunctural and structural changes) cannot be absorbed by the demands generated by the labour market'. The problem is essentially one of keeping the unemployed employable, of keeping them available for employment when employment is not available for them. It is tackled in two main ways. One is through programmes of ersatz work experience (see Watts, 1983). In projects of vocational preparation this work experience is a vehicle not so much for learning skills or applying knowledge learned in school, but for learning something of what it feels like to be employed. The other main response is the development of programmes of 'social and life skills'. One aspect of these programmes stresses the importance of acquiring non-academic, interpersonal skills which are useful in getting and keeping jobs, especially white collar jobs; content focuses on how to behave at interviews, how to take and give messages and instructions, and so on. The other aspect stresses adjustment to a likely long period of unemployment, coping with its impact on personal, social and family relationships.

The other major strand of influence of the MSC's experience in youth training and youth unemployment is rather more difficult to pin down. It is essentially a new kind of pedagogy, rooted in the work of the Further Education Unit, whose publications have done much to define this approach. There is space here to do little more than list some of these shifts, but it is worthwhile to do so because they are evidently beginning to affect the work of TVEI schools, especially through the introduction into schools of courses leading to qualifications of the Business and Technician Education Council, the City and Guilds of London Institute, the Royal Society of Arts, and other bodies whose work had previously been confined to the post-compulsory sector. This 'new FEU pedagogy' involves, then, among other things, a move towards teaching courses rather than subjects, 'experiential' and 'problem solving' rather than 'academic' learning, criterion – rather than norm-referenced assessment, competence rather than age-related courses, the introduction of profiling on a wide scale and qualifications that are 'work-related'. These features are not, of course, being taken on wholesale by schools (though it is important to note the desire of BTEC and CGLI to gain very much more than a foothold in the pre-16 curriculum; see 'Schools to be offered new practical curriculum', *Times Educational Supplement*, 6 January 1984), but it is clear that some of them, especially perhaps profiling (which is part of all TVEI projects), are being introduced across a range of schools.

One final aspect of the experience of the MSC's youth programmes, which cross-cuts all those discussed so far, should be mentioned at this point. This is the connection between practicality and relevance, and student motivation. Those 'turned off' schools by an academic diet are frequently reported as blooming when carrying out relevant or practical work, and to become 'different people' on work experience.

The third major strand of the diagnosis which appears to underlie TVEI is the educational consequences of the pace and nature of technological change. Again, the issues are well known, and by no means exclusive to TVEI, and I will do no more than mention them here. The educational implications of the pace of technological change have usually been derived from an assumption that it will mean that very few people are likely to stay in the same job, or even the same broad area of work, all their lives. There is a consequent need for 'education for flexibility', and specifically an emphasis on 'generic' rather than 'specific' skills. This does not seem to have been nearly such a prominent feature in TVEI, however, as those associated with the *content* of technological change, and especially the growth of Information Technology (IT). There are at least three assumed consequences of this growth that are built into the diagnosis. First, it is held that future employment prospects are likely to be most propitious in IT-based industry and commerce. Secondly, even those who are not employed in IT-related jobs will live their lives in a society where relationships of all kinds, and especially of individuals to institutions, will be transformed by IT. And, thirdly, teaching and learning themselves will make ever-increasing use of IT, altering both what it is possible to teach, and how it is possible to teach it. These three features combine to place a heavy emphasis on IT in TVEI.

The three aspects of the diagnosis which I have identified so far – the legacy of the Great Debate, the rise of youth unemployment, and the consequences of technological change – are by no means exclusive to TVEI. They are, rather, part of the *zeitgeist* and I have merely tried to indicate the particular emphases which seem to underlie the specific TVEI diagnosis. However, there is one further element which underlies much of the distinctiveness of the TVEI diagnosis and it is peculiar to TVEI. This derives from David Young's close personal association with the Jewish charity ORT, the Organization for Rehabilitation through Training, which, it is clear, provided something of a model for TVEI:

> ORT's philosophy is to incorporate job specific training into a broad education beginning at the age of 14, with an emphasis on the individual pupil .... The British ORT trust [of which David Young was an original trustee] was founded in 1980 out of a concern that schools here were failing to develop the potential of a large proportion of their pupils, and a desire to make education more relevant to the world outside, by developing practical and marketable skills (Hofkins, 1984, p. 180).

■ Putting TVEI into practice

While most of the elements of the diagnosis which produced TVEI were common currency, they had had rather little impact on the education system. Privately sponsored programmes like Project Trident, which concentrated on providing work experience for school pupils, and Young Enterprise, which aimed to show them how business worked, had had some impact (see Jamieson, 1986), but neither they nor any more official efforts seemed likely to bring about the kind of redirection of the education system called for in the Great Debate and Green Paper.

There are a number of reasons for this. Among the more important are:

(1) The DES's constitutional position prevented it from making central interventions in the school curriculum. It had therefore to rely on what it could achieve by means of advice, persuasion and whatever pressure it could bring to bear.

(2) The funding base of schools made them less vulnerable to the kind of incursions that the MSC had been able to make into the curriculum and structure of colleges of further education.

(3) It is by no means certain that the DES's own field representatives and organic intellectuals, the HMI, were convinced either of the correctness of the diagnosis or of the value and appropriateness for schools of the approaches contained within MSC youth programmes.

(4) The schools and teachers had always quite explicitly opposed attempts to divert them in a more employment-related direction. They, too, did not accept the diagnosis, which they felt made them scapegoats for the nation's economic decline.

Thus, while the problem of the kind of education required by the diagnosis outlined above was being taken seriously, and a range of possible solutions was available, the problem of school, teacher and education system autonomy and accountability remained. There was not in the existing framework a way of reorienting schools in the desired direction. That is why the MSC had to be given the job of delivering TVEI.

What the education service was confronted with when TVEI was announced, then, was a broadly familiar package to be delivered by quite new means to a body operating with a style, expectations, and under a set of constraints, quite different from those it was used to [...]. How the LEAs and schools reacted to this situation, and the effect of that reaction on the shape of TVEI in practice, will make up the remainder of this chapter.

For the essential point is, of course, that being acquainted with the origin and framework of the project does not necessarily tell us a great deal about how it works. It certainly does not tell us conclusively and comprehensively what TVEI is. This is so for the general reason that practically every study ever published of an educational or curriculum innovation concludes that the form it actually takes is different from what was intended, that the process of implementation itself alters the shape and emphasis of the project. It is also true in the particular case of TVEI both for the reason that, as suggested in the last section, the diagnosis is a fairly broad and flexible one, which does not entail or specify particular remedies for particular problems, and that there was no pressure from MSC for LEAs to conform to particular kinds of programme in their submissions. They had, of course, to fit in with the guidelines, but there was a clear acceptance, and even encouragement, of the diversity across the local projects; this is demonstrated clearly in the first 14 projects selected, which differ very considerably from each other in their interpretation of the common guidelines, their institutional arrangements, and so on. Even where the same subjects appear near universally, like Technology or Business Studies, the level and content through which they are to be approached differs across the schemes.

What TVEI is, then, in any particular LEA or school, is the outcome of continuing interplay between the requirements of participation in the initiative, as spelled out in the authority's contract with the MSC, and what existed before, and continues to exist alongside, TVEI in the authority and schools. TVEI has to be accommodated to the existing patterns of practice; however great the sums of money involved in any particular local project may appear as extra funding, they are a very small proportion of the overall budget, and certainly not sufficient to cause an LEA completely to reorganize itself as the condition of accepting TVEI money – though this is rather less true at the level of the school.

It will be useful to go very briefly through the structures and processes through which the design and implementation of local TVEI schemes have to pass to get an idea how, and how far, the broad guidelines of the initiative are shaped to meet local requirements, conditions and traditions. The obvious place to start is the LEA's decision to prepare an application for participation in TVEI. It seems that in each of the three rounds of TVEI there was in some authorities a great deal of discussion over whether to bid for TVEI or not. As I stated above, the main grounds of opposition (apart from the initial, and continuing, anger over the manner of announcing the scheme) were that the scheme was divisive and that it would have a narrowing effect on the curriculum. One further objection was that the money came from the MSC, which led to fears of a takeover of the school system similar to that which it was felt MSC was carrying out in the further education sector. The continuing strength of these objections is apparent in the fact that 21 LEAs in England and Wales and 4 in the north of Scotland are still (1986) refusing to submit bids for TVEI money. So why did the majority of LEAs apply to take part in the scheme? After all, the initially hostile reception to the scheme was practically universal. The answer is, undoubtedly, because of the money. Though some LEAs were already carrying out TVEI-like projects, and others were eager to do so, it is unlikely that so many of them would have volunteered to take part in a scheme with the aims of TVEI if there had not been such large sums of money involved. At a time of falling rolls and declining funding for education, most authorities felt that they could not afford not to bid for the TVEI money, and they invested much time and effort in preparing their bids in an extremely short time. The extent to which local authorities were *only* 'doing it for the money', that is, the nature of their commitment to the principles of TVEI, varied considerably. There are some missionaries among the first round of TVEI authorities, and also perhaps some who were hoping to be able to 'take the money and run'.

Differences between the various schemes deriving from the nature of the authority's ideological commitment to it became wider through the process of the preparation of the bid. At least three rather different models, with different consequences for the eventual shape of the scheme, appear to have been followed. In some authorities, the initial approach from MSC was passed to the authority's senior officer dealing with further education, because he or she was the person responsible for all contact with MSC. This led in some of those cases to the scheme being drawn up within the further education section of the LEA and consequently inscribed with at least some of the elements of the FEU pedagogy mentioned above. A different pattern, and one which I suspect was much more common among the second round authorities who had a little longer than the first round to prepare their bid, was to devolve responsibility for drawing up the scheme to a consortium, or competing consortia, of heads in the authority. These groups were obviously likely to be primarily committed to getting what they could out of the scheme for the schools. A third pattern was for the authority to select the schools to take part in the scheme first, and draw up a proposal in collaboration with them. A further dimension of difference within this pattern comes from the different criteria used to select the schools. Some TVEI schools have been included because they have demonstrated that they could make it work, others because they are thought to need a new challenge. In some cases it has been used to equalize provision across the authority by bringing extra resources to the worst-off schools, in others it has been used to smooth school amalgamation. In yet others, TVEI funds have gone to the schools in the areas of the most powerful councillors.

So, just as the guidelines did not clearly imply or promote any particular kind of scheme, nor did they suggest any 'profiles for the TVEI school'. In this situation, though their initial motivation may have been the money, when it came to preparing the applications which showed how the money would be used, local authorities fitted the requirements of TVEI to their own particular circumstances. How they did this varied with the way the bid was prepared, but typically TVEI money provided solutions to other problems in addition to that of changing the provision of technical and vocational education according to a specified set of guidelines.

It should not be assumed, however, that LEAs have been able to take on TVEI without cost, that they are doing nothing they would not have done anyway, given the funding. At the simplest level, it seems highly unlikely that any LEA would have been willing to suggest, or able to get away with, such an uneven distribution of such large resources across its schools. The concentration of those very significant extra resources within, in most cases, a very small proportion of their schools, has undoubtedly created major problems for LEAs. It seems unlikely, too, that LEAs would voluntarily have surrendered even that part of their control of what goes on in their schools which is required by participation in TVEI.

TVEI's reception in the schools largely parallels that in the LEAs. Initial suspicion of its background and purpose mixed with morale levels depressed through the 1980s by curtailment of funding and poor career prospects leave schools uncertain about what was required, and also about what they might have to concede. In this situation, TVEI represented for most schools almost the only prospect of funded curriculum development at all, let alone of such lavish funding, and like the LEAs, this made it difficult for those identified by whatever processes the LEA used as TVEI schools to say no to participation in the project. As with the LEAs it is difficult to point to a typical school reaction to TVEI. Some of those involved were clearly very anxious to be included in the scheme, others were wary of it; some staffs were divided on it, while others were agnostic. The motives of schools were as varied as LEAs, but again the money and resources involved were critical factors.

The TVEI schools have, though, had to change in a number of ways, and while certainly almost every one of them I have consulted insist they are doing nothing they would not anyway have wanted to do if the funding had been available, it is not so clear that the *particular* changes entailed by TVEI would have been at the top of their priority list, or that, given a free hand, they would have spent the available money in precisely, or even broadly, the same areas.

At one level, indeed, the most immediate and obvious impact of TVEI on schools has been the vast amount of extra work it has involved for staff, especially, but not only, those directly involved in the project. They have been involved not just in 'new' or 'additional' projects, like attempting to mitigate sex-stereotyping, or creating a profiling system, but also in what they would, pre-TVEI, have recognized as hard core curriculum development, in drawing up new courses to fit in with the local interpretations of TVEI. And though this has in some schools reinforced any divisiveness inherent in TVEI, in rather more it has provided a boost to morale, and rekindled the professional fires of a large group of teachers, many of which had been dampened, apparently for good, by the depressed state of the profession in the years before TVEI came on the scene.

In the end, the surest guide to what comprises TVEI in any particular LEA or school is what that LEA or school was like before November 1982. But though LEAs and schools have not been forced to do anything they would not have wanted to do, given the funding, this does not mean that they are spending TVEI money as they would have, given a free hand. To this extent, at least, the initiative has succeeded in shifting the pattern of education in the schools involved in it.

■ The TVEI effect

Both the structure and the ideology of TVEI constrain the breadth of possible interpretations of the TVEI guidelines. They do not do this in a denotative way, however, and the scope for possible interpretations of the guidelines remains wide. The most important effect of the structure and ideology is that they make treating TVEI as merely a piece of curriculum reform, in the narrow sense of changing the subjects taught to a particular group of students, extremely difficult. Conceiving of, and delivering, an acceptable interpretation of TVEI almost necessarily involves a combination of factors. Critical differences between TVEI schemes come not only from their emphasizing different aspects of the guidelines – such as subject development, profiling or work experience – but from the particular combination of those aspects in each school. This combination is a key component of what I will call the 'TVEI effect', and its precise formulation is shaped by the reaction to, and interpretation of, the TVEI guidelines, and the resources available in the changing context of each school.

The TVEI effect, what TVEI means within any school, is not

produced only by each school's interpretation and combination of the set guidelines, however. It is also a function of the *salience* of the scheme within the school. This is made up of a number of factors, which will be discussed below. Like the combination of TVEI guidelines adopted within a school, the salience of TVEI results from the reaction of the headteacher and staff to the introduction of the scheme in the context of a particular school at a particular point in its history. The combination of TVEI guidelines and the scheme's salience within a school are mutually influential, whether mutually supportive or mutually hostile, and their relationship, together with the effect on the scheme of any changes in what is going on in the major part of the school, gives the TVEI effect its internal dynamic and determines the nature of the school's response to external factors.

In this final section of this chapter, then, I first of all consider something of the range of variation in the interpretation of some of the guidelines. I then go on to look at the idea of the salience of TVEI in the school, and finish by suggesting some of the key conditions within schools under which the guidelines are interpreted and the salience determined.

Most obviously, introducing TVEI into a school might be expected to involve some change in what is taught, either through the introduction of new subjects to the curriculum or in the modification of existing subjects. There is, however, considerable variation in the extent of change in what is taught, from the introduction of a whole new slate of 'TVEI subjects' that did not previously exist in the school, to the use of TVEI resources to teach existing, and unmodified, syllabuses more effectively. It is important to recognize that the degree of subject change brought about by TVEI is not the only nor necessarily the most important index of its effect on schools. Though we would be right in assuming that it will typically be a central component of the TVEI effect, it is possible to conceive of a potent TVEI effect being achieved in a school with little modification of pre-TVEI syllabuses.

A key 'non-subject' aspect of the TVEI is profiling. Though the guidelines speak only of 'records of achievement', in the great majority of TVEI schemes that requirement is met by something called 'profiling'. The possible variations of practice under that heading are very wide. Some schemes have adapted 'off the shelf' existing forms of profiling, while others have devised their own, often at great cost in teachers' time and effort. A variety of possible uses of pupils' profiles exists. They can be summative or formative, for teacher use only or available to parents and students too, and so on; but the major distinction in their contribution to the TVEI effect is between those (relatively few) schemes where that contribution is substantive, where profiling is a key organizing axis of the whole scheme, and those where it is limited to a more or less important service function.

The contribution of work experience to the TVEI effect can be appreciated in a rather similar way, in that its extent and nature vary with the degree to which the two periods of work experience that students must undergo in the course of the 4-year scheme are integrated into the scheme as a whole, or treated as a quite separate part of it. It is possible for the curriculum as a whole and the period of work experience to be organized in full recognition of the mutual benefit they could provide; or it is possible for the organization of work experience to be seen as just another chore entailed by taking the TVEI money and using it for things that are really important. The reaction to, and integration of, work experience can, indeed, stand for the perceived place and importance of 'links with industry' as a whole within TVEI schemes.

Residential education's contribution to the TVEI effect also varies with the nature and extent of its integration into the scheme as a whole. This applies to both of the two main forms it appears to have taken: the 'outward-bound' form, where the 'adventure and self-reliance' medium is a more central part of the message than the actual context in which it takes place; and the 'curriculum enrichment' form, where students are brought into contact with aspects of their subjects that lie outside the ability of the school to provide.

Besides the guidelines contained in the contract there are some other necessary accompaniments of bringing TVEI into a school, which may be important components of the TVEI effect. One of these, which has already been mentioned, is the prominence of the scheme in the school. Another very important one, which it is easy to take for granted, is the need for schools to spend in a relatively short time relatively large sums of money (though the precise amount of money available for spending by schools and the precise degree of control they have over that spending vary). This presents both technical and political difficulties. The technical difficulties arise as much as anything from schools' sheer inexperience of disposing of large sums of money in a short time in the most appropriate way. This inexperience, together with the short time-scale, may indeed lead to a conservatism in spending the money, that is, a tendency to spend it on somewhat more advanced equipment for teaching essentially the same content. More time for deliberation, and the consideration of alternatives, may have led in some cases to rather more 'radical' uses of the money.

The political problems associated with the distribution of the extra funds may also tend to push it into a similarly conservative direction. Any distribution, whether it is of equipment or additional salary points, is likely to be perceived as threatening by one or other subject departments or groups of staff within a school, and again there is some pressure towards changing as little as possible, 'doing more of the same', or introducing initiatives that cross the whole curriculum.

The magnification of the TVEI impact in the school through monitoring and marginality clearly enhances its prominence. This relates to what I have called the 'salience' of TVEI in the school. This contributes a great deal to the TVEI effect. It is made up of three components: identity, integration and compass. Identity refers both to the amount and to the nature of what is known about the scheme within the school. The public identity of a school's TVEI scheme can be found in the way the scheme is publicized to the staff and to the pupils and parents. It appears perhaps most clearly in the way TVEI is 'marketed' to pupils and parents. Is it separately identified in the options booklets? Is there a preferred target audience implicit in the way the scheme is described (and especially in the subjects it is possible to take alongside TVEI)? How far is its technical and vocational nature stressed, and especially its 'job-getting' potential? The clarity, popularity and divisiveness of the TVEI identity within a school are rooted in part in the kind of public face presented. They are also rooted in the less public aspect of TVEI in practice, which itself derives from the kind of changes entailed by the way the school interprets and combines the guidelines.

Together with its identity, the extent of its integration into the school as a whole determines the 'profile' of TVEI in the school. It is possible, for instance, for TVEI pupils, their parents and those who teach them not to be aware of their TVEI status. The degree of integration of TVEI into the school is associated with the degree of separateness of the TVEI group(s). This is a function of the number of hours they spend being taught as a separate group, the number of teachers teaching them, whether or not they are a group for non-TVEI purposes – especially whether they are a distinct registration group – and whether or not they have their own accommodation. The extent of TVEI's integration into a school is associated not only with the degree of isolation of those directly involved in it. It is also determined by the spread of information about it among those teachers not directly involved, whether they are made aware only of what they 'need' to know for the smooth operation of the scheme – which in many cases will be nothing – or of the broader details and ramifications of the scheme as a whole as it develops.

What I am calling its 'compass', the degree to which it penetrates and affects the workings of the rest of the school, is another part of its salience, but it is not directly linked to the height of profile. The compass of TVEI in a school comes about through a combination of articulation and infection. Articulation refers to the changes necessarily implied for the rest of the school by TVEI; for instance, in the timetable, or the need to construct viable classes in particular subjects. Infection refers to the 'voluntary' reactions in the rest of the school to TVEI. These can be positive – as might occur, for instance, in a decision to profile whole year groups and not just the TVEI/pupils – or negative, as might occur in the refusal of departments teaching 'core' subjects to accommodate any changes in approach implied by the introduction of TVEI; such as, for instance, a shift from English to 'communications', or Mathematics to 'numeracy'.

It is crucial to realize that the form taken by both components of the TVEI effect, the combination of the guidelines and its salience, emerges, and continues to change, through a complex process of negotiation between what was before TVEI and what might emerge as a result of it. These negotiations, explicit and implicit, between head and staff, coordinator and departments, members of the same department and so on, do not take place in a neutral arena. That arena is defined and marked by the history of previous negotiations, which are unique to each school. TVEI both heightens the importance of some facets of that history, and brings new aspects of it into play, as well as filtering the effect of external events into and on the negotiations. Among the especially prominent conditions of negotiation over TVEI are:

(1) The generally low level of morale within the teaching profession, following some years of declining funds, falling rolls and apparent decreasing public esteem. This meant a warm welcome for almost anything that promised extra funding and the possibility of professional development.

(2) Considerable resistance among both the leadership and the rank and file of the teaching profession to a narrowly defined 'vocational education' – the preparation of factory fodder – and to anything that threatened the principles of comprehensive education.

(3) The heightening of this resistance through the apparent attribution to teachers of blame for national decline in the debates that prefigured TVEI, where teachers appeared as scapegoats, as part of the problem rather than part of the solution.

(4) The existence of a growing pressure towards some kind of differential reward for different performance in the payment of teachers.

(5) The possibility that some subjects might disappear from the curriculum with declining staffing levels.

(6) Apprehension over the effects of the entry of the MSC into the area of further education.

(7) A heightened awareness of competition between secondary schools, possibly involving their very survival, as a result of falling rolls.

Not all the factors apply in all cases. More importantly, they do not all carry equal weight. For instance, the need for extra funds in most cases outweighed any reservations about TVEI. It did not remove those reservations, though, and a common pattern of acceptance of TVEI into a school is to attempt to do it with minimum infringement of those reservations. But that is only one form of response, albeit fairly typical. The main point is that whatever the orientation towards TVEI, however significant the various conditions of negotiation may be, TVEI is never merely imposed on schools. It is always accepted on certain implicit or explicit conditions based largely on the existing history, ideology, structure and location of the school, to produce a TVEI effect unique to that school.

■ Conclusion

I have argued here that although TVEI varies immensely across authorities and schools, it does not vary infinitely. The variations are constrained by the origins of the initiative and the problems it was created to solve. These led to it taking on a particular broad structure and ideology, both of which allowed a very wide range of local variation. The nature and extent of that variation are shaped in the schools into the unique TVEI effect by their own history and the conditions under which TVEI was accepted into the schools. In the end, although it may be changed or even transformed by TVEI, the surest guide to understanding TVEI in a school is what the school was like before.

References

Bates, I. (1984) 'From vocational guidance to life skills: historical perspectives on careers education', in Bates, I. *et al.*, *Schooling for the Dole? The New Vocationalism*, pp. 170–219 (London: Macmillan).

Beck, J. (1983) 'Accountability, industry and education: reflections on some aspects of educational and industrial policies of the Labour administrations of 1974–9', in Ahier, J. and Flude, M. (eds), *Contemporary Education Policy*, pp. 211–32 (London: Croom Helm).

Esland, G. and Cathcart, H. (1981) *Education and the Corporate Economy*, E353 Unit 2 (Milton Keynes: Open University Press).

Farley, M. (1985) 'Trends and Structural Changes in English Vocational Education' in Dale, R. (ed.) 1985 *Education, Training and Employment: towards a new vocationalism* (Oxford: Pergamon).

Grubb, W. N. and Lazerson, M. (1981) 'Vocational solutions to youth problems: the persistent frustrations of the American experience'. *Educational Analysis*, Vol. 3, No. 2, pp. 91–103.

Hofkins, D. (1984) 'ORT: Confidence through skills'. *Education*, Vol. 163, No. 5, p. 100.

Jamieson, I. (1986) 'Corporate hegemony or pedagogic liberation?', in R. Dale (ed.), *Education, Training and Employment*, pp. 23–40 (Oxford: Pergamon Press).

McGowan, E. E. and Cohen, D. K. (1977) 'Career education – reforming school through work'. *Public Interest*, 46 (Winter), 28–47.

Moore, R. (1984) 'Schooling and the World of Work', in Bates, I. *et al.*, *Schooling for the Dole*, pp. 65–103 (London: Macmillan).

MSC (1984) *TVEI Operating Manual* (London: MSC).

Offe, C. (1984) *Contradictions of the Welfare State* (London: Heinemann).

Reeder, D. (1979) 'A recurring debate: education and industry', in Bernbaum, G. (ed.), *Schooling in Decline*, pp. 115–48 (London: Macmillan).

Watts, A. G. (1983) *Education, Unemployment and the Future of Work* (Milton Keynes: Open University Press).

Chapter 13

From the Decade of the Enterprise Culture to the Decade of the TECs

F. Coffield

This article looks back at the rise of the enterprise movement in the 1980s and forward to the establishment and performance of 100 Training and Enterprise Councils (TECs) in England and Wales during the 1990s. Both strategies are thought to be part of an ideological project of the Conservative Government to transform Britain's economy and education by means of the enterprise culture. The main initiatives designed to promote such a culture are described, the concept of enterprise as used on enterprise courses is examined, and the conclusion drawn that there is no generic skill of enterprise whose essence can be distilled and taught. A number of crucial issues in relation to the new TECs (the need for a national plan for education, training and employment, the commitment of employers, future remit, accountability and representation, etc.) are discussed and some constructive suggestions made. The next ten years will show whether TECs prove to be an ambitious, forward-looking and productive strategy or an ill-advised, risky and unsuccessful gamble with the future prosperity of Britain.

■ Introduction

A few years ago the word 'enterprise' was fashionable: it has now become pervasive and is in danger of becoming compulsory or at least very difficult to avoid. When social historians come to assess Britain in the 1980s they

Source: Coffield, F. (1990) 'From the decade of the enterprise culture to the decade of the TECs', *British Journal of Education and Work*, September. © Trentham Books Ltd.

are likely to emphasize this key word which has come to stand for a collection of political, economic and social values. Perhaps more than any other term it summarizes the *zeitgeist* created by the Conservative Government during the last decade. James Hamilton Dunn in a prophetic article written in 1977 argued that a change in the direction of British politics was seen by the New Right to require:

> ... the creation (or rediscovery) of what the New Right call a 'myth' or 'spirit'. In order for these myths to be accepted, politicians must appeal to the imagination of the British people .... This new spirit can be called the spirit of enterprise. It should create greater economic freedom but it requires faith to maintain it .... As with religious faith, the faith in the spirit of enterprise takes the shape of a way of life, which becomes the driving force of the community (Dunn, 1977, p. 226).[1]

In the words of one of the leading exponents of enterprise, Allan Gibb: 'The entrepreneur in the UK has become the god (or goddess) of current UK political ideology and a leading actor in the theatre of the "new economics".' (Gibb, 1987, p. 3). The 1980s witnessed a sudden mushrooming of schemes, courses, agencies, and publications all specializing in the promotion of enterprise and in the creation of the enterprise culture. In 1989 at the national launch of the new Training and Enterprise Councils, Norman Fowler, the then Secretary of State for Employment, described them as a 'genuine revolution in the way Britain develops its people and stimulates business growth' (*Employment Gazette*, April 1989, p. 155). The Training Agency (1989a, p. 2) believes that enterprise will play an important role in '... the restructuring of the British economy, the starting of small businesses, the revival of the inner cities and the expansion of European markets in 1992.'

It is, however, Lord Young (Chairman of the Manpower Services Commission and then Secretary of State for Employment), who is most identified with the policy of promoting an enterprise culture, and his explanation for the decline of British industry neatly encapsulates the ruling ideology of the Conservative Government in the 1980s. 'The problems of our economy,' he wrote in 1986 (p. 25), 'have largely stemmed from a lack of enterprise. But don't pick on the managers in British industry today. At least, they made the choice to go into industry and commerce, they took on the challenge of producing goods and services and they are fighting to create wealth and jobs. The real culprits are bedded deep in our national history and culture.' Of the four culprits who are mentioned by name, the first is the education system 'which had little contact and no regard for industry – which looked down on scientific and technical subjects and which disdained vocational preparation.' (The other three culprits listed by Lord Young are 'a financial system ... with little concern for small businesses,' a protectionist industrial system and a confrontational industrial relations system.)

The first section of this article critically examines the House that

Lord Young has Built, and explores what is euphemistically described as 'the philosophy of enterprise', the growth of the enterprise movement and issues surrounding its meaning and role in educational and social policy. In the final part, a number of questions are asked about the latest development of Government thinking on education, training and employment, namely, the establishment of the new TECs.

■ The rise of the enterprise movement

A broad enterprise movement is now in full swing and includes the following initiatives, most of which arrive with a virtually compulsory acronym attached to their official title: more detail is provided on those projects thought to be less familiar or more recent.

(a) *Technical and Vocational Education Initiative* (TVEI) is now regularly included in the list of enterprise initiatives issued by the Training Agency (for example, Training Agency, 1989a, p. 2). [...] The national extension of TVEI is estimated to cost about £90 million per year over the ten years of its development from the Autumn term, 1987 onwards (Dept of Employment *et al.*, 1986, p. 10).

(b) *The Mini Enterprise in Schools Project (MESP)* began as a national scheme in England and Wales in 1985 for 'children from any age, from primary to sixth form' to run 'a small business, making or selling products or services' (MESP, 1988). It was launched by the Industry/Education Unit of the Department of Trade and Industry under Lord Young, has been supported by the Society of Education Officers and has been backed financially by the National Westminster Bank which provides a £40 grant to every participating school, and a business account combining a low interest loan of up to £50, if required. It remains to be seen whether the project develops the enterprise culture within pupils or whether 'their experience of business in school may stimulate in them a critical penetration of the exploitative relations involved in capitalist production' (Shilling, 1989, p. 122), or indeed whether students learn to form price-fixing cartels. Questions also need to be asked about the quality of the products offered for sale by these mini-companies. Do any of them become in any way commercially viable and, if so, what happens if they begin to pose a serious challenge to existing local firms?

(c) *Enterprise in YTS* was launched by Lord Young and Geoffrey Holland (then Director of MSC) in 1986 with the aim of developing an enterprise culture among young people. The MSC responded to this initiative by setting up a series of projects to develop different approaches to the training of enterprise and their stated objective was as follows: 'By 1990, Enterprise training will be sufficiently developed to be available to all trainees in all YTS schemes as an integral part of their training' (MSC leaflet, *Enterprise in YTS*, 1987). In the same way as the role of MESP has grown to include the promotion of mini-companies in other vocational schemes such as CPVE and TVEI (see Shilling, 1989), so enterprise training is conceived by the MSC as not only relevant to YTS trainees but to a wide range of unemployed people on the New Job Training Scheme, the Community Programme and their successor, Employment Training.

(d) *Training for Enterprise Programme* (TFE) aims to 'equip potential and existing entrepreneurs with the skills and knowledge successfully to launch, manage and develop a small business' (National Audit Office, 1988, p. 16). The number of trainees has grown very rapidly from 32 in 1977–78 to over 115,000 in 1987–88 at a cost of over £64 million. The main programmes on offer under TFE are:

(1) Business Enterprise Programme (BEP): up to seven days of basic training covering the skills needed to set up and run a small business.

(2) Private Enterprise Programme (PEP): a series of thirteen one-day training modules for existing businesses, for which there were 60,000 places in 1987–88.

(3) Management Extension Programme (MEP): offers unemployed managers three weeks of training in small business management, followed by a secondment to a firm for up to 23 weeks.

(4) Graduate Gateway Programme (GGP): designed to encourage graduates to consider a career in business. In addition, there are Enterprise Introduction Days and Enterprise Rehearsal, which allow participants to try out a business idea in a commercial setting, from which they can then be transferred to the Enterprise Allowance Scheme.

(e) *Enterprise Allowance Scheme* (EAS) was introduced in 1983 with 25,000 places after pilot schemes had been tried in five areas. It expanded rapidly with 80,000 places available in 1986 and 110,000 places for 1988/89. By 1988 over 329,000 people out of work for at least eight weeks (originally thirteen weeks) had taken up the offer of £40 per week for a year at a cost to the Government of £545 million (National Audit Office, 1988, p. 7). Applicants must also be over 18 and have £1000 (which could be a loan or an overdraft) to invest in the new business they wish to start up.

The National Audit Office in 1988 evaluated the efforts of the Training Agency to achieve their objective of helping unemployed people create viable new businesses which would not otherwise exist. They found that 13 per cent left before completing their year on the scheme, that the overall survival rate three years after entering the scheme was 57 per cent and that the commercial viability of the proposed businesses had never been tested. In addition, the claims made by the Department of Employment for the new jobs created by the scheme needed to be substantially reduced by both deadweight (those who would have set up in business anyway without the scheme) and displacement (the amount of existing output and employment which is lost as a result of the new business). In the words of the report, the Department 'assume that half of EAS businesses displace existing businesses' (National Audit Office, 1988, p. 9). All participants on EAS are visited once a year and another fifth are revisited if they are thought to be high risk, a situation which forced Sir Geoffrey Holland (by now, Permanent Secretary at the Department of Employment) to admit to the House of Commons Committee of Public Accounts that the participants '... are quite certainly out on their own and they often feel very isolated from each other' (House of Commons Committee of Public Accounts, 1989, p. 6). All these findings point strongly to the same conclusion: the scheme was introduced and has been expanded because of its 'register effect', namely, it has been highly successful in lowering the unemployment figures. The scheme is also based on an act of faith by Government ministers that self-employment and small firms will by themselves regenerate the economy, a belief for which, as Finn (1986, p. 10) has pointed out, there is no substantial evidence.

(f) *Enterprise and Education.*The Department of Trade and Industry which acquired the subtitle of the Department for Enterprise in January, 1988, issued a White Paper at that time which argued that employers have much to contribute to the development of the curriculum, the management of schools and colleges, and the promotion of enterprise activities in these institutions. The Government then set itself three objectives: to involve 10 per cent of teachers in industrial placements every year; to provide all secondary pupils with two or more weeks of work experience; and to impress on every trainee teacher 'an appreciation of the needs of employers and of the importance of links between schools and employers' (Department of Trade and Industry, 1988, para. 4.5). These objectives could easily serve as performance indicators of the Government's willingness to fund such enterprises because LEAs, schools and employers have since appeared loath to move beyond the resourcing of pilot projects, pointing to the competing demands on them from the National Curriculum and Local Management of Schools.

(g) *Enterprise in Higher Education (EHE)* is an initiative of the Training Agency which was introduced in December 1987 'to assist institutions of higher education develop enterprising graduates in partnership with employers' (Training Agency, 1989a, p. 2). Over one hundred institutions submitted proposals for funding of up to £1 million over five years and eleven institutions (four Universities and seven Polytechnics) were then invited to participate in round one of the initiative; and there has since been a second round of grants awarded. The main objective is that 'every person seeking a higher education qualification should be able to develop competencies and aptitudes relevant to enterprise (Training Agency, 1989a, p. 5), and staff in higher education are to be involved in training programmes so that not only the curriculum is changed but also the processes of learning and teaching. The significance of EHE is that the Training Agency has been able to buy its way into the curriculum and pedagogy of higher education by using the same technique that the MSC employed with TVEI, namely, dangling large sums of money in front of schools which had been starved of resources. As Jamieson (1989, p. 73) writes, institutions of higher education have been falling over each other to ensnare themselves upon the golden hook. It remains to be seen whether the participating institutions seize the opportunity to develop creative local programmes and abandon the deadening jargon of the Training Agency. It may, however, transpire that the institutions simply use the money provided by the Training Agency for developments which were already planned but shelved for lack of funds.

(h) *Enterprise Awareness in Teacher Education* (EATE). This project was launched by the Department of Trade and Industry in September 1989 with the aim of acting as a catalyst to promote staff and course development focusing on enterprise, economic and industrial awareness within institutions of initial teacher education. EATE has been funded by the DTI initially for two years with the possibility of an extension for a third year.

(i) *Evangelical Enterprise* works in partnership with the DTI's inner cities Task Force and the Evangelical Alliance, a grouping of black churches, to provide enterprise projects to help unemployed people. In the words of Michael Hastings, Director of Evangelical Enterprise: 'Our ongoing vision is for a new and determined Christian activism that will bring healing to Inner City areas by grasping creative opportunities to help people into real work and by supporting constructive enterprise' (quoted by Roberts, 1988, p. 371).

(j) Over 400 *Local Enterprise Agencies*, which began as a response to high unemployment, 'are non-profitmaking companies. Typically they represent a public/private partnership, are private sector led (with) the job of providing a free, confidential business advice service for unemployed people wishing to explore the self-employment option ...' (Grayson, 1989, pp. 534–535).

(k) *The Training and Enterprise Councils (TECs)* were launched in March, 1989 by the Prime Minister and the then Secretary of State for Employment, Norman Fowler. Eventually there will be 100 TECs throughout the country, responsible for a budget of almost £3 billion annually, although the budget for each TEC is more likely to be in the range of £20 to £50 million per year. Local TECs will set up as independent companies, entering into a commercial contract with the Secretary of State for Employment to develop training and enterprise in their area. Handing over the main responsibility for training all our young people, the unemployed and all adults requiring retraining to local employers may be, as the *Unemployment Bulletin* (Issue 30, Summer 1989, p. 1) argues, a smokescreen to disguise central Government's retreat from funding industrial training, but the advisability of such a move needs to be examined in detail and it is discussed in the final section of this article.

(l) *Scottish Enterprise (SE), and Highlands and Islands Enterprise (HIE).* The Training Agency in Scotland is to be replaced by these two bodies, with SE being formed from an amalgamation with the Scottish Development Agency, with an annual budget of £500 million and a staff of 1500. According to Raffe (1989, p. 9) 'the most obvious difference between these proposals and the parallel creation of TECs in England is that the new Scottish bodies will have broader responsibilities .... The word "training" is absent from the title of the proposed local enterprise companies; they will be LECs not TECs.'

The above list is by no means complete: in addition, there are programmes sponsored by the Training Agency (for example, New Enterprise Programme, Graduate Enterprise Programme); by the Department of Trade and Industry (for example, The Enterprise Initiative with Enterprise Counsellors); by the Department of Employment (twenty-four Enterprise zones, Enterprise centres, Freephone Enterprise and the Regional Enterprise Unit); and by independent, national or local organizations (for example, Young Enterprise, the Industrial Society's Enterprise Unit, the Community Enterprise Trust, British Coal Enterprise Limited, and so on).

The first conclusion to be drawn from this massive investment of resources is that enterprise is not just the latest fashion or bandwagon in Conservative thinking; rather a whole new world of enterprise has been brought into being and its influence is spreading in so many directions simultaneously that few people are likely to escape whether they are children in primary school, students in university, unemployed miners or redundant executives. The intention is nothing less than to change the culture in education, training and employment from what is termed dependence to enterprise.

As significant as the number of initiatives has been their style: under the leadership of Lord Young, programmes have been launched with all the razzamatazz normally associated with show business; an example is The *Enterprise Express*, a seven carriage, special exhibition train which left Euston station with a fanfare of trumpets from the band of the Royal Marines to 'spread the message of enterprise throughout the nation' (*In Business Now*, April/May, 1986, p. 22). The BBC Radio Four programme on Enterprise also arranged for the *Express* to make an unscheduled stop at Borchester, the fictional market town featured in *The Archers*.

■ The concept of enterprise

The plethora of organizations and initiatives has created in turn an over-abundance of competing definitions and contrasting lists of different enterprise skills or attributes. The debates earlier this century about the nature of intelligence, where psychologists were generous to a fault with their definitions, each writer putting forward his or her own definition and some offering over the years two or three which were logically incompatible, are now being repeated over the word enterprise.

One of the main producers of enterprise materials has been Durham University's Business School (DUBS) which has published *Key Skills* in enterprise for 14–16 year olds (Johnson *et al.*, 1987a), for 16–19 year olds (Johnson *et al.*, 1987b) and *Primary Enterprise* (DUBS, 1989). These teaching materials, which had been bought by 'over 75 per cent of secondary schools in Britain' by 1989 (Johnson, 1989), find their academic justification in Allan Gibb's monograph on *Enterprise Culture – its Meaning and Implications for Education and Training* (Gibbs, 1987). He claims that there are at least twelve entrepreneurial attributes (Gibb, 1987, p. 6):

(1) initiative;
(2) strong persuasive powers;
(3) moderate rather than high risk-taking ability;
(4) flexibility;
(5) creativity;
(6) independence/autonomy;
(7) problem-solving ability;
(8) need for achievement;
(9) imagination;
(10) high belief in control of one's own destiny;
(11) leadership;
(12) hard work.

No argument is advanced to explain why these particular twelve have been chosen. Gibb does concede that not all of the twelve 'are measurable at present, and many are controversial, in that the evidence associating them with particular forms of behaviour is as yet weak' (Gibb, 1987, p. 7).

Such a reasonable and qualified assertion is, however, omitted from the introductions to the resource packs on enterprise skills for schools and colleges produced under Professor Gibb's leadership. There it is claimed that 'These attributes – the essence of enterprise – have been extensively researched over the years in many countries with consensus in their findings' (Johnson *et al.*, 1987, p. x). Although a table is produced by Johnson *et al.* to show 'how the research findings on enterprise attributes guide the educational aims' (Johnson *et al.*, 1987, p. xi), there are no references to the literature which would enable such claims to be checked.

Gibb, on the other hand, does refer to US psychologists such as McClelland and Rotter to provide a theoretical justification for including, for example, in his list of attributes 'need for achievement' and 'high belief in control of one's own destiny'. But what is missing is any evidence that links internal locus of control and all the other attributes into a unitary concept called enterprise. Readers also need to be directed to the literature (for example, Kilby, 1971, p. 19) which has examined the claims made by psychologists like McClelland and which has judged that they failed to achieve an acceptable level of empirical verification.

A reading of the original source material is even more revealing. [. . .] McClelland, for example, studied the relationship between economic development and 'the need for achievement' which he defined as 'a desire to do well, not so much for the sake of social recognition or prestige, but for the sake of an inner feeling of personal achievement' (McClelland, 1971, p. 110). He took as his measure of 'the need for achievement' the number of references to 'doing a good job' [*sic*] in children's readers from twenty-three countries around 1925 and from thirty-nine countries around 1950; and 'for a measure of economic development, we relied on the amount of electricity produced in each country' (McClelland, 1971, p. 111). The two measures are then claimed to be statistically correlated at a highly significant level in Western, Communist and underdeveloped countries and McClelland concludes '. . . it is startling to find concrete evidence for psychological determination, for psychological developments which precede and presumably cause economic changes' (McClelland, 1971, p. 112). No argument is offered in support of the almost imperceptible slide from correlation to presumed causation. Moreover, Abercrombie *et al.* (1986, p. 183) claim that arguments about motivation explain only part of the relationship between individualism and capitalism: 'However, they provide neither a necessary nor a sufficient condition for that explanation. There are other ways in which individualism and capitalism relate to one another that are not dependent on motivation. For example, there is the familiar argument of Weber and Marx that a capitalist economy will constrain individuals to behave appropriately, regardless of their beliefs and motives, if they are to survive economically.'[2]

But perhaps the most serious omission of all from the publications on enterprise from the Durham University Business School is the failure to provide alternative views on enterprise and to admit what a hotly contested and inadequate concept enterprise has always been. Kilby (1971, p. 6), for example, explores seven competing theories of enterprise in his book, the four psychological theories (of Schumpeter, McClelland, Hagen and Kunkel) and the three sociological theories (of Weber, Cochran and Young) and finds them all wanting. To give the impression that researchers have reached a consensus and to offer students of enterprise a closed world which excludes controversy and debate is anti-intellectual. Gibb also leaves aside the 'degree to which they (the attributes) are innate or not' – but in what way could, for example, 'moderate, risk-taking ability' or any of the other culturally laden attributes be considered 'innate'?

Instead of the consensus claimed by Johnson *et al.*, an immediate problem in identifying the core skills of enterprise is that every organization has its own list. *Community Enterprise in the Curriculum* (Turner, 1988, p. 15) also has exactly twelve core skills but, as can be seen, only two are the same as those in Gibb's list:

(1) assess one's strengths and weaknesses;

(2) seek information and advice;

(3) make decisions;

(4) plan one's time and energy;

(5) carry through an agreed responsibility;

(6) negotiate;

(7) deal with people in power and authority;

(8) problem-solve;

(9) resolve conflict;

(10) cope with stress and tension;

(11) evaluate one's performance;

(12) communicate.

So the number of 'core' enterprise skills has jumped from twelve to twenty-two. The City and Guilds of London Institute (1988) talks of six main enterprise skill areas, three of which correspond with Gibb's list. Pitman's course on enterprise skills (1987) has five transferable skills, none of which are mentioned in Gibb's list.

The Scottish Vocational Education Council's module on Enterprise Activity seeks to develop four skills, one of which 'task management skills'

could generously be said to be close to 'problem-solving ability' as Gibb
has it. Finally, the Royal Society of Arts has produced a profile of thirty-
one sentences 'defining the skills and competencies involved in enterprise'.
These range from such sophisticated skills as No. 9 'the ability to resolve
conflict' and No. 15 'the ability to solve problems', on the one hand, to
such routine tasks as No. 18 'open, conduct and close a brief transaction by
 telephone' and No. 23 'use alphabetical order and index systems to locate
information in dictionaries and reference books', on the other. What kind
of a concept is it that has, at a conservative estimate, more than fifty 'core'
skills? How many peripheral skills are there likely to be? There is a close
parallel here with the core skills of the Youth Training Scheme. Jonathan
(1987, p. 112) quotes examples of these skills such as 'filling a supermarket
shelf', 'sorting incoming mail' and 'counting items singly or in batches',
and then adds: 'This is not "learning through doing"; it is simply "doing"
and not doing anything very stimulating at that.'

All the lists and courses mentioned in the previous paragraph are
making a series of assumptions about the nature and function of knowledge
which have been challenged by Jonathan (1983) and Thompson (1984).
Jonathan, for instance, attacks what she describes as 'The Manpower
Services model of education' for arguing that 'the process of learning
matters more than the content learnt', as if 'insight that the learning
process is itself important is replaced by the false claim that it is all-
important' (Jonathan, 1983, p. 8). Second, '... it is quite overlooked that
the very success of say, science depends upon steeping practitioners in the
content of disciplines before they are able to strike out on their own and
add to that content' (Jonathan, 1983, p. 8). Thirdly, generic, identifiable
and transferable skills cannot be epistemologically divorced from content:
'What sort of questions are intelligent and what answers are sensible
depends upon context' (Jonathan, 1983, p. 8).

To sum up at this point. First, we are not dealing with a tightly
defined, agreed and unitary concept but with a farrago of 'hurrah' words
like 'creativity', 'initiative' and 'leadership'. Too many of the definitions
tend to be circular or consist of managerial tautologies, tricked out with the
rhetoric of progressive education. Part of the confusion stems from the fact
that the word 'enterprise' is used in different ways, sometimes referring to
an individual ability considered amenable to improvement and at other
times to a form of economic activity, usually in small businesses. For
example, ' cause one can be enterprising both by making a million before
one's fortieth birthday and by shepherding passengers out of a burning
aeroplane, does not mean that there is a generic skill of enterprise whose
essence can be distilled and taught.

Second, some notions which are central to most definitions of
enterprise, problem-solving for instance, have been taken from psychology
and then simplified, decontextualized and invested with a significance and
power which few psychologists would be prepared to support. Problem-

solving is treated within the enterprise literature as if it were the highest form of thinking or as if it were to be equated with thinking itself. The more fundamental issues of finding and accurately formulating problems, or learning to live with problems which are not amenable to easy (or any) solution are nowhere discussed. Instead of an approach which seems to suggest that the student of enterprise need only apply a set of techniques (the core skills) to be guaranteed success, a more powerful and educative model of thinking could have been presented by emphasizing the critical role of argument, controversy and debate in developing the mind (see Billig, 1989). [. . .]

Third, as Thompson (1984, p. 204) has argued about the Education for Capability movement, the potential terms of reference of words like 'capability' or 'skills' (or 'enterprise') are so wide that to call someone 'capable' or 'skilful' (or 'enterprising') without specific context is meaningless. And yet Gibb (1987, p. 11) redefines 'enterprise' as 'the exercise of enterprising attributes in *any* task or environmental context.' (Emphasis added.) Fourth, the enthusiasm for enterprise seems to be based on the mistaken notions that there is no distinction between the words 'education' and 'training' (see Dearden, 1984), or between 'vocational education' and 'vocational training' (Pring, 1987), that *how* you learn is more important than *what* you learn, and that a general, liberal education somehow excludes the practical application of knowledge. Perhaps we all need to collapse the polarities in the centuries old debate between the liberal and the vocational in favour of a liberal vocationalism (see Silver and Brennan, 1988). Fifth, enterprise tends to be viewed (for example, by Gibb, 1987) as an individual attribute and both structural factors and local economic conditions are ignored. As the National Audit Office argued in reference to new products and services offered by the Enterprise Allowance Scheme, 'success depends upon the adequacy of local demand.' (National Audit Office, 1988, p. 8). Sixth, where is the independent and convincing evidence of the success of enterprise education or enterprise initiatives?

When accountability and value for money have become such standard management tools, why have so many enterprise initiatives been 'doomed to success' from day one? The national extension of TVEI, for example, was announced in the White Paper of July, 1986 (Dept of Employment *et al.*, 1986, p. 9) but the fourteen pilot projects were launched in September 1983 for four years, so no summative evaluation could have been available to influence the decision to create a national scheme.

The problems with the enterprise movement do not end with the terminological mare's nest described above. Attention also needs to be paid to the key role in enterprise education which is given to skills. Maurice Holt in 1987 edited a collection of essays which exposed the fallacy of generic, transferable skills and challenged the superficial and reductionist use of the term 'skills' to analyse professional activities such as teaching (for example, Smith, 1987). But even those contributors who had already become anxious at the current obsession with skills failed to predict how inflated the claims were to become. Witness the stance taken by Johnson *et al.* (1987, p. xi): 'The components of Enterprise are a mixture of attitudes, skills and motivations (in this book we describe all three as "skills").' Complexity is dispensed with, words become interchangeable and the concept of 'skills' becomes impossibly inflated. To paraphrase Wittgenstein's (1978, p. 232) famous criticism of psychology: in enterprise education there are experiential learning activities and conceptual confusion.

The definitional and epistemological problems surrounding the concept of enterprise tend to be dismissed by those working within the burgeoning enterprise industry who act, speak and write as if they were all using the same concept. Such intellectual confusion has not prevented the expenditure of much commendable effort and commitment in the interests of young or unemployed people, but the problems of definition and the mistaken assumptions about the nature of knowledge will not simply go away. It is perfectly possible that a number of challenging and satisfying jobs have been created by means of, for instance, the Enterprise Allowance Scheme despite the linguistic and epistemological muddle, but the quantity, the quality and the durability of these jobs can only be assessed through empirical research.[3] Nor is it any part of my argument to defend pedagogical practices in schools or in universities which may be in need of change. What is contested is the implicit assumption in say, the Enterprise in Higher Education initiative, that combining academic excellence and practical application is a new departure for engineering, law, medicine, education, or the creative arts. Just as there is nothing as practical as a good theory, there is also nothing as impractical as misunderstood or misapplied theory (see Fullan, 1982).

One attempt to bring some order to the different kinds of alternative employment projects which stretch right across the whole ideological spectrum is the typology suggested by Rees (1986, p. 15):

> ... self employment, small businesses run by young capitalist entrepreneurs; worker co-operatives, competing in a capitalist economy but operating an egalitarian management structure; and community businesses, offering socially useful goods and services to those that need them, usually without making much of a profit.

Law (1983) describes the various shades of enterprise projects by saying that they can be 'blue' (self-employment or mini-companies), or 'pink' (a profit-sharing co-operative) or 'green' (concerned with a community or environmental issue). Perhaps there are also some 'rainbow' enterprises which adopt a mixed approach, combining profit-making and community involvement. But what studies have been done in this country show that 'the majority of people who describe themselves as self-

employed do not have any employees at all – not even a part-time assistant'
(Hakim, 1988, p. 429). The emphasis in most courses on enterprise
remains firmly on the setting up of small businesses; alternative approaches, although sometimes alluded to in the introduction, are from then
on quietly forgotten (for example, Johnson *et al.*, 1987).

Others, however, like Turner (1989) the author of *Community
Enterprise in the Curriculum*, explicitly stress a wider range of commitments. This training package sets out to link the 'fields of community
involvement and enterprise skill development' (p. 1) and employs a broad
definition of the concept of enterprise which is '... relevant to all people,
meaning a project, venture or undertaking' and '... aims at fostering a
process of empowerment for participants which will provide skills and
experiences that are relevant to the achievement of social, economic and
political goals.' (p. 15). What may be termed 'the official version of
enterprise' is, however, confined to the 'blue' corner, as can be seen from
the video produced by the Training Commission on *Enterprise Training in
Employment Training*, which defines Enterprise Training as 'training in
how to start a new business, to develop that business and, of course, to
make it a success.'

■ The decade of the TECs

As the enterprise movement has grown, so too have the responsibilities
given to employers who are now becoming increasingly involved in the
management of hospitals, polytechnics, universities and schools. The
establishment of the new TECs, however, can be seen as a radical
development of this policy whereby the training of young people, of the
unemployed and all those in employment has been handed over to bodies
controlled by industrialists; two-thirds of each TEC board must consist of
the senior managers of national or major companies at local level. The
move is presented as not so much another government programme as yet
another national strategy to harness the energy and commitment of
employers '... to help provide the country with the skilled and
enterprising workforce it needs for sustained economic growth and
prosperity' (Training Agency, 1989c, p. 3). In more detail, TECs can be
described as a national network of independent companies, led by chief
executives from private industry in order to deliver training and enterprise
locally.

The model being followed is not the German *Dual System* of
vocational training but rather the US Private Industry Councils (or PICs)
which appear '... to have more impeccable free enterprise credentials.

But the truth is that in regard to training, it is free enterprise which has failed over many decades to deliver the goods. Why should we expect it to do so now?' (*Times Educational Supplement*, 16 December 1988). TECs have also grown out of the importation into this country of US initiatives like the Boston Compact, whereby employers offer jobs to young, working-class people in the inner city who achieve previously agreed standards in schools. It will be one of the first tasks for the TECs to signal to their local communities that their remit goes way beyond coping with school leavers with few, if any, qualifications. The plan is not only for TECs to manage existing programmes such as YTS, Employment Training, Business Growth Training, Small Firms Counselling, the Enterprise Allowance Scheme, Training Access Points, and the Training of Trainers, and to be involved in the development of TVEI and Work Related Further Education. TECs will also be charged with assessing the economic and social needs of their locality, deciding on priorities and allocating resources to stimulate local economic development. In the words of Norman Fowler, then Secretary of State for Employment: '... if we are to expect employers to take the reins locally, we must give them real powers to make real decisions' (*Employment Gazette*, April 1989, p. 156). Later he issued strategic guidance (Training Agency, 1989b, p. 6) which described the role of the TECs as follows: 'Each TEC will need to establish a clear vision of training and enterprise in the community ... [and] develop its ideas and plans in partnership with the community, and ... publish them widely.'

The TECs have also been set up with great speed: within a year of their announcement in the White Paper *Employment for the 1990s*, issued at the end of 1988, 44 had been set up with development funding, and within two years it was envisaged that more than 80 would be in operation. The first generation of TECs assumed full responsibilities from April, 1990.

The establishment of the TECs provides an opportunity to review policy in this area and some of the key issues are as follows:

1. *A national plan for education, training and employment* Why are all these new structures, plans and activities necessary? Together they constitute the latest attempt to provide what has been missing in Britain for the last one hundred and fifty years, namely, a coherent and comprehensive national plan for education, training *and* employment (or ETE[4]). Governments of both main parties have come and gone, the main Departments of State concerned (DES, Department of Employment, DTI, and to a lesser extent the Home Office) continue to divide the responsibilities among themselves and we are still without a coordinated policy for ETE. Since 1945 we have witnessed successive reorganizations of the education system and of the national provision of training; and during this period, industry has undergone a series of structural changes. Each of

these developments, however, has taken place more or less independently, and what we have always needed is an imaginative, overarching policy which would emphasize the vital links between education, training and employment, and how various groups progress from one stage to another. Commentators tend to discuss the relationship *either* between education and training *or* between training and employment, but what we lack is the vision to create a policy which embraces all three together.

In the early 1980s the concentration of the current Government was on training (YOP, YTS, Community Programme, etc.), and *only* on training; as a result we ended up with some of the most highly trained dole queues in the world. In July 1988, the Secretary of State for Education acquired numerous new centralizing powers through the passing into law of the Education Reform Act (ERA); within six months the Department of Employment was decentralizing the system of training. In what ways have the ERA (1988) and the legislation establishing the TECs been planned and coordinated in advance? If such coordination *had* taken place, there might now be a National Curriculum for 5 to 18 year olds rather than for 5 to 16 year olds. Perhaps one can detect the vague outline of a grand design to restructure and to privatize[5] both the education and training systems (see Edwards *et al.*, 1989, p. 220 on this point), but on the ground at local level, staff in education and in the TECs will be left to develop what links they can in very changed circumstances.[6] The leader in the *Times Educational Supplement* (16 December 1988) reflected thus on the publication of *Employment for the 1990s*: '... it is extraordinary that, having at last got round to creating a national system of *education*, the Government should now abdicate all responsibility for the *training* of school-leavers.' (Emphasis as in original.) The third corner of the triangle – employment – has been the most neglected as can be seen from the dismantling of regional policy, the unprecedented high levels of unemployment, the lack of continuing education and training for workers, and the disappearance of the debate about the quality of jobs. Has society no responsibility, for instance, to those who have done everything in their power to find employment, who have conscientiously attended one training course after another and still find themselves unemployed? (see Ashby, 1989). The interim judgment is that TECs will make the creation of a national strategic plan for ETE less rather than more likely because their programmes are designed to be local and tactical.

2. *The commitment of employers*   The establishment of TECs is a high risk strategy which hopes finally to secure the commitment of employers to training. The historic failure (Wiener, 1981) and the continuing complacency (Coopers and Lybrand, 1985) of most British employers in relation to training is well known to Government because much of the recent evidence has been produced by reports commissioned by them. What has changed since the MSC passed the following judgement:

'Training is perceived by many employers as a disposable overhead dropped at the first sign of lowering profit margins'? (New Training Initiative, 1981).

Employers themselves would not care to be judged by their record of attendance at the Area Manpower Boards of the MSC, but it is still possible that the highest trade deficit in our history in 1989 will prod them into working collectively to enable them to face and began to beat international competition (see Godley, 1989). Local pride and concern for the future prosperity of their area may provide an additional spur to action.

3. *Representativeness and accountability*   It is, of course, part of the official strategy for the Boards of TECs, to be controlled by the chief executives of large companies with few, if any, directors of small businesses and only token representation from trade unions, education, local government or voluntary organizations. There is a genuine (but not insurmountable) problem in an area like, say, Oldham; it has been estimated (*Focus on Training*, October 1989, p. 7) that there are as many as 15,000 small enterprises 'who could benefit from the TEC but who may be too busy or preoccupied with their own immediate survival to participate.' Out of the fifteen seats on each Board, education and voluntary organizations in North East England are tending to be given one place each with the trade unions being invited to join by some TECs and not others, but the final composition is not yet complete in some cases. To give a national plan for ETE (see point 1 above) any chance of working, the composition of the Boards would need to be changed to: one-third employers, one-third trade unions, and one-third education, training, local authorities and voluntary organizations, with the Government taking full responsibility for leadership and the future direction of policy.

To whom will the TECs be accountable? Performance is likely to vary from those who were first to be set up to those who have still to apply for development funding. No doubt there will be knighthoods for those judged to be successful, but what is to stop a TEC responding to the short-term needs of local employers and sacrificing the long-term education, training and employment prospects of young people and adults? What happens to those chief executives who are unable to take a more far-sighted view? How are they to be removed from the Board? Do they simply return to their firms and another employer is chosen to rectify the damage done?

The Training Agency (*Guide to Planning*, 1989c) has laid down that each TEC will be required to:

- make its 3 year Corporate Plan available for public inspection;
- publish an Annual Report;
- hold at least one public meeting each year.

In addition, the contract each TEC enters into with the Secretary of State will be for a finite period; its Business Plan has to be approved by the Training Agency, planning guidelines with specific objectives will be issued each year by the Department of Employment, as will performance indicators and performance-related bonuses (of around 2 per cent of the total budget). This battery of control mechanisms (or performance-related funding or PRF) makes clear that the TECs will be accountable not so much to the local community as directly to the Training Agency and Government. Should there not be an independent, national and comprehensive evaluation of such a radical measure?

4. *Future remit?* No-one would be surprised if the TECs were to take over the responsibility for the Enterprise Initiative from the Department of Trade and Industry, but in whose interest would it be for the Careers Service, for instance, to lose its independent status as honest brokers between young people and employers and be answerable directly to local TECs? Are TECs more likely to look favourably on the CBI proposal to issue to all young people who leave school at 16 credits or vouchers which are cashed in when employers provide them with training?[7] Their remit *could* be extended to cover all further education, advanced as well as non-advanced. And if further education, is it too speculative to suggest that higher education could be absorbed to ensure that universities and polytechnics respond appropriately to the needs of local employers and open up access to their local communities? A strategic plan which identifies skill shortages and the need to attract inward investment from hi-tech firms will fairly soon have to examine the quality of the available housing stock and of the transport system; and so the remit of the TECs may grow by leaps and bounds. The outcome is more than usually difficult to predict because all three of the main political actors involved in the conception of the scheme (Fowler, Young and Baker at the Departments of Employment, Trade and Industry and Education) have all moved on. The development of a coordinated, comprehensive policy for ETE is likely to be postponed again as new Ministers work to understand their new responsibilities, never mind those which transcend those of their Departments.

5. *National, regional and local levels* The Training Agency's *Guide to Planning* (1989c, p. 4) explains how the national framework of TECs will operate 'at three levels: the national level, the industry level and the local level.' Two serious problems suggest themselves right away. First, it is by no means certain that the aggregation of 100 local business plans produces an adequate response to national needs in education, training and employment. And if the national priorities, as laid down by the Secretary of State, are seen to conflict with the objectives of a local TEC, which will be given precedence? Second, one strategic level is missing altogether from the plan – the regional. The North East of England, for instance, will have

five TECs, each responding to the specific needs of a small, geographically-defined area, but who will be responsible for regional planning and for the production of structural plans to cope with the deep-seated economic inequalities within and between the regions? It would be a constructive step if groups of TECs came together to address the problems of the region in which they are situated, but years are likely to pass before they are in a position to act in such a concerted manner.

6. *What levers on change?*   What mechanisms will the TECs employ to encourage or to enforce change? There appears to be excessive reliance on peer pressure whereby good employers are expected persistently and amiably to cajole their more recalcitrant brethren into training their own workers – or paying for others to do so. What is to happen to those employers who do not experience sudden Pauline conversions to training on the road to Moorfoot, Sheffield or to their local TEC? Some TECs are already discussing the inclusion of quality controls when they sub-contract training, but they may need to introduce contract compliance or local levies on companies who resist all exhortations to train their workers.

The contrast between the treatment of employers and of members of the education service is particularly marked in this regard. Why, for example, has the Government not even taken reserve powers to enforce change on employers who resist all other forms of pressure, in the way that it has been felt necessary in education to legislate the National Curriculum into existence with all the force of statutory orders? It is predicted that a future Government will have to introduce legislation to enforce the commitment to training of the rogue, fly-by-night or just the uncommitted employer. Even Universities and Polytechnics have only recently begun to invest in the training of their own employees.

7. *The values of the board*   With chief executives holding down two-thirds of the seats on the Board of every TEC, their values will prevail and so the ethos will tend to reflect in the main the views of successful, self-made, entrepreneurial, white males. How many seats will be found, for example, in the Boardroom for women or blacks? Will either group believe the rhetoric of how important they are becoming in the workforce, if they are excluded? What attention will be paid to the education, training and employment needs of the handicapped or of ethnic minorities or of rural communities? The Training Agency is presently engaged in piloting performance indicators for TECs, one of which concerns the involvement of the handicapped in training; but is it conceivable that a TEC would have its contract ended or its budget cut significantly if particular targets regarding disadvantaged groups were not met?

8. *Partnership or control*   The advent of the TECs has been cloaked in the language of partnership. But when elite groups insist on using and re-using

the word 'partnership', it is reasonably certain that a major shift in power is taking place in favour of one preferred group at the expense of another. The word 'partnership', like the word 'consultation', has fallen upon hard times. The questions which need to be asked are: who will drive this partnership? What is the relative power of the various participants? What entitlement have minorities to a hearing or to funding? What appeals procedure will there be against the decisions of the Board?

■ Conclusions

No matter what Government had been in power in the 1980s, some radical measures would need to have been taken to cope with the continuing decline of the British economy, relative to its major international competitors. This article has sought to raise the question of whether those which have been taken will prove to be the most appropriate, but the problems to which they are directed are not in dispute.

The wide-ranging study *Training in Britain* (Training Agency, 1989d, p. 55) claims that 'In 1988 one in three individuals of working age reported having no qualifications' and, perhaps more serious still, 'one third of 19–34 year olds and almost one-half of those aged 35 and over, could not foresee circumstances which would lead them to undertake education or training' (p. 53). The task facing the TECs in changing the attitudes of such a substantial minority of the workforce is not to be underestimated.

Coupled with this, we need to assess the significance for the European Community of the growth in numbers of young people in developing countries. In a speech given in December, 1989, Norman Fowler gave the figures as follows:

> 'Between now and the year 2010 the population of Western Europe will increase by 2 per cent; that of Japan by 8 per cent; that of the United States by 17 per cent; but that of the developing world by no less than 45 per cent. In that period the numbers of those aged 15 to 24 in the developing world grow by 20 per cent, and the numbers of those aged 25 to 54 by a staggering 60 per cent.'

The implications for Britain were thought to be obvious: 'we must become a high productivity, high skill, high technology economy' (Norman Fowler, 1989). Our chances of achieving that goal depend largely upon developing and implementing a national policy for ETE with sufficient resources to give it vibrant life.

Successive Conservative Governments have sought to reverse our economic decline by replacing what they have termed the dependency culture with the enterprise culture. Enterprise has helped to provide the ideological basis for the radical changes in education, training and industrial policy. The word 'enterprise', however, is best understood *not* as a coherent set of logically related ideas but as a short-hand way of referring to a clutch of values such as individualism, self-reliance, competition, self-employment, profitability, minimal government and capitalism unfettered by rules and regulations on the US model. Levitas (1986, p. 80) has rightly emphasized 'the two dominant strands of thought within the New Right – neo-liberal economics and social authoritarianism'.

It could, however, be retorted that, if the notion of enterprise is such a conceptual quagmire, then surely its effects are likely to be diffuse, the unintended consequences manifold and the internal contradictions an endless source of confusion? On the other hand, logical incoherence and lack of an agreed definition did not prevent concepts like 'intelligence' or 'maladjustment' from exerting a powerful (and at times baleful) influence on social policy and on the lives of millions of children.

An example of one internal contradiction within the ruling ideology of the Conservative Government is the virtual exclusion of enterprise education from either the core or the foundation subjects or even the cross-curricular issues within the National Curriculum; and not even the rather anxious attempts by the authors of *Primary Enterprise* (DUBS, 1989, p. 3) to show how attainment targets can be met by primary pupils through enterprise activities are likely to rescue enterprise education. The subject has run up against the buffers of another strain in Conservative thinking – the traditional conception of knowledge as a body of facts (like the curriculum for Science in the National Curriculum) to be memorized and retold in examinations like A level. [. . .] In any dispute within the Conservative party between knowledge and skills (entrepreneurial or otherwise), high-status knowledge will be reserved for those destined for high-status occupations while new, progressive-sounding courses like enterprise education which might threaten academic standards will be thought appropriate for those who are to be trained for (un)employment. For the sake of both groups, we need to collapse this false dichotomy which continues to bedevil the education, training and employment of *all* our young people. Hall (1988, p. 10) has followed Gramsci in arguing that ideologies are rarely logically consistent or homogeneous but tend to be internally fractured: 'It is because Thatcherism knows this that it understands why the ideological terrain of struggle is so crucial.' Logical contradictions within the ideology may, as Levitas (1986, p. 11) argues, 'be a strength rather than a weakness, enabling the New Right to switch the grounds of its legitimations at will.'

For ten years now, the enterprise culture has been at the centre of the political stage in Britain and this article has sought to begin the process of evaluating what has been achieved in our name and with our money.

The massive resources that have been lavished on making a success of this ideological project could have been invested in other ways; in British manufacturing industry, in regional development and, in a comprehensive, national plan to create dynamic interactions between education, vocational training and employment.

In the 1990s, Government will look increasingly to the TECs for improvements in our economic performance because they have entrusted the task of creating a new society to the praetorian guard of the enterprise culture – the chief executives of British industry. Within ten years we shall know whether this strategy proves to be bold, forward-looking and productive or risky, retrograde and redundant.

Notes

1. I am grateful to John Ritchie's (1987) article for bringing this article and Lord Young's (1986) to my attention.
2. Ralph Glasser, for example, describes in his autobiography (1988, p. 19) how Richard Crossman 'in silver grey suit and dove grey silk tie' asked towards the end of the 1930s his Oxford study group on social mobility the following question: why do people work? 'To have no money, for instance, no money at all, was to them (people like Crossman) inconceivable. How *could* they ask, so innocently, "Why do people work?" I said, curtly "Because they'd starve if they didn't!" ' (Emphasis as in original.)
3. The attempt to transform the so-called dependency culture of Cleveland into an enterprise culture is being independently evaluated by Dr MacDonald and myself as an associate study of the ESRC's 16–19 Initiative whose funding is here gratefully acknowledged. The term 'dependency culture' just like its counterpart 'enterprise culture' is an ideological rather than a neutral phrase and is so treated in this article.
4. The acronym – ETE – is produced, after the fashion of the Training Agency, in the hope that it will catch on.
5. Stephen Wilks has argued (1987, p. 9) that in Britain, especially since 1983, 'traditional industrial policy has been submerged under a new "enterprise policy" .... The privatization argument has moved from ideology to doctrine to dogma in a very short period of time and is being pursued for its own sake.'
6. Another example of the *lack* of coordination between the DES and the Department of Employment can be seen in the establishment of the Certificate for Pre-Vocational Education by the DES in July 1984 to counteract the march stolen on them when the MSC set up TVEI in November 1982.
7. In March 1990, the Government announced the introduction of training credits for 16 and 17 year olds leaving full-time education 'to help create a more efficient and responsive market in training' (Michael Howard, Employment Secretary, *Insight*, No. 19, Summer 1990, p. 10). The TECs will be invited to run a range of pilot schemes to cover a total of 45,000 school

leavers. The history of such initiatives suggests that training credits will be judged an immediate success and extended nationally.

Acknowledgements

I wish to acknowledge my thanks to Tony Edwards, Gerald Grace, Jackson Hall, Robert MacDonald and Bill Williamson who read and commented on earlier drafts of this article. The argument and the mistakes, however, remain my own.

References

Abercrombie, N., Hill, S. and Turner, B. S. (1986) *Sovereign Individuals of Capitalism* (London: Allen and Unwin).

Ashby, P. (1989) *Citizenship, Income and Work* (St George's House, Windsor Castle).

Billig, M. (1989) 'Rhetoric and psychology', Lecture at Durham University, 22 January.

City and Guilds of London Institute (1988) *Enterprise Skills Record of Achievement* (Portland Place, London).

Coopers and Lybrand Associates (1985) *A Challenge to Complacency: Changing Attitudes to Training* (Moorfoot, Sheffield: Manpower Services Commission).

Dearden, R. (1984) 'Education and training'. *Westminster Studies in Education*, 7, pp. 57–66.

Department of Employment *et al.* (1986) *Working Together – Education and Training*, Cmnd 9823 (London: HMSO).

Department of Employment (1988) *Employment for the 1990s*, Cmnd 540 (London: HMSO).

Department of Trade and Industry (1988) *DTI – the Department for Enterprise*, Cmnd 278 (London: HMSO).

DTI/National Westminster Bank (1988) *Mini-Enterprises in Schools 1987/88*.

Dunn, J. H. (1977) 'The language and myths of the New Right'. *New Society*, 5, May, pp. 225–226.

Durham University Business School (1989) *Primary Enterprise: A Primary School Approach to Enterprise Education within the National Curriculum* (Durham: Casdec).

Edwards, T., Fitz, J. and Whitty, G. (1989) *The State and Private Education: An Evaluation of the Assisted Places Scheme* (London: Falmer Press).

Finn, D. (1986) 'Free Enterprise?'. *Unemployment Bulletin*, Issue 22, pp. 5–10.

Fowler, N. (1989) Speech to the Business in the Cities Conference, December.

Fullan, M. (1982) *The Meaning of Educational Change* (Ontario: Oise Press).

Gibb, A. (1987) Enterprise culture – its meaning and implications for education and training. *Journal of European Industrial Training*, Vol. 11, No. 2, pp. 1–28.

Glasser, R. (1988) *Gorbals Boy at Oxford* (London: Chatto and Windus).

Godley, W. (1989) 'Economic disaster in slow motion'. *The Observer*, 27 August.

Grayson, D. (1989) 'At the roots of enterprise'. *Employment Gazette*, Vol. 97, No. 10, October, pp. 534–538.

Hakim, C. (1988) 'Self employment in Britain: recent trends and current issues'. *Work, Employment and Society*, Vol. 2, No. 4, pp. 421–450.

Hall, S. (1988) *The Hard Road to Renewal: Thatcherism and the Crisis of the Left* (London: Verso).

Holt, M. (ed.) (1987) *Skills and Vocationalism: The Easy Answer* (Milton Keynes: Open University Press).

House of Commons Committee of Public Accounts (1989) *Assistance to Small Firms*, 8th report (London: HMSO).

Jamieson, I. (1989) 'Education and the economy: themes and issues'. *Journal of Education Policy*, Vol. 4, No. 1, pp. 69–73.

Johnson, C. *et al.* (1987a) *Key Skills: Enterprise Skills through Active Learning, 14–16* (London: Hodder and Stoughton).

Johnson, C. *et al.* (1987b) *Key Skills: Enterprise Skills through Active Learning, 16–19* (London: Hodder and Stoughton).

Johnson, C. (1989) Personal communication.

Jonathan, R. (1983) 'The Manpower Service model of education'. *Cambridge Journal of Education*, 13, pp. 3–10.

Jonathan, R. (1987) 'The Youth Training Scheme and core skills: an educational analysis', in Holt, M. (ed.), *Skills and Vocationalism: The Easy Answer*, pp. 89–119 (Milton Keynes: Open University Press).

Kilby, P. (1971) 'Hunting the heffalump', in Kilby, P. (ed.), *Entrepreneurship and Economic Development* (New York: Free Press).

Law, B. (1983) 'The colour-coded curriculum'. *NICEC Training and Development Bulletin*, No. 23, pp. 2–3.

Levitas, R. (ed.) (1986) *The Ideology of the New Right* (Cambridge: Polity Press).

Manpower Services Commission (1981) *A New Training Initiative: An Agenda for Action* (Selkirk House: London).

McClelland, D. C. (1971) 'The achievement motive in economic growth', in Kilby, P. (ed.), *Entrepreneurship and Economic Development*, pp. 109–122 (New York: Free Press).

National Audit Office (1988) *Department of Employment/Training Commission: Assistance to Small Firms*, Report No 655 (London: HMSO).

Pitman Examinations Institute (1987) *Enterprise Skills* (Godalming, Surrey).

Pring, R. (1987) 'The curriculum and the new vocationalism'. *British Journal of Education and Work*, Vol. 1, No. 3, pp. 133–148.

Raffe, D. (1989) 'Scotland v England: the place of "home internationals" in comparative research'. Paper presented to TA Conference, Manchester, September.

Rees, T. (1986) 'Education for enterprise: the state and alternative employment for young people'. *Journal of Education Policy*, Vol. 3, No. 1, pp. 9–22.

Ritchie, J. (1987) 'Explaining enterprise cutures'. Paper presented to Tenth UK

Small Business Policy and Research Conference, Cranfield.

Roberts, J. (1988) 'Pie in the sky? Or sharing the cake on the plate? Lessons from evangelical enterprise'. *Employment Gazette*, July, pp. 365–371.

Rotter, J. B. (1966) 'Generalized expectancies for internal versus external control of reinforcement'. *Psychological Monographs*, 80, No. 609.

Shilling, C. (1989) 'The mini-enterprise in schools project: a new stage in education–industry relations?'. *Journal of Education Policy*, Vol. 4, No. 2, pp. 115–124.

Silver, H. and Brennan, J. (1988) *A Liberal Vocationalism* (London: Methuen).

Smith, R. (1987) 'Teaching on stilts: a critique of classroom skills', in Holt, M. (ed.), *Skills and Vocationalism: the Easy Answer*, pp. 43–55 (Milton Keynes: Open University Press).

Thompson, K. (1984) 'Education for capability – a critique'. *British Journal of Educational Studies*, vol. XXXII, No. 3, pp. 203–212.

Training Agency (1989a) *Enterprise in Higher Education* (Moorfoot: Sheffield).

Training Agency (1989b) *Training and Enterprise: Priorities for Action 1990/91* (Moorfoot: Sheffield).

Training Agency (1989c) *TECs: Guide to Planning* (Moorfoot: Sheffield).

Training Agency (1989d) *Training in Britain – Main Report* (Moorfoot: Sheffield).

Turner, D. (1989) *The Enterprise Factor: Community Enterprise in the Curriculum* (London: CSV).

Unemployment Bulletin (1989) *Developing TECs*, Issue 30, Summer, pp. 1–3.

Wiener, M. J. (1981) *English Culture and the Decline of the Industrial Spirit 1850–1980* (Harmondsworth: Penguin).

Wilks, S. (1987) 'From industrial policy to enterprise policy in Britain'. *Journal of General Management*, Vol. 12, No. 4, pp. 5–20.

Wittgenstein, L. (1978) *Philosophical Investigations* (Oxford: Blackwell).

Young, Lord David (1986) 'Enterprise – the road to jobs'. *London Business School Journal*, Vol. 11, Pt 1, pp. 21–27.

Chapter 14

Some Alternatives in Youth Training: Franchise and Corporatist Models

J. Chandler and C. Wallace

Radical approaches to training have tended to come from the New Right in recent years, reflecting philosophies of entrepreneurship, free enterprise and the private market. This is in contrast to the approach previously offered in Britain and in other countries. In order to consider what alternatives might be desirable we critically assess developments in training both here and in West Germany before considering the foundations for a progressive training strategy in Britain.

In this paper we examine two alternative models of youth training – the 'corporatist' model in West Germany involving a high degree of collaboration between industry and the state and the 'franchise' model in England whereby youth training has been subcontracted to small and mostly private agencies but at public expense. Models of training need to be set within the political economy of the nation and of the capitalist system as a whole, and are crucial in the social reproduction of class, race and gender divisions. The organization and delivery of youth or adult training need to be seen in their historical and cultural context. However, this does not mean that particular systems are determined entirely by external factors; 'better' and 'worse' models still exist according to whether they are able to meet training needs nationally and the needs of young people more specifically.

Source: Chandler, J. and Wallace, C. (1990) 'Some alternatives in youth training: franchise and corporatist models', in Gleeson, D. (ed.), *Training and Its Alternatives*, The Open University Press, Milton Keynes, pp. 92–109.

■   The value of comparison

Youth unemployment became an issue in most industrial societies in the 1970s and 1980s and those countries – such as West Germany, Austria and Switzerland – which already had established training schemes, expanded them, whereas others which had no such schemes – such as Australia, Britain and Canada – started to construct them. In all these countries the unqualified, bottom end of the school spectrum were identified as the 'problems', the ones least likely to get jobs. Likewise, other traditionally disadvantaged groups such as young women and migrant workers or those from ethnic minorities were also identified (OECD, 1981).

The various new schemes introduced were designed to 'mop up' the unemployed and compensate for their disadvantages. However, this needs to be set within the context of pre-existing education and training systems. Table 14.1 gives some comparison of Britain and other European countries in the late 1970s, when these schemes were introduced. It can be seen that comparatively more young people entered the labour market directly in Great Britain than most other countries and the 'youth unemployment' problem was correspondingly greater. (Youth unemployment is in inverted commas here since to some extent it is an artefact of the education/training system. Thus, in West Germany, and now in Britain, too, there is no official unemployment for young people who have not worked before.)

Despite differences in national economic performance, certain themes remain in common to all such schemes: first, there is the issue of whether training should be universal or selective in its approach (Benn and Fairley, 1986; Dale, 1985). Second, there is the extent to which youth training programmes should recruit on a voluntary or compulsory basis; and third there are debates about the status and quality of training and skills imparted (Ainley, 1988; Cockburn, 1983; Peck and Haughton, 1987). The structure and legitimation of youth training may also respond differently to the ebb and flow of economic and demographic tides.

Sheldrake and Vickerstaff (1987) devised a classification of the relationship between vocational training systems and their funding structures and philosophies. In their classification, the German system is seen as embodying a 'corporate' solution to training provision. West Germany has a long tradition of vocational training for young people, an apprenticeship system which is a product of the close alliance of public and employer interest. The USA relies on the free market where it is left to companies to fund the training of their employees or individuals to fund their own vocational development. By contrast, France has followed a more interventionist path in the provision of state funding and provides a legal entitlement for each individual to avail themselves of training.

Sheldrake and Vickerstaff (1987) describe the infertile ground in Britain for the growth of any system of vocational preparation – the

Table 14.1 Occupation of young people immediately after the end of compulsory education (per cent). (*Source*: Council of Europe, 1981.)

	Switzerland	Austria	Netherlands	Federal Republic of Germany	Denmark	UK
Grammar school courses	10	13	10	25	60	10
Technical and vocational courses	16	25	65	15	60	10
Vocational training (apprenticeship)	60	50	3	40	10	20
At work and unemployed	14	12	22	20	20	60

reluctance of private companies to pay for training, the commitment of trade unions to training only so long as it enhanced the position of craft workers over the rest, the state's commitment to training only in times of national emergency (such as war) or as an *ad hoc* response to unemployment. They chart the failed and half-hearted corporatist solution embodied in the Industrial Training Boards following the 1964 Industrial Training Act. According to these authors there is no identifiable training 'system' in Britain and hence it is left out of their classification. Ainley and Corney (forthcoming) bring their historical account further forward as they chronicle the rise, the reshaping and the fall of the Manpower Services Commission (MSC). Amid the squabbling, the interdepartmental rivalry, the mercurial switches of organizational tack and the spawning of a host of vocational schemes, they argue that an approach to training is discernible. We shall begin therefore by describing the system in Great Britain.

■ Great Britain: the 'franchise' model of youth training

The development of vocational training in Britain needs to be seen in the context of the history of social change. Through the nineteenth century, the dominant economic model in Britain was that of *laissez faire*, whereas in Germany the state took a more active role in social policy. Britain had industrialized with a workforce largely uneducated and untrained. Educational institutions were attended by a gentlemanly elite and wedded to aristocratic, landed and imperial values. Education for the masses was largely in the hands of voluntary organizations, and trade schools served the needs of local employers. Nevertheless, it was considered important for mass education (introduced in 1870) to inculcate girls and boys with the right attitudes for working life – in the factories, farms and as domestic servants: in this sense it was 'vocational'. Although apprenticeships were selectively available, until quite recently the majority left school at the minimum age without any training and drifted between 'dead end' jobs, absorbing the culture of the workplace as they learned to labour. This situation was identified as early as the 1920s as the 'problem of boy labour'; it continued more or less until the 1970s. The expansion of education from the 1960s onwards took the form of an expansion of more academic style education, particularly at the university level, providing an avenue of mobility for some working class young people and a source of class continuity for the sons and daughters of the middle classes. There remained the continuing problem of the 'Newsom child' who benefited little from the improved education system, felt alienated from its goals and fled jubilantly into the workplace at the first opportunity. Thus, while the mood of the times was to erode selective education at the secondary school level, it nevertheless continued in terms of routes out of school.

Further education and industrial training, despite the 1959 Crowther Report, remained the Cinderella of the education system, providing courses to meet the needs of local employers according to demand (Dale, 1985; Gleeson, 1985). At the same time more progressive models of pedagogy argued that children needed a broad humanistic introduction to knowledge rather than a narrow vocational curriculum. At that time, too, a range of official and academic reports decried the unsupervised and random 'floundering' into work which was characteristic of this system (Maizels, 1970; Ashton and Field, 1976). However, until the late 1970s the solution was always seen in terms of expanding the existing primary, secondary and higher educational provision to foster equality of opportunity by providing more avenues of upward mobility. This sort of education was seen as a 'good thing' in itself and for a short while this liberal educational ideology was influential. However, it never reached the minimum age school leavers, the working class lads who saw this kind of education as boring and irrelevant to their needs (Willis, 1977; Ashton and Field, 1976). Even those further up the academic hierarchy tended to have an instrumental approach to education, seeing it as a means to achieve better qualifications for a job rather than having a genuine thirst for learning (Brown, 1987). Marsden and Ryan (1988) describe this situation as one of a trade off between high wages for young people and low quality training; in Germany, by contrast, there was a situation of high quality training and low youth wages.

From the 1970s however, the mood changes and mass youth unemployment together with Britain's poor economic performance led to the Great Debate initiated by James Callaghan in a speech at Ruskin College in 1976. Fears about a wasted generation of idle and rioting young men soon became a reality. The 'liberal' education system and lack of training were blamed for Britain's declining place in the world economy. The response took the form of the introduction of a new form of vocational rhetoric into education and later various new vocational qualifications – the Technical and Vocational Educational Initiative (TVEI), the Certificate of Pre-Vocational Education, and so on. In a sense, these were not new at all; they were no more than a return to the traditional arguments for mass education, that it should turn out well socialized workers to fit the needs of the economy. The Manpower Services Commission (MSC), set up at the beginning of the decade as a modest quango, took on the job of providing training schemes for the unemployed to overcome their disadvantages in the labour market and became the vehicle for later training strategies.

Sheldrake and Vickerstaff see this as an embryonic system of training in Britain which was swallowed up by rising unemployment, but for Ainley and Corney this was evidence of the MSC being given the scope to follow its expansionist ambitions and attempt to introduce a training culture into Britain (under the redoubtable Lord Young). The sensitivity to policy change was a virtue, permitting the rapid establishment and disbandment of schemes and the introduction of the Trojan horse of training into both the school system and the workplace. By the early 1980s the MSC commanded a budget twice that of the university sector; without direct responsibility to any government department or local authority, it was able to effect rapid and sweeping changes. It was directed by representatives from employers, trade unions and local interest groups but also enjoyed considerable autonomy. At this stage (the early 1980s) the MSC could be said to embody a 'corporatist' solution to youth training. Its move into education was later followed by an attempt to set up a unified and compatible system of national qualifications under NCVQ.

In 1981, with the introduction of the New Training Initiative, the MSC was able to replace the existing mish-mash of temporary schemes with a broad training initiative available to everyone; the Youth Training Scheme was born. Although many aspects of this initiative were never in the end implemented, the Youth Training Scheme was actually expanded into a two-year scheme in 1986 and absorbed most of the older apprenticehsip training, along with many of the Industrial Training Boards, to provide a full-time bridge between school and work. The increasing intervention of the state in the youth labour market was also linked to undermining craft privileges and union control of skills. Attempts to drive down youth wages at the same time (and thus allow them to 'price themselves back into work', in the phrasing of the 1985 Employment White Paper) perhaps indicated an attempted shift towards what Marsden and Ryan might call a low wage, high quality training trade off. Marsden and Ryan (1988) argue that what had traditionally existed in Britain was training for the internal labour markets of employers so that training was often informal, often job-specific and not transferable elsewhere. Germany by contrast, trained people for 'occupational labour markets' whereby training was generalized and transferable between firms. In this way German workers enjoyed greater flexibility and the country as a whole had a highly skilled workforce. There was an attempt to introduce this in Britain under the New Training Initiative by developing training around 'core' and 'transferable skills' and by setting up 'occupational training families' within which these skills were transferable.

Superficially, youth training appeared more established than its forerunners to make work schemes more than the adult equivalents. It appeared to lack any alternatives. As Geoffrey Holland declared, 'If the two-year YTS fails then we are at the end of the road. There is nowhere else to go' (*Times Educational Supplement*, 3 September 1985).

Nevertheless there are strong suggestions that youth training is shallowly planted in Britain. Ainley and Corney catalogue the political expediency and policy shifts characteristic of the history of the MSC. As the MSC has moved through Training Commission to Training Agency, the structure and constitution of the organization was – and still is – kept administratively fluid. Demographic changes have led to fewer young people seeking work and a more buoyant economy has led to shrinking dole queues. In the process, YTS is threatened and is disappearing in some areas such as the south-east (although it always involved a smaller proportion of young people there). It may well survive as a scheme for labour market 'unemployables' in depressed areas, but its regional diversity would appear to be increasing. This decline is compounded by older doubts as to whether YTS can provide good quality training or lead into jobs. Altogether, the YTS is becoming an increasingly rickety bridge to work.

When first established, YTS contained both employer-based and workshop-based schemes. When the scheme was reorganized in 1986, the shift was towards the former for both political and financial reasons. A grant is allocated to each scheme which can be either on a 'basic' or a 'premium' level, the premium funding being available for trainees with special needs and for trainees in areas of poor employment. In addition, permanent additional funding can be obtained for those with significant learning difficulties. The funding assumes that wherever possible the trainee will be receiving on-the-job training on employer's premises and that the scheme will be receiving employer contributions. Premium funding is designed to cover the additional cost of containing a first-year trainee within a workshop unit, but assumes that in the second year these will move to placement with an employer.

It was in this context that we undertook a research project into the role of managing agents and the organization of training in two contrasting labour markets: Liverpool and the south-west. The one was urban and declining, the other was rural and while it was prosperous in some parts, in others the employment prospects were similar to those in Liverpool. Altogether 56 managing agents were interviewed in Liverpool and in the south-west. This study was complemented by one of off-the-job training and a cross-sectional survey of young people themselves. These pieces of research form the basis for the discussion here.

■ The 'privatization' of training

In the atmosphere of accelerated 'privatization' operating since 1979, it is perhaps inevitable that the YTS should have developed in ways which increasingly prioritize the interests and influence of the private employer. However, as LeGrand and Robinson (1983) illustrate, there are many models of privatization. After the failure of extreme privatization – *laissez faire* – which characterized this area more or less until recently, and the brief moment of corporatism in the early 1980s, a new model of privatization has emerged. In the same way that schools have been encouraged to become more financially and managerially independent or even to opt out of the state education system (albeit retaining state funding), and departments within higher education have become cost centres, with their own budgets and line managers thus creating internal markets within institutions, so the YTS and employment training which is to follow it is based upon the idea of 'franchising' to small local employers or managing agents. Managing agents have been moving towards this model for some time, becoming more and more like state-funded small businesses, but the creation of Training and Enterprise Councils (TEC), with the task of subcontracting training and enterprise activities to local providers on a performance-related basis, strengthens the tendency for the British state to act like a holding company (modelled obviously on the private sector) which subcontracts parts of itself at different levels.

Since the 1980s employment-based training has increasingly been favoured over workshop- and community-based training because of its lower costs and higher likelihood of leading to jobs. Financial pressures on managing agents have encouraged them to have more trainees defined as having 'employee status'; the numbers of these have risen from 9 per cent to 16 per cent. Now under proposals in the new White Paper *Employment and Training for the 1990s*, the managing agents are likely to be controlled even more by local employer interests, as is the off-the-job training element. In itself, the MSC never ran nor devised training programmes, but set broad guidelines within which it vetted, then licensed and funded, schemes proposed by a wide assortment of bodies and individuals. Some groups had been approached by MSC and asked to submit proposals whereas others simply tended them. Hence, the scheme could incorporate schemes run by employers, local authorities, private agencies and voluntary organizations and could encompass both employer-based and workshop programmes. The dominant organizational structure is thus the agency, enabling youth training to be publicly funded but privately contracted to a diverse range of sponsoring bodies. Within this franchise system, all individual schemes were routinely monitored for cost, recruitment, occupancy and performance. With changes in funding, administration began to take a primarily financial form.

Local employment conditions influence the structure of YTS and the job opportunities available to YTS leavers. In Devon the proportion of people unemployed approaches the national average of 11 per cent, while in Liverpool the proportion rises to 18 per cent. Although the same proportion of young people enter YTS in Devon and Liverpool (43 per cent), young people in Liverpool have half the chance of getting a job at 16 and three times the chance of being unemployed. The structure of YTS differs between the two regions. In Liverpool the absence of employers to lead YTS and the reluctance of the local authority to become involved in training initiatives has meant that over a third of trainees are occupying premium places in quasi-workshop schemes, primarily run by voluntary associations. The more buoyant economy in Devon gives more scope for local employers and private training agencies, and the local authority is also more involved in youth training provision. Premium funding is available for those who are 'difficult to employ', but the numbers designated as such depends upon the nature of the local economy as much as the characteristics of trainees; hence 10 per cent in Liverpool. Raffe (1987) argues that the degree of 'attachment' or 'detachment' from employers' own internal labour markets determines the likelihood of being premium-funded and the likelihood of schemes leading to jobs afterwards. The greater detachment of schemes from the labour market in Liverpool is reflected in the poorer employment prospects for leavers, with 78 per cent of YTS leavers finding work in Devon compared with 43 per cent in Liverpool.

However, although YTS guaranteed a place to all school leavers, it could not guarantee equal quality of training, nor jobs at the end, and the scheme was regarded with cynicism by many (Raffe, 1988). Attempts to counteract this with a widescale publicity programme were bolstered by changes in the social security system which abolished unemployment benefit for those under 18 (and thus official unemployment for this age group) making the YTS one of the only ways in which they could get any money. Responsibility for young people's welfare was thrown back on to the family by offering a lower benefit rate for those under 25 (Wallace, 1988; Abbott and Wallace, 1989).

The organization of the YTS in this way has a number of advantages. First, it allows for considerable regional diversity to meet local conditions. Second, it promotes competition between managing agents to recruit, place and otherwise 'sell' training. Thirdly, it enables very rapid changes to be introduced.

But is this really privatization? It certainly mirrors developments in the health service, education and housing; the USA rather than West Germany is increasingly being seen as the model to emulate. However, we could argue that this is in fact a form of 'state-induced enterprise'. It enables an ideology of market capitalism in terms of market trading and financial management to be introduced, and a small business ethos thus permeates the franchised sections of the welfare state. In fact, however, the whole system exists because of state subsidy and state intervention, and does not therefore represent the withdrawal of the state. In other words, 'privatization' is introduced as an organizational principle rather than because there is a genuinely free market. This organizational principle means that problems can be privatized, too. The state accepts no responsibility for the shortfall in places or their quality at the level of delivery. Control can, however, be exercised by withdrawing the franchise if targets are not met and this is a very powerful sanction. In this way, while responsibility is decentralized, power is further centralized.

This leads in turn to an 'enterprise ideology', with managing agents seeing themselves as 'selling trainees'. It is not just the labour of trainees which is commodified but the trainees themselves, as they are the product to be sold. This was embodied in the 'buy two and get one free' idea, and in the idea expressed by one managing agent that you could have one (trainee) for £10 or two disabled for £5 each. Indeed some at the Adam Smith Institute tend to see this kind of franchising: – which has just been suggested for primary health care – as a form of interim arrangement of the way to full privatization.

Since early this year (1989), this model of training has applied not just to youth training but to adult training, which has been subsumed under Employment Training (also to be run by managing/training agents).

■ Problems with the British system

The operation of managing agents as profit centres can serve to compromise the quality of the vocational training provided, since more global concerns about training are replaced by getting and keeping placements or making enough money to survive. The schemes are of differing quality, too. The hierarchy of training schemes is based upon proximity to employers' internal labour markets, so that schemes with close proximity to these recruit young people selectively for further development later, whereas those schemes which are relatively detached from private sector internal labour markets – particularly those being sponsored by local authorities and voluntary organizations – tend to recruit the less able (Raffe, 1987). As Raffe points out, while YTS works in relation to internal labour markets, it has yet to prove itself in external labour markets; employers are not yet showing sufficient preference for YTS trainees in their recruitment practices and until they do so, the YTS will continue to suffer from a lack of legitimacy (Raffe, 1988).

As we move down the training hierarchy and further from internal labour markets, placement rates for trainees fall and contributions from employers become more negotiable or non-existent. It is in this sector that employers are likely to default on their payments altogether. These issues are illustrated in the charging rates of three different schemes in Devon which were run by the same managing agent. The agent ran a forestry scheme with a regional catchment area, which obtained employer contributions of £13.50 for first-year trainees and £19 for second-year trainees. He ran a basic scheme which served a local population and offered from £12 for first years to £17.50 for second years. He also ran a premium scheme where employer contributions would be individually negotiated within the range of £8–15 per week. The greater number of detached schemes with premium trainees in Liverpool and the fewer employers offering placements amplifies the scope for negotiation and increase the chances of employers defaulting altogether on their contributions. In this type of competitive market, managing agents start to see themselves as 'selling trainees', charging what the market will bear for the qualities under consideration, forming price cartels through managing agents associations and, where there is a scarcity of placements, undercutting other agents.

The managing agents therefore have a strong financial interest in pleasing the employer. If a trainee loses a place, the employer may look elsewhere, and to avoid this schemes engage in rigorous pre-placement screening. This is especially the case with young people who are less attractive to employers. Hence, whatever the requirements of the MSC, managing agents are reluctant to move trainees for fear of upsetting the employers and because they would then be less likely to be employed afterwards. Where valued training places are few, agents are forced to be as unobtrusive as possible in their monitoring and to turn monitoring exercises into surreptitious marketing.

Changes in YTS have had a marginal impact on schemes run by companies and incorporated into their own recruitment. However, for schemes less linked to employment, the changes have been considerable. The moves towards employer-led schemes has led all independent schemes to regard themselves as profit centres, irrespective of whether their sponsoring body is a private firm, local authority or a voluntary organization.

Linked to this has been the growth of the training manager, the person with administrative and accounting skills who organizes elements of training and marshals the essential support of employers. Agencies have become more uniformly business-oriented. Financial self-sufficiency and the entrepreneurial approach have led many agencies to seek sources of income outside the YTS. For example, most managing agents in the sample also derived an income from the sale of scheme products and services, and here premium schemes predominated. Much of this production was described as incidental and minor, but it ranged from doing small electrical motor or dress repairs, to the manufacture of soft toys, mirrors and furniture. Predictably it was the schemes more detached from the labour market which were thinking more seriously of income-generating sidelines. Some have expanded their training to include private training for employers and adult training for the government. Others have sold the goods and services of trainees so that agents have diversified into small products or service companies.

As YTS has moved towards employer control so it has become more diversified and decentralized. Suggestions following the recent White Paper are that local boards will become more autonomous and employer-composed. This raises the question of their commitment to the low achieving youngster, the least attractive and 'employable' trainees, and the extent to which a regionalized YTS can deliver a national training programme.

For these reasons, it can be seen that although YTS was intended to train people for occupational labour markets', in Marsden and Ryan's terms, it in fact trains them for 'internal labour markets', as the transferability of skills is undermined by increasing employer control (and was subverted in any case during placements). As union and craft control has already been removed by previous 'reforms', this effectively deregulates the training market. A low wage, low quality training scheme has been developed.

Another problem identified with the scheme elsewhere is the perpetuation and reproduction of gender and race divisions. Cockburn (1987) has described how, despite the commitment to equal opportunities, girls are clustered within a small range of schemes and that where they try to cross out of traditionally gender stereotyped jobs, they still end up doing the more 'feminine' work.

Wrench and Cross (1989) have described how the employer-led nature of the recruitment process leads careers officers and managing agents to send the sorts of recruits they know the employer will like – and these are often not black ones. Black and Asian young people are less likely to be on the schemes at all, and where they are, are found in the more stigmatized 'premium' place schemes.

Class divisions are likewise reproduced through youth training, since it does not affect the more academically oriented young people who are headed for more middle class careers at all. Although the refrain of vocationalism is heard more and more in the ivory tower of higher education, no one has yet suggested that graduates do a compensatory course of training after they have graduated and before they enter work.

Hence the divisions into 'academic' and 'vocational' training perpetuated through the schemes reflects older divisions between 'grammar' and 'secondary modern' schools, between Newsom courses and others (Burgess, 1988).

As the economy has been restructured and liberalized through the Thatcher years, so a more casualized and flexible labour force has been created and the MSC and YTS are no longer needed as battering rams to break down established and restrictive practices. The form of flexible franchising is also reflected in the contractual employment relations used for trainers and trainees alike. Thus, the managing agent can be closed down almost overnight and the training organizers and tutors are all on similarly temporary and performance-related contracts.

The new employment White Paper *Employment for the 1990s* will reinforce the trends we have been describing. It will reinforce the tendency towards regional decentralization and the devolution of training into more and more localized units. This makes the possibility of a coordinated training strategy ever more remote. Second, it will reinforce the tendency for schemes to be employer-led – indeed they will now become employer-owned; the proposed Training and Enterprise Councils will have to have at least two-thirds private employers and were set up to circumvent the more uncooperative trades unions. Third, it will reinforce the link between training and unemployment by making the unemployed face even more stringent tests to prove that they are looking for work and forcing them into training schemes as an alternative.

■ Qualifications and education

Courses and counselling offer a concerted programme of moral training as trainees are tutored in social and life skills and personal effectiveness. Reliability and self-discipline are stressed and work experience seen as the opportunity for trainees to make themselves indispensable, as the opportunity to create a real job for themselves. Courses in enterprise are also available, designed to implant the ambitions of self-employment and promote the entrepreneurial culture among the unemployed. The content of courses and the profiling and monitoring of trainees individualizes training issues and trainees' conceptions of the workplace. Youth training contains a manifest and not-so-hidden curriculum.

Theoretically, all trainees should follow an approved training programme leading to a qualification, and this is within a hierarchy of courses and qualifications. Fifty to sixty per cent of trainees in basic places had obtained a qualification in their first year of training, compared with 40 per cent of trainees in premium places. Premium trainees were also much less likely to be attempting qualifications in their second year. City and

Guilds and RSA qualifications, tied to skilled occupations, continue to dominate. Many premium scheme managers regarded vocational quali- fications as beyond the capacities of their trainees and irrelevant to their needs. They preferred to concentrate on basic numeracy and literacy, and had devised assessment systems where any change in the response of trainees could be marked as an improvement; these were courses which no one could fail.

These figures give an official picture of expanding credentialism, but in practice it is rather different. Vocational qualifications themselves continue to be valued only in traditional areas of skilled and non-manual work. In other areas of the occupational and training hierarchy, quali- fications play a more symbolic role. Schemes catering for the low achiever may regard qualifications as beyond their capacity, and argue that they may operate as a disincentive if the trainee drops out. Hence, many of the training courses become nominal in character. The development of scheme-based competence objectives are designed as much to teach worker disciplines as specific skills, and hence (as has been observed elsewhere) this form of training has served to redefine skills behaviourally.

There has always been some tension between on-the-job and off- the-job training, as off-the-job training is sometimes seen as irrelevant by both employers and trainees (for an analysis of trainer's perspectives on this see Parsons, 1989). In this way the division between vocational and academic learning (job-based and classroom-based) is perpetuated. The off-the-job training is organized in skill centres and sometimes in further education colleges where there may be specific YTS tutors or where other tutors may have taken on YTS courses. The present reformulations of the YTS do nothing to integrate these forms of learning, and indeed the off- the-job element is being played down by becoming more flexible and less obligatory. Yet much of which is taught, such as basic literacy and numeracy, has direct vocational impact.

The divisions emerging seem to be those holding to traditional lines of segmentation in the labour market. There is a growing polarization between schemes which serve to lead into 'better jobs' with training and those which serve as 'workfare' for the unemployed. In this context, schemes will continue to have a legitimacy problem.

■ Germany: the corporatist model of youth training

The vocational training and education system in West Germany rests upon ancient foundations of craft apprenticeship dating back to the Middle

Ages, but legally instituted under the Prussian state and Weimar Republic. The importance of the state as an instrument for overcoming factional, religious and class conflicts has to be emphasized in this context, and in the context of German history and social policy. Since then a whole package of 'youth welfare' legislation has evolved. The vocational training system – known as the 'dual system' because young people had to continue in education but could also go to work and be trained – was expanded into a near universal scheme in the 1960s as a way of developing a highly qualified workforce in an export-oriented economy; it has since developed even more multifoliate layers.

This has been described as a 'corporatist' model (Sheldrake and Vickerstaff, 1987) because it depends upon agreement between the different interested parties – employers, educationalists, unions, and the local and national levels of the state – and is monitored, validated and coordinated by the state centrally. The system is supported by a legal framework which, on the negative side, prohibits untrained people from passing themselves off as craftsmen or training apprentices themselves, and on the positive side guarantees the legitimacy of qualifications obtained. However, the cost of training is met largely by private industry who accept 'cheap' employees on low wages in return for training them, but also by the trainees themselves who accept lower wages while training in return for the prospect of higher wages later on.

Here I shall describe the main features of the German system before going on to look at how it has responded to the crisis of youth unemployment and industrial restructuring in the 1980s. The German system relies upon a highly stratified education system which retains young people for longer than most other national education systems (see Table 14.1). For the first nine or ten years of compulsory education, young people attend one of three levels of school: a *Gymnasium*, a *Realschule* (these account for about a quarter each of each age cohort) or a *Hauptschule* (accounting roughly for the other half). Pupils are selected into these different academic tracks during their fourth or fifth year of schooling. After the first nine or ten years (which is completed at roughly the age of 16) young people are obliged to undertake another two years schooling for at least eight hours per week. They can do this at full-time school or in some sort of vocational technical college as the day release part of their apprenticeship. If they undertake no form of training at all, they are still obliged to do the extra two years part-time schooling, although in practice some 'disappear' from the education system at this stage. In this 'sponsored' system of educational mobility (Hamilton, 1981, 1987), the *Gymnasium* represents the 'academic' track and those who leave with appropriately high marks in their final certificate are assured a place at university (which they enter at 19 or so and which takes a minimum of five years if they do a full degree course). These students later enter professional jobs. The *Realschule* do not prepare young people for university entrance but provide another certificate which equips them for technical and white collar training at an intermediate level. At the bottom of the hierarchy, the *Hauptschule* offer only a basic certificate after nine or ten years' schooling leading to more manual trades and training. Those leaving *Hauptschule* are the ones least likely to obtain apprenticeship places. At vocational and technical schools, their off-the-job training consists of German, social studies and theoretical and practical aspects of their trade such as book-keeping, accountancy and law. A variety of technical and vocational colleges exists where people can improve their credentials through part-time study or evening classes, or full-time pre-vocational courses of various kinds. There are some regional variations in this pattern, and there are also a few comprehensives (*Gesamtschule*) in some areas.

Only about 10 per cent manage to fall out of this dual system altogether, but the remaining school leavers undertaken training lasting between two and three years, although not everyone finds a place straight away. Those not getting an apprenticeship the first time round can undertake a pre-vocational course at a college and this can count towards the off-the-job training element of their apprenticeship. Those who do *not* get apprenticeships at all are more likely to be the children of *gastarbeiters* or girls – although girls are becoming increasingly vocationally minded (Seidenspinner and Burger, 1982). However, there is also stratification within the apprenticeship schemes with the less prestigious schemes – such as in catering and retail – requiring only two-year courses, having lower allowances and being more likely to be staffed by girls. We are led to speculate that if it were not for the fact that girls and *gastarbeiters* are predisposed towards the less prestigious schemes and are less likely to take up training in any case, the whole system may have generated an unbearable backlog of frustrated ambition since the majority of school leavers aspire to an apprenticeship.

The apprenticeship system is monitored centrally from Berlin by the *Bundesinstitut für Berufsbildung* where regular meetings of the interested parties for each craft meet to thrash out what is required for that skill. The BIBB is also responsible for reclassifying, realigning and even abolishing skills, in line with the changing requirements of industry. The whole elaborate system of education and training (which I have described only very cursorily here) is set up so as to offer a parallel career hierarchy to that of *Gymnasium*–higher education. The vocational technical colleges of various kinds and the apprenticeship system itself are part of a tiered structure of examinations which people can work their way through, improving their position on the job and through evening classes and eventually going on to higher education in a polytechnic type establishment (*Fachschule*) and obtaining a degree. Alternatively, people can work their way up through night school and professional courses into positions of senior management, bypassing the higher education system altogether.

This is possible because the different vocational and academic qualifications are coordinated in a national scheme of equivalence and these
are linked to internal ladders of promotion.

Employers pay for this system by losing employees for the off-the-
job training element of their scheme. There is a division between small and
large employers in this respect. Small employers are among the main
employers of craft apprentices and they are able to offer an all-round
introduction to the craft but can seldom offer jobs to their trainees
afterwards. In large firms, on the other hand, trainees are more likely to be
trained in specialist parts of the firm.

The system is sanctioned formally by the fact that no one is able to
train an apprentice unless they have the certificate of *Meister*, which
requires training in addition to the basic apprenticeship. Informally,
employers prefer workers with some training as they are deemed more
reliable and able to turn out better quality work. The apprenticeship
system enjoys a high degree of status and legitimacy in the community
generally. The desirability of obtaining training is reinforced by better
wages later, more secure employment, access to ladders of promotion, and
consequently, better welfare – such as health schemes, pensions and
unemployment benefits which are all linked to employment through the
national insurance system.

How did this German system cope with rising youth unemployment
in the 1980s? It did so basically by expanding the education and vocational
training systems, making the employment of apprentices more attractive to
employers (lifting various protective legislation), by adding another year to
compulsory schooling in many places to make it ten years, and by
threatening to apply a payroll tax to employers who did not recruit
sufficient apprentices (OECD, 1981). Pre-vocational courses were provided for those who did not find a place straight away (Koditz, 1985). They
were assisted in this by the fact that more people opted to stay for longer
periods in the education system so that more went to *Gymnasium* – and
therefore university – and more to *Realschule* where they stayed for
longer. The *Hauptschule* started to empty of all but the migrant workers'
children in many areas. Where young people were unable to enter the
apprenticeship of their choice, they undertook another and then took a
second apprenticeship later (Heinz and Krueger, 1987). Thus while there
was trading up by many trying to improve their chances through spending
longer in academic education, there was also a trading down as people took
courses which were lower than those they had hoped for and those
(especially girls) leaving *Gymnasium* started to undertake apprenticeship
training rather than going straight to university. This tended to inflate the
entrance qualifications, making entry to schemes more competitive.
Instead of a 'first phase' transition problem – from school to training – a
'second phase' transition problem was identified – from training into work.
It is still not certain how this will affect German youth since the bulk of

them are still at present absorbed within the expanded education and training system. Other alleged flaws in the system are in terms of youth attitudes: a number of surveys have tended to show that young people are becoming disillusioned and cynical about work and tend no longer to see work as a central life goal (Shell, 1981). Whatever the value of such surveys, they tend to provoke wide publicity in a country where the political allegiance of the young generation has been a point of concern since the war.

Critics have argued that the German system is not as ideal as is supposed because it rests upon highly stratified divisions within education and work (Holt and Reid, 1988). Indeed, the whole process is highly bureaucratized – and some would say, rigid. Hence, in West Germany, far more trades can be classified as 'skilled' and this social construction of skill is heavily reinforced at all levels. Classroom learning plays an important part in this construction of 'skill' and this perhaps avoids the mental/manual divide of the kind found in Britain (Browne, 1981; Wallace, 1987). However, the gulf between the elite 'academic' track and less prestigious 'vocational' ones is nevertheless wide. Furthermore, since young people can remain at university into their 30s, this means that at the academic end of the spectrum they can emerge relatively older and with no practical experience at all to take up elite jobs. Another consequence of this system is that young people are strongly socially controlled by dependence upon their parents (the training allowance does not allow them to become economically independent) and through being socialized into a hierarchical workforce from the beginning as apprentices. Finally, there are the divisions between good and less good apprenticeships which we mentioned previously.

This system discriminates against women (Heinz and Krueger, 1987). Girls are less likely to go for the more prestigious trades and career ladders, and they are perhaps less likely to be 'sponsored' by employers. Second, it reinforces a masculine hierarchy of wages work and the notion of unbroken 'careers', also based upon masculine models of work and skill. Despite evidence that girls are increasingly seeing their lives in terms of work roles (Seidenspinner and Burger, 1982; Shell, 1981) as well as family roles, this does nothing to challenge the male division of labour and merely fits girls into a world where they are sure to be disadvantaged. Finally, the system rests upon the menial and unskilled work being carried out by migrant workers who make up a significant proportion of the German workforce and have few rights in terms of employment protection. These are the ones who end up in the secondary labour market jobs.

Thus, despite the apparent advantages of the German system, it also has a number of drawbacks. Nevertheless the coordinated commitment to education and training controlled but not paid for by the state enables us to characterize this as the 'corporatist model'; for Germans it would be unthinkable for training to be run as a 'business' in itself.

■   Implications and lessons for the future

Raffe (1987) has indicated that the success or otherwise of the Youth Training Scheme must depend upon the *context* in which it is set rather than the actual content of the schemes. By examining these different national contexts we can speculate as to the different directions which youth training might take and the problems associated with each. In this sense, the future of youth training (as Raffe points out) will depend upon the nature of divisions within the labour market and the demand for youth labour in any given regional context.

Three main points of contrast spring to mind. First, because the German system – irrespective of its quality – was introduced at a time of full employment and relative prosperity, it was built upon and still retains a high degree of *legitimacy* in the eyes of employers, trainers and the general public. The Youth Training Scheme, by contrast, introduced during times of rising unemployment and as a way of concealing unemployment, has had difficulty establishing any kind of legitimacy, especially when its already fragile status is undermined by cuts in funding as youth employment starts to rise once more. We would argue, however, that the survival and legitimation of training has less to do with its effectiveness in terms of jobs than to the relationship between the state and the employers. The differences in the structure of training between Britain and Germany are symptomatic of the differences in the political economies of the two countries and the cultural valuation and definition of training and 'skill'.

Second, the crisis in training in Britain stems from rising employment rather than rising unemployment. In Germany the system is undermined when there are more trained young people than employers want – although this seems to have been solved by certificate inflation and providing people with even more training. In Britain it is the fall in unemployment which causes problems as there is then no reason to have schemes – except in a minority of cases.

Third, while the German method is to respond with a nationally coordinated strategy of integrated academic and vocational training, in Britain the solution is a variety of regionally diverse local initiatives which would seem to make NCVQ more difficult to implement. We are returning to the locally specific, locally based training to fit the needs of local employers, reminiscent of the system which existed before the 1964 Industrial Training Act. Training in Britain will become increasingly employer-controlled, whether or not it is employer-based, and this means it is tied to short-term economic goals rather than long-term national interests.

Finally, while the German system is based upon negotiations between a number of different interest groups – including trade unions and educationalists as well as employers – in Britain this corporatist approach has been abandoned, the educational content of courses eroded and given low priority, and the needs of employers given primary status. While the needs of private employers are important in making any scheme work, they cannot guarantee that the interests of young people, or indeed the national requirement for a trained workforce, can be met. So far, education has been blamed for not producing an appropriately trained workforce and new schemes introduced at all levels to make education more vocationally relevant. However, there is little point in improving the education and training system if, as Raffe's work (1988) suggests, employers do not recognize these skills and qualifications. It would seem that only a coordinated intervention is employers' recruitment practices – such as by making it illegal to employ untrained personnel in certain capacities – would have any effect in helping to legitimate new skills.

It has been fashionable in academic circles to be sceptical of the value of youth training. It may seem strange, therefore, that we are defending it. However, a nationally coordinated series of vocational qualifications and training, providing an alternative career route out of unskilled jobs for non-academic school leavers, seems preferable to throwing them into the labour market to sink or swim at 16. This would help to integrate young people into the employment system and go some way towards mitigating the more extreme alienation of youth from the sort of 'shit jobs' which they are expected to do (Wallace, 1987). The MSC almost delivered this; but the scheme was stillborn when the MSC was severely scaled down and finally abolished in September 1988. Would it have been possible to make it into somethiing which served the needs of youth people? The MSC appeared mainly to serve the needs of political expediency, to be a way of circumventing the educational establishment. How could a better system of training have been implemented? In order to answer this question we need to be cognizant of the shortcomings of the schemes we have examined.

We recognize that the danger inherent in suggesting alternatives is that these are utopian and that any alternatives we are likely to suggest must take place within the reality of a capitalist system which ultimately serves to exploit the labour of young people for the lowest cost. We recognize that within a capitalist divided labour market, where young workers are commodified labour and the ultimate goal is profitability, there is limited scope for humanitarian alternatives. Such alternatives would need to take into account inequalities of class, race and gender which – while they may be endemic – can at least be loosened.

A nationally coordinated system of vocational qualifications built on to existing educational provision and evening classes would provide a framework for occupational mobility for those not able or preferring not to enter academic 'tracks'. Genuine gangways between the vocational and the academic routes and re-entry tracks for those who missed out first time round would mean that there would be the possibility of movement between different levels. Age restrictions on apprenticeships would need to be removed since these make possible only a once-and-for-all choice, and discriminate against women who might like to take up a trade after having a family.

Such a national training framework would need to be negotiated with the various different members of the community in order to obtain legitimacy – trades unions, voluntary organizations, the education establishment – and in order to ensure that all views were represented. This would be achieved not by advertising hype but by consultation. Such schemes would be worthless simply as a sop to unemployment – a problem which has bedevilled them all along. They would need to be introduced in the context of an expanding labour market of the kind we are entering in the 1990s. They would also be worthless if they were part of a 'no choice' situation such as that introduced in the recent White Paper, which linked training opportunities with forcing people off the dole.

The price for accepting some idea of skill training would be that it would have to lead to better jobs at the end of it – meaning better rewarded, more secure, more linked to ladders of promotion and exchangeable in an external, occupational labour market. The creation of skills inevitably leads to the creation of segmented labour markets and, therefore, to inequality. However, our argument is that a progressive notion of skilled training would provide more open access to primary sectors instead of limiting these jobs by race and sex. Formal forms of social closure are perhaps easier to tackle than informal forms of social closure.

The dichotomy between useful (but low status) vocational training and useless (but high status) academic training would need to be broken so that a general social awareness and human understanding, as well as high standards of literacy and numeracy, should be seen as an essential part of training for jobs. However, in saying this, we would also need to recognize the antipathy which many students have to more 'academic' learning.

One problem we have identified with traditional skilled training is that it is a way of buttressing divisions of race and gender in the labour market and acts as a form of exclusion by more privileged groups. This reflects a masculine view of work and the labour market. A more progressive training policy would need to take a broader view. This use of skills would need to be challenged and the fact that a shortage of skilled workers is predicted in the 1990s gives scope to include non-traditional groups: middle-aged women training as car mechanics; young women training as North Sea divers; young Asians training for the police force and so on. Cockburn (1987) raises the issue of the problems for men crossing to women's jobs as well as vice versa; these gender stereotypes would need to be tackled, too.

However, we can go further than this and challenge the whole way in which skill is constructed. Given that some recent research in the sociology of work raises the notion that skill is socially constructed rather than being some sort of inherent quality existing in some types of work, it would be important to redefine skill to include the sorts of activities undertaken by a variety of other groups, especially women. Hence, youth training could take into account the sorts of voluntary activities, domestic work and community care undertaken by man women, and encourage young men to perceive these as worthwhile and useful. This would require some sort of training and reward for work outside of employment as well as inside.

Finally, this entire youth training scheme would need to be built upon a foundation of youth incomes policies coordinated in such a way as to afford genuine choices to young people between employment, training, and education and work outside of employment. As part of this, we would need to accept the right to be unemployed and to receive benefits as such, otherwise training and education become compulsory and lose legitimacy as time-serving schemes. Thus, young people would have the right to an independent income at the age of 16 whichever course of action they pursued, and if the government was concerned to encourage young people to stay in education or go into training rather than employment or unemployment it would need to offer financial incentives to do so.

So far, we have talked of national interests or national training strategies and in terms of research and policy carried out so far, that would seem to be appropriate. However, in 1992, Britain becomes part of a European labour market and British workers will need to compete against German ones for jobs. Given that they will be unqualified legally to perform many skilled jobs in Germany and that their qualifications are not transferable but job-specific, we would expect them to be disadvantaged in any European competition. It could be that they are in demand to perform the sorts of unskilled work currently carried out by migrant workers from Southern Europe or they may also perform skilled jobs illegally as *Schwarzarbeiters*. Either way they will be both exploited and disadvantaged. Surely it is now time to think of integrated and compatible training systems?

References

Abbott, P. A. and Wallace, C. (1989). 'The family', in Brown, P. and Scase, R., *Beyond Thatcherism* (Milton Keynes: Open University Press).
Ainley, P. (1988) *From School to YTS* (Milton Keynes: Open University Press).
Ainley, P. and Corney, M. (forthcoming) *The MSC: Rise and Fall of a Quango*.
Ashton, D. N. and Field, D. (1976) *Young Workers* (London: Hutchinson).
Benn, C. and Fairley, J. (eds) (1986) *Challenging the MSC on Jobs. Education and Training: Enquiry into a National Disaster* (London: Pluto).
Brown, P. (1987) *Schooling Ordinary Kids* (London: Tavistock).

Browne, K. (1981) 'Schooling, capitalism and the mental–manual division of labour'. *Sociological Review*, Vol. 2, No. 3, pp. 445–473.

Burgess, R. (1988) 'Whatever happened to the Newsom Course?', in Pollard, A., Purvis, J. and Walford, G., *Education, Training and the New Vocationalism* (Milton Keynes: Open University Press).

Cockburn, C. (1983) *Brothers* (London: Pluto).

Cockburn, C. (1987) *Two Track Training* (London: Macmillan).

Council of Europe (1981) *Living Tomorrow: An Inquiry into the Preparation of Young People for Working Life* (Strasbourg: Council of Europe).

Dale, R. (ed.) (1985) *Education, Training and Unemployment: Towards a New Vocationalism?* (London: Pergamon).

Gleeson, D. (1985) 'The privatisation of industry and the nationalisation of youth', in Dale, R. (ed.), *Education, Training and Unemployment: Towards a New Vocationalism?* (London: Pergamon).

Hamilton, S. (1981) 'Inequality and youth unemployment: can work programmes work?'. *Education and Urban Society*, Vol. 14, No. 1, pp. 103–126.

Hamilton, S. (1987) 'Apprenticeship as a transition to adulthood in Germany'. *American Journal of Education*, Vol. 95, No. 2, pp. 315–345.

Heinz, W. and Krueger, H. (1987) *Hauptsache eine Lehrstelle. Jugendlichee vor den Huerden den Arbeitsmarkts* (Weinheim: Duetscher Studien Verlag).

Holt, M. and Reid, W. A. (1988) 'Instrumentalism and education: 14–18 rhetoric and the 11–16 curriculum', in Pollard, A., Purvis, J. and Walford, G., *Education, Training and the New Vocationalism* (Milton Keynes: Open University Press).

Koditz, V. (1985) 'The German Federal Republic: how the state copes with the crisis – a guide through the tangle of schemes', in Marsden, D. and Ryan, P. (1988), 'Apprenticeship and labour market structure: UK youth unemployment and training in comparative context'. Paper submitted to *International Symposium on Innovations in Apprenticeship and Training, OECD, Paris*.

LeGrand, J. and Robinson, R. (1983) *Privatisation and the Welfare State* (London: Macmillan).

Maizels, J. (1970) *Adolescent Needs and the Transition from School to Work* (London: Athlone Press).

Marsden, D. and Ryan, P. (1988) 'Apprenticeship and labour market structure: UK youth unemployment and training in comparative context'. Paper submitted to *International Symposium on Innovations in Apprenticeship and Training, OECD, Paris*.

OECD (1981) *OECD Monitor* (Paris: OECD).

Parsons, K. (1989) 'Off the job training: tutors' perspectives'. Paper presented to the *BSA Conference, Plymouth Polytechnic*.

Peck, J. and Haughton, G. (1987) *Training and the Contemporary Reconstruction of a Skill*. Working Paper No. 19 (Manchester: Industry Research Unit).

Raffe, D. (1987) 'The context of the Youth Training Scheme; an analysis of its strategy and development'. *British Journal of Education and Work*, Vol. 1, pp. 1–33.

Raffe, D. (1988) 'Going with the grain: youth training in transition', in Brown, S. and Wake, R. (eds), *Education in Transition*, pp. 110–123 (Edinburgh: Scottish Council for Research in Education).

Seidenspinner, G. and Burger, A. (1982) *Maedchen '82* (Munich: Forschungs-bericht Deutsches Jugendinstitut).

Sheldrake, J. and Vickerstaff, S. A. (1987) *The History of Industrial Training in Britain* (Aldershot: Gower).

Shell Survey (1981) *Jugend '81 Lebentswurfe, Altagskulturen, Zukunftsbilder* (Hamburg: Jugendwerke der Deutscher Shell).

Wallace, C. (1987) *For Richer, For Poorer: Growing up in and out of Work* (London: Tavistock).

Wallace (1988) 'Between the family and the state: young people in transition'. *Youth and Policy*, Vol. 25, pp. 25–37.

Willis, P. (1977) *Learning to Labour* (Farnborough: Saxon House).

White Paper (1989) *Employment and Training for the 1990s* (London: HMSO).

Wrench, J. and Lee, G. (1983) 'A subtle hammering – young black people and the labour market', in Troyna, B. and Smith, D. I., *Racism, School and the Labour Market* (Leicester: National Youth Bureau).

Chapter 15

The Youth Training Scheme and Core Skills: An Educational Analysis

R. Jonathan

In the budget speech of March 1985, the Chancellor of the Exchequer announced the expansion of the YTS into a two-year programme, as a measure to combat unemployment by improving the education and training of young people. The expansion of the scheme will clearly improve the unemployment figures, by removing up to half a million young people from the unemployment register for a further year. Whether the scheme or its expansion will reduce unemployment in other ways depends upon the validity of two assumptions: the claim that unemployment in the young results from inadequate education and training, and the related claim that the provisions of the YTS represent a programme of worthwhile education and training for young people.

There has been much discussion of the first of these claims, casting serious doubt on the suggestion that attention to the supply side only of the labour market will have significant economic effects in the short or medium term. Whether or not education and training provision will have beneficial social and economic effects in the long term, in combination with other measures, depends of course on the quality of the provision offered, together with further discussion about what counts as beneficial, and to whom. Thus even as an economic measure the value of the YTS depends in the long term on evaluation of the content of its learning programme.

However, it is one of the distinguishing features of a free society that

Source: Jonathan, R. (1987) 'The Youth Training Scheme and core skills: an educational analysis', in Holt, M. (ed.), *Skills and Vocationalism: The easy answer*, The Open University Press, Milton Keynes, pp. 89–119.

sections of the population cannot be centrally drafted into particular economic activities for the presumed good of the economic collective. We must suppose then that the YTS is not to be seen as a purely bureaucratic measure, designed simply to improve collective economic efficiency, but rather as an initiative for the improvement of education and training which is hoped to have, as well as beneficial consequences for its clients in terms of cognitive gains and improved life chances, some wider economic effects which would in turn be to their advantage as well as that of others. Clearly, individual and collective dimensions of benefit cannot be neatly separated, whether in economic or (less obviously) in educational terms, but neither should they be conflated, for many of the relations between individual and collective benefit are contingent upon alterable social circumstance. When the modification of social circumstance is itself one of the aims of public policy, the prime focus is appropriately placed on benefit to individuals, with benefit to the wider society as indirect consequence. Thus as an education and training measure, the YTS is to be evaluated primarily in terms of its benefits to trainees, for it is in any case only through these that social and economic improvements in which they could share might accrue to the wider society.

Moreover, in evaluating a programme of education and training from the public policy point of view, we are required to understand trainee benefit in terms of cognitive gains and increased life chances related to them which might be achieved by the cohort of trainees. For incidental advantages of a purely positional sort gained by particular individuals make no contribution to the increased collective welfare sought through improved education and training. Thus, for particular individuals, benefits to trainees in terms of increased employability in the immediate future may well relate, not to the content of the scheme or its worth, but to employers' perceptions of that content and worth. When too many young people are chasing too few jobs, it may well be prudent from the young person's viewpoint to undergo any form of preparation which is seen as giving a competitive edge in the job market. Similarly, it may well be useful for employers to select young recruits from an otherwise undifferentiated pool of candidates by using any yardstick which seems to suggest motivation and persistence. But though such reasoning may be rational for individuals in crisis conditions, it is no basis for policies intended to have long-term beneficial effects. Unless the learning content of the programme of education and training offered has inherent value in addition to its usefulness as a screening device, it will provide neither individual nor collective long-term gains. Though some individuals rather than others may secure existing jobs, as a result partly of attendance, they will neither secure more demanding work than they otherwise would have done, nor perform what they do secure more effectively. Though existing jobs may be more readily allocated to motivated individuals, there will not be those cognitive gains in the pool of labour on which is posited the more skilled, versatile and capable labour force which would facilitate quantitative increase and qualitative change in economic activity.

Thus on all counts, fundamental questions to be asked of the YTS relate to the quality of the learning experiences it offers to the trainee. It is on that matter that this paper will focus, rather than on questions of those social effects (on wage expectations, on the hierarchy of economic rewards, on the power of trade unions) which depend not on the content of the scheme, but on the manner and circumstances in which it is developed. This is not to suggest that educational questions can be neatly separated from social and political questions, or that only the former should be addressed in examining the scheme: an analysis of the content of the YTS learning programme will show that its education and training content is highly charged with a range of political and social commitments. It is simply to insist that the rewards and status of trainees, though important, are modifiable secondary questions, which have up to now distracted attention from a more fundamental issue: what is the value of this one/two year programme of education and training as a learning experience for its young clients?

It should be noted on this point that when we are talking of a programme put together at great speed for nearly half a million clients, which subsumes pre-existing training provision as well as extending it to a mass clientele for radically altered purposes, it is clear that the individual experiences of trainees will be very diverse. A small proportion of selected trainees will find themselves being trained for a particular occupational role, as under the apprenticeship system, with a prospective employer, and another relatively minor group will be following FE courses with considerable carry-over of content and method from earlier provision, though now under the umbrella of the YTS. Since these arrangements predate the scheme and are not typical of the experience of the mass of its clients, these are not the experiences of individuals by which it is to be judged. Just as the worth of the scheme tends to be judged by its clients in terms of the incidental effects of their participation, so its merits and demerits are often weighed by providers and managers in relation to what they are able to offer, incidentally, under its umbrella. While both of these are important considerations, the worth of any particular scheme of education and training relative to other actual or possible schemes must relate to the central distinguishing features of the scheme under consideration. Intended consequences should not blind us to important side effects, but attention to side effects alone precludes relative evaluation of alternative policies where side effects are common.

The hallmark of the YTS, which is claimed by its designers to be its central element, is the Core Skills programme – a collection of 103 'skills' which are generic and transferable, can be learned and assessed in quite diverse contexts, and which as well as equipping young people for an unspecified range of occupational roles, also make good prior failures of education and socialization. We are told that 'it is the core areas ... that provide the content of YTS'[1]; that they are 'an essential element of the YTS (which) could lead to the setting up of a work-based alternative to O-levels and CSE as a route into further education and employment'; and that they could provide 'a common framework for accrediting performance in vocational and pre-vocational education and training'[2]. If the Core Skills comprise the content of the scheme, if it is this central part of the programme which permits its extension to half a million youngsters, and which furthermore legitimates its claim to be a programme of education as well as training, this is the element which must be examined in order to evaluate the scheme as a learning programme. If, moreover, transferable Core Skills are claimed to have a significant part to play in the reform of secondary schooling, an analysis of that central element in the YTS will be of interest to educators in general.

This paper, then, will attempt to examine the content of the YTS learning programme by focusing on the Core Skills which provide its central element. It will become clear that this is a far from straightforward task, since the system of training embraced by the scheme is not only pluralist in practice, with differences in aims and philosophies both within and between groups of teachers and policy makers; this pluralism is encouraged by the ambiguity of policies formulated to secure maximum support across a range of interest groups who have not traditionally been in concert. The crucial question to be asked about the Core Skills programme is whether this is indeed the meat common to a range of incidentally varying sandwiches, or whether it is an opaque packaging device which simultaneously permits variety and inhibits quality control.

The examination will fall into four parts. Section 2 will look at the background of ideas and circumstances which gave rise to this radically changed approach to training. Section 3 will examine the development of the programme's rationale which followed the publication of the New Training Initiative. Section 4 will examine the final recommended content of the programme in the light of this rationale, paying attention to its hidden as well as its overt curriculum. These three sections together are designed to provide an evaluation of the learning programme, but first a preliminary section is required to establish the criteria according to which this evaluation should be conducted.

■ Evaluation criteria for this 'programme of education and training'

The YTS presents us with an interesting problem: it purports to be a programme of education and training – should it be evaluated according to criteria appropriate to training, or according to the more complex criteria normally applied to education? Traditionally, there has been a sharp dichotomy in Britain between education and training, both in theory and in practice.

In practice, the divide between education and training has become considerably blurred during the past decade. Accelerating demands that education should become more relevant and useful, to individuals and to society – with relevance and use being understood in economic terms – are currently the prime force for curriculum change. The introduction of TVEI in Britain as a whole, and in Scotland the Standard Grade in Social and Vocational Skills and the modularization of the curriculum post-16, are evidence of a growing vocational impetus in schooling. The YTS, on the other hand, imports educational aims to a mass post-school training programme just as those other initiatives import training objectives to schooling. The acceptability of this blurring of the divide *in practice* between education and training depends upon claims about the existence of certain skills and their transferability. The skills in question are not the narrow mechanical skills of the operative or fitter, they include life skills, social skills, reasoning skills, survival skills, problem-solving skills etc. Since these, it is claimed, once learned, can be readily transferred to a vast range of contexts and since, collectively, they comprise the cognitive, social and emotional equipment needed by tomorrow's adults, skill training is no longer the limited addition to education that it was once thought to be. It is presented as an adequate alternative or even a desirable substitute.

Moreover, the aims of a *generic* training programme such as the YTS represents go far beyond the specific vocational training purposes of the apprenticeship schemes and Industrial Training Board programmes which preceded it. For the skills it seeks to promote are not particular technical facilities, but a range of general developmental attributes, dispositions and capacities. This is not 'training' as hitherto understood in vocational preparation, for only in the military context has training overtly encompassed attitudes and dispositions. Although troops are drilled not just so that they will march and reload efficiently, but also so that they will obey orders, respect rank and respond predictably, plumbers are trained simply to solder pipes, so that the pipes will not leak. It might here be objected that any learning has a dispositional carry-over, or that even the most task-related training contains or implies an aspect of professional socialization. Nonetheless, though consequences are ultimately what matter, these are likely to be more far-reaching if they are deliberately promoted as well as incidentally produced. Outside the military context the aims of training have hitherto been specific and limited in scope, with the development of personal attributes, dispositions and capacities thought to be the province of education and socialization. Where these broader personal developments are the aim of learning programmes, broader questions of justification arise concerning the aims, method and content of those programmes.

It is thus not surprising that the YTS is billed as a programme of education as well as training, since its aims go beyond those of traditional vocational preparation. For the scheme does not offer (as might be supposed) traditional training plus added educational features: it embodies a concept of training which is itself so radically revised that it no longer exhibits the three distinguishing features which formerly helped to characterize vocational training, and which legitimated the divide between education and training which has existed in theory as well as in practice. Although there are no doubt historical and sociological reasons for an overemphasis in Britain on that divide, there were in the past three sound reasons for that professional demarcation line, which allowed theorists to apply different evaluating criteria to the two activities.

Firstly, where training is task-specific, the ends of the activity are not matters of dispute, and what is the most effective means of securing that end is an empirical matter. Secondly, this type of training is generally separated from and subsequent to the process of general education, assumed to have already proceeded to a satisfactory minimum level. Thirdly, training programmes have been thought to require less stringent moral justification than the processes of compulsory education, since their clientele are volunteers and no longer children. None of these traditional features of training are applicable to the learning programmes of the YTS, as will be briefly indicated. If that case can be made, then the sort of evaluation appropriate to the scheme will be an educational analysis.

Why then does generic training require the more complex and stringent criteria of justification which have long been thought appropriate to educational programmes? If training is task-specific, it can be judged simply on whether it achieves its objective. If an adult is taught to drive, or a child to tie his shoelaces, we merely ask if the end has been achieved efficiently and subject to the normal moral constraints. These, of course, are more stringent when trainees are children or non-volunteers. But generic training, such as the YTS claims to offer, is not specific to tasks, and its objectives cannot therefore be defined in terms of specific tasks. It might be supposed that they can be defined in terms of a *range* of tasks, but the more this range is extended, the more any definition of prerequisite competencies undergoes a change of focus, from skills to be mastered to capacities necessary for mastery. When maximum adaptability is the watchword, as in the YTS, then learning objectives are rather defined in terms of changes sought in the dispositions of the trainee. The Core Skills of the YTS aim to develop the trainee in cognitive, social and personal terms, remedying prior failures of education and socialization. It is therefore not enough to ask whether such a scheme achieves its objectives: the objectives themselves need careful examination.

How stringent our evaluation of means and ends needs to be

depends upon the moral status of the trainee. It is generally accepted that we have a greater moral responsibility towards those who are in our power, than towards those who by reason of maturity or circumstance are in a position to reject or refuse the treatment they are offered. Since entrants to training programmes are adult volunteers and school pupils are under-age conscripts, we require distinctive moral justification of schooling programmes in terms of their long-term benefit to the learner. We justify compulsory education on the twin grounds that those being taught have insufficient knowledge and understanding to decide for themselves how they can best develop henceforward, and that the learning experiences offered them are such as to enhance their development of rational autonomy. Since entrants to training programmes are adult volunteers, these strictures traditionally have not applied to them.

It is of course true that children are obliged by law to undergo a process of education, and it is true that no one is compelled to join the YTS (I am not concerned here with proposed extensions of the scheme, since policy statements vary on that matter[3]). However, to leave the matter there is rather like insisting that we are all free to dine at the Ritz, as there is no law or rule which would bar any one of us from admission. At the age of sixteen the choice for over half of our young people is between courses at school or in FE, paid employment (obtained by 21 per cent of the age group in 1983[4] and by roughly similar proportion subsequently), unemployment with or without supplementary benefit, or the YTS. The first option often demands academic prerequisites these young people lack, the second is clearly not open to that majority of sixteen-year-old leavers who have failed in recent years to find employment within six months of entering the labour market, and the third option has been declared undesirable and subject to review by the governments.[5] The prospective trainee might well echo Charlie Brown: 'Life is full of choices but you never get any'. I would therefore argue that most trainees, by force of circumstance, can scarcely be considered volunteers. If that is a fair point then its implications for evaluation criteria are substantive but negative. Where learning programmes are devised for non-volunteers, they must be compatible with further development of the learner's rational autonomy: they must not stunt critical faculties, narrow horizons, lower expectations or diminish moral discrimination.

If, in addition to not being a volunteer, learners are also at such a low level of cognitive and emotional development that others have the right to make developmental decisions for them on the grounds of their incapacity (as we do with children), then along with those rights of decision go corresponding duties of a more positive kind. In such circumstances, teachers are normally thought to have positive duties to develop critical faculties, to broaden horizons, to inform expectations and to develop moral discrimination in the learner. I would be happy to argue simply for the negative criteria enumerated in the preceding paragraph, but the designers of the generic training programme for the YTS seem to be working on assumptions about the capacities of trainees which would logically bring the second, more stringent, set of criteria into play. If, on examination, the Core Skills turn out to be very rudimentary, then either they are redundant, or a scheme in which they are central should be subject to the strictest evaluation of an ethical sort.

Thus, whatever additional criteria are relevant on economic and political grounds, the content of the scheme and the status of its clients point to the necessity of evaluating the YTS firstly according to educational criteria. If these points of principle are not sufficiently compelling, there are further pragmatic considerations which imply that an educational evaluation of the scheme is urgently required. Whatever the force of the arguments above, it would be simplistic to view the YTS as a training measure quite separate from policies and practice in education, and thus to be evaluated by training policy makers according to their own criteria; the scheme is part of the educational context, for four main reasons.

Firstly, if the designers of the scheme have, as they claim, identified developmental needs in trainees which society endorses and which the schools have failed to meet, then either the education system is failing large numbers of young people, or schools and society are at cross purposes concerning the aims of education. Either case requires a response from educators, whether in modifying methods and broadening aims or in presenting the case for aims and methods worthy of retention.

Secondly, the YTS (and particularly its generic training element) is likely to have a significant backwash effect on the secondary school curriculum for the less academic pupil, not only through direct import into the period of compulsory education via the measures of TVEI, but also indirectly. The assessment profiles of the YTS have been frequently referred to by the MSC and the IMS as an alternative to O-levels. Indeed the Director of the MSC announced in September 1984 that:

> The package extends backwards into schools to catch that group numbering 20 per cent or more of the age cohort who are given nothing by the formal 16-plus examinations and, despite nine years of formal schooling, so very little by way of basic cognitive skills.[6]

At the time of writing it is hoped to introduce a new YTS Certificate in April 1986, covering the four key areas of the scheme.[7]

Thirdly, the rationale for generic training and the eventual Core Skills programme is not something dreamt up by the MSC simply to provide an educational legitimation for a national scheme of youth training. The momentum for the rapid implementation of the proposals of advisory bodies such as IMS could scarcely have been secured by a huge input of funds alone. In the development of the YTS, as in the general blurring of the distinction between education and training, political expediency coincides happily with certain popular (though misguided) trends in educational thinking. Many of these (such as the claim that what you learn does not matter, it is *how* you learn that is *all* important; that we should teach what is relevant and useful, and that those judgements are straightforward; that the economic needs of the group should determine the learning experiences of the individual; that equipping the young 'for life' means equipping them to fit into and 'cope with' circumstance, not to evaluate and possibly modify it, etc.) are taken careful account of in the specifications of learning programmes in the YTS. With some exceptions (such as the Social and Vocational Skills course for 14–15 year olds in Scotland, some elements of the Scottish Action Plan for 16–18 provision and various elements of TVEI), the emphasis in schools on 'skills' ('life-skills', 'social-skills', 'survival-skills', 'coping-skills') is still at the level of exhortation and exploration: the YTS Core Skills programme offers an opportunity to evaluate the 'skills' movement when it is translated from rhetoric to reality.

The fourth reason for scrutiny of the scheme on educational criteria is that curriculum change, direct or indirect, is not simply a matter of whether the innovation in question is acceptable in itself. Time and resources are finite, and to include A in a curriculum is to exclude B. In FE Core Skills threaten Liberal Studies courses, in secondary schools TVEI pre-empts the development of courses for its clients which are not subject to the approval of an extra-educational quango. We therefore need to be satisfied not simply that these programmes are unobjectionable, but that they are equally or more worthwhile than alternatives which could be offered to the client groups concerned, whether these are conscripts by statute or by circumstance.

I would therefore argue that the YTS, because it is a formal learning programme designed to influence the development of a captive audience, and because furthermore it is indissolubly linked with past and future educational practice, should be subjected to scrutiny in educational terms. There are other bases for scrutiny, but these fall outside the focus of this chapter.

■ Educational and social change and the Youth Training Scheme

In order to understand the development of the Core Skills programme and its centrality to the YTS rationale, reference must be made to the background of interlinked economic, scoial and educational circumstances which gave rise to it. Although, for political reasons, *something* has to be done about the alarming rise in youth unemployment, precisely what should be done depends upon a set of diagnoses of past economic failure, present educational ills and future social trends. Before we can evaluate the treatment, we should examine the diagnoses and the symptoms on which it is claimed to be based. From the late 1970s to the present there has been a growing tendency to redefine the problem of youth unemployment as a problem of inappropriate or inadequate education and training for young people. What trends in thinking have lent plausibility to that redefinition?

When explanations are sought for past economic failure, comparisons between the UK and its major trading partners are inevitable. Although of course the political, social, economic and educational arrangements of any given society are indissolubly linked in complex ways, attention in this instance has been focused heavily on *educational* differences between the UK and its trading partners, singling out a causal factor which was both politically acceptable and potentially remediable. And indeed there is ample evidence that youngsters in the UK find themselves in the labour market earlier, in greater numbers, and with less preparation than in comparable industrialized countries.[8]

The diagnostic focus on educational shortcomings was the more persuasive at a time when cracks in the educational consensus were widening. Growing awareness that comprehensive reorganization had still left a secondary school system geared principally to the needs of the more able and offering little to motivate the many who leave school uncertificated, gave ample scope for orchestration of public demands for more say in the aims and content of education. Over the past decade, the 'Great Debate' was followed by the accountability movement, curriculum review, proposals for examination reform, the introduction of market forces via the Parents' Charter, increased central interest in curriculum content and assessment, central attention to teacher quality and training, and the introduction of the Technical and Vocational Education Initiative. Though the grounds for dissatisfaction with present educational policies and practice varied widely within and between groups of interested parties (parents, teachers, employers, pupils, politicians), the general breakdown of consensus created a climate in which firm diagnoses and hard-headed remedies appear particularly attractive. The more so, of course, when those remedies accord or appear to accord with current fashions in education thought.

This latter point is also relevant to the diagnosis of future social trends. The restructuring of the economic base is more easily presented as a manageable problem of education and training when many educators themselves stress knowledge obsolescence and the primacy of discrete procedural skills, and when 'continuing education', 'recurrent education' and 'lifelong education' are presented as inevitable and desirable developments. Against this background, youth unemployment becomes, not a result of economic recession, but a concomitant of inadequate education and training, now seen as a significant cause of recession. The case for a large-scale programme of nationally organized youth training becomes persuasive on educational, economic, social and political grounds, the more so as it allows a range of lobbies in education, training and employment to secure support for independently favoured measures.[9] Thus the Youth Opportunities Programme was swiftly replaced by the more extensive YTS, and in September 1984 the Director of the MSC envisaged 'an end to youth unemployment when no one would enter the labour market until the age of 18.'[10] Although at the time of writing the YTS is still technically a voluntary scheme, this prognostication was brought one step nearer to realization by the expansion of the scheme into a two-year programme, announced in the Budget Speech of March 1985. The new two-year programme is planned to be in place in April 1986, consisting of foundation training for the first year (compare the present programme of the YTS), followed by more specific vocational training in the second year, to the extent to which the availability of places with employers or in training workshops makes that possible.

Criticism of the YTS has initially focused on both the purposes of policy makers and the effect on trainees in political and economic terms. Objections have been raised to a measure which disguises the true level of unemployment and also depresses the wage expectations of trainees and hence of related disadvantaged social groups. Notwithstanding the force of these objections, they divert attention from the central point which concerns the quality of the learning programme offered. They are too easily answered – at cross purposes – by the opposing faction which urges us to welcome a policy that promises to provide initially a year and subsequently two years of structured learning and attainable qualifications for that large segment of school leavers whose alternatives are aimlessness or at best unskilled labour. That *some* programme of education and training, open to all 16-year-old school leavers, would in principle be desirable (provided its claimed harmful side effects were mitigated) is hard to deny. But endorsement of any particular programme must depend upon an evaluation of its content.

As noted earlier, this cannot be, with the YTS, a straightforward evaluation of the efficiency of means to prespecified ends, since the key innovation of the scheme is that this is not training with a particular occupational task in view. In this respect the New Training Initiative of 1981[11] represents a turning point in training policy from employer-based training for specific jobs, and the boosting of key occupational skills through Industrial Training Boards (partially financed by pay-roll levies on employers), to the provision of a period of planned education, training and work experience for all under 18 and not at school.[12] The £1,000 million per year YTS is intended to initiate a universal foundation training for 16-year-old leavers which would provide a broader and more generic type of vocational orientation than hitherto with, if circumstances permit, more specific training in the second year of the proposed two-year scheme.

Indeed the avowed rationale of the scheme[13] echoes liberal demands for a vocational preparation characterized by generic rather than specific skills, flexibility and choice of training, and attention to the social and personal as well as the technical development of trainees.[14]

At the policy level this shift from specific to broadly-based training is justified primarily in economic and social terms.[15] Though it is also noted that a broad base is educationally sounder for the trainee, actual and envisaged economic circumstance is stressed as requiring the change. A decline in unskilled work, the increased pace of technological development and consequent structural changes in the industrial base, are seen as necessitating a more competent, broadly trained and adaptable work force. The MSC's Corporate Plan for 1985–89 reiterates this point:

> ... the need will be for people with dual or cross trade experience and it is likely that job prospects will be best for people with transferable skills they can use in several industries. Britain's international competitiveness will depend to some extent on the rate at which those new skills are acquired.[16]

A cynic might add that since one cannot train for particular jobs when there are few of these available to graduates of the training, the strategy likely to cause least frustration is to train for 'jobs in general' – a strategy which appears to coincide happily with liberal demands that learning should open doors rather than close them. Again, we should ask not whether this apparently virtuous change of policy was born out of necessity, but where its presumed virtue for the trainee is supposed to lie. And the answer to that is of course in the identification and development of the Core of the programme.

Basic to the shift in training emphasis is the assumption that it is possible to identify Core Skills which would be transferable across a broad range of related occupations and which could be taught and assessed during a one- or two-year period of education and training, in order both to remedy deficiencies in the previous education and socialization of trainees and to enhance their future employability. While government stresses the economic benefits of training, the designers of the YTS initially stressed its social and educational benefits, in contradistinction to YOP which is widely acknowledged to have served primarily to remove youngsters temporarily from the unemployment register.[17] Thus transferable skills are seen as the key to three separate sorts of problems: economic, social and educational. In education, the identification and promotion of such skills promises to solve the perennial problem of worthwhile content and also the pedagogical problem of motivation for 'non-academic' pupils.[18] Socially, the fostering of these claimed skills legitimates the occupation, off the labour market, of hundreds of thousands of young people who would not willingly remain in education, and for whom there are few jobs waiting for which they could be specifically trained in the traditional sense. Economically, the decline in unskilled work, the increased pace of technological development and the consequent restructuring of the industrial base, are seen as requiring a more adaptable work force. Clearly, it is precisely in virtue of the Core – the very element claimed to be of educational value to the trainee – that the extension and expansion of training post-16, and the introduction of an allied 'vocationally enhanced curriculum' for the 14–18 age group in schools, is legitimated. It is therefore this element of the YTS which requires educational evaluation.

■ Core Skills: the design rationale

The large claims made for the Core Skills programme cannot be assessed by looking at the programme itself and its guides and manuals, for in those presentations the rationale for the scheme is nowhere to be found, except in the vaguest rhetorical terms. However, there *is* a detailed rationale, and it is crucial to understanding how these transferable skills have been identified and why they are to be learned and assessed in the manner eventually prescribed. I shall be concerned here to offer a critique of the design rationale of the Core Skills programme, before discussing subsequent revisions of design, for these are entirely pragmatic and obscure its underlying rationale. I shall not explore shortcomings in the implementation of the scheme.[19]

The IMS was commissioned by MSC in 1981 to prepare a report on *Foundation Training Issues* which would underpin implementation of the New Training Initiative.[20] It noted that to avoid the unevenness of YOP provision, a more precise specification of learning objectives was required, and further noted that:

> Possible growth points and innovations come under five headings: additional basic skills; world of non-employment; broadly related skills; personal effectiveness skills; and ability to transfer and ownership of skills. The first three are extensions of the YOP achievement.[21]

The last two are thus the areas of innovation. The innovations are justified by the changing economic and social conditions noted earlier, so that 'To strengthen young people's adaptability, versatility and employability, it will be necessary to formulate learning objectives at a higher level.' The writers of the report note, however, that 'there is, as yet, no common understanding of what they are or how they can be learnt, although some YOP schemes are moving in this direction'.[22] [*sic*] This mixture of disarming candour about ignorance of the destination, and blithe confidence concerning how to get there, was to characterize the Core Skills development programme. Thus, less than eighteen months before the launch of the Core, this report asserts that even with level-one skills (for World of Work and World of Non-Employment) there is 'insufficient collective wisdom for syllabus writing'; and that, worse still, for levels two and three (Personal Effectiveness and Transferability) 'we are on much thinner ice'.[23] The report's authors state that they are not at all sure that there is teachable content here at all:

> There is no clear understanding yet whether they are learning objectives which 'govern' other learning and for which it is impossible to devise content organization and methods, or whether they are learning methods, i.e. policy instruments for use in implementing learning objectives.[24]

These doubts notwithstanding, the same body then set about investigating relationships between these dubious entities. Their report, published within the year,[25] was designed not only to identify learning objectives, but to suggest assessment procedures and to 'consider the relationship between the learning objectives within a framework consisting of specific and broadly related work skills, the world of non-employment, personal effectiveness, and the ownership of skills'.[26] Achieving the impossible in this way was facilitated by the fact that 'The remit asks that this project be concerned with *outcomes*, not with the processes by which they are to be achieved'.[27] In layman's language it is thus a question of stipulating what changes the YTS should seek to bring about in the understanding, capacities, attitudes and responses of young people, and of devising assessment procedures for the changes desired, without giving thought to how these might be brought about. The report states openly that the criteria behind this stipulation of desirable change in competences, attitude and behaviour are that they should be non-controversial and consistent with envisaged shortcomings in provision. The report thus announces:

> Opinion among educational and voluntary organizations is divided. We have tried therefore to produce proposals that would meet with general acceptance, would benefit the economy as well as the individual trainee, and could accommodate the unavoidable stresses involved in setting up a voluntary, multi-agency Scheme with limited resources for 460,000 young people.[28]

The first point to need comment here is that in the design of a programme whose rhetoric constantly reiterates the primacy of process over content in learning, no consideration of process plays any part in the establishment of desirable learning outcomes. Programmes of learning normally take account of three differing types of criteria: psychological considerations relating to the cognitive and emotional capacities of the learner, epistemological considerations relating to the logic and structure of what is to be learned, and ethical constraints on both process and content. Matters of public acceptance and practical implementation are the cart that these horses have to pull. In the development of the Core Skills programme it is not that the cart has been put before the horse: all the horses concerned have been ceremonially shot dead at the outset.

Given the criteria remaining for recommendations – general acceptability and consistency with an uncontrollable diversity of provision – their principal characteristic is inevitable, namely specification of outcomes at a high level of generality, allowing for radical ambiguity in interpretation. And indeed this is the case. There are plenty of things that we are all in favour of: personal development, responsible behaviour, clear thinking, freedom, fresh air and fun. These are also the very things about whose nature we argue most. There are plenty of things that are so self-evidently desirable that we all agree with promoting them, while disagreeing radically about what they are and how that should be done. We are all in favour of a broader, rather than a narrow, preparation for working life; we would all support the promotion of skills which prepare for many activities rather than one; we all prefer adaptability rather than lack of it or social adjustment rather than its converse, and we would all endorse systematic rather than haphazard learning. At the level of broad specification, the outcomes proposed for trainees are likely to secure general assent. What then are these broad specifications?

■   Types of competence recommended

These are divided broadly between competences required in employment and those required in 'the world outside employment'. There is no space here to explore the assumption that an individual's economic activity is the most significant feature of his life, nor the even more questionable assumption (revealed when employment competences are discussed under the heading of 'The Benefits to Employers and Young People'[29]) that the interests of capital and labour necessarily coincide in a free-market economy. To be competent in the world of employment seems *prima facie* of benefit to the individual, and this is therefore the aspect of a programme of education and training traditionally thought of as least problematic. However, things are less straightforward when employment competences are to be generic, rather than task or occupation specific, for it still has to be decided what competences are relevant to the future employment situation of trainees. With generic training we do not know what this employment will consist in, so that relevance in this case may be to the assumed capacities of the trainee or his envisaged social role, rather than to the prespecifiable demands of a particular job.

Demands for the liberalization of training have long suggested that young people should be prepared for a broad range of occupations, in order to keep options open as long as possible. If broad ranges of occupation could be identified and prepared for generically, the problem of relevance seems avoidable, for in that case relevance would once again be simply instrumental, though broader. This is the approach adopted by the YTS designers in establishing what competencies are relevant to the world of employment as it will be experienced by graduates of the scheme.

If employment competencies are to be generic, occupations must be aggregated into groups, unless we are talking of competences thought desirable in all types of employment. Any competences so generally applicable, whether personal attributes and social skills or the basic skills of numeracy and literacy, would also seem to be prerequisites for full adult autonomy in an advanced society. They thus could not comprise the innovative element in a generic training programme, since they should constitute the minimum (though not always achieved) objectives of a programme of general education. By 'generic' is thus intended 'widely applicable' rather than 'universally applicable'.

Accordingly, the IMS established eleven Occupational Training Families (OTFs),[30] each with an identified 'Key Purpose' (KP). For example: OTF 2 Agriculture, Horticulture, Forestry and Fisheries – KP Nurturing and gathering living things; OTF 8 Food Preparation and Service – KP Transforming and handling edible matter; OTF 11 Transport Services – KP Moving goods and people. According to the IMS, competences relevant to training within any OTF can be broken down into two sorts: those which directly reflect the key purpose of related activities within the group, and those common to all. Additionally, there are Transfer Learning Objectives (TLOs) 'concerned with the ability to find out rather than to do',[31] so that the trainee can later extend his acquired competence.

For the wider world outside employment, the report summary can be quoted directly:

> Six roles were identified. Two essential roles were *Personal Survival* and *Exercising Citizenship*. The four optional roles were Contributing to the Community; Self-Employment; Continuing education; Pursuit of Leisure Activities.[32]

At this level of generality, who could fail to endorse these goals, which seem to accord well with liberal requirements for the sort of vocational preparation which is of lasting benefit to the trainee? This has been thought to require the identification of 'broad ranges of vocational competence as the basis of courses of study which underpin a variety of crafts and within a broad occupational field'[33] and further to constitute 'a genuine educational experience in that it inculcates knowledge, skills and attitudes which lift the worker's perspective beyond the demands which the job itself imposes'[34]. Closer scrutiny, however, may qualify that endorsement.

■ Competences for the world of employment

Though it seems desirable in principle to group various occupations, the value in practice of doing so depends upon the criteria used to establish a group. Such criteria will of course also determine what competencies are common to the group. The best way to see what effective criteria have been used in this case is to look at the occupations comprising OTFs. OTF 2 (Agriculture, Forestry and Horticulture) lists 34 occupations including beekeeper, florist, market gardener, fisherman and market porter. OTF 4 (Installation, Maintenance and Repair Occupations) lists 27, including cobbler, electrician, garage mechanic and window-cleaner. OTF 8 (Food Preparation and Service Occupations) lists 22 including baker, kitchen porter and vending machine operator. OTF 1 (Transport Services Occupations) lists 25, including air traffic control assistant, milkman, refuse collector, lift attendant and ship's agent.

One of two interpretations can be placed on these rather surprising groupings. If criteria relate primarily to the notional 'key purpose' of a general field of employment activity, irrespective of the competence differences of both level and type which obtain within that field, then there is clearly no basis for common competence and consequent skill transfer between occupations within the family which would adequately prepare for any, let alone all, of the named occupations. OTFs established on this basis would defeat the purpose for which they were set up. The second possible interpretation is that while the key purpose generates a list of occupations, the competence envisaged is not for the trades, crafts and skills listed, but for low-level tasks in their general area. It certainly appears that whatever occupational competences are required in common by both a florist and a fisherman, or an electrician and a window-cleaner, or an air-traffic control assistant and a lift attendant, they must be at a very low level of skill content, since it is possible to train somebody to be either an electrician or a window-cleaner as well as an electrician. But if that person is trained *generally* for either rather than *specifically* for both, he or she ends up competent in neither role, though the shortfall in necessary competence will vary with the skill demands of each role. Where the level of skill demand is highly variable within an OTF (as in OTF 1 from air traffic control to lift attendant) or where the types of skills are very diverse (as in OTF 4 between cobbler and garage mechanic), any commonality between competences required will be in the area of rudimentary prerequisites, which as they stand can only prepare for unskilled work in the general area of these trades and tasks rather than for the trades and tasks themselves.

These groupings are supposed to benefit both employers and trainees. From the employer's point of view, there is clear benefit, in terms of employee transferability, in the grouping of jobs. That the OTFs are not discrete suggests that they are indeed a convenience for the groupings of trainees, rather than a coherent grouping of occupations, for the benefit of trainees. Indeed, benefit to the trainee depends upon which of the above interpretations of groupings criteria is justified. To trainees and their parents it matters a great deal whether traineeship in OTF 11 will prepare learners for a career in transport or whether it promises to teach them part of what they need to know to be a lift attendant. Or again, will traineeship in OTF 8 prepare a youngster for a career in catering or does it offer some of the competence needed to fill a vending machine? For any educational evaluation of the scheme we need to know whether the OTFs, by broadening the skill base, keep options open and horizons broad for the trainee, or whether, by offering only training in and habituation to rudimentary performances, they do precisely the reverse. To suggest this is not to subscribe to any conspiracy theory, merely to assert that unless the *genus* on which generic training is founded is coherent in terms of both type and level of skill, such training will necessarily be a blend of compensatory socialization and preparation for unskilled labour.

Detailed *Work Learning Guides* were produced for each OTF, breaking down the prerequisites for relevant competences: a study of these guides leaves little doubt that here this is indeed the case. Thus for OTF 8 (Food Preparation and Service) the learning objectives are either devoid of content, since context is unspecified (for example, 'perform own role to standard of timeliness and hygiene') or, if specific, devoid of skill ('dress correctly', 'maintain clean and tidy work station', 'avoid safety hazards', 'use appropriate language and behaviour', 'create attractive environment'). These typify learning objectives related to the 'key purpose' of this OTF. As for the second sort of competence arrived at, that which is transferable to other ranges of occupation, the overall competence of 'contributing to the efficient running of the organization' breaks down into 'adapt working hours to customer needs', 'stand in for others', 'perform others' jobs', 'carry out allocated group tasks on time' and 'keep utensils clean'. No doubt all these so-called competences would contribute to the efficient running of the organization, but what do they contribute to the vocational preparation of the trainee, other than to fit him, by modifying his attitudes, behaviour and expectations, for the role of flexible operative? The reality of the vocational element of the skill programme is thus diametrically opposed to its rhetoric. When the broad specification of goals is translated into detailed (and assessable) learning objectives, we have moved away from liberal demands for generic training to the illiberal social reproduction of a pliant underclass.

The point to be emphasized here is that once training becomes generic in the sense implied by OTFs, based on skills claimed to be transferable across activities which vary enormously in the type and level of demand they make on practitioners, the identification of relevant learning objectives ceases to be a straightforward empirical matter, since they can no longer be related instrumentally to a particular training outcome. Relevance is now related to the assumed characteristics of trainees and the social roles envisaged for them, rather than to a particular task for which they have themselves chosen to be trained. Judgements of relevance thus entail social and political evaluations concerning the appropriate future activities of trainees. Superficially, transferable skills look like an escape from the murky waters of ethical justification, in that they apparently keep options open for youngsters. In reality, they require close ethical scrutiny, since they necessarily define the parameters in which those options will be exercised.

It might be supposed that this would be remedied by the incorporation in the programme of Transfer Learning Objectives, since the 'ability to find out rather than to do' seems to echo current educational emphasis on 'learning how to learn' as an answer to the claimed obsolescence of knowledge. Current emphasis on process in education arises in reaction to the bad old stereotype of rote learning and in over-reaction to a new awareness that knowledge is open to development and revision. Insight that the learning process is itself important is replaced by the false claim that it is all-important: learning skills are no longer seen as a means of applying and extending knowledge, they are offered as a replacement for it.

A recent Bow Paper on 'lifelong learning' typically describes as a skill 'The ability to frame an intelligent question and to recognize a sensible answer'[35], apparently unaware of what is involved in doing so. What sorts of questions are intelligent and what answers are sensible depends upon context: knowledge and understanding of context is required to make these judgements. The YTS claims to prepare the trainee for changes of employment context by means of increased competence in learning skills. Thus, we are told, the aim is to enable the trainee, in a new context, to answer two questions '*What* do I need to be able to find out about the thing with which I am unfamiliar?' and '*What* do I need to ask myself about where and *how* to find out?'[36]. Imagine someone stranded by the roadside with a car breakdown, or puzzled about why a recipe has failed to produce the expected result. If they can answer either of these key questions, it is surely not that they now know how to develop the knowledge and understanding needed, but that they have it already. As Humphrey Lyttelton remarked 'If I knew where jazz was going, I'd be there already!'. If the value of 'learning skills' is that they facilitate the acquisition of new knowledge, their success depends in part on an attitude of confident inquiry, but much more importantly on the possession of a considerable fund of existing relevant knowledge.

However, once again, when the TLOs are translated from vague goals into explicit learning objectives (LOs) it becomes clear that the ability to develop and acquire worthwhile knowledge is not what is at issue. From the TLO 'Behave in order to create and maintain satisfactory work relationships' the LO is derived 'Find out how to behave in order to create and maintain satisfactory work relationships'[37]. The list of items headed

'What you need to know' includes 'What style of language the other person would like you to use', 'at what time the other person would like to communicate with you', and 'What rules or requirements the organization has about how to behave' etc.[38]. Under 'How to find out' various suggestions about whom to imitate and whom to obey are listed. It may well be useful to know what others expect of one, and to be able to adapt, chameleon-like, to different situations. But transferable learning skills are promoted in education precisely on the grounds that they increase initiative, non-dependence on authorities, and a reflective, critical attitude. The TLOs of the YTS, on the other hand, are designed to foster malleability and conformity. Thus this innovation in the vocational element of the YTS again reinforces its anti-educational characteristics.

If the 'vocationally enhanced curricula' proposed for secondary schools exhibit similar features, as the Director of MSC has promised[39], then the educational climate will have turned full circle in two centuries. In 1806 Colquhoun wrote 'Let it not be conceived for a moment that it is the object of the author to recommend a system of education for the poor which shall pass the bounds of their condition in society'[40]. In 1981 the Bow Paper quoted above announced 'You don't need O-levels to be a road-mender .... Too high a qualification is really a disqualification for a contented, competent employee'[41]. When Colquhoun was writing, it was unremarkable to presume that any education charitably provided for the poor in society should primarily serve the interests of the providers. For the past decade the presumption that education provided by the state should serve the interests of the state, viewed primarily as an economic collective, has been quietly growing in strength. I have argued elsewhere that even in social and economic terms this policy trend is misguided[42], but those are by no means the primary criteria which should be used to evaluate YTS as a scheme of education and training. The benefit *to the trainee* of the vocational element in the content of YTS is hard to discern unless we assume:

(1) that up to half a million school leavers each year are potentially capable of only the lowest-level tasks;
(2) that such tasks will exist at an adequate level of reward;
(3) that it is in the individual's interest to be socialized into his/her inevitable role in a hierarchical social and employment structure.

All the above relates of course only to intended benefit and core content, and it will again be objected that the redeeming features of the scheme are to be found in its unintended effects and contingent consequences. For some, it is true, this vocational programme may stimulate interest in and determination to acquire the specific training which the Core does not offer. And for some the circumstances of their work placement may offer worthwhile learning experiences which make the rationale for the Core irrelevant. But again I would maintain that it is a poor justification of any learning programme to support it either on the grounds that it does not work or that it does not matter.

■ Competences for 'the world outside employment'

The scheme's designers give four reasons why 'any proposals for the learning content of YTS should include consideration of the world outside employment'[43]. Firstly, for this group, unemployment will be an inevitable feature of life: 'YTS would not be helping young people to prepare for the reality of adult life if it did not attempt to help them to cope competently outside the world of employment'[44]. Secondly, this being the case, if 'employment competences' are not used outside the context of a job, they will atrophy during the trainee's inevitable periods of unemployment. Thirdly, it is argued that those who 'come to terms with unemployment' and 'develop alternative activities' are more likely to find eventual re-employment. It is suggested that an 'employment ethic' should be replaced by a 'work ethic'[45]. Fourthly, the YTS will lack credibility, it is argued, if it prepares largely for employment in an age of mass unemployment.

Thus the next important point to be noted about this scheme of education and training is that it is not to consist, as one might expect, of a training element to prepare for working life and an educational element to prepare for personal, social and cultural development in adulthood. Rather, the training element seeks to fit the individual for his place in a pool of adaptable unskilled labour, and the so-called educational element aims to adapt him for his place in the economically (and, often, politically) marginalized pool of the unemployed. The 'World Outside Employment' looks, on closer inspection of consultative documents, like the world of unemployment. In a scheme of education and training one would expect the content of the educational element, at least, to be determined by the capacities and interests of the trainee, in order to broaden his choice of potential social role. In the rationale for the YTS this element also is determined by envisaged constraints of the labour market, claimed to be inevitable, which are beyond trainees' control and to which it is therefore in their interest to adapt. The economic lot which policy makers envisage for these young people is the central consideration in *both* the training and the 'education' elements of the scheme.

It would be hard to find a clearer demonstration of the fact that 'relevance' and 'usefulness' are very dangerous criteria for learning programmes to adopt, since both of those concepts are context and purpose dependent. We need therefore to examine what context is being prepared for and whose purposes are being served, before we endorse any programme of learning characterized by its 'relevance' and 'usefulness'.

Once again, at the level of broad specification, no one could object to the six roles in the world outside employment in which the scheme's designers aimed at trainee competence. These are: Personal Survival, Exercising Citizenship, Contributing to the Community, Self-Employment, Continuing Education, and the Pursuit of Leisure, the first two being essential, the others optional. If, as claimed, young people are to be given the competences involved in 'deciding what goals are personally important to pursue' and in 'beginning to direct their own lives'[46], this seems highly educationally desirable. Leaving aside the point that they are to pursue these goals and live these lives in circumstances which are taken as given, and which may be highly unfavourable to the individuals concerned, a study of the *Work Learning Guides*[47] gives no clue as to how these laudable aims might be achieved through the programmes proposed.

As with the occupational competences examined earlier, the learning objectives and their prerequisites listed are either devoid of content or devoid of skill, though in this case the former type predominate. In order to achieve Personal Survival, the trainee should be able to 'Maintain physical and mental health'[48]. On the physical side he should be able to 'obtain heating' and 'obtain housing' – no further prerequisites being listed for these abilities. On the mental side he should be able to 'undertake a range of activities each day', 'create and maintain satisfying relationships with others' (divided significantly into family, friends and 'authority figures'). Satisfying relationships will be maintained by the ability to 'make assessments about own and others' influence on situations that seem realistic to other people'. It is clear that what counts as a reasonable assessment of situations or appropriate behaviour in them, is again not for the trainee to decide; he is to defer to the judgements and standards of others on these matters. The trainee is scarcely 'beginning to direct his own life': he is being trained to take responsibility for coping with adverse circumstances which he has not chosen, and also for conforming to expectations which he is not expected to question.

The other essential area of personal development is outlined in the *Exercising Citizenship Learning Guide*[49] which aims to enable the trainee to 'obtain rights and fulfil responsibilities as a citizen'. Again, nowhere is it considered that an important part of adult citizenship in a free society is understanding, evaluating and possibly seeking to modify the currently accepted rights and responsibilities of citizens in the society to which one belongs. Moreover, in a society where citizens, however equal they may be before the law, are certainly not equal in social circumstances, different clusters of rights and responsibilities will appear relevant and appropriate to different types of citizen. This *Learning Guide* leaves no doubt as to what type of citizenship trainees are to be prepared to exercise. The overall aim is broken down, unexceptionably, into 'contribute to society' and 'obtain social, financial and legal benefits to which entitled as a citizen'. Now, every member of a social group is expected both to contribute and to benefit; but what the type and manner of these transactions are to be for a given individual is revealing.

The contribution to society envisaged for these young people consists in, 'Help other people in the everyday life of the community' and 'Exercise right to vote in elections'. The obtaining of rights is clearly not to be a matter of seeking parity of equality or freedom with more privileged citizens, but simply of obtaining welfare relief entitlements by rule-following and subservient behaviour. Thus to exercise their rights these young people need just three prerequisite competences: 'Apply to the right body/person at the correct time'; 'Apply by means seen as appropriate by body/person'; and 'Create a favourable impression'.

I do not question that one of the skills of citizenship is to be able to operate within the social system obtaining; but there are two major objections to the YTS interpretation of citizenship training which require that the label 'education for citizenship' be withheld from the programme. Trainees are firstly required, not to understand and evaluate the social structure and its institutions, but to fit into it and secondly, they are offered only the competence to fit into it at the lowest level of personal control and power.

It would be tedious to repeat this analysis from high-level aims to specific learning objectives and their contributory competences for each of the six 'Learning Opportunities' which the YTS was originally designed to foster (Basic Skills, World of Work, World outside Employment, Job-Specific and Broadly Related Skills, Personal Effectiveness and Skill Transfer). In each of these areas there is the same slide from fashionable and high-minded but empty phrases ('YTS aims to ensure that young people take responsibility for their own learning'[50]) to the recommended fostering and testing of low-level skills and dependent attitudes (find out how to behave by imitating and asking others). The competences envisaged for trainees in each of these six areas are either:

(1) meaningless without specification of some content and context (perform own role to appropriate standard);
(2) meaningless altogether (use senses correctly);
(3) of dubious value to the trainee (behave ethically by finding out what counts as ethical behaviour in an unfamiliar situation);
(4) at a very low level of skill (count items singly or in batches).

We are told that 'It is the core areas, as part of the learning opportunities, that provide the content of YTS'[51], yet the initial problem which IMS noted – that there may be no teachable content here after all – is unresolved. It is avoided in practice by declaring that:

The core areas are a tool for developing and organizing the training programme. They must be incorporated into the planned work experience. They are not 'subjects' to be taught in the off-the-job element. They must be integrated into all aspects of learning throughout the 12 months' training programme[52].

Thus, the remit given to the designers of the YTS was to identify transferable skills, which could be acquired and assessed in a diverse range of contexts, and which would meet with general public endorsement. Lest anyone suggest that at the end of the YTS development exercise, the Emperor still does not appear to have any clothes, we are warned pre-emptively that these are special, invisible clothes. Moreover, being invisible, they are all the more serviceable, for they are suited to all shapes and sizes, fitting for all occasions, usable in all climates, and not subject to changes in fashion.

■   The design revised: the Core Skills Programme

Without an examination of the bulky IMS reports which detail the development of the YTS recommendations, the final glossy presentation of the Core Skills programme to managing agents, sponsors and trainers would be quite baffling. For the elaborate rationale for the YTS, the detailed design which underpins its claim to be a programme of education as well as training, is a complex set of posited generic occupational competences and of personal and social attributes which are not to be explicitly taught at all, since they are 'embedded in tasks' and 'inferred from task performance'.

The Core Skills Programme was accordingly announced in May 1984. In a press notice, Dr G. Tolley, head of the MSC Quality Branch [sic] unveiled 'an essential element of the YTS [which] could lead to the setting up of a work-based alternative to O-levels and CSE as a route into further education and employment'[53]. A model for schooling is also explicitly envisaged since we are told that 'It could also provide a common framework for accrediting performance in vocational and pre-vocational education and training'[53]. The equivocations and hesitations of the IMS feasibility studies have now disappeared – as indeed have many of the more liberal notions of bodies such as the Youth Task Group – and a tidy programme of skills which are claimed to underlie the successful performance of almost all tasks at work and many practical activities outside the workplace is presented. The skills are now grouped into four core areas of number, communication, problem solving and practical, which itself represents a paring down of the scheme's scope, emphasizing remediation of prior failures of education and socialization.

The Practitioner Guide to the YTS Core[54] and the *Core Skills Manual*[55] were published a month later in June 1984, together with a *Guide to the Revised Scheme Design and Content*[56]. The Revised Guide reiterates 'the emphasis on the "transfer" of skills to new situations and personal effectiveness', although under the heading 'What are the benefits?', the trainee is no longer separately mentioned:

> the overall aim of the YTS will be to produce a better motivated and more adaptable workforce, capable of developing skills to meet changing employment needs. This will have the effect of reducing training costs as well as minimizing wastage and should prove in the long term to be of benefit to employers and to the economy as a whole[56].

Four simplified outcomes are now specified: trainers should achieve:

'(1) competence in a job and/or a range of occupational skills;

(2) competence in a range of transferable core skills;

(3) ability to transfer skills and knowledge to new situations;

(4) personal effectiveness[56]'.

These indeed have been endorsed as the four key outcomes for the proposed two-year scheme. The last three of these look consistent with educational criteria, and indeed it is envisaged that the trainee should become consciously aware of the Core Skills they possess, should learn to analyse those required in new situations and should be able to find out how to acquire them. In developing personal effectiveness, trainees would be encouraged to 'use their initiative, think for themselves, find out things for themselves, solve problems and plan, handle interpersonal relationships, accept responsibility and become independent[56]'.

Although, then, the aims of the programme make no reference to the trainees' benefit except in so far as it is in their interest to be adapted to whatever employment they are offered, the content of the programme (within a more limited range) sounds as if it would accord with educational demands that young people's autonomy be encouraged and respected and their rational development fostered. The methods of learning advocated also seem to echo up-to-date educational thinking, since stress is to be on 'experiential learning, learning through doing, an emphasis on skills and tasks rather than knowledge or theory (that is, taking an *active part* in the learning)[56]'.

Again, however, the latent ambiguity in all these fine phrases is exposed by the list of Core Skills to be promoted and by the context in which the trainee is to acquire them. Since learning is to be through doing, and these skills are prerequisites to the performance of tasks, the trainee will acquire them in the context of a task. The tasks most frequently used as illustrative examples in the *Practitioner Guide* are 'filling a supermarket shelf' and 'sorting incoming mail'. A surprising number of Core Skills are implicit in both of these activities, from 'plan the order of activities' (9.1), through 'decide which category something belongs to' (10.2), 'estimate quantity of observed items or materials' (3.2), to 'count items singly or in batches' (1.1). However, since it is clear that all of these skills are involved in getting oneself up and out of the house in the morning, it is hard to see what *new* skills the trainee is acquiring. This is not 'learning through doing'; it is simply 'doing', and not doing anything very stimulating at that.

The important point here is that when emphasis is to be on skills common to tasks, this is necessarily the case, since the learning potential of a new situation lies in its distinguishing features. It would be objected to this that there are two aspects to a new situation: the changed context and the procedural skills a person brings to it – conscious awareness of the facility in these skills serving to minimize contextual variation. This indeed is the assumption behind demands for the promotion of 'problem-solving abilities' and 'thinking skills' in education, and it exhibits all the same difficulties.

One of the reasons for the downgrading of content in education is the observation that after years of studying 'subjects', pupils are frequently unable to solve real problems or to think critically. It is therefore easy to suppose that content is unimportant and that the skills of problem-solving and critical thinking should be approached directly. However, although a knowledge of content – badly taught – is not enough to promote these skills, they can be neither acquired nor exercised without it. For there is no such thing as 'problem solving' or 'thinking': there is only solving this particular problem, or thinking about this particular matter. Not only is a great deal of relevant understanding required to solve a problem: this understanding is required to recognize that there is a problem in the first place. Moreover, this understanding is not simply a matter of appropriate information, for different *procedures* are necessary for the solving of different types of problems and for effective thinking in different areas of life. An education with adequate depth and breadth of content is essential to these valued 'skills' precisely because technical problems, social problems, aesthetic problems and moral problems differ from each other in both content and procedures.

There is thus no shortcut to the acquisition of basic (or core) skills, if by basic we mean *fundamental*. Human thought and activity are richly varied and there is no Holy Grail of skills or competences which can substitute for broad knowledge, understanding and experience. If, however, by basic we mean *rudimentary*, then there are certainly common prerequisite competences for most tasks which reflect the mental and physical capacities of ordinary human development. What is needed for 'successful performance' in a given context in addition to these common human capacities is an understanding of that context. Where a context is complex the understanding required will be considerable, and the ordinary capacities will be taken for granted. Where a context is trivial, little understanding will be required, and there will be little task content beyond the exercise of rudimentary capacities. This does not show that in the new context trainees are learning by doing – it rather shows that there is nothing here for them to learn.

Four representative Core Skills will illustrate this[57]. *Skill no. 1.1* 'Count items singly or in batches' requires the ability to count (which we can suppose a trainee to have) and sufficient familiarity with the situation to know what counts as an item or a batch. *Skill no. 10.2* 'decide which category something belongs to' is both more rudimentary and more context-dependent. Fishermen and florists both do this, because in addition to an ordinary human brain they have, respectively, a knowledge of fish and a knowledge of flowers. *Skill no. 13.3* 'manipulate objects and materials' is yet more rudimentary and hence more context-dependent. Abstracted from context it does not even require a human brain – ants and sparrows do this too. What makes this activity *skilful* is an understanding of the nature and purpose of context: the florist might display it arranging flowers to best effect, and the fisherman setting his trawl, but no amount of flower arranging will promote skill in fishing. *Skill no. 9.8* 'diagnose a fault' is as vacuous as 'problem-solving', since to diagnose a fault, say, in the engine of a car I need to know something about cars – a lot of fault-diagnosing skill, developed in finding out why my cakes do not rise, will not get me very far.

It would be objected that I am wilfully misunderstanding the nature and purpose of skill transfer here: I may need additional information, but past success in diagnosing faults will give me an attitude of confidence and a procedural head start. Even this more modest claim is false. Unless confidence is based on an awareness of the limits of my knowledge and the extent of my ignorance, it will only mislead. I need a real understanding of what differentiates the unfamiliar from the familiar context before I can decide what sort of additional information I now need. I may either need to understand a different set of technical principles, or, worse still, I may need to bring quite other principles into play – a design fault will involve aesthetic considerations, a breakdown in customer relations will call for social and personal understanding. Even if we consider problems which are purely technical, there are no skills of fault diagnosis which are necessarily transferable. Trial and error, or a process of elimination are the sorts of procedures which might be effective in some situations in the absence of relevant knowledge (as in trying to get a car engine to fire by adjusting the plug gap), but in a different situation such techniques would be disastrous (a dentist searching for the cause of toothache or a hairdresser investigating the cause of her client's thinning hair).

I am not arguing here that people cannot be helped to get better at solving problems or at diagnosing faults: clearly a thorough knowledge of car mechanics, dental disease or hair treatments will enable practitioners in those areas to understand and possibly solve related problems and faults. I am also not suggesting that people cannot be taught to be more effective in solving problems or in diagnosing faults in an enlarged range of relevantly similar situations. The careful teaching of appropriate procedures (whether this be the identification of causal chains, the recognition of cyclic systems, or the ability to test assumptions), together with plenty of opportunities to practise them in situations which motivate the learner, will certainly enable him/her to extend acquired knowledge and further develop specific skills. None of that is new, and has characterized good educational practice from the time of Plato[58].

What is novel in the fashionable skills-based approach to learning are the twin suggestions that procedural learning supersedes content learning, and that the transferability of procedural skills is independent of context[59]. What is truly innovative about the YTS approach to skill training is that these assumptions are compounded by the claim that those transferable skills are not to be taught at all, but simply to be picked up by trainees in whatever situation they find themselves. If, while 'sorting incoming mail' or 'stocking a supermarket shelf' trainees show that they can readdress mail to a relocated department, or remove misplaced sausages from the jam shelves, it is no help to them, or to future employers, to assess them favourably on the skill of 'diagnosing a fault'. And it is highly misleading to claim that they are learning to diagnose faults, or are being taught to solve problems in general.

This brief examination (which has avoided both the most rudimentary of the Core Skills, such as 'Find out information by speaking to other people' and the most vacuous, such as 'decide between alternative courses of action') should demonstrate that not only is there nothing here for trainers to teach – as the MSC admits – there is nothing for trainees to learn, at least in the cognitive sense. However, there is plenty for them to learn about attitude. In accordance with the rationale of the YTS developed in the IMS reports examined in section 3, trainees are learning the habits and attitudes appropriate to individuals who will join the pool of the marginally employed. They are being habituated to routine tasks – checking, sorting, cleaning, loading, running errands. They are expected to accept the hierarchy of the workplace, and their position in it, to be cooperative and obedient, to 'show willing', to 'be prepared to do more than the minimum', to 'find out what is expected' etc.

Of course, none of these dispositions as they stand is objectionable: rational autonomy is all very well, but few organizations would run efficiently if everyone exercised it all of the time. It is clearly important for adults to understand the purposes and structure of the institutions in which they have a role, and a scheme of education and training might well be expected to promote understanding of that aspect of adult life. A YTS Core Project *Starting Work* claims to teach this understanding. But it does so, typically, by means of a booklet in which trainees fill in the names of the people who give them instructions, the instructions, and the names of 'your boss', 'his/her boss' and 'his/her boss' in ascending hierarchical order. The transfer learning here is limited to 'Find out who is in charge of you when you are doing a particular job'. Far from promoting an understanding of the structure and purpose of an institution, this type of learning is anti-educational, leading trainees to believe that what happens to be the case socially must be accepted without question. What is offered to these young people is indeed mere information rather than knowledge and understanding, and information selected in such a way that possibilities for the development of understanding are foreclosed. Similarly, the social and personal development involved in these Core Projects consists in trainees finding out what authority figures want and in learning to act accordingly. To persuade young people, as do these *Work Learning Guides*, that ethical behaviour consists in doing whatever one's immediate superior believes to be acceptable, is not just to fail to promote moral autonomy: it is to subvert it.

Thus, though there is little in YTS to develop the minds of those hundreds of thousands of sixteen-year olds who, for want of a real alternative, find themselves on the programme, there is a great deal to mould them for their envisaged social role. Though they are to 'use their initiative, think for themselves, find out things for themselves, solve problems and plan, handle interpersonal relationships, accept responsibility and become independent'[56], they are to do this in a prescribed manner and in a particular context. Indeed, here as elsewhere, it is context which puts flesh on the bones of empty phrases. In effect, trainees are rather to adopt instructions, find out who is in charge, discharge their allotted tasks efficiently, comply with expectations, and internalize the supervisor.

Though there is nothing to teach in the Core, and little to learn which could claim value in either educational or training terms, there is much to assess. Trainees are to be assessed on their supervisors' judgement of whether they show competence in the Core Skills in going about their allotted tasks. Schemes provided by managing agents (voluntary organizations, colleges, LEAs, large firms, small employers in shops and workshops) are to be judged by the same supervisors' judgements of trainee attributes and competence. There are two potential kinds of benefit to a person undergoing a course of education and training: the inherent value of the course he follows, in terms of his own personal development, and its exchange value in enabling him to use his qualifications as economic or social bargaining counters. I have suggested that the inherent value of this programme to the trainee is dubious to say the least. Though the certification offered by the scheme is spoken of by its designers as 'an alternative to O-levels', it is hard to see what could be the exchange value of a certificate of competence with the inevitable characteristics of the YTS.

Where competences are meaningless without specification of content and context, there will be no comparability between levels of competence exhibited in a bewildering and uncontrollable variety of contexts. Where competences are altogether meaningless, they are open to the wildest variation in judgement. Where competences are so low-level that it is assumed trainees will be able to achieve them without teaching, then by definition graduates of the scheme are either being judged on competences they started out with, or on trivial gains in competence. Finally, given the characteristics either of vacuity or of redundancy which characterize the basis of the assessment, and given the fact that in making these nebulous assessments, the judges of the trainees are also judging the quality of their own schemes, then neither objectivity nor precision in judgement seems likely. Since these are the two characteristics on which the exchange value of a criterion-referenced assessment is based, then it would appear that for the trainee the exchange value of the YTS is as dubious as its inherent value.

Once again, this is not to say that a YTS training will not give a competitive edge in a severely restricted job market to some trainees. Employers may regard graduates of the scheme, generally, as likely to be more motivated than those who rejected it, just as they will be likely, specifically, to take what recruits they require from those who have responded well to placement with them under the YTS umbrella. But as has been argued above, to note this merely indicates the desirability of *some* training programme from the individual's point of view: it neither endorses this particular programme from that point of view, nor does it answer the expectations of benefit from the cohort of young people as a whole, nor from the wider society. Any such endorsement of a particular programme should be dependent upon favourable evaluation of its distinctive characteristics.

■ Conclusion

This paper has concentrated accordingly on the Core Skills programme, following its development from the first announcement of NTI to the Revised Scheme at the end of the first year of implementation. Plans to date for the new two-year scheme leave Core Sills in their central position, albeit endorsing the desirability of some more specific vocational training in the second year, in so far as circumstances permit this development. Since the Core Skills are claimed to be 'the Heart of YTS', the locus of benefit to the trainee, and the rationale for conflating education and training, it is this element of the scheme which requires scrutiny.

There are several basic questions to be asked in judging the value of learning something – let us call it X:

(1) What is X?

(2) Is it teachable?

(3) Do the learners know it already?

(4) Of what value will it be to them?

(5) Of what value will their learning X be to others?

(6) Is the balance between (4) and (5) morally acceptable if the learners are not volunteers?

Only if satisfactory replies can be offered to those questions is it worth pursuing further questions of how X can best be taught or learned.

I have tried in this analysis to suggest answers to those basic questions in respect of the content of the YTS. If we let X here stand for the Core Skills around which the Youth Training Scheme is built, the answers seem to be as follows:

(1) X may be anything or nothing, depending on context.

(2) X is here not even claimed to be teachable, but rather learnable in any undemanding context through exercise.

(3) But X can be exercised without teaching only if the context is so undemanding that the learner knows X already.

(4) The value of X is claimed to lie in its transferability, but since that part of X which is transferable (a rudimentary capacity) is already known, and that part which is context-dependent (the element of skill) must be taught in context, X itself has no value without teaching.

(5) The attitudinal learning promoted may have considerable value to others, given acceptance of certain moral premises about what social arrangements are desirable. These premises, far from representing social consensus, are at the heart of public moral and political debate.

(6) Even if such disputes were settled in favour of the premises adopted by the designers of the Core Skills programme, the balance between (4) and (5) would not be morally acceptable unless trainees were genuine volunteers, neither penalized for rejecting the programme nor lacking viable alternatives to it, and unless they were already in possession of the normal human capacities which the Core Skills describe when abstracted from context. Thus as the central element of the YTS, X – the programme of Core Skills – is either redundant or it is morally unacceptable.

I referred earlier to the normal criteria for educational evaluation – soundness on epistemological, psychological and ethical grounds – and it is my contention that the Core Skills programme fails on all counts. This critique should not be construed as a defence of our arrangements for education and training before the advent of NTI. There is clearly a need for reform in the secondary sector, most urgently for those pupils who leave at sixteen, but also for those who are sufficiently motivated to suspend their disbelief in the value of what is offered to them. There is also a need for a programme which prepares young people to bridge the transition from school to adult life, which builds confidence, enhances skills and provides an understanding of our social and economic institutions. Such a programme is needed and should be welcomed, but the Youth Training Scheme, built as it is around the concept of Core Skills, is not such a programme.

Notes and references

1. *The Youth Training Scheme Minimum Criteria*, 1984–5, produced by Community Schemes Unit of NCVO, 1984, p. 10.
2. MSC Press Notice 72/84, *Skills Training at the Heart of YTS*, MSC press office, May 1984.
3. The 1981 White Paper, *A New Training Initiative: a Programme for Action* (Cmnd 8455), suggests that YTS should eventually cater for all 16-year-old school leavers, as do many MSC policy statements. However the 1984 White Paper, *Training for Jobs* (Cmnd 9135), in March 1985, still leaves it technically voluntary.
4. Statistics for destinations for 16-year-old school leavers from *DES report by HMI on the Youth Training Scheme 1983–4*, DES, 1984, p. 4.
5. This review is again shelved at the time of writing, but it is not unreasonable to suppose that it may well reopen when the two-year scheme is in place.
6. *Training News*, no. 10, September 1984, p. 2 (Newsletter of Advisory Committee, Education and Training, Scottish Local Government Employers).
7. i.e. (1) Competence is a job and/or range of skills.
   (2) Competence is a range of core skills.
   (3) Ability to transfer skills and knowledge to new situations.
   (4) Personal effectiveness.
   See Cmnd 9482, April 1985, 'Education and training for young people', HMSO; and Interim paper issued by MSC Working Group on Funding and Administration, 1985, 'Possible framework for development of the youth training scheme', paras 8 and 12.
8. *Competence and Competition* (1985). London, National Economic Development Office.
9. For the exponential growth in initial training, see Ryan, P. 'The new training initiative after two years', *Lloyd's Bank Review*, April 1984, p. 33.
10. Quoted in *Training News*, no. 10, *op. cit.*, p. 2.
11. White Paper, *A New Training Initiative: a Programme for Action*, Cmnd

8455, December 1981; see also Manpower Services Commission, *A New Training Initiative: a Consultative Document* (May 1981), and *A New Training Initiative: an Agenda for Action* (December 1981).

12.   See also White Paper, *Training for Jobs*, Cmnd 9135 (January 1984).

13.   See Manpower Services Commission, *Youth Task Report* (April 1982).

14.   e.g. Entwistle, H. (1970), *Education Work and Leisure*, Routledge & Kegan Paul.

15.   Institute of Manpower Studies, report no. 39 *Foundation Training Issues*, C. Hayes, A. Izatt, J. Morrisson, H. Smith, C. Townsend, February 1982.

16.   Manpower Services Commission, *Corporate Plan for 1985–9*, MSC, 1985, para. 3.

17.   The above report (14) largely accepted the board condemnation of YOP expressed in an unpublished working paper of OECD, 1981.

18.   It has been noted that when training becomes generic, much of its motivating force appears to be lost, compare HMI report on first year of YTS.

19.   For such a critique, see *The Youth Training Scheme in Further Education 1983–4: an HMI Survey*, DES report, 1984. Ryan (1984) *op. cit.* Raffe, D. (1984), 'Small expectations: the first year of the Youth Training Scheme', paper presented at *Young Person's Labour Market Conference*, University of Warwick, 1–2 November 1984. Dutton, P. (1982), 'The new training initiative: what are its chances?'. *Discussion Paper, 18*, Institute for Employment Research, University of Warwick, 1982. *Times Educational Supplement*, 22 October and 24 December 1982; 25 March, 4 April, 13 May, 22 July 1983; 6 January 1984.

20.   IMS report, no. 39, *op. cit.* 1982.

21.   *ibid*, p. 4.

22.   *ibid*, p. 3.

23.   *ibid*, pp. 46 & 47.

24.   *ibid*, p. 47.

25.   IMS Report no. 68, 1983, *Training for Skill Ownership*, C. Hayes, N. Fonda, M. Pope, R. Stuart, K. Townsend.

26.   *ibid*, p. 9.

27.   *ibid*, p. 9.

28.   *ibid*, p. 9.

29.   *ibid*, p. 27.

30.   *ibid*, p. 50 for full list.

31.   *ibid*, p. 14.

32.   *ibid.*, p. 5.

33.   Entwistle, H. (1970), *op. cit.*, p. 89.

34.   *ibid*, p. 56.

35.   Virgo, P. 'Learning for change, training, retraining and lifelong education for multi-career lives', *Bow Paper*, 1981, p. 2.

36.   IMS Report no. 68, p. 14.

37.   *ibid*, p. 228.

38.   *ibid*, p. 228.

39.   Training News, no. 10, *op. cit.*, p. 2.

40.   Colquhoun, *Treatise on Indigence*, 1806.

41.   Virgo, 1981, *op. cit.*, p. 9.

42.   Jonathan, R. 'The Manpower Service model of education', in *Cambridge Journal of Education*, Vol. 13, No. 2, 1983; and Jonathan, R. 'Education and the "needs of industry" ', in Hartnett, A. and Naish, N. (eds), *Education and Society Today*, Falmer Press, 1986.

43.   IMS report no. 68, *op. cit.*, 1983, introduction.

44.   *ibid*, summary 4.2.

45.   *ibid*, summary 4.5.

46.   *ibid*, summary 4.19, 4.20.

47.   IMS Report 1968, *op. cit.*, 1983, Annex C, pp. 161–175.

48.   *ibid*, Annex F, p. 246.

49.   *ibid*, Annex F, p. 247.

50.   YTS information booklet for Managing Agencies. *ESF Youth Training Scheme Core Project.*

51.   *The Youth Training Scheme Minimum Criteria* 1984–5, produced by Community Schemes Unit, NCVO, 1984, p. 10.

52.   *ibid*, p. 10.

53.   MSC Press Notice 72/84, *Skills Training at the Heart of YTS*, MSC press office, May 1984.

54.   *Manpower Services Commission Round Robin No. 8/84 – Core Skills in YTS, Quality Branch*, MSC, 15 June 1984.

55.   *Core Skills in YTS, Part 1: Youth Training Scheme Manual*, Quality Branch, MSC, June 1984.

56.   *Guide to the Revised Scheme Design and Content*, YTS, 84(a), MSC, Quality Branch, 1984.

57.   The full list of 103 Core Skills is to be found in the *Core Skills Manual* (55 above).

58.   cf. the development of the slave-boy's geometrical skills in 'Meno'. Plato, *Protagoras and Meno*, trans. W. K. G. Guthrie, Penguin, 1956.

59.   For a critique of this approach, see McPeck, J., *Critical Thinking and Education*, Martin Robertson, 1981.

Chapter 16

16–18 on Both Sides of the Border

D. Raffe and G. Courtenay

■ Introduction

[...] People in the rest of Britain, even educationalists, tend to be poorly informed about the Scottish education system. Their ignorance is understandable given the centralized politics and media of Britain. Debates about 'British' education tend to be internal to, and specific to, the English system; when Scottish developments are noted they tend to be appraised for their relevance to England.[1] Not that developed media coverage necessarily provides the answer. The *Times Educational Supplement* publishes a separate Scottish edition, in which several pages carry Scottish news not published south of the Border. While it improves coverage of Scottish affairs within Scotland, this arrangement has the unfortunate side-effect that English readers 'learn a great deal more about education in China and the Republic of Ireland than they do about [the] Scottish system' (Roberts, 1984). Scotland is not a nation-state, and is often left out of comparative studies by representative international organizations as well as by independent academics. Writers comparing the British and other systems often treat England as representative of Britain or use the terms interchangeably.

Many of these studies seek to learn from foreign experience and draw conclusions that can be applied in Britain. Yet they often find that the lessons of other countries can only be applied very indirectly, because of confounding differences in each country's history, economy, culture and politics. Yet the irony is that fewer studies have sought to learn from comparisons *within* the UK, where these confounding differences may be

Source: Raffe, D. and Courtenay, G. (1988) '16–18 on both Sides of the Border', in Raffe, D. (ed.), *Education and the Youth Labour Market*, Falmer Press, Basingstoke, pp. 12–39.

much smaller. A second aim of this chapter, therefore, is to offer an assessment of the extent of the differences between Scotland and England and Wales, and to see if we can identify a point where, institutional differences having been discounted, the essential similarities prevail.

We use data from the Scottish Young Peoples Surveys of 1985 and 1986 and from the 1985 and 1986 surveys of the first cohort of the England and Wales Youth Cohort Study. The design of the England and Wales study was influenced by the Scottish experience (Clough and Gray, 1986) and there are several similarities between them. Both surveys were conducted by post, collected data on a wide range of educational, training and labour-market topics from a cross-section of young people, and have followed up their samples longitudinally over (at least) three data-sweeps. This chapter is based on the first two sweeps. The Scottish sample covered the year group who entered fourth year of secondary school in 1983, nearly all of whom were eligible to leave school by the end of 1984. Pupils normally transfer to secondary school at 12 in Scotland and at 11 in England and Wales; the Scottish fourth year is roughly equivalent to the English/Welsh fifth year, in that both mark the 'normal' end of compulsory schooling. The English and Welsh sample covered young people aged 16 on 31 August 1984, who were all eligible to leave school either at Easter or summer 1984.

Before we present data on the two samples, we note three differences between the studies that may affect the comparison.

First, there are differences in method. [...] Perhaps the most important difference is that the first sweep survey in England and Wales was required to distribute many of its first-sweep questionnaires, together with reminders for non-respondents, through the schools. This produced a relatively low response rate, 69 per cent compared with 84 per cent for the Scottish first-sweep survey when the figures are calculated on the most nearly comparable basis. There were knock-on effects on response to the second sweep, since the survey team in England and Wales lacked addresses for some of their first-sweep respondents. As a result, the proportion of first-sweep respondents who returned usable questionnaires at the second sweep was again somewhat lower in England and Wales (75 per cent) than in Scotland (82 per cent). The data in this chapter are based on young people who responded to both sweeps.[2] They are weighted to compensate for differential non-response, using population figures for qualifications at 16, gender, staying-on at school, and (for English and Welsh leavers only) region and school type. Early data from the second cohort of the English and Welsh study, from which the response was much higher, suggest that the weighted estimates from the first cohort are not seriously affected by non-response.

Different questionnaires were used in the two studies – necessarily, since institutional differences made many of the questions asked in one study inappropriate to the other. In addition the Scottish questionnaire was differentiated into types, with randomized versions within each type, whereas the English and Welsh study used a single questionnaire. We have restricted our comparisons to items included in all Scottish questionnaire versions and to data which are, we believe, comparable between the studies.

The second difference between the surveys is that the Scottish sample includes young people from independent schools and the English and Welsh sample does not. Since one purpose of this chapter is to describe the Scottish system we have not excluded independent schools from the figures presented below. Excluding them from the Scottish figures would reduce the percentage staying on at school by about one percentage point for girls and two percentage points for boys. It would make no discernible difference to any estimates based on labour-market entrants. However the independent sector is smaller in Scotland where it accounts for less than 4 per cent of the age group, compared with England and Wales where it accounts for 7 per cent. Adding independent schools to the English and Welsh data might make much more difference than subtracting them from the Scottish data.

Third, the Scottish survey describes a school year group, all of whom were in the fourth year of secondary school in 1983/84, whereas the English and Welsh survey describes a birth cohort, all of whom were aged 16 on 31 August 1984 and became old enough to leave school either at Easter or in the summer of that year. In practice, the English and Welsh sample roughly coincided with a school year group – most were in fifth year in 1983/84 – and most members of the Scottish year group were eligible to leave school by the end of 1984. However arrangements both for entry to primary school and for the end of compulsory schooling differ between the two countries. The Scottish year group was some four months younger, on average, than the English and Welsh birth cohort. One in seven were 16 years old by the end of February 1984 and had therefore been eligible to leave the previous Christmas (or in a few cases at the end of third year) although most in fact stayed on to complete the fourth year. (The two statutory leaving dates in Scotland are 31 May and at Christmas). A majority of the Scottish year group became 16 between 1 March and 30 September 1984, and was eligible to leave school on 31 May. However nearly three in ten of the Scots were still only 15 at the end of September and had to remain at school until Christmas 1984 (or, in a very few cases, summer 1985). The proportion of these 'conscripts' in each year group has grown in recent years, a consequence of changes in primary entry arrangements a decade or so earlier (Burnhill, 1984). The autumn term in Scotland is by far the longest, starting in August, and most schools start the new session at the beginning of June, during the summer term. This means that a substantial minority of each age group must stay on at school for about half of what is notionally the first 'post-compulsory' school session. [. . .]

Table 16.1 shows the statuses of the two samples at four time points from October 1984 to April 1986. These time points cover the fifth and sixth years of Scottish secondary schooling and (for most sample members) the two years of the English Sixth form, together with their non-school alternatives. The Scottish data are based on questions asked in the 1985 and 1986 questionnaires, in each case asking respondents what they had been doing 'at the beginning of last October' and what they were doing 'now'. Since both Scottish surveys were despatched in the middle of March, we shall interpret the 'now' figures as referring to the beginning of April (in fact, they describe a spread of dates as some respondents replied earlier than others). The data for the first three time points for England and Wales are obtained from 'diary' items that asked what respondents were doing for all or most of each month from September 1984 to February 1986. The 'April 1986' figures refer to respondents' current status at the time of the England and Wales survey. Since the questionnaires were despatched at the end of February, the median response referred to a date some two or three weeks earlier than the beginning of April; but for simplicity we shall refer to the current data from both 1986 surveys as describing April.

Our discussion focuses in turn on two main institutional locations of young people in each country: full-time education and the labour market.

■ Full-time education

☐ Institutional framework

At the first time point, in October 1984, twice as many of the Scottish sample as of the English and Welsh sample were still at school: 57 per cent compared with 28 per cent. However, half of these Scots were 'conscripts', still too young to leave. By April 1985, the second time point, virtually all members of both samples were eligible to have left school. There were still more Scots at school, but the differential had narrowed: 42 per cent compared with 28 per cent. However, apart from the younger average age of the Scottish sample and the exclusion of the independent sector from the English and Welsh sample, this comparison must be further qualified by reference to institutional differences between the systems.

First, the institutional structure and balance of full-time post-compulsory education differs between the two countries. In Scotland most young people continuing in full-time education beyond 16 to do at school; except in some sparsely populated areas, nearly all of these continue in the same school where they have spent their previous four years. The only

Table 16.1   Status at six-monthly intervals (percentages).

Date:	October 1984		April 1985		October 1985		April 1986	
Country:	Sc	E&W	Sc	E&W	Sc	E&W	Sc	E&W
Median age (approx.):	16yr 3m	16yr 7m	16yr 9m	17yr 1m	17yr 3m	17yr 7m	17yr 9m	18yr 1m
School stage:	5th yr	Lower 6th	6th yr	Lower 6th	6th yr	Upper 6th	6th yr	Upper 6th
Full-time FE/HE	5	15	4	14	12	13	8	13
School	57	28	42	28	20	21	20	19
Full-time job	11	17	17	22	33	43	40	45
YTS	18	28	23	24	16	6	7	3
Unemployed	7	8	11	9	15	13	19	15
Others	2	1	2	1	4	3	5	4
NK	1	2	1	2	1	2	*	0
Total	101	99	100	100	101	101	99	99
n	(5292)	(6075)	(5292)	(6075)	(5292)	(6075)	(5292)	(6075)
Males								
Full-time FE/HE	3	10	2	9	9	9	6 ⎱	29
School	54	27	38	26	19	20	19 ⎰	50
Full-time job	12	21	19	26	35	47	43	3
YTS	21	30	26	27	17	5	8	15
Unemployed	7	8	12	9	17	14	21	15

Others	2	1	1	1	1	2	3	3
NK	1	2	2	2	3	2	*	0
Total	100	98	100	100	101	99	100	100
n	(2598)	(2825)	(2598)	(2825)	(2598)	(2825)	(2598)	(2825)
Females								
Full-time FE/HE	7	20	6	18	14	16	11 }	36
School	59	30	46	29	22	21	22 }	
Full-time job	11	13	16	19	30	39	38	41
YTS	15	26	20	21	14	6	7	4
Unemployed	6	8	9	8	13	12	16	14
Others	2	1	2	1	6	4	7	6
NK	1	2	1	2	1	2	*	0
Total	101	100	100	98	100	100	101	101
n	(2654)	(3250)	(2694)	(3250)	(2694)	(3250)	(2694)	(3250)

Note The England and Wales sample covered a birth cohort, not a school-year group, so the sample members may have been at different school stages.

* = <0.5.

other full-time education option is to study a vocational course in a college of further education. In England and Wales the range of options at 16 is wider, and is more likely to involve a move to a different institution. In addition to schools and colleges there are sixth form colleges (included with schools in our data) and tertiary colleges (included with colleges); the range of courses offered in college is considerably wider, and includes General Certificate of Education (GCE) courses, overlapping (and sometimes competing) with the options available at school. In some respects the transition beyond compulsory education is more clearly defined in England and Wales, whereas in Scotland it is more simply a matter of continuing or not continuing at school. This difference is reinforced by the statutory leaving regulations discussed above: for nearly half of Scots, the end of compulsory education comes mid way through a school session.

So although in April 1985 more of the Scottish than of the English and Welsh sample were still at school, this was partly balanced by the smaller proportion entering full-time further education: 4 per cent in Scotland compared with 14 per cent in England and Wales. By October 1985 participation in further education appears to have evened out between the two systems: 12 per cent in Scotland compared with 13 per cent in England and Wales. However the 12 per cent in Scotland included 4 per cent, mostly on short courses, who had left by April 1986, and a further 2.5 per cent who were in full-time *higher* education. The opportunity to enter higher education at 17 years is a traditional feature of Scottish education, associated both with the 'myth' of wider educational opportunity and access and with the four-year structure of honours degree courses (Gray *et al.*, 1983). In practice, only a minority of higher-education students enter at 17. Despite the greater average age of English and Welsh sample members only a negligible proportion had entered higher education by spring 1986.

☐   **Transition patterns**

This leads us to a further institutional difference between the two systems: their different transition patterns. In England and Wales there is a clearly defined transition point at 16 (summer 1984 for our sample members). Another will follow at 18, in summer 1986, although our present data do not extend this far. Some young people leave at 17 but for the majority post-compulsory education (below higher education) can be represented as a two-year stage with clearly defined start and end points, at 16 and 18 years respectively.

Scotland has the same two transition points, although we have suggested that the first of these is less clearly defined. However there are two additional transition points. The first occurs half way through the fifth year when the 'conscripts', who were too young to leave from fourth year, become eligible to leave school. The second occurs at the end of the fifth year, when half the voluntary school stayers leave school. This is not the result of dropping-out: most fifth-year students take one-year courses, and the sixth year usually comprises a discrete stage.

Not all fifth-year leavers end compulsory education at this point; about three in ten of those who left school at the end of fifth year in summer 1985 were in full-time further education in the following October, and a further one in ten were in higher education. More Scots entered full-time further education at 17 (from fifth year) than at 16 (from fourth year). Moreover, some two-thirds of the students who entered from fourth year left after a year, at 17. The 17-year-old transition point is therefore particularly significant for Scottish further education, which experiences a substantial turn-round of its full-time students at this point.

Some of these differences are summarized in Table 16.2, which shows transitions between April 1985 and April 1986. The table only records *net* transitions: it does not, for example, show short full-time courses which young people entered and left between these dates. Of young people at school in England and Wales in 1985, nearly four in five were still in full-time education a year later, and more than two-thirds were still at school. By contrast, less than half (47 per cent) of the Scots who were at school in April 1985 were still there in April 1986. In England and Wales 11 per cent of those at school in April 1985 were in full-time further or higher education a year later. The comparable figure in Scotland was 14 per cent, and a further 5 per cent had already entered short courses and left (compared with almost none in England and Wales). Two-thirds of the full-time further education students in England and Wales in April 1985 were still there a year later, twice as many as in Scotland.

To summarize: in England and Wales we can identify two clear transition points at 16 and 18, with separate and largely alternative streams covering the intervening stage, and with relatively small movements between streams or out of full-time education at 17. In Scotland, by contrast, the 16-year-old transition is less likely to accompany an institutional break; it is more staggered, with a few young people leaving from the winter of fourth year and a significant exodus of 'winter leavers' in the middle of the fifth year; and there is a further and major transition at 17, when there is not only substantial movement out of full-time education but also significant movement between sectors, especially between school and further or higher education.

☐   Courses in post-compulsory education

These institutional differences are reflected in the structure and content of post-compulsory courses in the two systems. This is evident if we consider

Table 16.2 Status in April 1986 by status in April 1985 (percentages).

Status in April 1985	Status in April 1986								
	FT FE/HE	School	Job	YTS	Unemployed	Others	NK	Total	n
Scotland									
Full-time FE	33	0	31	18	10	7	2	101	(182)
School	14	47	19	12	4	3	*	99	(2683)
Full-time job	1	0	84	1	11	2	0	99	(808)
YTS	2	0	56	2	36	4	*	100	(1022)
Unemployed	2	0	25	9	53	12	*	101	(448)
Others	3	0	26	3	29	39	1	101	(80)
NK	9	22	28	16	20	4	1	100	(69)
All	8	20	40	7	19	5	*	99	(5292)
England & Wales									
Full-time FE	65	3	20	7	4	2	0	101	(799)
School	11	68	13	5	2	2	0	101	(2741)
Full-time job	1	*	88	*	9	2	0	100	(1020)
YTS	2	*	65	1	24	7	0	99	(1049)
Unemployed	2	*	25	6	54	12*	0	99	(325)
Others	8	1	36	9	19	26	0	99	(62)
NK	2	2	50	1	37	8	0	100	(79)
All	13	19	45	3	15	4	0	99	(6075)

Note * = <0.5.

the main school-based courses for post-compulsory students: in England and Wales the 'A' level of the GCE, in Scotland the Higher grade of the Scottish Certificate of Education (SCE). Both are subject-based and largely 'academic' courses; both provide the principal qualification for entry to higher education; both have proved relatively resistant to change. However they differ in length – 'A' levels are normally taken over two years, whereas Highers are normally taken over one year – and in content and level. The (very notional) qualifying level for higher education is two 'A' levels in England and Wales and three Highers in Scotland.

The traditional 'norm' for the curriculum for an academically successful student after 16 comprises three 'A' levels over two years in England and Wales and five Highers in one year in Scotland (Gray et al., 1983). Five subjects were required for the pre-existing Scottish group certificate course. The possibility of completing them after five years of secondary school is of considerable symbolic importance: the Scottish system has seen itself as providing more scope for educational mobility than in England where seven years of secondary schooling are usually needed to qualify for university entrance. The larger number of subjects at Highers is the basis of the Scottish claim to offer greater breadth than the highly specialized English system.

However, the Scottish system diverges considerably from this norm. In the first place, the structure of courses encourages many students to spread their Highers attempts over two years, although typically the decisions are taken incrementally and piecemeal (McPherson, 1984a, 1984b). Second and relatedly, the shorter length and lower level of Highers encourages many students to take one or a few subjects, usually in conjunction with resits or new subjects at 'O' grade. Thus, of the sample members in full-time education in spring 1985, 57 per cent of the English and Welsh were attempting at least one 'A' level, and more than three-quarters of these studied three or more (Clough et al., 1988); many more of the Scots in full-time education attempted at least one Higher – about four in five – but only a quarter of these attempted five Highers in fifth year.

It follows that in the Scottish system the distinction between high-status 'academic' and other educational routes after 16 is both less sharp and less final: less sharp, because of the wide variation in numbers of Highers subjects studied in fifth year; and less final, because at least in principle the sixth year allows young people to upgrade their qualifications by taking further Highers or resitting old ones. In practice, many young people leave school after a predominantly academic fifth year to enter YTS or non-advanced vocational courses at college. The fifth year may keep young people's mobility chances alive, but it also performs an important 'cooling out' function.

The corollary is that the balance of the curriculum changes much more between the first and second post-compulsory years in Scotland than it does south of the Border. In England and Wales, 19 per cent of those in full-time education in spring 1985, and more than half of those at college, were taking vocational courses only (Clough *et al.*, 1988). These included courses offered by the Business and Technician Education Council (BTEC), the Royal Society of Arts (RSA) and the City and Guilds of London Institute (C&GLI). More than two-thirds said they were on two-year courses. A further 10 per cent – again, rather more of the college students – combined vocational with 'O' level or equivalent courses, and 14 per cent took 'O' level or equivalent courses only; a third or fewer of these students described their courses as lasting two years. Thus, between the first and second post-compulsory years in England and Wales, the proportion of students following 'O' grade courses or combinations of 'O' grades with vocational courses might be expected to fall; but the broad balance between 'academic' 'A' level courses and the more traditional full-time vocational courses remained roughly constant.

By contrast, in Scotland in the first post-compulsory year very few school students and most of the college students were taking predominantly vocational courses; but college students comprised only 8 per cent of Scots in full-time education in spring 1985. A year later this proportion had risen to 23 per cent. This figure excludes higher education and takes no account of those who had already passed through short full-time vocational courses after the end of fifth year.

One final aspect of post-compulsory courses in Scotland must be noted. In January 1983 the Scottish Education Department published its 16-plus Action Plan (SED, 1983), which proposed to replace all non-advanced vocational courses by a system of modules, each of notional forty hours' duration. The modules were to be available at school or college, to full- or part-time students, and were to be accredited through a single certificate, the National Certificate of the Scottish Vocational Education Council (Scotvec). The proposals were implemented very swiftly, and our year group was the first to experience the new modular system after fourth year. [...] In principle, the new modular system keeps options open and provides mobility ladders in respect of vocational education: something which the structure of Highers courses, again in principle, may do for academic education.

☐ **Differentiation**

Beneath the various institutional differences we have described, there may be underlying sociological similarities. In saying this we do not deny that sociological processes are influenced by their institutional context; nor do our data allow us to compare sociological processes in the two systems as comprehensively as their institutional structures. We will simply point to two aspects of differentiation, by gender and by previous qualification level, which hint at sociological similarities. First, in both systems more girls than boys continued in full-time education, and among those who continued more girls entered college. Second, in both systems continued full-time education, especially at school, was strongly related to attainment at 16. Table 16.3 shows the proportion of 'higher-' and 'lower-qualified' young people in different statuses in April 1986. In England and Wales young people with at least one GCE 'O' level at grades A–C or at least one Certificate of Secondary Education (CSE) at grade 1 are counted as 'higher-qualified'; in Scotland young people with at least one SCE 'O' grade in bands A–C are so counted. The Scottish 'O' grade is roughly equivalent to the English 'O' level; in 1984 these were the main examinations taken at the end of compulsory schooling. However, most parts of Scotland lacked an equivalent to the English CSE; as a result, 'O' grades were taken by a larger proportion of the age group than typically took 'O' levels in England and Wales. Consequently the benchmarks used to define qualification groups in the two countries are not fully comparable: 65 per cent of the Scots, compared with 57 per cent of the English and Welsh, count as higher-qualified in Table 16.3. Comparisons should therefore be made between qualification groups within each country, rather than between countries within each qualification group. Within each country, the proportion continuing in full-time education is much larger among the higher qualified; almost none of the lower qualified is still at school. Conversely the proportion in the labour market, and especially the proportion unemployed, is much larger among the lower qualified.

□   **Later transitions**

When discussing transition points earlier in this section, we were unable to present data on the transition at 18 years; this occurs in summer 1986 for our year groups, as we will only have data on it when the third sweeps of our respective samples have been completed. Earlier data for Scotland showed that some two-thirds of young people still at school in the sixth year continued in higher or other full-time education (SED/SEB, 1982; Raffe, 1984a). If these patterns have continued we infer that only a third of our sixth-year school students, equivalent to some 6 or 7 per cent of the age group, would enter the labour market at 18; they would probably be joined by a smaller number (but larger proportion) of college students. It is probable that rather more young people in England and Wales would enter the labour market at 18, since fewer of them had done so at 17. Nevertheless, it is clear that most of the young people in our two samples who were to enter the labour market as teenagers had already done so by April 1986. With this in mind, we turn to consider differences in the youth labour markets of Scotland and of England and Wales.

Table 16.3   Status in April 1986 by qualifications at 16 (percentages).

	Scotland		England and Wales	
	Higher qualified	Lower qualified	Higher qualified	Lower qualified
Full-time FE/HE	11	3	18	6
School	30	1	33	1
Full-time job	38	45	37	57
YTS	8	7	3	4
Unemployed	9	36	6	26
Others	4	7	3	7
NK	*	*	0	0
Total	100	99	100	101
n	(3931)	(1349)	(4341)	(1734)

Note   Higher qualified: Scotland: any S4 'O' grade at A–C.
England and Wales: any ABC1 at 16.
Lower qualified: all others.

■   The youth labour market

□   Key differences

Our surveys point to two key differences between the youth labour markets of Scotland and of England and Wales. Most other apparent differences, we shall argue, can be explained in terms of these two; beyond them, the similarities are far more striking.

The first key difference results directly from the institutional differences described above. That is that entry to the labour market among members of each cohort is more staggered in Scotland than in England and Wales. Of young people in the labour market in April 1986, 25 per cent in Scotland had been in full-time education a year earlier, compared with 15 per cent in England and Wales. This reflects the greater transition at 17 in Scotland. This difference is significant but not huge; many of the transitions at 17 in Scotland are between sectors of full-time education rather than out of them and into the labour market. The more striking contrast is in the proportion who were in full-time education eighteen months earlier, in October 1984: 48 per cent in Scotland compared with 18

Table 16.4   Employment rates.

	All		Males		Females	
	Sc	E&W	Sc	E&W	Sc	E&W
Full-time jobs as % of labour market (incl. YTS)						
October 1984	32	32	30	35	34	28
April 1985	34	41	33	42	36	39
October 1985	51	70	51	71	52	68
April 1986	61	72	59	73	62	69
Full-time jobs as % of employed and unemployed						
October 1984	63	68	62	72	65	62
April 1985	62	72	60	74	63	70
October 1985	68	77	67	77	69	76
April 1986	68	76	67	77	70	74

per cent in England and Wales. This difference is due to the Scottish winter leavers, the 'conscripts' who had to stay on at school beyond summer 1984 but left when they were able to, in December.

The second key difference is that the Scottish labour market is weaker. However, because of the institutional differences we have just described it is impossible to summarize this relative weakness in a single pair of statistics. Table 16.4 shows the employment rates of the two year groups at each of the four time points shown in Table 16.1. The first set of employment rates is based on all in the labour market, and includes YTS trainees with the non-employed. The second set of rates is based on young people who were either in full-time jobs or unemployment, and excludes YTS.

Among year-group members in the labour market in October 1984, the proportion in full-time jobs was 32 per cent in both countries. Excluding YTS trainees from the calculation considerably boosts the estimated employment rate but results in a slightly lower rate in Scotland (63 per cent) than in England and Wales (68 per cent). (This appears to reflect a slower rate of entry into YTS among unemployed young people in Scotland: see Raffe and Courtenay, 1987.) Employment rates were higher among girls in Scotland and among boys in England and Wales. However, comparisons based on October 1984 may be inappropriate, since more of the Scottish year group were still in full-time education. By October 1984 the Scottish labour market had had a little more than a third of the year group to absorb, compared with more than a half in England and Wales (see Table 16.1). More Scots entered the labour market over the following winter and summer; by October 1985 there was a wide gap between the two countries' employment rates, which stood at 51 per cent of the labour market in Scotland compared with 70 per cent in England and Wales. However, this comparison is also inappropriate: at least it must be interpreted in the knowledge that more Scots had recently joined the labour market and had had less time to look for work, and that more Scots were still on their one-year YTS schemes. In April 1986 the gap had narrowed – employment rates stood at 61 per cent in Scotland and 72 per cent in England and Wales – but there were still more Scots on YTS. If the YTS trainees are excluded, the difference in employment rates is slightly narrower: 68 per cent compared with 76 per cent. These two figures may provide as good a summary as can be found of the relative strengths of the two countries' labour markets, given that no single set of statistics can adequately express the difference. This is because it is impossible to find data that are simultaneously comparable with respect to duration in the labour market, age and season without restricting the comparison to an unrepresentative subset of young people in one or other of the countries.

The relative disadvantage of Scottish males, however, is well established despite these problems of measurement. In April 1986 their employment rate (net of YTS) was 10 percentage points lower than in England and Wales: 67 per cent compared with 77 per cent. Among females the gap was narrower: 70 per cent compared with 74 per cent.

There are, therefore, two key differences between the youth labour markets of Scotland and of England and Wales. Institutional differences in full-time education result in different patterns of entry to the labour market; and the Scottish market is weaker, especially for males. Once these differences are allowed for, the similarities between the two systems are more remarkable than the differences.

☐   **Occupational structure**

The (all-age) labour market in Scotland is often perceived to be biased towards manual occupations relative to that of England and Wales. To some extent the perception is true: the share of the workforce taken by manual jobs is some 4 percentage points higher in Scotland than in England and Wales (Kendrick, 1986). But this difference is largely due to Scotland's smaller proportion of managers, especially in the private sector: many firms operating in Scotland have headquarters based elsewhere, for example in the south-east of England. The relative scarcity of managers in Scotland is unlikely to have a large effect on the teenage labour markets.

Table 16.5 shows the occupations of sample members who were in full-time jobs in April 1986. There were fewer Scots in the first two (non-manual) occupational categories shown in the table, especially clerical occupations. But these two categories were distinctive in Scotland because they had recruited around half their current (April 1986) employees from young people leaving school at the end of fifth year (at age 17). (No other occupational category had recruited more than 21 per cent of its current employees from young people leaving at the end of fifth year.) Moreover, in both countries many clerical employees had been recruited from YTS. It is therefore probable that the number of non-manual employees in Scotland in April 1986 would subsequently be swelled by 17-year-old school leavers who were then still on YTS; in England and Wales many fewer YTS trainees were still on the scheme. (However, if we are correct in anticipating a larger influx of 18-year-olds to the labour market in England and Wales, they may in turn boost the relative share of non-manual employment south of the Border.)

In other words, the main difference between the countries' occupational distributions shown in Table 16.5 may be at least partly attributable to the more staggered pattern of labour-market entry in Scotland, rather than to 'underlying' differences in the labour markets. All other differences in Table 16.5 are small. Scotland had more young people working in personal services, in farming, fishing and related occupations and in materials processing, making and related (excluding metal and electrical) occupations. The last difference affects females and may reflect the relative importance of the textile and clothing and food and drink industries in Scotland.

There were slightly greater industrial than occupational differences between the two countries (table not shown). Construction accounted for 14 per cent of Scottish employment compared with 8 per cent in England and Wales; 7 per cent of Scots were employed in the metal goods, engineering and vehicles industries compared with 10 per cent in England and Wales. In most other respects the industrial structures of the two countries were similar: for example, in both countries manufacturing only accounted for a small proportion of young people's employment (23 per cent in Scotland, 28 per cent in England and Wales).

One particular feature of the two countries deserves comment. The scale and character of gender differentiation in employment was very similar. In both countries more than half of all girls worked in just two occupational categories (clerical and personal services), and two more categories (selling, and materials processing, etc., excluding metal and electrical) accounted for most of the remainder. Other categories (notably metal and electrical processing) were largely the preserve of boys. The table almost certainly underestimates the extent of this differentiation. Several of the categories shown in the table are broad and include a wide range of constituent occupations which are themselves gendered. To the

Table 16.5 Occupations of all in full-time employment in April 1986 (percentages).

	Males and females		Males		Females	
	Scotland	England & Wales	Scotland	England & Wales	Scotland	England & Wales
Professional, managerial and related	4	5	3	5	5	6
Clerical and related	20	26	7	10	35	46
Selling	8	8	6	6	11	11
Security and protective services	3	2	5	4	*	*
Catering, cleaning, hairdressing and other personal services	12	9	5	5	20	15
Farming, fishing and related	5	3	9	4	1	1
Materials processing, making and repairing (exc. metal & electrical)	16	14	16	17	15	9
Processing, making, repairing and related (metal and electrical)	14	13	24	22	2	1
Painting, repetitive assembling, product inspecting, packaging and related	5	7	5	7	5	7
Construction, mining and related not identified elsewhere	4	4	8	6	0	0
Transport operating, materials moving and storing and related	3	4	6	7	*	*
Miscellaneous	1	1	2	2	*	*
NK/inadequately described	6	4	6	5	6	2
Total	101	100	102	100	100	98
n	(2007)	(2261)	(1046)	(1124)	(961)	(1137)

Note * = <0.5.

gender differentiation between the categories shown in Table 16.5 must therefore be added a further substantial amount of differentiation between occupations within each of these categories. In both countries fewer girls than boys reported receiving training in their current job, and, of those that did, girls reported considerably shorter average periods of training.

☐   **The Youth Training Scheme**

YTS is a British-wide scheme, run by the Manpower Services Commission, and its framework and structure are essentially the same in Scotland as in England and Wales. It aims 'to provide a foundation of broad-based vocational education and training, and planned work experience' for young people leaving full-time education before 18 (MSC, 1986, p. 2). When our year groups entered it, it was a one-year scheme; a minimum of thirteen weeks were spent off-the-job, and the balance largely consisted of work experience with one or more employers. All 16-year-old school leavers were eligible to enter, and 17-year-old leavers could enter if they were unemployed. YTS has since been extended to a two-year scheme, for 16-year-old leavers; it remains a one-year scheme for 17-year-olds but they no longer have to be unemployed to enter. The aims of YTS have been extended to give 'all trainees the opportunity to obtain a vocational qualification related to competence in the workplace, or to obtain a credit towards such a qualification' (MSC, 1986, p. 2).

In both countries YTS, despite its standard framework, is internally heterogeneous. It has been used by employers as a way of inducting, screening and training young workers; about a third of trainees find work with the employers responsible for their schemes (Gray and King, 1986). However, YTS also provides a safety net for unemployed young people. At the time our year-group members were 16, minimum-age school leavers who could not find jobs, training or further education places by the following Christmas were guaranteed the offer of a suitable place on the scheme. (The guarantee has since been extended to all leavers under 18.) YTS is therefore torn between its function as an unemployment-based scheme and its aims of developing and extending a new youth training framework: a conflict of purposes that has been diagnosed in both countries (Bevan and Varlaam, 1987; Mansell and Miller, 1987; Raffe, 1987).

The pressures on YTS to function primarily as an unemployment-based scheme are evident in our data. The relative scale of YTS in the two countries is in inverse relation to the relative strengths of their labour markets: 42 per cent of the Scottish year group had entered YTS by spring 1986, compared with 37 per cent of the English and Welsh.[3] More young people entered YTS in Scotland, we suggest, because fewer could find jobs instead. This interpretation is supported by the observation that the difference in participation rates was smaller for girls (39 per cent compared with 35 per cent) than for boys (46 per cent compared with 39 per cent); as we have seen, the relative weakness of the Scottish labour market was also less pronounced for girls. In both countries YTS tended to attract less-qualified members of each year group. Thirty per cent of the higher qualified in Scotland (see Table 16.3) entered YTS compared with 66 per cent of the less qualified; in England and Wales the difference between higher and lower qualified, defined on a different basis, was broadly similar: 24 per cent compared with 54 per cent. This difference is largely due to the greater proportions of the better qualified continuing in full-time education, but it also reflects a tendency for better qualified leavers to enter jobs rather than YTS.

YTS trainees in Scotland had more difficulty finding jobs at the end of their schemes. In April 1986 56 per cent of former YTS trainees in Scotland were in full-time jobs compared with 67 per cent in England and Wales. Table 16.2, which shows transitions between April 1985 and April 1986, tells a similar story: among those on YTS in April 1985 the employment rate one year later was 56 per cent in Scotland compared with 65 per cent in England and Wales. The difference was slightly greater among males (57 per cent compared with 67 per cent) than among females (56 per cent compared with 63 per cent).

In each country the same proportion of full-time employees in April 1986 had been on YTS (49 per cent), with little difference between the male and female proportions (Table 16.6). In Scotland this figure would probably grow further after April 1986, when those still on YTS entered employment. In both countries more young people could be expected to enter employment from full-time education in summer 1986, without going on YTS, with a somewhat larger influx in England and Wales than in Scotland. In the longer term, therefore, the role of YTS as a route to employment may be slightly greater in Scotland than in England and Wales, reflecting the relative weakness of the Scottish labour market and the role of YTS as, in part, an unemployment-based scheme.

In neither country, apparently, had YTS monopolized access to particular sectors of employment. [...] YTS trainees were widely spread across the differential occupational categories shown in Table 16.6. The only categories in either country in which fewer than 40 per cent of their employees had been on YTS were security and protective services (which largely comprises the Armed Forces) and professional, managerial and related occupations. However in Scotland, at least, the latter category, which recruits the largest proportion of 17-year-old school leavers, would probably increase its proportion of former YTS trainees when young people still on YTS in spring 1986 entered it. Conversely, in neither country did YTS trainees account for as many as two-thirds of the employees in any occupational category. The highest proportion was 64

Table 16.6 Percentage ever on YTS, by occupation: all in full-time employment in April 1986.

	Males and females		Males		Females	
	Scotland	England & Wales	Scotland	England & Wales	Scotland	England & Wales
Professional, managerial and related	24	37	(18)	39	31	37
Clerical and related	43	46	39	31	44	50
Selling	57	55	56	54	57	55
Security and protective services	18	24	18	(23)	*	*
Catering, cleaning, hairdressing and other personal services	51	55	(53)	(45)	51	60
Farming, fishing and related	55	(48)	54	(44)	*	*
Materials processing, making and repairing (exc. metal and electrical)	56	48	57	51	56	44
Processing, making, repairing and related (metal and electrical)	43	56	43	57	*	*
Painting, repetitive assembling, product inspecting, packaging and related	56	46	(58)	51	(54)	40
Construction, mining and related not identified elsewhere	64	46	64	46	*	*
Transport operating, materials moving and storing and related	61	57	62	59	*	*
Miscellaneous	(68)	(60)	(71)	(61)	*	*
NK/inadequately described	44	45	49	50	39	32
All in full-time jobs	49	49	49	48	48	50

Note Bracketed numbers indicate unweighted base *n* less than 50; asterisks denote base *n* less than 20.

per cent, for the residual 'construction, mining and related (not identified elsewhere)' category in Scotland. More detailed occupational categories would probably reveal tighter associations between particular occupations and YTS; nevertheless it remains clear that YTS did not monopolize access to any broad areas or segments of employment.

There is one difference between the two countries which, although it results from the institutional differences discussed earlier, may have important consequences both for YTS and for the education system. This is that in Scotland there is more overlap between YTS and full-time post-compulsory education, in terms of students attending both. We have seen that in England and Wales post-compulsory education and training can reasonably be represented as a two-year stage, with relatively little movement between institutions during that stage. The different options entered at 16 are, by and large, alternatives; few young people enter more than one. As a result, few of those who opt for school or further education at 16 ever enter YTS: only 7 per cent of those in further education in spring 1985, and only 5 per cent of those at school, were on YTS a year later (Table 16.3). In Scotland, by contrast, the comparable figures are 18 per cent and 12 per cent; decisions at 16 typically commit the student only for one further year; there is a further transition point at 17, when many young people leave full-time education for YTS. (Relatively few young people in either system move in the other direction, from YTS to full-time education.) The conversion of YTS to a two-year scheme will not remove this national difference, and may even consolidate it; it will confirm the 16–18 period as a two-year stage in England and Wales, but 17-year-old school leavers will still be entitled to a one-year YTS.

The overlap between full-time post-compulsory education and YTS in Scotland becomes far greater if we include fifth-year winter leavers, some two-thirds of whom go on to enter YTS. Strictly these young people have not left 'post-compulsory' education: they have stayed at school compulsorily because they were not old enough to leave after fourth year. However they tend to follow 'post-compulsory' courses so their experience reinforces our general point. This is that the greater overlap between post-compulsory education and YTS in Scotland, as well as between different types of post-compulsory education, makes for greater problems of integration and articulation.

□   **Labour-market dynamics**

Table 16.7 summarizes much of our argument concerning differences and similarities in the two countries' labour markets. The table is restricted to early entrants, that is to young people in the labour market in October 1984. It therefore partly 'controls' for one of the two differences noted earlier, that is the different pattern of labour-market entry arising from institutional differences in full-time education. This 'control' is imperfect since the young people covered by the table are less representative of their

Table 16.7 Typology of labour-market experiences by sex: all in labour market in October 1984.

	All		Males		Females	
	Scotland	England & Wales	Scotland	England & Wales	Scotland	England & Wales
In full-time job in April 1986:						
no previous YTS	25	29	25	33	25	25
previously on YTS	35	39	35	38	33	40
On YTS in April 1986:						
no previous job	1	1	1	1	1	1
previously in a job	*	1	*	1	*	1
Unemployed in April 1986:						
no previous job or YTS	3	4	4	3	3	5
previously in a job, no YTS	4	5	4	5	5	5
previously on YTS, no job	14	9	16	9	12	8
previously in a job and on YTS	9	5	8	5	10	5
Not in labour market in April 1986	8	8	6	6	11	10
Total	99	101	99	101	100	100
n	(1576)	(2263)	(884)	(1151)	(692)	(1122)

Note * = <0.5.

year group in Scotland than in England and Wales. The table summarizes young people's 'careers' up to April 1986 by showing their April 1986 status and the other labour-market statuses they had experienced up to this point.

In both countries a majority of these young people were in jobs in April 1986, but more were in jobs in England and Wales (68 per cent) than in Scotland (60 per cent). The difference was smaller among girls than among boys. More than half of those in jobs had been on YTS; this proportion is larger than that shown in Table 16.6, reflecting the fact that these early entrants to the labour market were particularly likely to go on YTS. Only a handful of these early entrants were still on the scheme in April 1986. In each country, 8 per cent of the early entrants had already left the full-time labour market; in each country, more girls than boys had done so. The remainder were unemployed: 30 per cent in Scotland compared with 23 per cent in England and Wales, with the differential again larger among boys than among girls. However, the difference in unemployment rates is entirely accounted for by the larger proportion of Scots who had been on YTS and then returned to unemployment. The proportion of young people in Scotland who remained or became unemployed without ever having been on YTS was fractionally smaller in Scotland (although when the Scottish figures are adjusted to exclude very early leavers from YTS, not recorded in the data for England and Wales, this proportion becomes the same as for England and Wales). In other words the 'hard core' of young people who remained unemployed and did not go on YTS was about the same size in the two countries; Scottish youth unemployment was higher, not because the coverage of YTS was less effective, but because fewer young people found jobs after going on the scheme.

In both countries the 'lower-qualified' early entrants were more than twice as likely to be unemployed as the 'higher qualified', and several times more likely to have remained continuously unemployed without going on YTS.

☐   **Geographical variation**

The common perception of Scotland as a part of the 'depressed north' of Britain tends to imply that Scotland is itself internally homogeneous. In presenting aggregate data on the two systems we may ourselves have encouraged this impression. Yet Scotland is far from homogeneous. The 'north/south' divide within England has a rough parallel in a 'west/east' divide within Scotland.

This is illustrated if we disaggregate the Scottish data in Table 16.7 to separate Strathclyde Region from the rest of Scotland. Nearly half the population of Scotland lives in Strathclyde, which includes Glasgow and the Clydeside conurbation. Of the early entrants to the labour market shown in Table 16.7, only 15 per cent in Strathclyde were in full-time jobs in spring 1986 and had not been on YTS; the proportion in the rest of Scotland was more than twice as large, at 33 per cent. The most striking contrast was in the proportion who were currently unemployed, had been on YTS but had never had a job: 22 per cent in Strathclyde compared with 7 per cent in the rest of Scotland. (The 'hard core' of young people who had remained unemployed without going on YTS was the same size, at 3 per cent, in both parts of Scotland.)

In spring 1986, employment rates (net of YTS) among our sample members stood at 68 per cent in Scotland and 76 per cent in England and Wales (Table 16.4): unemployment rates were therefore 32 per cent and 24 per cent respectively. Within Scotland this rate differed between Strathclyde (39 per cent) and the rest of Scotland (25 per cent); at a more local level it ranged from 10 per cent (Grampian) and 15 per cent (Borders) to 44 per cent (Lanarkshire) and 48 per cent (Glasgow). (Orkney and Shetland had the lowest unemployment rates, but based on small sample numbers.) Similarly, the average unemployment rate of 24 per cent in England and Wales masks a wide variation ranging from 11 per cent (South-east) and 17 per cent (Greater London) to 32 per cent (North-east), 33 per cent (Yorkshire and Humberside) and 34 per cent (Northern England and Wales).

■ Discussion

It is with respect to the 16–18 stage that the structure – and perhaps also the philosophy – of Scottish education differs most visibly from its southern counterpart. We have described these differnces in terms of institutional structures, with less institutional variety in Scotland and a smaller further education sector; in terms of the greater number of transition points, and in particular a significant transition point at 17 years; in terms of the weaker definition of many of these transitions; and in terms of the weaker boundaries between the educational tracks followed beyond 16, with a larger number of students taking Highers and a wider range in the number of Highers taken. On the other hand the curricular boundaries between institutions, that is between vocational college courses and largely academic school courses, are stronger in Scotland than in England and Wales, although the Action Plan reforms and current proposals for institutional restructuring in some local authorities seek to weaken them. Alongside these differences are contrasting systems of qualifications, both academic and vocational, although vocational qualifications have recently been reformed in Scotland and are currently undergoing reform in England and Wales.

The 'myth' of Scottish education views the system as offering greater breadth and wider access than the English system, and many of the differences we have noted can be rationalized in these terms. The interplay of myth and practice is complex (Gray et al., 1983), but several aspects of this myth deserve further sociological scrutiny in a comparative context. For example, the Scottish system has been described as being closer to a 'contest' model of mobility through education than England, which was Turner's (1961) original example of 'sponsored' mobility (McPherson, 1973). In contest systems selection decisions are postponed, and the bases for selection are less clearly prescribed, whereas in systems of sponsored mobility future members of the elite are identified at an early stage and given separate educational preparation for their future roles. The weaker boundaries between educational tracks after 16 (at least within school), and the opportunities which the one-year Highers course provides for students to add further subjects in the sixth year, brings the Scottish system closer to the contest model than in England and Wales where the tracks entered at 16 appear to be more clear cut and more final. The Action Plan reform of vocational education, with its aim of providing ladders of progression that climb over institutional and status boundaries, can also be represented in 'contest' mobility terms (Raffe, 1985).

If the educational horizons of Scottish post-compulsory students remain broader for longer, it may follow that the 'cooling-out' function is also emphasized more in Scottish post-compulsory education (Clark, 1961). We have seen that several of the transitions among 17-year-olds in Scotland were 'downwards' in terms of conventional status distinctions: from academic school courses to non-advanced further education, from college to YTS, or from school to YTS. We do not know the educational and occupational ambitions of our sample members when they entered fifth year, but it is likely that for many of them the end of fifth year was the time when they had to lower their sights. We have already noted that the frequent transitions during the post-compulsory stage in Scotland make the need for coordination, integration and coherent lines of progression more urgent; our argument suggests that often these lines of progression can be seen as leading 'downwards' rather than 'upwards' as the term is more usually understood. Of course the notion of level is more complex than this, but our analysis points to a sociological view of progression that must be added to the educational and curricular one. The importance of the 'cooling-out' function is emphasized by evidence from earlier surveys suggesting that some of the 17-year-old leavers entering the labour market might have done better had they left at 16 (Raffe, 1984a).

We conclude that the institutional differences between the two countries' education systems may be theoretically, and practically, significant. On the other hand these differences occur within contexts, reflected in the two countries' labour markets and in patterns of differentiation among young people, which appear to be very similar. It follows that more focused comparisons between the two countries may offer considerable scope for teasing out the specific effects of institutional and policy differences. Earlier in this chapter we referred to 'confounding differences' which reduced the value of comparisons with overseas countries: many of these are indeed smaller within Britain. England and Wales could learn from Scotland, and vice versa.

The scope for such learning may be further increased by the fact that the institutional differences between the two countries are small in an international context. In comparison with most European countries, North America or Japan, both the Scottish and the English and Welsh systems have characteristics that mark them out as distinctively 'British': a relatively low level of participation beyond 16; a relatively small full-time technical or vocational sector; and a significant, if untidy, part-time vocational sector, now further complicated by the distinctively British YTS.

Several factors have prevented too great a divergence between the Sottish and the English and Welsh systems. One is the fact of centralized political control; another is the influence of the universities, which tend to promote uniformity across the UK. A third factor, which we have examined more closely in this chapter, is the influence of the labour market.

Whereas our discussion of the two education systems has focused on their differences – albeit slight, in international context – our discussion of the two countries' labour markets has focused on their similarities. Some educational differences have knock-on effects on labour markets, resulting for example in a more staggered pattern of entry in Scotland; and the Scottish youth labour market, particularly for boys, is weaker. Once these two factors are allowed for, there are no substantial differences between the youth labour markets of Scotland and of England and Wales that we can discover. The occupational structure, the role of YTS, differentiation by gender and qualifications, patterns of movement in the labour market – all of these are broadly similar in Scotland and in England and Wales. Even the relative weakness of the Scottish labour market is small beside the geographical variation *within* each country.

This similarity helps us to point to the labour market, and the 'context' for education which it helps to provide, as a source of some of the common problems facing British education systems (Raffe, 1984b and 1987). For example, the relatively low participation in full-time education after 16, and in particular the lack of a developed technical or vocational sector, may largely reflect employers' preferences for recruiting at 16, and their stigmatization of young people who have followed lower-status 'non-academic' courses. It also follows that in areas where educational policy is closely tied to the labour market, such as the development of vocational courses and qualifications, Scotland's freedom of manoeuvre is restricted.

With respect to education, we suggested that comparisons between Scotland and England and Wales might yield conclusions that are of both theoretical and practical value. With respect to the labour market, on the other hand, it is not wholly misleading to treat Scotland as a 'microcosm' of Great Britain. This is not to say that the Scottish labour market is precisely representative of Britain, rather that the Scottish market is internally varied and contains most of the ingredients contained in the wider British market, if not always in the same proportions, and that labour-market processes are very similar.

Acknowledgements

The Scottish Young Peoples Survey is carried out by the Centre for Educational Sociology (CES) at the University of Edinburgh in conjunction with the Scottish

Education Department (SED). It is funded by the SED, the Manpower Services Commission (MSC), the Industry Department for Scotland and the Department of Employment (DE). The England and Wales Youth Cohort Study is carried out by Social and Community Planning Research in collaboration with the University of Sheffield. It is funded by the MSC, the DE and Department of Education and Science (DES). Work on this chapter was supported by the Economic and Social Research Council (grant number C00280004), of which the CES is a Designated Research Centre. The authors are responsible for the opinions expressed in this chapter.

Notes

1.   We refer to Britain rather than the UK because in certain respects Northern Ireland provides an exception to the centralized politics of the UK, although many of our other comments may apply at least as strongly to Northern Ireland as to Scotland. We apologize to Welsh readers that for simplicity of expression we occasionally refer to England and Wales as a single country.
2.   Some estimates therefore differ very slightly from earlier papers (Raffe and Courtenay, 1986, 1987) based on all first-sweep respondents.
3.   The gap between the countries may be slightly exaggerated as the English and Welsh study does not record spells on YTS concluded before September 1984 and spells too short to appear in the month-by-month 'diary' data. The effect of the former exclusion, at least, is slight: excluding spells concluded before September 1984 from the Scottish data only reduces the proportion who had ever been on YTS by a single percentage point.

References

Bevan, S. and Varlaam, C. (1987) 'Political pressures and strategic aspirations in the Youth Training Scheme', in Harrison, A. and Gretton, J. (eds), *Education and Training UK 1987* (Newbury: Policy Journals).
Burnhill, P. (1984) 'The ragged edge of compulsory schooling', in Raffe, D. (ed.), *Fourteen to Eighteen: The Changing Pattern of Schooling in Scotland* (Aberdeen: Aberdeen University Press).
Clark, B. (1961) 'The "cooling-out" function in higher education', in Halsey, A. H., Floud, J. and Anderson, C. A. (eds), *Education, Economy and Society* (New York: Free Press).
Clough, E. and Gray, J. (1986) *Pathways 16–19: National Youth Cohort Study (England and Wales) 1985–1990* (Sheffield: University of Sheffield, Division of Education).
Clough, E., Gray, J. and Jones, B. (1988) 'Curricular patterns in post-compulsory provision: Findings from the National Youth Cohort Study'. *Research Papers in Education, 3*.

Gray, D. and King, S. (1986) *The Youth Training Scheme: The First Three Years*. Research and Development Series No. 35 (Sheffield: MSC).

Gray, J., McPherson, A. F. and Raffe, D. (1983) *Reconstructions of Secondary Education: Theory, Myth and Practice since the War* (Henley: Routledge and Kegan Paul).

Kendrick, S. (1986) 'Occupational change in modern Scotland', in McCrone, D. (ed.), *Scottish Government Yearbook 1986* (Edinburgh: University of Edinburgh, Unit for the Study of Government in Scotland).

McPherson, A. (1973) 'Selection and survivals: A sociology of the ancient Scottish universities', in Brown, R. (ed.), *Knowledge, Education and Cultural Change* (London: Tavistock).

McPherson, A. (1984a) 'Post-compulsory schooling: The fifth year', in Raffe, D. (ed.), *Fourteen to Eighteen: The Changing Pattern of Schooling in Scotland* (Aberdeen: Aberdeen University Press).

McPherson, A. (1984b) 'Post-compulsory schooling: The sixth year', in Raffe, D. (ed.), *Fourteen to Eighteen: The Changing Pattern of Schooling in Scotland* (Aberdeen: Aberdeen University Press).

Manpower Services Commission (1986) *Guide to Content and Quality on YTS/ Approved Training Organisations* (Sheffield: MSC).

Mansell, J. and Miller, J. (1987) *The Organisation and Content of Studies at the Post-Compulsory Level: Country Study: England and Wales*, OECD Educational Monographs (Paris: OECD).

Raffe, D. (1984a) 'The transition from school to work and the recession: Evidence from the Scottish School Leavers Surveys, 1977–1983'. *British Journal of Sociology of Education*, Vol. 5, No. 3, pp. 247–265.

Raffe, D. (ed.) (1984b) *Fourteen to Eighteen: The Changing Pattern of Schooling in Scotland* (Aberdeen: Aberdeen University Press).

Raffe, D. (1985) 'The extendable ladder: Scotland's 16+ Action Plan'. *Youth and Policy*, 12, pp. 27–33.

Raffe, D. (1987) 'The context of the Youth Training Scheme: An analysis of its strategy and development'. *British Journal of Education and Work*, Vol. 1, No. 1, pp. 1–31.

Raffe, D. and Courtenay, G. (1986) *Post-16 Transitions in Scotland and in England and Wales Compared* (Edinburgh: University of Edinburgh, Centre for Educational Sociology).

Raffe, D. and Courtenay, G. (1987) 'Wha's like us? Post-16 transitions in Scotland and England and Wales compared'. *Scottish Educational Review*, Vol. 19, No. 1, pp. 28–38.

Roberts, A. (1984) 'The (not so) famous four'. *Times Educational Supplement (Scotland)*, 23 November, p. 22.

Scottish Education Department (1983) *16–18s in Scotland: An Action Plan* (Edinburgh: SED).

Scottish Education Department/Scottish Examination Board (1982) *Full-time Education after S4: A Statistical Study* (Dalkeith: SEB).

Turner, R. H. (1961) 'Modes of social ascent through education: Sponsored and contest mobility', in Halsey, A. H., Floud, J. and Anderson, C. A. (eds), *Education, Economy and Society* (New York: Free Press).

Chapter 17

Policy and Response: Changing Perceptions and Priorities in the Vocational Training Policy of the EEC Commission

G. Neave

The perspectives involved in the study of vocationalization are many. From a sociological–historical context, it may be regarded as yet another step in the protracted process that has extended the period of childhood and, at the same time, reinforced institutional dependence. It may be seen from an economic context where vocationalization stands as one element or response to the twin imperatives, of on the one hand, 'stocking up' skills which prolonged youth unemployment might cause to be lost or, on the other, as a way of dealing with that massive occupational change which, we are led to believe, a high-technology-based economy will bring about. Similarly, vocationalization may be interpreted from the standpoint of its curricular aspect, that is, from the operationalization of particular skills and their location in relevant points of the education or training systems. A further perspective from which this issue could be examined is that of educational planning and its various techniques, budgetary, human resource allocation and training, the levels and type of labour force to which they contribute. Last but not least, there is what, *faute de mieux*,

Source: Neave, G. (1987) 'Policy and response: changing perceptions and priorities in the vocational training policy of the EEC Commission', in Langlo, J. and Lillis, K. (eds), *Vocationalizing Education*, Pergamon, Oxford.

could be called the perspective of political sociology. This latter might see vocationalization as an example of how governments seek to alter prevalent and established value systems in education towards what some might call 'a new realism' and others, less charitably disposed, might see as a 'new utilitarianism'.

Thus, in discussing vocationalization, there is a plurality of interpretations that can be brought to bear. What most of these have in common, however, is their focus on policy at the stage of implementation – that is, within the school or within the training system, irrespective of whether these are located in the public sector, which is more likely to be the case, or in the private sector, which tends increasingly to be a major growth area as firms assume responsibility for the training of their work force.

Examining policy at the implementation stage is vital. It gives us a notion of how far set objectives have been met. It also gives us equally important indications of how they have not. But there is another aspect to policy and to this vocationalization is no exception. This is the matter of policy formulation. It turns around the perceptions of priorities, how the *problèmatique* is conceived and negotiated by those who have either responsibility for developing such measures or, alternatively, who occupy a key role in scanning a range of options which set the outer bounds within which implementation is itself set. It is to the formulation aspect that this paper is addressed.

■ The Commission of the European Communities

There are several reasons that justify the choice of the Commission of the European Communities as a case study. The first is that policy formulation rests upon a 'comparative dimension'; the second is that the Communities, unlike other international bodies, rest upon a juridical base which, in certain instances, provides for legislation that is binding upon Member States and enforceable by sanction. This, of course, is rarely used. But it is this feature that separates the Commission from say, OECD, the Council of Europe or UNESCO. From a constitutional point of view, the Commission occupies a rare and unique situation: it has powers both legislative and executive. Third, it provides a permanent and high level forum to debate, to consider proposals for action at Community level and, sometimes, to exercise a surveillance and monitoring function. Among these the Education Committee, composed of permanent delegates from the Member States and the Commission's representatives, and the

Advisory Council for Vocational Training, made up of government, employers' and employees' delegates and the Commission officials, are the most salient. Fourth, considerable financial resources may back policy development. Without monetary backing, what passes for policy is little more than the hortatory statement of the impotent and the hamstrung! As an indication of the resources available, in 1984, some ECU 1,437,000,000 was disbursed by the European Social Fund in support of a range of measures to assist young people – in retraining, relocation and job creation (*Educational and vocational training* . . ., 1985, p. 14).

■ Origins of community policy

If we take the process of vocationalization as being broadly aimed at introducing new skills into the curriculum as a means of creating a better match between the output of school and training systems on the one hand, with the perceived requirements of industry on the other, then it is evident that Community developments in this area have a dual origin. This dual origin is not merely organizational and administrative, it is also juridical. Organizationally, vocational training remained a responsibility separate from education. The former came under the purlieu of the Directorate General V in charge of Social Affairs. The latter was added to the general oversight of Directorate General XII whose remit covered research and science. To this, education was added in 1974 (*Education in the European Community*, 1974).

Legally, vocational training is a matter of Community competence based on Articles 57, 118 and 128 of the Treaty of Rome. Education, however, is not formally mentioned and resides on a special formula designed to stress the *voluntary* nature of the meeting of Member State Ministers of Education (*Mise en oeuvre d'un programme* . . ., 1976).

There were, in effect, two clearly differentiated organizational contexts from which the issue of vocationalization emerged. The first of these involved vocational training *per se* and was defined in 1963. A number of general guidelines were set out as part of a general strategy to move towards a common policy in this area (*Council decision* . . ., 1963).

In essence, vocational training policy was seen as an instrument for encouraging mobility of labour across the then six Member States, an interpretation which corresponded to the prevalent view of the Community as primarily an *economic entity*. And the major element in such a policy was informational, that is, enhanced vocational guidance as a lever to this end. Though intentions were to move towards a policy common to all Member States, intention does not imply capability. Several reasons account for this. First, vocational guidance did not enjoy a high priority on the agenda of Member States; second, resources inside the Commission were relatively limited and third, because responsibility for this area tended to be dispersed across different Ministries – Education, Labour, Agriculture, etc. – within the Member States.

The second organizational context began to emerge in the course of the early 1970s urged on by a reinterpretation of the Community's long-term *raison d'être*. This interpretation took the view that the Community could not remain simply as an economic conglomerate, but had, if it were to engage the support of its citizens, to assume a *cultural* commonality as well. The establishment of an education service in 1974 and the creation of a Community Education Action Programme in 1976 was a response to an expanded view of the Communities' spheres of interest. However, in contrast to the basic goal of a vocational training policy which was to work towards harmonization, the education service, from the first, set its face against this imperative. 'Harmonization of these systems and policies', it was stated, 'cannot be considered as an end in itself' (Resolution of 6 ... June, 1974).

Issues involving vocationalization were split between two different services, with a different juridical base and different strategic assumptions permeating their respective remits. This organizational duality was heavily reflected in the basic areas from which each service sought to build its individual policy of vocationalization. Working from a traditional perspective, Directorate General V conceived policy formulation in terms of the effectiveness of various apprenticeship schemes in the Member States, to continue with exploring the potential for guidance for those moving from full-time schooling to full-time employment and to analyse current trends in Member State vocational guidance services (*Activities of Directorate General V . . .*, 1979a). The central assumption behind their activity was, first, to uphold the historic dichotomy between education on the one hand and training on the other, while seeking to extend the range of activities included in the former to wider target groups – for example, women and girls or those school-leavers with no opportunity for vocational training.

The stance taken by Directorate General XII ran parallel to this. The crucial difference lay in the fact that the education service was not prepared to accept the validity of the 'binary model' of education *versus* training. From very early on after the drawing up of the Community Education Action Programme, the education service argued strongly in support of 'integrating' vocational training into the education system (*Preparation of young people . . .*, 1976).

The policy to be pursued, it suggested, ought to be initiatory rather than responsive. It ought to be part of a long-term strategy, developed across broad areas of Commission responsibility and bear down on the linkage between education and work rather than industrial strategy and training. Beneath this disagreement about the focus and goals of the two series lay a more understandable, though covert, agenda – namely, was education to be ancillary to vocational training or, on the contrary, should vocational training be regarded as a service item in a policy whose running was made by education?

■ Different policy approaches

The concept of vocationalization therefore, had, like Janus, two faces. It also had two vastly different approaches in its development, depending on which particular section of the Commission's services had responsibility for it at a particular time. For those responsible for 'vocational training' *sensu stricto* it was a matter of extending into compulsory education elements to strengthen the 'vocational element'. For those working within the framework of the education service, it involved strengthening within the vocational training system those elements of general education which might serve in a remedial function for 'at risk groups'. The former built from the training system back into school. The latter sought to build from school into the training system. Complementary though these strategies might be, wide differences existed in what might be termed 'the formulative stage' of their development. It is probably correct to say that 'policy formulation' as enacted by DGV tended to stick more closely to formal bureaucratic procedures and to involve negotiation within a legislative framework through the Advisory Committee on Vocational Training, the Economic and Social Affairs Committee and the 'social partners', that is, government employers and trades unions. This was not the approach espoused by the education services. Here policy formulation was, at one and the same time, more extensive, more protracted and, equally important, based on the belief that educational research ought to be a prior stage to the formulation of policy. To be sure, the education section of Directorate General XII engaged in regular discussion and consultation with the Education Committee, the main forum representing the education ministries of the Member States. Nevertheless, the development of its policy relied on an extensive programme of 'action research', designed not merely to ascertain the most fruitful ways of tackling the transition from school to work, but also to involve the education world from the grass roots upward.

This programme, perhaps one of the most sustained examples of collaborative research at international level to be undertaken, was launched in the autumn of 1977. Then, it involved some 28 projects, ranging from Denmark to Sicily, from Berlin to Ireland. Today, it is in its 'second phase', the first having ended in 1981–82. Some degree of its scale can be gathered from its financial profile. In its first year of operation, total funding from all sources – Commission as well as Member State – was in the order of ECU 6,000,000 (*Implementation of the Resolution* ..., 1980).

The focus of this 'action research' lay in six areas: These were:

(1) education and training needs of school-leavers facing difficulty in obtaining employment;

(2) problems of poor motivation towards study and work, and ways of stimulating greater participation by young people;

(3) compensatory action to provide better opportunities for specific groups, namely girls, migrants' children, the handicapped;

(4) the association of vocational preparation before and after school-leaving age by strengthening cooperation between education and employment sectors;

(5) development of continuing guidance and counselling services;

(6) improvements in both initial and in-service teacher training the better to enable them to prepare young people for adult and working life (*Preparation of young people . . .*, 1976).

From the standpoint of policy development, the transition project had two main purposes: first, to provide a series of networks across Member States, in which examples in one might inspire initiatives in another; second, to cut across formal administrative boundaries which separated education from training and labour market bodies in an attempt to move towards a broadly coordinated policy. In short, the 'transition programme' stood as an operational expression of the conviction, aired earlier by the education service, which refused to recognize the established division between education and training.

Such a 'bottom up' networking approach stood in marked contrast to the legislative 'top down' perspective embarked upon by the vocational training services, an approach which emerged clearly in the Recommendation issued in July 1977, which called for the extension of vocational *preparation* to those categories of young people who were unemployed or faced the threat of unemployment in the future (*Activities of Directorate General V . . .*, 1979b).

■ Intervention of external factors

Complementary though the two strategies for vocationalization might be, and despite the very marked differences in procedure, both services shared a common assumption at least up to 1978. This central assumption was the nature of youth unemployment itself. Prior to 1978, youth unemployment was held to be a cyclical phenomenon, a temporary fluctuation that would readjust itself once the economy began to pick up again. From this it followed that measures to extend vocational training were conceived in the same light as the problem they were designed to tackle – namely, as short-term responses of a sectoral nature. From the standpoint of the education service, the main task to be tackled involved a more thorough grounding in the basic skills the better to improve insertion to the labour market once the latter picked up. From the standpoint of the vocational training services, the goal of policy was, in essence, to extend provision by expanding the capacity of vocational training systems. This, effectively, was little more than a policy of holding youngsters off the labour market in a labour market context which itself, would remain broadly similar once recovery set in.

By 1978, few of these basic policy parameters held good. Unemployment in general and youth unemployment in particular appeared to have assumed a permanent dimension. Unemployment was then, not transitional, but structural. Second, unemployment itself hid more wide-ranging shifts in the structure of industry – a marked shrinkage in the secondary sector and an even more marked change in the nature of work and the skills required by the 'new technologies'.

These external factors had wide-ranging consequences for the 'frame' in which policy was considered. First, they cast doubts on the validity of a policy based on short-term *ad hoc* responses. Second, and more specifically, they called into question the strategy of extending the intake capacity of traditional vocational training systems. They seemed to suggest that a prior requisite for policy development should be a reassessment of the role of traditional training systems and their ability to meet fundamental changes in the structure of the labour force. Finally, they re-opened a point that the education service had made virtually from the time that education had been included as part of Commission responsibilities – namely, the high degree of 'administrative compartmentalization' in Member State systems between authorities with an educational remit and those with responsibility for vocational training. Though not recognized as such at the time, the upshot of these external factors was to give added weight to the strategy which the education service had been forced to adopt as a result of the absence of a firm legal base for education in the Communities' founding treaties.

■ Alternance: a new approach to the relationship between education and training

Thus shifts in the 'contextual framework' brought about shifts in the 'conceptual framework' in which discussion took place. The fact that youth unemployment was no longer confined to either 'the disadvantaged' or to 'marginal' groups caused the Commission's services to revise their approach. Such a revision took place over the four years from 1979 to 1983. Essentially, it turned around the development of what might be termed a coordinated, cross-sector strategy designed to bring together education, vocational training and employment authorities. It brought to an end what is best described as a 'reactive' policy and replaced it by a medium-term, forward-looking perspective, in which vocational training was interpreted not as a vehicle for 'stocking up' skills, so much as an active instrument for generating new skills and, no less important, new employment (*The development of vocational training* ..., 1982).

Naturally, such changes did not come overnight. The move towards a coordinated, cross-sector approach was, however, marked by two developments. The first of these involved recasting the 'conceptual framework', the second, changes in the organizational context in which Commission policy was worked out. Central to the former was the emergence of the so-called 'alternance model' of vocational training. Essentially, the alternance model combines a 'sandwich' course format with the principle of permanent education. It seeks to link practical knowledge derived from the workplace with a more theoretical grounding in training establishments. It takes the view that work experience is a central element in experiential learning. The significance of this concept is obvious, and may be seen as a key element in 'vocationalizing' education. Seen from the school perspective, it seeks to supplement knowledge conveyed in the classroom with 'real-life' experience. Seen from the perspective of vocational training, alternance departs from the view that such training is limited only to the under-25s or that it should take place on a 'one-off' basis. The importance of the alternance model did not lie simply as a way to impart greater flexibility to established systems of training, nor yet as a means of re-skilling both the younger generation or those in mid career. It also had a particular significance in the conduct of policy inside the Commission. For just as the alternance model predicated a new type of linkage and relationship between work and training, so it also predicated a closer collaboration between the two services of education and training whose policies had, hitherto, operated like the classic definition of political parties in 18th-century England – two stagecoaches going down the same road, occasionally spattering one another with mud!

Changes in the organizational framework were equally significant. In January 1981, responsibility for both education and vocational training was brought together under a single Directorate. Directorate General V now assumed the remit for employment, social affairs and education. The bringing together of the two services set the stamp on the move towards a comprehensive strategy first, to use vocational training as an instrument to attack unemployment and second, to link in with policy developments in other areas of the Commission's activities (*The development of vocational training* ..., 1982).

How far the two services were now agreed on the basic priorities may be seen from discussions in the Education Committee early in 1981. The Education Committee identified two areas as crucial to the Commission's policy development. These were:

(1) the preparation of young people for working life;
(2) the development of continuing education and training (*Outcomes of the proceedings* ..., 1981).

Beneath these two priorities ran a particular vision of the school system which, itself, might eventually move towards the principle of 'integration', at the upper secondary and the post-secondary levels. Included in this pattern would be general education, vocational training and certain elements of work experience.

■ Coordinate planning: towards vocationalization?

The relocation of both education and vocational training inside a single Directorate accelerated the trend towards coordinate planning. By June 1981, the Ministers of Education endorsed the notion of interlinked planning for vocational training and education. Similarly, the previous month, their colleagues in charge of Social Affairs gave their blessing to this same principle. The following year, on 27 May 1982, the Social Affairs Council passed a Resolution on Community Action against Unemployment which marked a further step along this road. The new approach rested on five major points:

(1) strengthening the general level of education during compulsory schooling;
(2) the development of initial and complementary training grounded on a broad range of related occupations (*famille de métiers*);
(3) the drawing up of new options for continuing education of a general character to be available throughout an individual's working life;
(4) the organization of such training, whether initial or in-service upon modular units in keeping with the alternance model;
(5) a corresponding reinforcement of guidance and vocational training services to underpin the development of vocational training.

A close examination of the documents circulated at this time among the Social Affairs Directorate reveals that coordinated planning had three levels. These were the political, technical and administrative levels. At the political level, the main objective was to bring together both the Ministers in charge of education in joint discussion at Community level with their counterparts in charge of employment policies, thereby securing agreement for the approach already under discussion inside the Commission. This objective was secured in June 1983, when for the first time in the history of the Communities, Ministers from both 'sides' met, and agreed on a five-year programme for vocational training policies up to 1988 (*Education and vocational training* . . ., 1985, pp. 11–13).

At the technical level, the main objective was to redefine vocational training by setting up what was termed a '*stage de préparation*' on the one hand, and, on the other, to redefine its content to include the development of social skills, and finally, to place it firmly within the context of *éducation permanente*. At the administrative level, the main objective sought was to bring about coordination between the various services – education, vocational training, employment and social services generally – by local or regional authorities. Local or regional coordination was important for several reasons. First, because it formed the implementation of the principle agreed at Community level; second, following the experience of the transition from school to work programme, local coordination was seen as key in developing successful transitional strategies (*Interim report* . . ., 1985). And third, because, seen from the standpoint of vocationalization, it showed most clearly that the process was not limited simply to those authorities in charge of schools or training establishments. If it was to be part of an overall plan both to re-skill and to create employment, then it had, perforce, to involve local labour market agencies as well as both sides of industry.

The central item in Commission thinking was contained in the concept of 'preparatory stage' which later emerged as the notion of a 'Social Guarantee'. From the standpoint of its location in education/ training systems, it was to follow on immediately after the end of compulsory education. Its purpose was threefold: first to operationalize the notion of 'alternance'; second, to develop a wider range of skills, including remediation, than the usual pattern of vocational training; third, to instil among its 'clients' the notion that training itself was not a 'one-off' activity, but rather part of life-long learning. Thus, what the Commission had in mind as an instrument of vocationalization was a parallel sector alongside full-time secondary schooling for all early leavers and those without formal qualifications. Originally, the notion of a Social Guarantee was to provide vocational training and work experience as a matter of right for all early leavers or youngsters without qualifications. Its salient features were one year's foundation training immediately after compulsory education with the additional possibility of a further year of a more advanced nature. This second year would be available at any period up to the age of 25.

If the nomenclature of the proposal was retained by the joint meeting of Education and Social Affairs Ministers in June 1983, the generous terms put forward were not. Instead the Council opted for a programme consisting either of basic training and/or initial work experience for six months – and certainly no more than a year. The idea of a further year was not looked upon with delight! Even in this diluted form, the Social Guarantee represented one of the most comprehensive statements about vocational training policy the Commission had made since the original guidelines were drawn up in 1963. In addition to the usual categories of early school-leavers and the unqualified, access of women, particularly those in rural areas, was also given priority.

The Social Guarantee was not, however, the only example of cross-sectoral planning within the Commission, for equally radical proposals were also put forward for compulsory education. Some of these may be seen simply as extensions into the school system of those principles developed within the alternance model. Foremost among them was the notion of using the Community itself as a learning resource. School authorities were to be encouraged to develop close links with employment authorities as a first step in creating direct work experience for the 14–18 age range, either in firms or in the community. This theme was taken up and elaborated the following year in the joint meeting of Ministers of Education and Social Affairs. Vocational guidance, counselling and careers' education, the meeting recommended, should span the whole period from secondary school to training and, moreover, they should be closely interwoven into the school curriculum (*Education and vocational training* ..., 1985).

These developments may, of course, be seen in terms of 'lateral policy coordination', that is, the bringing together of administrative areas, both within the Commission and, hopefully, within the Member States as well, which cover a similar age range. But there is also an element of 'vertical coordination'. By 'vertical coordination', I mean extending the planning perspective either to cover an older age range and thus other types of educational establishment relevant to it or introducing another issue transcending both areas of 'lateral coordination' and thus linking them with a common theme. Two examples may serve to illustrate this process and, at the same time, show how vocationalization, first applied within the usual domain of post-compulsory links with training and the labour market, has been extended recently to embrace higher education.

■ The emergence of a 'human resources' strategy

The emergence of 'vertical coordination' as a policy mechanism can be traced back to 1978 and in particular to the Heads of State Conference at

Bonn. One of the topics discussed was the potential of the so-called 'new information technologies' and their possible impact on employment, culture and education. From the viewpoint of the education service, the new technologies merely emphasized, once again, the validity of its original thesis, namely closer coordination between education and training on the one hand, and better articulation with the alternance model on the other. Thus while the advent of the new technologies was seen as a catalyst to the overall task of redrawing the map of education and training, it did not change the overall policy perspective which the Social Affairs directorate had embarked upon. On the contrary, it appeared to add a new urgency to bringing education, training and labour market agencies into closer collaboration.

Even though the education service regarded the new information technologies as an element of reinforcement and thus, of continuity in their objective to redraw the links between education and training, they did introduce a new perspective into Commission thinking. This perspective involved wider consultation with other Commission services and at the same time brought education and training into a broader policy planning context. In effect, employment and social policy – the overall setting in which both the education and training services operated, was itself only part of a more complex issue. This issue was nothing less than the future industrial viability of the Communities, faced with the challenge in the field of high technology from the USA and Japan. As such, it touched upon such areas as industrial policy, the Communities' research and development strategy, the planning of regional affairs and finally, the question of innovation strategies and the development of what is known as 'the internal market'. The latter, scheduled to be complete by 1992, involves removing the final obstacles to the free movement of goods and services within the Communities. Within this 'ecology' of different policy fields, the Ministry of Social Affairs occupied a very specific niche. Its main task lay in the development of a 'human resources' strategy. This, in turn, meant that from the first, the measures designed to introduce the new information technologies into the education and training systems required extended consultation with Directorate Generals III (Industry), XII (Research and Development), XIII (Innovation and the Internal Market) and XVI (Regional Affairs) (*Nouvelles initiatives* . . ., 1982).

The human resources strategy has come to dominate much of current Commission views on the development of both education and training, and was instrumental in changing, once again, the policy context in which vocationalization was placed. If, in the early 1980s, reform of vocational training was seen as a way of creating employment, now it became part of a broader plan to re-equip European industry by updating the knowledge base on which it rested. And, as Commission documents make clear, the central element in this knowledge base lay in raising the level of technical knowledge not only in the active labour force, but in those likely to join it in the future. From the particular confines of education and training, the advent of the new technologies imposed three specific priorities:

(1) training and in-service education of teachers and instructors through application of the new technologies;

(2) the appropriate adaptation of training programmes for young people and, in particular, the young unemployed;

(3) recognition of the needs of specific client groups, including women and older workers.

By introducing the new information technologies into the policy equation as an element in re-skilling, the human resources perspective extended the scope in which vocationalization was set. If this served to reiterate the relevance of 'alternance education', it also raised the issue of balancing opportunities and provision for re-skilling between young people and the older generation who, without it, were in a position no less precarious than that of their children. This latter consideration occupied a key place in redefining vocational training as a process of permanent updating, rather than a 'once-for-a-lifetime' induction into industry.

Furthermore, just as the human resources strategy posed the need to cross-link policy options across a wide range of Commission activities, so it also posed the question of 'highly qualified manpower', both in the field of research and in its supply and interlink with industry. The role of research in general and that carried out by higher education specifically in the development of 'high technology' is a matter of record. A number of programmes designed to accelerate knowledge transfer between universities and industry have been put in place by the Commission. ESPRIT (European Strategic Programme for Research into Information Technology), RACE (Research and Development in Communications Technology) and, more recently, COMETT (Community Action Programme for Education and Training in Technology) are among the more visible (*University–industry cooperation* . . ., 1985).

Strictly speaking, these programmes – with the exception of COMETT – lie outside the purlieu of Social Affairs. They are important, however, in that they seek to develop closer ties between research, industry and universities and also because such links, originally laid down within the ambit of other directorates, are now becoming a central part of the human resources strategy being developed by Directorate General V. From this point of view, they are perhaps less an illustration of the vocationalization of higher education – though there are signs of this too, see below – than of the process of 'vertical coordination' between different sectors of the education/training systems. To the extent that they involve higher education as a research base for industrial change on the one hand,

and, on the other, as a source of supply of graduates qualified in the areas deemed relevant to the 'high technology imperative', such programmes are complementary to the objectives assigned to vocational training systems. They are, in short, a prolongation at a higher level of those objectives we have already seen applied both to schools and to training – realigning of skills in keeping with economic change, the expansion of 'work experience programmes' during undergraduate training while, at the same time, serving as a knowledge base to sustain the transition to a high technology economy.

■ Conclusion

In any organization with responsibility for defining policy and setting resources to achieve particular goals – and here the EEC Commission is no exception – the priorities chosen are in function to the perception of the particular issue and the organizational context in which perceptions are apprehended. The development of vocational training measures over the 10 years from 1975 to 1985 shows this clearly. From being an instrument for improving mobility of labour and confined within the usual bounds of training systems, vocational training has, over the years, assumed a central and crucial role not merely as a vehicle for modernization, but also in gaining some measure of acceptance of the consequences, social, occupational and cognitive, of that process. The role of vocational training, at least as it is reflected in documented discussion and proposals put forward by the EEC Commission, appears to have gone through three stages; the first when it was seen as responding to an established pattern of industry stocking up skills and acting as a palliative to what was held to be short-term youth unemployment; the second, as part of a broader policy sweep designed to create better coordination between education authorities on the one hand and employment creation on the other; and the third when it assumed the status of a medium-term plan to accelerate the changeover to a new industrial base, and as such locked in firmly with compulsory schooling on the one hand and the university system on the other. These changes in role, as I have argued, reflect equally pronounced changes in the way the basic problem was understood, first in terms of youth unemployment, second as a vehicle for job creation and re-training and third, as a sectorial element in a more general mission, namely to ensure the industrial renewal of Europe.

Some may care to see these developments merely as the growth of the 'vocational imperative' and the rise of a technocratic view in which education is subordinated to the overriding demands of industry. There may be some validity for such a view, though it should perhaps be pointed out that what is one generation's utilitarianism turns out often to be its successors' accepted orthodoxy until the next round of reforms hoves in to view, at which point it becomes – for those opposed to it – a new utilitarian ideology. What this view tends to forget is that while it may be the individual's right to refuse the opportunity to develop those competencies that may stand her or him in good stead at a time of social and economic change, this right can only be exercised once such provision is available.

There is, of course, another viewpoint on the issue of vocationalization and one which, if implicit throughout much of the Commission's thinking on the subject, remained largely unpursued. This is the question of control and authority. New elements in the school curriculum, new training policies for teachers or vocational educators, changes in the balance of student flows through higher education – all of which, in varying degrees, have been touched upon in the elaboration of the Commission's proposals – beg the question 'control by whom to do what?' Even if aspects such as these have no part in Community level responsibility – which in essence, resides in drawing up an agreed framework within which national authorities operate *selon leur gré et selon leurs capacités* – the way the policy frame is drawn up implies some measure of shifts in the balance of power and responsibility.

The prevalent view of vocationalization tends to see the process in terms of an illegitimate intervention by authorities or agencies whose priorities do not accord with established practice and convention. The 'industrialization' of the school curriculum can be seen as a particular instance of this. In point of fact, the process engaged in is a rather wider one. As it emerges in the reflections of the education of vocational training services of the EEC Commission, vocationalization contains another dimension which is often underplayed in the debates on this subject. This dimension involves the application of 'power sharing' or co-responsibility which, first developed in the field of industrial relations, is now inserted into education or vocational training. The clearest expression of this principle, which can just as well be understood as a dispersal of power from a single monolithic administration or, for that matter, from a similar professional grouping, emerges in the various schemes for linking the school with its local community or in the various proposals for coordination between regional and local authorities as a way of developing more flexible vocational training initiatives. Not surprisingly, no specific details were mentioned as to the particular format to be used or to the exact balance of responsibility to be assigned to different interests. Nevertheless, the principle of 'partnership' or co-responsibility is clearly stated. How it is to be effected remains a matter for the respective Member States to work out.

From this point of view, the evolution of vocational training policies in the EEC Commission casts a rather different light on the controversy surrounding the rise of vocationalization. For what can be seen as a negative development when viewed from the standpoint of corporative interests, may equally well be regarded as a positive one for those 'social partners' hitherto excluded from the enterprise. At the present time, we tend to identify opportunities for acquiring new competencies and updating old skills in terms of 'education' or 'training' simply because that is the way they were defined in the past. But it is no less evident that, by redefining location in the education system, content, length and availability, what is emerging is not merely a different type of relationship between the two areas education and training, but an entirely different 'learning system' – despite the ghastly jargon of the phrase. It would be surprising if such a new concept did *not* require new partnership arrangements. That we happen to interpret this 'new provision' in terms of the old – and, to be frank, in terms of ancient conflicts which accompanied the development of 'education' *versus* 'vocational training' – tells us nothing about the potential of the 'new provision'. What it does show is perhaps our inability at the present time to go beyond hide-bound concepts, or to maintain our debate within them.

In taking the EEC Commission as a case study in changing concepts and priorities, I am not suggesting that discussion of this issue has necessarily to follow the same path. But, by dint of being the focal point at which this issue has been debated at a supranational level, and proposals for dealing with it elaborated at a similar level, we can recognize more clearly some dimensions which are less evident within a national context.

If, as I have suggested, the process of vocationalization disguises the emergence of a 'new learning system', whether such a system gives due recognition to established authorities or brings about changes in the hierarchy of status among subject areas, is magnificently irrelevant. What is relevant, surely, is whether such new provision will contribute significantly to 'life, liberty and the pursuit of happiness' in a time of massive economic change.

References

Activities of Directorate General V in the field of vocational training (1979a) Document V/585/79, 29 May (mimeo).

Activities of Directorate General V in the field of vocational training July 1977 to May 1979 (1979b) Document V/535/79, 28 May.

Council decision of 2 April 1963 laying down general principles for implementing a common vocational training policy (1963) Document 63/226/EEC, *Official Journal*, 10 April.

Education and vocational training within the European Community: activities of the Commission of the European Communities in 1983 and 1984 (1985) COCM (85) 134 Final, Brussels, 29 March (mimeo).

Education in the European Community (1974) *Bulletin of the European Communities* (supplement) No. 3.

Implementation of the Resolution of 13 December 1976: progress report on measures taken at Community level (1980) Document 5471/80 (EDUC 30), 5 March.

Interim report on the development of the Programme to the Education Committee concerning the implementation of the second series of pilot projects (1985) Document CAB/XIV/170–EN, Brussels, Sept.

Mise en oeuvre d'un programme d'action an niveau communautaire (1976) Document SEC (76) 216, 21 January.

Nouvelles initiatives communautaires pour la période 1983 à 1987 concernant les nouvelles technologies de l'information et le changement social (1982) Projet de Communication de la Commission au Conseil (version no. 5), le 11 février (typewritten).

Outcomes of the proceedings of the Education Committee, 23–24 April 1981 (1981) Document 6502/81 (EDUC 14), 29 April.

Preparation of young people for working life and for transition from education to work (1976) Document R/32290/e/76 (EDUC 52), 8 October.

Resolution of 6 June 1974 (1974) Official Journal No. C982, 20 August.

The development of vocational training policies in the European Communities in the 1980s (1982) Draft Communication to the Council, Bruxelles, 8 July, pp. 1–2.

University–industry cooperation in promoting training policies to meet the challenges of social and technological change and industrial development in the European Community (1985) Draft Communication to the Council, 13 June.

Index